THE NOT-SO-GOLDEN YEARS

THE NOT-SO-GOLDEN YEARS

CAREGIVING, THE FRAIL ELDERLY, AND THE LONG-TERM CARE ESTABLISHMENT

Laura Katz Olson

ROWMAN & LITTLEFIELD PUBLISHERS, INC.
Lanham • Boulder • New York • Toronto • Oxford

ROWMAN & LITTLEFIELD PUBLISHERS, INC.

Published in the United States of America
by Rowman & Littlefield Publishers, Inc.
A Member of the Rowman & Littlefield Publishing Group
4501 Forbes Boulevard, Suite 200, Lanham, Maryland 20706
www.rowmanlittlefield.com

PO Box 317, Oxford OX2 9RU, United Kingdom

British Library Cataloguing in Publication Information Available

Library of Congress Cataloging-in-Publication Data
Olson, Laura Katz, 1945–
  The not-so-golden years : caregiving, the frail elderly, and the
long-term care establishment / Laura Katz Olson.
    p. cm.
Includes bibliographical references and index.
  ISBN 0-7425-2830-8 (cloth : alk. paper) — ISBN 0-7425-2831-6 (pbk. :
alk. paper)
  1. Aged—Long-term care—United States. 2. Frail elderly—Long-term
care—United States. 3. Aged—Government policy—United States. 4.
Caregivers—United States. 5. Aged women—United States. I. Title.
  HV1461.O47 2003
  362.1'9897—dc21

                                                      2003011860

∞™ The paper used in this publication meets the minimum requirements of American
National Standard for Information Sciences—Permanence of Paper for Printed Library
Materials, ANSI/NISO Z39.48-1992.

To William O. Winter
and
his late wife, Alice

CONTENTS

ABBREVIATIONS

AARP	American Association of Retired Persons
AHCA	American Health Care Association
ALF	Assisted Living Facility
AMA	American Medical Association
BBA	Balanced Budget Act
BBRA	Balanced Budget Refinement Act
BIPA	Benefits Improvement Act
CCRC	Continuing Care Retirement Community
CIA	Corporate Integrity Agreement
CIP	Complaint Improvement Project
CMHC	Community Mental Health Facilities
CON	Certificate of Need
COP	Community Options Program
DOJ	U.S. Department of Justice
FCA	False Claims Act
FHA	Federal Housing Administration
FMLA	Family and Medical Leave Act
GAO	U.S. General Accounting Office
HB	U.S. House, Committee on the Budget
HCC	U.S. House, Committee on Commerce
HCFA	Health Care Finance Administration
HEC	U.S. House, Committee on Energy and Commerce
HEW	U.S. Department of Health, Education, and Welfare
HGR	U.S. House, Committee on Government Reform
HGRO	U.S. House, Committee on Government Reform and Oversight

HHS	U.S. Department of Health and Human Services
HIPAA	Health Insurance Portability and Accountability Act
HSB	U.S. House, Committee on Small Business
HWM	U.S. House, Committee on Ways and Means
IOM	Institute of Medicine
IRCA	Immigration Reform and Control Act
MCO	Managed Care Organizations
MERFA	Medicare Education and Regulatory Fairness Act
MFCU	Medicaid Fraud Control Units
MIP	Medicare Integrity Program
MMIS	Medicaid Management Information System
NAC	National Alliance for Caregiving
NCC	National Citizen's Coalition for Nursing Home Reform
NCHS	National Center for Health Statistics
NCPSSM	National Committee to Preserve Social Security and Medicare
NEAIS	National Elder Abuse Incidence Study
NME	National Medical Enterprise
OAA	Older Americans Act
OBRA	Omnibus Budget Reconciliation Acts
OIG	U.S. Office of Inspector General
OSHA	Occupational Safety and Health Act
PCA	Progressive Corrective Action (initiative)
PPS	Prospective Payment System
PRWORA	Personal Responsibility and Work Opportunity Reconciliation Act
PSRO	Professional Standard Review Organizations
RHHI	Regional Home Health Intermediaries
SA	Senate Committee on Appropriations
SEIU	Service Employees International Union
SF	Senate Committee on Finance
SHMO	Social Health Maintenance Organizations
SJ	Senate Committee on the Judiciary
SNF	Skilled Nursing Facilities
SSCA	Senate Special Committee on Aging
SSI	Supplementary Security Income
SURS	Surveillance and Utilization Review Subsystem
TEFRA	Tax Equity and Fiscal Responsibility Act

ACKNOWLEDGMENTS

THIS BOOK OWES A PARTICULAR DEBT to a number of people who have read all or selected chapters of this book and who have offered helpful comments. My deepest thanks go to Sheila Neysmith, Sharon Keigher, and Colette Brown for their invaluable comments and suggestions. I am especially grateful to Joe Hendricks for his guidance, constructive criticism, and support.

I am grateful to my colleagues in the Women's Studies Council at Lehigh University for offering a supportive environment in which to pursue my research. Because of the commitment of people such as Pat Ward and Gayle Nemeth at Lehigh's interlibrary loan, I always had the articles and books that I needed readily available. During my innumerable computer "emergencies," Sandy Edmiston and Bill Bettermann provided me with immediate and cheerful assistance.

I am indebted to Jennifer Knerr, vice president and executive editor at Rowman & Littlefield, for her ongoing support of my books and to Renee Legatt, assistant editor, for her overall dedication and commitment to this project. Renee kept me informed and kept the book on track during all stages of the publishing process with great efficiency and professionalism. I also appreciate the efforts of Kärstin Painter, my production editor, who exhibited an extraordinarily keen eye for detail and improved the overall quality of the manuscript.

I want to thank my family, who is always there for me. I appreciate the love and support of my husband, George, especially the pleasure he took in the book's development and completion. He was a receptive listener and careful reader, finding the random spelling error or misplaced word. Over the years my daughter, Alix, has inspired me with her stimulating conversations, important feedback, emboldening poetry, and warm smile. I am eternally grateful to my mother for her perpetual faith in my ability to accomplish whatever I try. I value my sister, Anne, for being a loving presence in my life. And I appreciate my English setters, Charlie and Fergie, for adding levity to my days with their ever present "chewie wars."

I also owe an intellectual debt to the many feminists who through discussions, shared experiences, and their own work have excited my imagination and stirred my thinking in these pages. Needless to say, I alone am responsible for what appears here.

1

INTRODUCTION: SOCIAL LOCATION AND THE POLITICAL ECONOMY OF LONG-TERM CARE

THE WORLD IS AGING RAPIDLY as the number of elders continues to grow faster than the population as a whole.[1] Although some observers are alarmed at what they call an impending worldwide economic crisis, the expansion of the elderly population can be viewed in terms of accomplishments, opportunities, and challenges as well as costs. Certainly among the achievements in First World nations are reduced infant and maternal mortality, decreased infectious and parasitic diseases, improved education and nutrition, increased life expectancy, and lessened morbidity among the aged itself.

Indeed, the fastest growing sector of the population worldwide is what gerontologists have labeled the oldest old—individuals aged eighty-five and over. Already 70 million strong, they are expected to swell to 350 million by 2050. In the United States, the first of the 76 million baby boomers will reach age sixty-five in 2010 and will inflate the more advanced age group beginning in 2030; by 2040, the eighty-five and over population is projected to triple to 14.3 million (U.S. Bureau of the Census, 2000e). The prevalence of chronic physical or cognitive diseases, especially multiple disabling conditions, climbs measurably as one ages.[2] Unlike acute illnesses, though they can be relieved, improved, or even slowed down, functional impairments are not curable. Thus, the lengthening of lives often translates into extended periods of frailty for growing numbers of older people.

Since most of the oldest old require at least some help in order to stay in the community, whether by themselves or with other family members, and others need more comprehensive nursing home services, the number of elders requiring long-term care over the next forty years will mount considerably, perhaps doubling or even quadrupling the total today. The extent to which such developments burden families and/or public budgets depends on a number of factors, such as a nation's perspective on societal responsibilities for the elderly; the extent to which individuals and families are charged with their care and the personal resources available to them; the magnitude and type of communal services actually distributed to those in need; the nature and structural features of the medical and long-term care systems, including their ownership and control; and the government policies that underlie and support them.

A Framework for Assessing Long-Term Care

It is my intention to examine long-term care by addressing the structural and ideological forces that have shaped our needs, values, options, and policies, both private and public. The situation of the frail elderly and their caretakers reflects the power relations, market structures, and ideological constructs that allocate and distribute benefits, privileges, and disadvantages in the United States. I will focus on the interrelationships among economic, social, cultural, and political processes and show how the dynamics of commercial values and practices have influenced social provisions for our vulnerable aged population.

The language of business interests and the corporate model increasingly have driven government policies, thereby allowing the profit motive and greed to eclipse social responsibility and public accountability. Within the logic of market forces and private accumulation, human needs and moral values are secondary to financial considerations.[3] In the area of long-term care, the ascendancy of a market-driven ethic has encouraged the state to subsidize business interests while disregarding the adverse consequences for elders who rely on others for their basic activities of daily living.

This book will analyze the many incongruities inherent in state efforts to meet the demands of capital while attempting to provide care for those in need. The ongoing, complex negotiations between political officials and nursing home owners clearly are entangled in such contradictions, an interplay that is intensified because of the preponderance of government funding. Public money has supported and molded the long-term care business empire, fostering the primacy of institutional facilities, private, for-profit ownership, and the eventual growth and domination of large-scale nursing home chains. Quality of care has taken a back seat to material interests despite numerous exposés of the industry over the years. Periodic government endeavors to impose controls have been consistently overshadowed by the corporate agenda.

The economic, social, ideological, and political processes pertaining to long-term care will be viewed from the standpoints of gender, class, race/

ethnicity, and age. I will show the extent to which these multiple, interlocking systems of oppression structure our life situation and experiences, including the trajectory of the aging process, frailty and dependency, the economic and social conditions of old age, and the ways in which care work, both informal and formal, is perceived and practiced. Within this conceptual framework, I will examine how various subgroups are affected by structural and ideological forces and social policies, measuring both similarities and disparities in their experiences.

State power and policies in the area of elder care create, perpetuate, and reinforce gender, racial, class, and age hierarchies in a number of ways. The effect on subgroups, however, varies considerably. As Calasanti (1996) points out, we shouldn't rely exclusively on white, middle-class, male-oriented assumptions. Rather, it is imperative to explore the issues through the vantage point of the various structures of domination and compare their diverse situations with those of more privileged subgroups.

The Political Economy of Long-Term Care

Elder care policy is linked to and circumscribed by the overall political, social, economic, and ideological issues and parameters of the times. The decades of economic prosperity and expansion from World War II through the mid-1970s coincided with a steady growth in social welfare spending, especially for the sixty-five and over population. The improvement and expansion of the Social Security system significantly reduced poverty among the elderly. In 1965, Medicare, Medicaid, and the Older Americans Act were enacted, providing health care, nursing home funding for the impoverished, and some social services. The aged also have benefited from Supplementary Security Income (1974), food stamps (1965), subsidized housing, special tax benefits, and a number of other national and state efforts, including congregate meals and senior employment programs.

By 1973, the heyday of American domination of world markets and the global economy had waned, productivity declined, and the United States experienced deteriorating economic conditions, including stagflation. During the 1980s, the nation's financial problems were accompanied by growing waves of corporate mergers, acquisitions, and downsizing as well as the movement of jobs overseas, resulting in a shift from manufacturing to a service economy. The number of jobs in heavy industry steadily declined while low-wage employment in the service and retail sectors proliferated. Despite a strong economy for several years after 1983, the decade witnessed a stagnation in real wages for American workers, a decrease in personal savings, growth in income- and wealth inequality, shrinkage of the middle class, and large tax cuts, especially for corporations and upper-income households. Many married-couple families escaped poverty or serious declines in household income only because more wives, including those with very young children, were working.

The postwar boom years also gave way to the age of fiscal austerity and the large-scale political mobilization of conservative forces. The economic crisis of the 1970s, along with huge and growing national budget deficits generated through President Reagan's tax cuts and rising defense spending, permitted political and corporate leaders to usher in an era of government retrenchment and change the dominant discourse of public policy. New "catchwords" abounded, such as "family values" and "choice," bursting with untold potential to shift the course of American social welfare policies, including those affecting frail older people.

According to Minkler and Estes (1991), the portrayal of the elderly changed after the 1970s from a needy and worthy population to that of a politically powerful, greedy sector of society who were financially better-off than younger generations. They now were depicted as grabbing more than their share of the national budget and contributing substantially to the fiscal crisis itself. As a result, those programs serving older people came increasingly under attack.

The new vocabulary of limited government was translated into dicta for undermining support for essential services, an anti-entitlement mentality, and the rejection of a national responsibility for social needs. The undermining of social programs was reinforced by calls for decentralization. In turn, as state and local governments experienced growing economic burdens, they advocated for even greater cost containment, especially for programs serving the poor such as Medicaid. "Home care" and "familism," euphemisms for unpaid family care, became the rallying cry of national, state, and local leaders determined to cut government spending, regardless of its human toll. Self-reliance and individual responsibility, major values underlying our society, were used to further curtail collective responsibility for dependent elders.

While denigrating government, the new conservative forces increasingly elevated the role of the market as the preferred means for supplying public goods. Large-scale vested interests cashed in on the growing commodification of elder services. Efficiency, maximization of short-term profits, and a focus on the "bottom line," values that are incompatible with quality care, became the reigning ethos guiding the provision of social services. The revitalization of privatization, "market competition," and deregulation of business generated greater profiteering, fraud, and escalating costs in the medical and long-term care industries. New opportunities for consumer "choice" in the private sector and greater program "flexibility" inevitably led to reduced publicly funded services and higher out-of-pocket expenses for older people receiving health care. For-profit companies began developing elder care services for those older people who could afford to pay; they also continued to dip into the public coffers, offering especially poor-quality care for the economically needy.

The political and economic climate of the 1990s remained grounded in the ideological precepts of the Reagan era. Despite the expansion of the economy after 1992 and some increases in wages for workers at the bottom of the economic order by 1996, cleavages between the rich and poor continued to increase as did household debt, personal bankruptcies, deindustrialization, the proliferation of poorly paid jobs, financial speculation by large-scale investors, and increasing tax burdens on the low- and middle-income classes (Mishel, Bernstein, and Schmitt, 2001). The regressive Social Security tax became a growing share of federal revenues relative to personal income taxes, and the latter, in turn, took prominence over corporate taxes. President Clinton and the New Republican Congress sought to balance the annual national budget on the backs of the elderly, the working class, and the poor. In particular, legislators attempted to cut Medicaid costs—and even dismantle the program—as well as curtail the growth of Medicare and privatize Social Security. In 1996, they abolished the federal Aid to Families with Dependent Children program, thereby ending welfare as an entitlement for young, impoverished, female-headed households. Many of these women have been forced into low-paying work, including elder care.

Prevailing conservative views have been strengthened with the election of George W. Bush in 2000. Consequently, public discourse over the "budget surplus," accruing mostly from the Social Security system, was limited to tax cuts and tax expenditures rather than any initiation or expansion of needed social welfare legislation. The current political climate encourages small tax breaks for caregiving and long-term care insurance, policies that primarily aid the better-off sectors of society while offering only limited supportive services for low- and middle-income frail elders living at home. Their situation certainly will deteriorate even further now that the projected "surplus" is no longer a reality.

Long-term care, which has long been the stepchild of medical services, is both embedded in and distinct from health care policy in our country. Although both concerns were conspicuously left out of the New Deal package of Social Security programs and the United States never achieved universal health care, the aged and the very poor obtained some medical assistance through Medicare and Medicaid in 1965, programs that accounted for about one-third of the $1.3 trillion in total national health care costs in 2000 (HCFA, 2001). In fact, the Health Care Finance Administration is the "largest single purchaser of health care in the world" (HEC, 2001, 1).

However, these programs primarily finance acute rather than chronic care and medical intervention (including highly technical treatments) over supportive community services. Thus, the essential service needs of the elderly frequently are not covered, although many of them are as important, and in some cases even more crucial, to their health and well-being. The limited long-term care provided though public resources is situated within this institutional, medical model and is subject to the vicissitudes of health care costs, financial markets, private delivery systems, and public policies.

Though various government-funded long-term care bills were proposed from 1989 to 1994 and though Clinton's 1993 health care package called for long-term care based on the need for services regardless of age, such legislation has had almost no chance of passage. And even these limited efforts have been abandoned; political leaders now continue to concentrate mainly on controlling costs for elder care, rejecting any serious consideration of a national, universal, long-term care policy.

Structures of Domination: Gender, Race/Ethnicity, Class, and Age

Until recently, feminists have not been concerned with the gender issues related to aging, ageism, and long-term care. When addressing the domestic sphere and the social division of labor, their focus has been on household duties and childcare. "No one was arguing over who got to take care [of] and credit for caring for 'grandma' in the development of the rhetoric of the 'new man' in the reconstructed family story" (Fineman, 1995, 175). Such concerns as the devaluation of motherhood and the lack of decent day care centers tended to eclipse the problems and consequences of unpaid elder care work.[4]

Beginning in the late 1970s, a small number of women's old age groups were formed, composed mostly of middle-aged and older females, that relied on a feminist framework to guide their social and political activism.[5] However, they were mostly removed from the mainstream feminist movement and had little impact on its thinking, concerns, or endeavors (Macdonald with Rich, 1983). The silence on the subject of aging women was broken to a limited extent by the mid-1980s when a few women scholars began to explore how gender informs the experience of aging, most notably Carroll Estes, Meredith Minkler, Nancy Hooyman, and Beth Hess, and more recently Colette Browne, Linda Gannon, and a few others.[6] Moreover, as second-wave radical feminists confront their own aging as well as that of their ailing elderly parents, even some literary works on the subject are emerging, particularly in the form of memoirs.[7] Two of the more prominent of these are Kate Millett's *Mother Millett* (2001) and Alix Kates Shulman's *A Good Enough Daughter* (1999), both centering on the author's own role as caregiver. As Millett finds herself back in her hometown, St. Paul, Minnesota, and in charge of her mother's care, she admits that this is the first time she has "come to see age"; she suddenly becomes aware of her own aging, along with her lack of economic preparation for it.[8] A limited number of feminist works on aging, including those by Toni Calasanti, Deborah Stone, Jill Quadagno, and Evelyn Nakano Glenn, also are starting to analyze the impact of other locations of oppression on older women's lives.

Nonetheless, both gerontologists and feminists still are not paying sufficient attention to the situation of frail older women or to the overall gender issues related to their care. There is even less regard for the racialized and class dimensions of the problems, concerns that are integral to a full understanding of aging and long-term care. This book will undertake the larger task of addressing both gender and the various social locations of oppression that cut across it. My analysis first will look at aging and elder care through a feminist lens, thereby rendering gender central to the inquiry. As such, the study will emphasize the relations of production and reproduction, the patriarchal power relationships that structure them, and the complex interplay between the two domains. Since the late 1800s, with the growth of commercial markets and industrial capitalism, the roles of White men and women became increasingly demarcated. Work, government, and markets, the "public" sphere, were reserved for men whereas the responsibilities of women were relegated to the "private" domain. These duties were socially constructed to entail the reproduction and maintenance of labor power, especially the bearing and raising of children, care for the sick and disabled of all ages, and other services outside the formal market economy. As Glenn (1992) puts it, the gendered character of labor in the home became essential to the successful performance of the industrial economy. The "separate spheres" ideology forced women to become responsible for unpaid family care throughout their life cycle, leaving large numbers economically dependent on their spouses and/or the state. Even though women increasingly entered the paid labor force and the vast majority now work, their caring obligations have not lessened commensurably.

As suggested earlier, the rapid growth of the eighty-five and over population in recent decades has led to a greater need for supportive services. At the same time, government policies have affirmed and reinforced women's obligations for their disabled aged kin. Because of the private wall surrounding family work, women's care of frail older people is invisible, undervalued, and lonely. On one hand, though our society is dependent on such caregiving activities, we tend to depreciate them. On the other hand, in the name of family values, current political discourse depicts informal assistance as preferable to paid, outside help. While celebrating spousal/filial domesticity and commitment, such rhetoric translates into a social disregard for the substantial financial, physical, social, and psychological costs experienced by those providing elder care. The not-so-hidden agenda is to save public money on the backs of women caretakers.

The residual approach to long-term care, such as limiting and strictly controlling public resources for home- and community-based assistance, and an ideological stress on self-reliance and individualism, place ever-increasing demands on wives, daughters, and daughters-in-law. Social policies and programs grounded in government retrenchment, decentralization, familism, and privatization disproportionately burden women in their prescribed role as kin keepers. Despite the separate spheres ideology, most females today are balancing caregiving—sometimes for both young children and older relatives—with their obligations at work. Nearly 60 percent of all females will face elder care tasks at some point in their lives (Abel, 2000).

The devaluation and invisibility of family caregiving spill over into the public sector: hired care work, which mirrors that in the private domain, is gendered social reproduction commodified (Glenn, 1992; Hooyman and Gonyea, 1995) These frontline, mostly female aides in nursing homes and private residences are underpaid and overworked, and they generally lack health care and other fringe benefits for themselves and their families. The long-term care workplace, with its clearly delineated gender-based structural, relational, economic, and power differentials, is a striking illustration of women's disadvantaged position in the dual labor market.

Older women themselves may be subject to particular indignities and affronts. As several feminist writers suggest, the oppression of women can be found in a number of places, including lack of control over one's body and vulnerability to violence. However, as with other issue areas, their analyses tend to center on younger females, emphasizing such key concerns as reproductive rights, domestic abuse, sexual harassment, sexual exploitation, and rape. I will broaden this analytic framework to include the encumbrances of a gendered old age as well as intergenerational questions. Many disabled female elders, particularly those with limited resources, lose complete agency over their person, their well-being, and, indeed, their lives.

Even deeper insights can be gleaned by centering on what Calasanti and Zajicek (1993) refer to as the multiple realities and oppressions that are shaped by the interactions among gender, race/ethnicity, and class. Stratification by race, ethnicity, class, and even age intersect with gender in significant and fundamental ways, often demarcating additional sites of social and power relations leading to inequality and privilege (McMullin, 2000). A focus on gender alone ignores "how complexly the factors of race and gender are interlocked with the variable of social class in the United States" (Dressel, 1999, 245). It masks some central and consequential dynamics underlying the policies and issues related to aging and elder care.

Thus, though care work tends to be the domain of women, it is experienced in vastly differing ways depending on one's race, ethnicity, and socioeconomic class. Because of socially constructed racial/ethnic hierarchies of power in the economy, women of color, Latinas, and immigrants typically have jobs at the lower ends of the gendered labor force. The relations of production in the long-term care industries are noticeably stratified: in nursing homes these workers hold jobs primarily as undercompensated nurse's aides (NAs) while their White sisters are more likely to serve in the somewhat higher but still poorly paid nursing positions. Immigrants, Blacks, and Latinas are disproportionately respresented among aides in the home health and institutional care workforce, often laboring under grueling conditions. White men, on the other hand, tend to be hired as well-compensated administrators, usually with ample benefits packages.

When caring for their own kin, groups disadvantaged by race/ethnicity and class tend to have limited access to paid help. Many of them are single mothers who experience enormous stress in balancing their low-paid jobs with childcare and elder care responsibilities. In contrast, White, middle-class, professional women tend to have greater flexibility at work and more choices, especially in their ability to hire others to assist them and their frail relatives. They are able to extract cheap labor from immigrants and women of color, sometimes within exploitive domestic situations.

Aging itself is a cumulative experience in American society, allowing some to reap more advantages of income, wealth, health care, and well-being over their life course. Minority and other deprived older populations, who have suffered a lifetime of poverty, poor nutrition, and limited access to medical care, tend to have greater mortality, morbidity, disabling conditions, and inferior health status overall than the more advantaged groups. There is substantial documentation that socioeconomic status is highly associated with the prevalence of certain diseases and chronic conditions, associations that increase steadily with age. For many of those leading more privileged lives and achieving longer life spans, "older is getting younger all the time" (Rubin, 2000). Gerontologists increasingly focus on productive aging, aging "as ripening rather than decline" (Shulman, 1999). Some financially secure, hearty elders go back to school, go mountain climbing and skiing, start second careers, and travel worldwide. Others, especially those who are struggling financially, may suffer from chronic disabling diseases and an inability to live on their own without assistance from others.

The ability of dependent elders to determine their own living arrangements, conditions, and types of care varies according to class, gender, and race/ethnicity. Control over their well-being often depends on the availability of supportive services which, in the United States, are accessible mainly to those who can afford to pay. Disadvantaged older people often encounter discrimination in nursing home placement, inadequate financial resources, language difficulties, transportation problems, and other barriers to obtaining formal services. Thus, those with the most substantial needs for formal assistance have the least prospects for obtaining them.

Divergent cultural values, attitudes, and expectations within the United States mediate the aging experience as well. Although many overburdened families turn to private and public assistance when they can, certain ethnic/socioreligious groups are particularly reluctant to do so. Some groups emphasize collectivism, interdependence, and family over individual interests, creating strong bonds within the extended family and an extensive support system for frail elders. Others, who expand the concept of kin to include friends and neighbors, have even larger and more diverse networks. Groups such as Asian Americans tend to focus on the immediate family; cultural mandates for filial piety oblige adult children, usually daughters or daughters-in-law, to provide hands-on care to dependent parents. A few socioethnic groups, and their organizations, have built elaborate community services for older people over the years.

The complex dynamics of gender, racial/ethnic, and class relations are further marked by age. Though structures of domination and the inequities fostered by them are patterned throughout the life cycle, they also tend to be uniquely conditioned by age relations (McMullin, 2000). Old age is a fluid concept, susceptible to multiple interpretations, definitions, and historical perspectives. To a large extent, the problems related to aging and long-term care are socially constructed. Therefore, the situation of the oldest old stems not only from lifelong structured privileges and disadvantages but also from prevailing notions about old age and the social, economic, and political context in which aging occurs. And, as Calasanti and Slevin (2001, 193) aptly point out, "Ageism is the one oppression that we will all face." In American society, certain ageist assumptions have been formalized in public policies and employer practices.

The experiences of vulnerable older people are shaped by our basic values, including attitudes about frailty and dependency. In extolling the virtue of independence and self-reliance, the dominant culture in the United States devalues those in need of assistance, often stripping them of their power, authority, and even dignity. We avert our collective eyes to the inhumane conditions in long-term care facilities in some part because of our discomfort with disability, neediness, and very old age itself. In those sectors of society where older people are venerated, the functionally impaired aged tend to be more empowered and affirmed.

Both capital and the state substantially influence the circumstances of older people, reproducing, reinforcing and in some cases intensifying earlier inequities. However, aging policies also have flattened some class differences, forcing downward mobility for some elders, especially White, middle-class females. Private pensions and the Social Security system reward such women mostly on the basis of their marital status, reducing their financial well-being considerably upon divorce from or death of a husband. Many young female workers are imbued with a false sense of economic security only to discover that because of caring responsibilities, lack of a private pension, and low Social Security benefits in their own right, they have insufficient income in their older years. And, under Medicaid, a significant number of chronically ill aged women are forced to impoverish themselves in order to receive publicly supported institutional or in-home care.

Moreover, there are some situations and circumstances that the very old share in common. Though chronological age per se does not define one's health or life situation, the oldest old are most likely to suffer from chronic conditions, declining functional abilities, and waning strength. At the most advanced ages, even those with decent income can become vulnerable to dependency on others for their basic needs before they die. As one researcher remarked when describing the nursing home she was studying, "Lying in bed are housewives, plumbers, retired nurses, school teachers, a symphony violinist, a ham radio operator, and a pediatrician in his nineties" (Tisdale, 1987, 15). Most of the frail, dependent elderly, despite their life experiences and any accomplishments or financial success, are treated as if they were babies, without a past; the focus tends to be on their bodily functions and ailments (Shield, 1988). Thus, under current structural arrangements, aging can serve as a leveler of sorts: financial resources of many middle-class individuals gradually decline while functional impairments steadily rise.

Regardless of gender, race/ethnicity, and class, elders also face an increasing loss of family and friends to death. In addition, generational location can be a critical variable in the understanding of certain aspects of the aging and long-term care experiences. Since historical conditions partly frame one's life situation, there may be generational affinities among today's older people as well as differences between them and their adult children caregivers. This is most stark among ethnic elders and their more Americanized adult children.

An understanding of domestic long-term care issues must be situated within the context of the global economy, as well. Worldwide economic, political, and social conditions, including the terms of trade and investment, markets, wages, and immigration, are significantly influenced by multinational corporations and the industrialized nations, especially the United States. Class interests are intrinsic to state actions encouraging the availability of cheap labor for elder care, as evidenced by immigration and other social and economic policies. Capital's relentless demand for cheap material resources and exploitable labor has promoted policies that force large numbers of people in Third World countries to leave their homeland. As Grace Chang (2000) points out, although immigrants have always been imported for their low-cost labor, today's global trade in workers has shifted to women, many of them mothers, who serve the needs of First World service industries and better-off private households. According to Chang, structural adjustment policies and fiscal austerity measures imposed on Third World debtor nations by the First World vastly increased poverty, forcing many Chinese, Filipino, Caribbean, and Latino women to seek "temporary" employment in other countries to support their children back home.

Organization and Overview of the Book

Chapter 2 provides an overview of long-term care in the United States and the interlinking sociocultural, ideological, political, economic, and demographic forces shaping its development. I argue that it is mostly a haphazard system, dominated by nursing home care and offering few community services to chronically ill elders who can't afford to pay. The chapter describes the major features of the Medicare and Medicaid systems, their escalating expenditures since 1965, and their subsequent cost-containment strategies, including managed care, revised reimbursement formulas, promotion of in-home family care, cost-shifting schemes, and intensified privatization and market-based policies. Throughout the section, I show who gains and loses from our expensive but sorely inadequate means of providing for our frail elders both nationally and at the state level.

In the next three chapters, I look at the elder care experience from three different vantage points: family caregivers, the workers who comprise the paid caring labor force, and the frail elderly themselves. The chapters seek to explain how each of these vulnerable players, mostly women, are affected by long-term care policies and practices.

Chapter 3 examines the family ethic of care that places women in the role of informal caregiver, the promotion of familization and privatization that increasingly shifts full care of the aged to wives and adult daughters, and the financial, emotional, psychosocial, and physical costs they bear. The section addresses such issues as duty versus choice within an environment of limited options, conflicts between women's workplace and in-home caring labor functions, and the class-based divide rooted in the gendered division of family care. The chapter points out that as the demands for women's kin-keeping labor are steadily growing, their capacity to discharge them is decreasing.

Chapter 4 takes a careful look at paid caregiving work and its gendered, racialized complexion. As an integral part of the largely low-wage female labor force, nursing home aides and home-based personal care attendants—mainly Blacks, Latinos, and immigrants—provide the cheap labor that absorbs much of the private and social costs of caring for the frail aged. The chapter concentrates on the workplace environment and conditions experienced by these frontline workers; the multiple demands, stresses, and abuses confronting them on a daily basis; the circumstances of their personal and working lives, including inadequate income, low—or no—employee fringe benefits, lack of opportunities for advancement in their jobs, inflexible schedules, and, in the case of personal care attendants, isolation, ill-defined boundaries, and extreme vulnerability to patient, family, and agency demands. The chapter also analyzes how caring labor has been influenced by globalization and international capital, driving a new second-tier transnational female domestic workforce from Third World to First World nations. While receiving countries, especially the United States, attempt to extract their labor at the least cost, this female labor diaspora also serves the elites in their homeland: remittances sent by these transnational mothers help sustain both family members and their national economies. American immigration laws encourage the inflow of such cheap labor while attempting to minimize any social or economic costs to society.

In chapter 5, I turn to the frail elderly themselves, portraying their world from the standpoint of women's experiences and positioning the elderly as subjects in their own lives. Devalued by society overall, they are at risk of low- or poverty-level incomes, loss of independence, reliance on adult children, and/or institutionalization. The chapter details the nursing home experience: chronically ill elders face isolation, demeaning and depersonalizing treatment, ineffective care, powerlessness, and constant violations of their privacy, dignity, and other basic rights. The chapter includes a brief overview of assisted living housing and the more luxurious continuing care retirement communities, alternatives available only to those disabled elders who can afford to pay their high costs privately.

Chapter 6 assesses in more detail how gender and elder care issues are experienced differently depending on one's race, ethnicity, and/or social class. It discusses the growing racial and ethnic diversity of the United States generally and the aged specifically, and the effects of immigration policy. The chapter reviews the specific situation of Blacks, Latinas, and Asians and considers the interplay of such factors as culture and cultural mandates, gender, race, and class. It scrutinizes each group's socioeconomic and health status; labor force issues; access to appropriate medical care, nursing homes, home health care and other services; the types and variety of "family" configurations; attitudes toward the aged and elder care; and, for Asians and Latinas, acculturation levels and immigration experiences. Both as caregivers and care recipients, the women in each of the three groups under discussion face some similar as well as unique stresses, burdens, and challenges; there are intragroup variations, as well. The chapter argues that the limited opportunities and deprived socio-economic status of many younger and middle-aged racial/ethnic females are not only perpetuated into their old age but also engender greater financial and personal costs for them as caregivers.

The next two chapters shift focus to the long-term care industries, directing particular attention to institutional providers. Chapter 7 describes the growth of proprietary nursing homes as a big business, their political power, their bilking of Medicare and Medicaid, and the ultimate bankruptcies of the largest chains. The chapter also covers the abuse, maltreatment, and neglect of the nursing home population and the lax, ineffective government attempts to improve the situation over the years. It contends that despite numerous hearings, exposés, and subsequent regulations over the years, policymakers have been unwilling to address the underlying structural problems, thereby allowing seriously harmful practices to persist. Overall, the chapter explains how national and state rules more often protect the proprietors than the frail elderly themselves.

Care of the aged in the United States is not only a multibillion-dollar business but also a gold mine for certain industries. Chapter 8 focuses on Medicare and Medicaid fraud and criminal misconduct among a significant number of medical and long-term care providers. It explores financial exploitation of the health care programs by home health agencies, hospitals, physicians, nursing homes, durable medical equipment firms, pharmaceutical companies, clinical laboratories, managed care organizations, and others. It assesses the economic magnitude of the problem, the various types of unscrupulous schemes, some of the ill-conceived attempts by public officials to identify and control them, and the inadequate, ineffective penalties imposed. The chapter also explains how fraudulent practices are masked as clerical "errors," allowing even otherwise legitimate providers to cash in on the public programs. Moreover, it analyzes the inextricable link between economic profiteering and the maltreatment of program beneficiaries. The chapter concludes by showing how even the limited efforts of public officials in the 1990s to control financial abuses are being undermined by the enhanced power of industry groups in the twenty-first century.

Chapter 9 will weave together and synthesize the complex issues related to elder care in the United States and the underlying structures, values, and norms on which they are based. It places long-term care in the context of the American health care system and the larger political economy. This final section briefly examines and discusses the future of long-term care in the nation and offers a few strategies for change, including the overhaul of nursing homes, deprivatization of services, and a revaluation of care work. It specifically calls for a universal, publicly supported system of care for physically and mentally impaired people of all ages. The chapter then turns to some broader social issues that connect the myriad cumulative disadvantages of younger women, especially minorities, to their later vulnerability in old age. In order to address elder care issues fully, policymakers must confront fundamental questions associated with the gendered and racialized social and economic inequities in the country overall.

Notes

1. The United States ranks twenty-fifth worldwide in the percentage of its population age sixty and over and has experienced relatively lower growth of its oldest old than other industrialized nations (U.S. Bureau of the Census, 1996).

2. This book will discuss long-term care issues associated with older people, leaving it to others to address the equally important concerns of the younger disabled population and their families. It should be noted that the sixty-five and over population comprises only about 55 percent of individuals in need of supportive services (Binstock, 1996).

3. As Hendricks and Leedham (1999) argue, our moral economy is grounded in exchange value rather than use value, the latter allowing public officials to take individuals, equity, the public good, and social utility into account when making policy. In societies such as the United States, which is predicated on exchange value, productivity and capital accumulation are viewed not only as dominant concerns but also as "ends in themselves, leading to judgment of policies almost exclusively on the basis of cost." Moral economy, according to Minkler and Cole (1999), refers to the "popular consensus concerning the legitimacy of certain practices, on the basis of shared views of social norms or obligations."

4. Cynthia Rich, a feminist and author, wrote of her growing awareness of aging, beginning in 1977: "Slowly, I begin to see that the fear of the stigma of age, and total ignorance of its reality in the lives of old women, flow deep in myself, in other women I know, in the women's movement" (Macdonald with Rich, 1983, 11–12).

5. The most prominent was the Older Women's League, founded in 1977.

6. One of the earliest scholars and activists for aging women was Barbara Macdonald. Along with her partner Cynthia Rich, she had to fight for four years to have issues related to ageism included in the National Women's Studies Association's 1985 national conference (Macdonald with Rich, 1983).

7. One of the first American novelists dealing with the subject of contemporary older women was May Sarton who has written a number of works, including *As We Are Now* (1973) and *The House by the Sea* (1977).

8. However, both Kate Millett and Alix Kates Shulman ignore race and class in their otherwise sensitive accounts.

2

POLICIES AND PROGRAMS: THE PUBLIC AND PRIVATE COSTS OF CARE

SINCE THE 1930S, American social policies have expanded national entitlements, benefits, and services for the elderly, with costs reaching about $820 billion or nearly 45 percent of the total national budget by 2001 (U.S. Budget, 2003). Despite the improved overall economic situation of older people, large pockets of poverty persist, especially among single women, Blacks, Latinos, and other minorities. Concomitantly, huge and growing public investments in medical services for older people, although providing greater access to hospitals and physicians and enriching providers, have failed to alleviate the elderly's enormous financial burdens or address their chronic care needs. Certainly, the most conspicuous absence of social provision for elders has been in the area of long-term care (LTC), a world mostly populated by women.

The United States has never consciously or systematically developed a national system of long-term care to provide for its frail older population, and there are woefully few government-supported services available to them. Instead, the vast majority of disabled elderly have had to rely on their own resources—and families—to meet their basic needs. Consequently, because of the high costs, a significant number of older people who become physically or mentally incapacitated are also vulnerable to economic devastation and dependency on unpaid care for their daily needs.

Services for the elderly developed haphazardly over the years, mostly in response to funding streams and political/economic power, especially in the states, generating a decidedly medical and institutional bias (Kane, Kane, and Ladd, 1998). From the disorder, a bifurcated structure of LTC emerged: a means-tested program for the indigent as well as those middle-class elderly who attain eligibility through impoverishment, and a residual system for older people generally. The first, Medicaid, consists of well-financed but sorely deficient nursing homes and a limited number of scattered, ad hoc, and severely underfunded home- and community-based programs. The second, Medicare, provides firmly circumscribed institutional and home-based services, primarily incidental to acute medical care needs.

The nursing home has dominated LTC funding over the decades. Despite the restricted scope of government programs and the small number of people assisted, public payments to nursing homes have increased rapidly, currently representing over half of their total revenues (SSCA, 2000a). By 2001, they were paid a whopping $58 billion from the public treasury, with $38 billion coming from the federal government, mostly through Medicaid (GAO, 2002i).[1] Currently, there are about 1.6 million aged living in about 17,000 facilities; it is projected that their population will quadruple by 2050 to about 6.5 million people (U.S. Bureau of the Census, 2000a; U.S. Bureau of the Census, 2001).

The overwhelming number of physically or mentally impaired elders, however—about 80 percent—live in noninstitutional settings, whether alone, with a spouse, or in multigenerational households (SSCA, 1998c). Though their needs vary considerably, most require some help with the activities of daily living (ADLs)—eating, bathing, grooming, dressing, walking, toileting, getting in and out of bed or chairs, or other difficult maneuvers; and instrumental activities of daily living (IADLs)—housekeeping, laundry, and other household maintenance chores, shopping, food preparation, managing money, and paying bills.[2] Individuals with mental impairments also may require custodial supervision to ensure their safety. At the turn of the twenty-first century, over 9 million adults—many of them seriously disabled—are dependent on others for assistance in their day-to-day existence. Of the total, 4.2 million are elders living in the community, representing about one-seventh of the sixty-five and over population (GAO, 2001c).

Forces Shaping Care

Long-term care policies have been driven by a number of intersecting sociocultural, ideological, political, economic, and demographic forces. First, population aging is generating a growing demand for supportive services. Though age-specific disability and morbidity rates have been decreasing somewhat, the overall number of elders relying on others for their basic needs will continue to expand, especially as the baby boomers approach more advanced ages.

Second, similarly to other areas of social welfare in the United States since the late 1970s, public discourse on LTC has been dominated by overall retrenchment goals, along with an intensification of privatization and market-based policies. Consequently, it is increasingly assumed that the private sphere should shoulder more and more of the caring activities that the state has undertaken in the past. Such a shift from the public to the private sector entails fewer directly delivered elder care services, a growing commercialization of existing programs, less popular control or accountability over them, and reduced government expenditures on older people overall. These changes were reinforced by linking the fiscal crisis of the American economy to old age programs, fostering an anti-entitlement mentality. Benefits for the aged were further undermined with narratives about their greed and prosperity, with many public leaders insisting that the elderly have become a drain on the economy.

Government downsizing and private-sector solutions for social problems, advanced under President Reagan and the "New Right" and normalized under President Clinton and his "New Democrats," have become the dominant policy approach under the current administration of George W. Bush. As Hooyman and Gonyea (1995) put it, the public sphere has been increasingly exonerated from the obligations of community responsibility. Consequently, a leading strategy for LTC has been to increasingly privatize the costs of growing old, regardless of the human costs.

High and rapidly accelerating budget outlays for health care have prompted an ongoing effort among public officials to contain expenditures and curtail access to services, especially for nursing homes. Policymakers have sought to restructure reimbursement methods, encourage managed care organizations (MCOs), impose a barrage of new regulations, reduce coverage, introduce efficiencies, and control usage while perpetuating the existing costly, deficient system of privatized care. As a result, they have not been able to significantly stem rising public spending on the elderly but have succeeded in shrinking the availability of services, particularly for the poor and those with low incomes.

Third, government budget cutting, along with a strengthening of individualism and familism, has promoted and reinforced the responsibility of older people to finance their own care. Though the frail elderly have always had to rely primarily on their own resources for LTC, they are now forced to bear even greater costs. For a significant number of these vulnerable, mostly dependent individuals, such self-reliance implies economic devastation, and for many it means impoverishment. It also places their care squarely in the hands of families, primarily wives and daughters.

Fourth, individualism is buttressed by our residual approach to care: public resources for home- and community-based care must be strictly limited and controlled, provided only as a last resort. Although the federal government has allowed the creation of some innovative home- and community-based services in several states, the central thrust of these initiatives has been to save money on institutional care.

Fifth, fiscal austerity has been accompanied by cost shifting at all levels of the American political system. Over the last several decades, the national government has embarked on greater decentralization and devolution of authority for social programs. Long-term care has long been embedded in the politics and policies of the states: though there is considerable national funding and general federal guidelines exist, they are mostly responsible for eligibility standards; licensing, regulating, and inspecting providers; and the extent and types of services available. However, states now have even greater control over programs but obtain diminishing federal funding with which to implement them. To compensate, they have attempted to transfer some of their LTC costs to federally funded programs, to the national portion of joint undertakings, and to the frail elderly and their families.

Sixth, public policies have served to feed the LTC industries and ensure profitability while endorsing untenable private sector practices as well as certifying and sustaining poor quality of care. They also have abetted the movement from nonprofit to for-profit organizations as well as the accelerating mergers and consolidation of profit-making provider groups into large-scale chains.

Moreover, under current political and economic arrangements, providers can exert significant pressure on policymakers, and ultimatums abound. Managed care organizations and nursing homes regularly threaten to jeopardize the well-being of clients by reducing access to care. Though nursing homes have always had considerable influence over state LTC decisions, they now command additional leverage: large chains can threaten to displace a massive number of residents if their demands are not met.

Seventh, frail, dependent older people require supportive services that allow them to cope with the irreversible effects of their multiple disabling conditions. Concomitantly, their incidence of acute diseases tends to be even higher than that of the population generally. However, there are no clear distinctions between their medical and long-term care requirements (Kane, 1993). Despite the growing need of elders for integrated services, current age-based policies perpetuate a medical bias; they provide generous funding for hospital care—and to a lesser extent physician services—while failing to adequately address the complexities, effects, and consequences of chronic illnesses and functional impairments.

Population Aging

The average life expectancy in the United States was only about 47 at the turn of the twentieth century, rising to 76.5 years today. In 1900, older people comprised less than 4 percent of the population, but their percentage grew steadily over the decades, from 7 percent in 1940 and 9 percent in 1960 to 12.4 percent, or 35 million people, by 2000.[3] It is projected that the size of the older population will continue to grow rapidly, reaching 70 million people, or 20 percent of the total, by 2030 (Federal Interagency Forum, 2000; U.S. Bureau of the Census, 2001a, 2001g). The steady increase in the number and percentage of elders during the coming years can be attributed to a number of factors. Among them is the aging of the baby boomers and a decline in birthrates: during the 1950s and 1960s, families averaged 3.8 children; today, the number is 2.1. However, partly because of a relatively low number of births during the early 1930s as well as a large influx of young immigrants, from 1990 to 2000 the percentage of older people temporarily—for the first time since the first census in 1790—increased less than the population at large, 12 percent as compared to 13.2 percent (U.S. Bureau of the Census, 2001g).

Because of reductions in mortality among middle-aged and older people, since the 1950s the nation has experienced an impressive lengthening of the life span (Dailey, 1998). In fact, the most striking change has been the rapid growth of the oldest-old population. By mid-century, the eighty-five and over age group began expanding rapidly, 154 percent between 1940 and 1960 and 142 percent from 1960 to 1980 (Abel, 1991). From 1990 to 2000, the eighty-five and older population increased by a whopping 38 percent. Consisting of 4.2 million people, they now represent 1.5 percent of the total population and 12 percent of the elderly. Indeed, the third-fastest growing sector of the population—45 percent since 1990—has been the ninety-to-ninety-four-year-olds, with 1.1 million people. About 337,000 older adults are aged ninety-five and older; slightly over 50,000 are centenarians (U.S. Bureau of the Census, 2001a, 2001g). And the first of the 76 million baby boomers, currently representing about 28 percent of the population, will begin swelling the ranks of the elderly in only a few years. As the elderly population enlarges, its makeup is increasingly more female—about 19.7 million older women compared to 13.5 million older men. The difference is even more dramatic among the oldest old: there are about 2.8 million women and only 1.1 million men aged eighty-five and over (SSCA, 1998c).

Improved longevity has been accompanied by increased dependency; at the most extreme ages, more elders develop multiple chronic disabling conditions, along with Alzheimer's disease and other dementia conditions, render them reliant on others for care. About 16 percent of elders aged sixty-five to seventy-four have physical or cognitive conditions that limit their activities of daily living, including bathing, eating, and dressing on their own; however, by age eighty-five about half need some help to sustain themselves at home (Abel, 1991; Dailey, 1998). In 2000 only 4.5 percent of the elderly resided in a nursing home at any one time, but the proportion increased to slightly over 18 percent for those aged eighty-five and over (U.S. Bureau of the Census,

2000a).[4] Because women tend to outlive men and because they represent about 72 percent of the oldest-old population, they are the largest consumers of long-term care; they also comprise over 70 percent of all nursing home residents (Hooyman, 1997). Certainly, despite slight decreases over the past two decades in the prevalence of chronic conditions among the elderly (about 1 or 2 percent a year) the overall number of baby boomers dependent on others for assistance in their daily lives will rise dramatically, perhaps double the number of today (GAO, 2002a). Consisting mostly of females, their total could reach over 14 million frail elders by 2020 alone (GAO, 1999a).

Medicare

Medicare is the largest single source of health care funding in the United States, providing health-related services to 40 million older and disabled people in 2001. Enacted in 1965, it is primarily an acute health care insurance program that provides inpatient hospitalization, skilled nursing facilities (SNFs), some home health assistance and hospice services under part A, and physician, outpatient hospital, and other noninstitutional services—such as diagnostic laboratory tests, durable medical equipment, ambulance transport, and home health care—under part B. In order to substitute for expensive hospital care during convalescence, the program allows up to 100 days in a certified skilled nursing home (with a daily coinsurance after 20 days) and unlimited home health visits from accredited agencies. While a Medicare recipient is in the nursing home, Medicare covers nearly all patient costs, including ancillary services such as drugs, laboratory tests, and rehabilitation therapies.

Coverage of social supportive/homemaker services is explicitly prohibited. Any allowable postacute nursing home stays are for short-term skilled nursing and/or rehabilitation services, thus precluding ongoing care for chronic conditions. The program provides for in-home help only under specific, restricted conditions: a physician must prescribe a plan for recovery and certify that skilled services are medically necessary; the older person requires part-time or intermittent nursing care and/or physical, occupational, or speech therapy; and the patient is confined to the house. If these criteria are met, Medicare will fund certain other services, including a home health aide and medical equipment and supplies. Any personal assistance must be directly related to the medical treatment of an illness or injury (Kane, Kane, and Ladd, 1998; SSCA, 1998a, 1998c).

After its enactment, Medicare, along with Medicaid to a lesser extent, became a major and steadily increasing source of income for hospitals. Reimbursed on a cost-plus basis, including capital investments, and with few controls over expenditures, they went on a buying and building spree. Hospitals invested in costly and often unnecessary specialized high-tech medical equipment, fancy offices and lobbies, parking garages, and large-scale construction and expansion. Inefficiency, duplication of resources, and exorbitant administrative costs prevailed. Physicians found that they had no limits on the number of laboratory tests, sophisticated procedures, and therapies they ordered or performed, resulting in unnecessary surgeries and excessive treatments. Their fees, based on customary, prevailing charges, were open-ended as well. The pharmaceutical and hospital supply industries and other medical markets also cashed in. Consequently, during the first two decades of Medicare and Medicaid, the medical-industrial complex garnered high profits and fueled double-digit inflation in health care, even greater than the cost of living.

Medicare's outlays expanded dramatically, primarily due to soaring hospital costs; in the first year alone, hospital prices increased by 22 percent (Marmor, 1970). From $2.8 billion in 1967 and $12.9 billion in 1975, program disbursements escalated to $32.1 billion by 1980. Despite the budget-cutting decades that followed, Medicare continued to grow considerably, reaching $98.1 billion by 1990. Over the next seven years, it increased by about 10 to 11 percent annually to $190 billion. Even after more cost constraints on the program since 1997 and a temporary two-year slow-down, its outlays reached $218 billion in 2001, about 2.3 percent of GDP (gross domestic product) (U.S. Budget, 2001b).[5] Medicare has become the fourth-largest expenditure of the national government (12 percent of the budget), following Social Security, defense, and interest on the debt. If Medicare spending continues to grow at the same rate, it could reach over 23 percent of total federal expenditures and 4.5 percent of GDP by 2030 (GAO, 2001n).

Medicare Cost Containment

The New Hospital Reimbursement System and Its Aftermath

By the 1980s, Medicare policy making had become dominated by cost-containment strategies rather than by any new initiatives for program improvement and expansion. One of the early, more consequential responses to escalating Medicare outlays was the attempt to control hospital costs. Beginning in 1983, cost-based hospital reimbursement was replaced by a prospective payment system that pays a fixed, predetermined sum of money per illness, based on 470 diagnosis-related groups (DRGs).[6] In other words, hospitals would be rewarded or penalized, depending on how efficiently and rapidly they could provide treatments. As a result, older people had considerably shorter hospital stays, with reductions averaging over 22 percent in the ensuing years (Lee and Estes, 1981). Between 1990 and 1998 alone, the average length of a hospital stay was reduced from 8.8 to 6.1 days (Federal Interagency Forum, 2000). Older patients were shoved out the door "quicker and sicker," shifting significant responsibility for intensive medical care to nursing homes, home health agencies, and especially the elderly and their caregivers.

In order to reduce Medicare outlays under part B, the government also began to regulate the high and growing physician charges. Driven by both an increased number of doctor visits and a greater intensity of services, costs had grown more than 12 percent per beneficiary annually during the 1980s (GAO, 2002h). In 1992, the "customary, prevailing, and reasonable" payment method was replaced with a fee schedule, slowing the annual increases measurably. In order to cut expenditures further, in 1997 Congress mandated that the rates be adjusted annually to meet newly established spending targets, thus lowering fees even more.[7] Although there were some concerns about consumer access to physician services, studies show that few eligible doctors actually have left the program or refused to treat new Medicare patients (AARP, 2002b; GAO, 2002h). In addition, participating providers now can either accept the fixed rate for medical services or "balance bill" their patients, charging them no more than 15 percent over the set amount. In 2000, 86 percent of all fee-for-service physicians were accepting the Medicare rate as payment in full, up from 75 percent in 1996 (GAO, 2001h).

Despite the curbs on hospital and physician reimbursements, most of the savings were shifted as costs to other parts of the Medicare program, Medicaid, and the beneficiaries themselves. Medicare outlays continued to grow, particularly for in-home and skilled nursing home care, both of which became the most rapidly increasing pieces of program costs. Because of DRGs, patients have been released from hospitals with serious conditions requiring skilled medical care. In order to discourage high-cost nursing homes, the government steadily encouraged the use of home care services. At the same time, under the Omnibus Reconciliation Act (ORA) of 1980, it had made coverage under the home care provisions less restrictive. For example, new rules eliminated the 100 visit per year cap, the requirement that a Medicare recipient had to be hospitalized for three days prior to receiving home health services under part A, and the deductible for home care under part B. It also shifted most home care financing to part A (Benjamin, 1993).

Hospital discharges to home health agencies rose by nearly 40 percent after the imposition of DRGs (Hooyman and Gonyea, 1995). With no ceiling on the number of visits per beneficiary and with no cost-sharing for clients except for a 20 percent coinsurance on durable medical equipment, the number of elders using home care services and the number of visits per recipient more than doubled from 1990 to 1997 (GAO, 2000e); nearly 4 million elders, or more than 10 percent of all Medicare beneficiaries, were receiving some care at home, including limited personal services. Home health care costs grew at an annual rate of over 25 percent, from $2.5 billion in 1989 to $17.2 billion in 1997, accounting for 8.7 percent of Medicare outlays (SSCA, 1998a). In 1973, they had accounted for less than 1 percent of the total, or only $64 million.

Spurred by lucrative profits under Medicare, the number of home care agencies, along with the volume of services, expanded rapidly. Home health care became the fastest-growing component of the health care sector in the United States, accounting for over $30 billion annually by the end of the twenty-first century (SSCA, 1998e). In 1967 there were 1,753 Medicare participating agencies nationally, a number that had grown to just under 5,700 in 1990 and reached 10,500 by 1997 (Kane, Kane, and Ladd, 1998). Between 1995 and 1998 alone, the number of home health care agencies increased by 20 percent (GAO, 1999c).

The Medicare largesse also intensified the ongoing growth of for-profit home care agencies, a process that had begun with the ORA of 1980 allowing their participation under the program in every state: in five years, the number of for-profit agencies reimbursed by Medicare had increased sixfold (Benjamin, 1993). From 1990 to 1997, the percentage of proprietary agencies, mostly corporate chains, rose from 36 percent to 58 percent of the total; mergers and acquisitions proliferated (GAO, 1999e).[8] Hospitals, too, cashed in on more liberal home health benefits. As their income from the Medicare hospitalization provision declined because of DRGs, a number of enterprising institutions included home care as part of their services; about a quarter of home health agencies are hospital based (Kane, Kane, and Ladd, 1998).

Outlays for nursing homes also expanded dramatically, representing a growing share of Medicare, along with large owner profits. Although nursing home proprietors rely on Medicaid for most of their public funding, about 12 percent of their total revenue accrued from Medicare by 1998 (GAO, 2001c). Payments to skilled nursing facilities increased by an average of 25 percent annually during the 1990s, rising to $13.6 billion in 1998. During that period, Medicare-certified SNFs grew by about 6 percent each year to 14,860 facilities, and the number of beneficiaries receiving care doubled, along with an increase in services per patient (GAO, 1999n; OIG, 2001d). Currently, about 2 million people receive Medicare-covered skilled nursing care annually (SSCA, 2000a).

As chapter 7 will show, nursing homes took particular advantage of cost-based reimbursement policies and limited government oversight over spending for capital costs and ancillary services (GAO, 1999n). Many investors acquired and developed facilities as Medicare rates rose during the 1990s. They also added home health units along with expensive onsite therapy services and specialized medical equipment (SSCA, 2000a). Medicare's average daily payment to nursing homes increased 12 percent annually—from $98 in 1990 to $262 in 1998—mostly because of excessive ancillary services; outlays for occupational, speech, and physical therapy more than doubled (GAO, 1999n; OIG, 2001d). Significantly, actual costs for the goods and services nursing homes provided grew by only 3 percent (SSCA, 2000a). But their markup on therapy services alone was as high as 800 percent. Because of higher reimbursement rates, many facilities replaced Medicaid with Medicare patients whenever possible, thereby reducing care for the poor (GAO, 1999n; SSCA, 2000a).

In order to control the burgeoning Medicare expenditures, policymakers proposed various budget-cutting methods aimed at providers and beneficiaries alike. In fact, Medicare and Medicaid became the centers of social welfare retrenchment policies. In particular, the Balanced Budget Act (BBA) of 1997 proposed to cut Medicare outlays by over $115 billion (and Medicaid by $10 billion) over five years by reducing payments to hospitals, home health agencies, MCOs, and other providers. About $40 billion of the first-year Medicare reductions was for hospitals; $5 billion for physicians; $22 billion for managed care plans; $16 billion for home health agencies; and $10 billion for skilled nursing facilities. Among other changes, hospitals could no longer discharge patients to subacute centers and still receive their full DRG amount. As a result, hospitals kept the patients themselves, which had a negative impact on home health agencies and nursing homes (Stahl, 2000).

The major approach to curbing costs was to develop and implement new payment methods for postacute services. For home health care, the legislation restructured the cost-based reimbursement system, mandating that HCFA (U. S. Health Care Finance Administration) develop a prospective payment scheme (PPS) for 1999 (later extended to 2000) and an immediate "interim payment system" (IPS) containing per visit cost limits and overall payment caps based on the HHAs' average Medicare payments per client during 1994. Under BBA 1997, revised in 1999, the rates paid to the agencies would be reduced by 15 percent across the board a year after the PPS was implemented (GAO, 2000e). The act also initiated a prospective payment system for nursing homes. In addition to per diem payments for patients based on a case-mix classification system of resource utilization groups (RUGs), it capped occupational and physical therapy at $1,500 each for all recipients.

Because of cuts in funding, Medicare grew by only 1.5 percent from 1997 to 1998 and even declined 1 percent—to $190,447—the following year. Home health care costs, one of the fastest-growing components of the program, were reduced from $18 billion in 1996 to $9.5 billion in 1999 (HWM, 2001). Many home health agencies, which had come to rely on the inordinately high and growing reimbursement levels, closed down or were bought out by chains. Nationwide, 14 percent of home health agencies closed between October 1997 and January 1999; over 1,200 went out of business during 1998 alone (Simun, 1998).[9]

Although it is against the law, some agencies began using assorted means for "cherry-picking" low-cost clients, leaving the sickest and/or those requiring expensive care without access to community-based services, despite the fact that over 40 percent of those requiring home health care are seriously ill with unstable medical conditions and functional impairments (SSCA, 1998a). They also threatened to discontinue their participation in the Medicare program. Under current structural arrangements, then, any cuts in home care funding could drive frail elders into nursing homes or force families to shoulder an increased burden of care. Moreover, because of "the lack of standards for what constitutes appropriate care," they threaten the quality of services within the agencies themselves (GAO, 2000e).

Since BBA 1997, it also has been harder to place more costly patients in nursing homes; these facilities have become cautious about which Medicare beneficiaries they will take from hospitals, "requesting medical records, reviewing drug administration charts, and even sending staff to the hospital for in-person assessments" (GAO, 1999n, 7). One chain admitted that they now take in patients requiring fewer ancillary services (SSCA, 2000a). According to a recent study, hospital discharge planners have to contact, on average, three nursing homes prior to finding a placement for their patients (OIG, 2001d). Therefore, although most beneficiaries continue to have access to nursing home services, they cannot choose among providers and may be forced into low-quality facilities. Moreover, in order to maintain high profits, nursing homes began replacing professional therapists with less costly physical and occupational therapy assistants, raising new quality-of-care concerns (Stahl, 2000).

As a result, senior advocacy organizations and their allies were forced to defend against the budget cuts. Concomitantly, provider groups—particularly nursing homes, hospitals, and home health agencies—"sought to work out their own deals with Congress to ensure that, whatever happened, their interests would be protected" (Torres-Gil, 1998, 82). Their primary weapon was to threaten reduced access to services, especially for beneficiaries most in need.

One of the largest and most exhaustive campaigns against revisions to the Medicare program ensued immediately. BBA 1997 engendered mass mailings and other grassroots campaigns, intense lobbying, television commercials, and newspaper ads by a vast array of interests during 1999. The National Committee to Preserve Social Security and Medicare (NCPSSM), the American Association of Retired Persons (AARP), and other senior advocacy groups put their efforts into the preservation of Medicare overall, along with a demand for prescription drug coverage; NCPSSM alone spent approximately $1 million. Citizens for Better Medicare, which represents the pharmaceutical industry, spent nearly $30 million to oppose any benefits that would entail cost controls over drugs. The Alliance for Quality Nursing Home Care, made up of eleven nursing home operators, spent approximately $15 million to influence Congress through lobbying, political contributions, and advertising. Along with the American Health Care Association, the nursing home trade group, it sought the restoration of cuts to old age facilities. While the American Hospital Association focused on funding for its member organizations, the Coalition for Medicare Choices, consisting of health maintenance organizations, lobbied for higher reimbursement rates for MCOs; and the Biotechnology Industry Organization (representing biotech firms) opposed pharmaceutical benefits that would limit drug research. These campaigns cost $10 million, $5 million, and $50,000, respectively.

Congress caved in to industry demands while ignoring key consumer interests. Over the next several years, national policymakers enacted legislation that steadily restored billions of dollars to the various providers, increased reimbursement rates for home health agencies and nursing homes, suspended the payment ceilings for nursing home therapy services, and raised the caps for home health agencies as well as delayed their 15 percent across-the-board cuts. Under the Balanced Budget Refinement Act of 1999 (BBRA), Congress enacted a $16 billion, five-year "give-back" package; the following year, Clinton proposed another $21 billion. However, the provider groups demanded much more. Another massive and expensive lobbying campaign ensued, with hospitals and MCOs taking the lead; hospitals alone planned to spend more than $30 million on advertising. As part of a grassroots effort, the organizations appealed to beneficiaries who were enlisted to take up their cause, arguing that the cuts were hurting them as well (*Congressional Quarterly,* 2000). Ultimately, Congress gave them additional money; even greater amounts were promised for future years (SSCA, 2000a).[10] At the same time, the legislators conspicuously failed to enact a nursing home patient bill of rights, measures protecting MCO beneficiaries, or prescription drug coverage.

Managed Care

In an additional attempt to moderate Medicare spending but using the rhetoric of greater consumer "choice," Congress restructured the program to include managed care. Beginning in 1985, under the Tax Equity and Fiscal Responsibility Act (TEFRA) of 1982, beneficiaries have been allowed to enroll in managed care organizations that would receive a monthly capitated payment per client. Promising beneficiaries lower out-of-pocket costs and improved benefits, these plans soon became the fastest-growing component of Medicare. With 3 percent of the Medicare population enrolled in 1987, the percentage quickly grew to 9 percent by 1995 at a cost of $11 billion (SJ, 1994; Sparrow, 1996). Under BBA 1997, additional "choices" became available under the Medicare+Choice (M+C) program, including preferred provider organizations (PPOs), provider-sponsored organizations (PSOs), and fee-for-service schemes that allowed higher physician out-of-pocket charges. By 1999, there were about 409 choice-plus plans serving 7 million elders (or 17 percent of program participants) at a cost of $37 billion (HB, 2000a; SA, 2000a). The government currently is the largest single buyer of managed care services in the nation.

Right from the start, MCOs successfully enlisted healthier elders—often through illegal or unethical marketing tactics—and removed higher-cost people from their rolls (Anders, 1997; SJ, 1994). They particularly shortchanged elders with disabling conditions that are ongoing and expensive to treat. One investigation found that of the chronically ill elderly patients studied, 54 percent of those participating in MCOs experienced a decline in their physical health as compared to 28 percent of the beneficiaries enrolled in fee-for-service plans (Jones, 1999). Many of the frail aged who found themselves with severely inadequate or low-quality services eventually disenrolled; Medicare beneficiaries could withdraw from their plans with one month's notice (Anders, 1997). However, dropout rates became so high that new rules were instituted that will lock participants into their MCO for a year, beginning in 2005.

During the 1990s, hospital stays for MCO beneficiaries grew even shorter than for those using conventional Medicare, thus enlarging the pool of seriously ill older people using nursing homes and home health services. Some managed care plans placed upper limits on the number of home care visits and rehabilitative services, shifting the burdens of care to families (SSCA, 1998e). Critically, a 1994 government-commissioned study by the Center for Health Policy Research found that MCOs "handled their home-care patients faster, cheaper and less effectively than conventional Medicare did" (Anders, 1997, 323).

In reaction to congressional Medicare cuts under BBA 1997 that reduced reimbursement rates, and in order to maintain their high profits, a large number of MCOs began steadily increasing out-of-pocket client costs and canceling or placing caps on the special benefits that had lured beneficiaries into their plans, including coverage for prescription drugs, eyeglasses, and hearing aids (HWM, 2001). Some others threw out participating doctors who they viewed as spending "too much time" with patients or performing "excessive" procedures.

In addition, many MCOs threatened to pull out of Medicare entirely, and increasing numbers actually did so. Between 1998 and 2001, over 150 MCOs either refused to renew their contracts or reduced their service areas, affecting about 2.1 million beneficiaries (GAO, 2001j).[11] Their tactics worked: Congress immediately began restoring much of the funding. Under BBRA 1999, Congress increased payment rates and established new-entry bonuses to encourage plans where they were not already available. Again, in 2000, reimbursements were raised: MCOs received a total of $1 billion more, averaging $16 per beneficiary every month; very little of this money was used to benefit the clients themselves. In fact, only 16 percent of all plans used even a portion of the extra funds for improved benefits. And the infusion of money did not stop the tide of closings or increases in patient cost-sharing requirements. Nor did it improve the availability of plans (GAO, 2001j). In 2002, over 536,000 beneficiaries were dropped by their MCOs; the majority of the remaining plans raised their premiums, lowered services, or both, especially for prescription drug coverage (AARP, 2001c).

BBA 1997 also made it easier for states to set up managed care plans that include long-term care, including social health maintenance organizations (SHMOs). Although there have been only limited efforts to date (Wiener and Stevenson, 1998), many states are looking at this option as yet another budget-cutting device. Given the current care problems associated with MCOs, especially for elders with chronic, disabling conditions, it is highly questionable whether these organizations can and will provide adequate, quality services to those who are frail and dependent.

Medicaid

Most public funding for long-term care comes through the Medicaid program, enacted in 1965.[12] Originally designed to cover medical costs for the welfare-eligible population, primarily the blind, aged, and single mothers, it was soon expanded to include people who met state-established "medical indigency" requirements. The program is jointly funded by the national and state governments; states contribute matching funds from 22 to 50 percent, depending on their per capita income. Though they must adhere to certain broad federal guidelines, the states and localities shoulder most of the responsibility for the program. They must provide hospital and physician services, skilled nursing home care, and home health assistance;[13] additional services, including prescription drugs, dental care, rehabilitation services and personal assistance services (PAS), are at their option. States have considerable discretion over most other aspects of the program. Consequently, there is considerable variation among them in terms of whom they cover; eligibility standards; types, amount, scope, and duration of services; payment methods and reimbursement rates; and the integrity of the programs themselves.

Medicaid was never intended to fund support services for older people requiring long-term services: "No one at the time anticipated that Medicaid might be the major payer of long-term care, especially nursing home care" (Kane, 1994, 290). Both the skilled nursing and home care provisions under the act were restricted to medically necessary services ordered by a physician, focusing on short-term rehabilitation from acute illnesses. Over the years, however, Medicaid gradually absorbed the costs of the indigent and medically needy elderly and younger disabled populations who require extended institutional care for chronic, disabling conditions; their long-term care now consumes about 20 percent and 14 percent, respectively, of total program outlays (Wiener and Stevenson, 1998). In 2001, the elderly and disabled represent one-third of the 33 million people served under Medicaid but two-thirds of its total spending (U.S. Budget, 2001b).

Institutional facilities have dominated LTC spending under Medicaid, despite their high and growing costs, inadequate care, and older people's preference for community and in-home services.[14] Clearly, public policies, regulations, and rules over the years have privileged nursing homes over every other type of LTC. First, Medicaid covers a recipient's room and board in nursing homes, but such subsidies generally are disallowed for elders residing at home or in assisted living and other residential dwellings. Second, in many places, it is easier to qualify for institutional care than for home- and community-based services. Medicaid beneficiaries are entitled to nursing home services as long as there is an available certified bed; personal care services are at the option of the state. Moreover, unlike institutional care, states must obtain a waiver for their home and community care programs. Third, because of special spousal impoverishment rules, greater financial protection is afforded partners of nursing home residents than those caring for their spouses at home. Fourth, federal regulations specifying that Medicaid funds be paid directly to nursing homes serve to increase their use relative to other forms of care (Kane, Kane, and Ladd, 1998). Fifth, hospital social workers tend to find it easier, quicker, and more efficient to discharge ill patients to institutional facilities than to arrange formal care in the community (HGRO, 1997). Sixth, in states that have included a medically needy category, an older person with limited assets is eligible for nursing home placement if his or her income is less than the cost of care, an amount that tends to be well above the pensions of most elders (Kane, 1994). Thus, elders who "spend down" their financial resources on institutional care can be partially or fully supported by Medicaid.

As a result, nursing home care is the largest single source of expenditure under Medicaid (Wallack, 1997). In 1999, about three-fourths of all Medicaid long-term care funding went to institutional facilities, as compared to only one-fourth for in-home and community services (SSCA, 2001a). The program supports about 52 percent of all nursing home costs in the nation; about 68 percent of all nursing home patients rely on Medicaid for at least part of their care, the majority having exhausted their savings first (GAO, 1999k; Wiener, Sullivan, and Skaggs, 1996).[15]

Disbursements under Medicaid grew rapidly over the years, with the program experiencing cost overruns immediately (Jesilow, Pontell, and Geis, 1993). Nursing home prices, which rose well above overall inflation rates in the nation, accounted for the largest source of the accelerating outlays (Vladeck, 1980).[16] Costing $1.9 billion in 1966, Medicaid outlays reached a whopping $219 billion by 2001, with the national and state shares amounting to $124 billion and $95 billion, respectively. The portion paid by the federal government represents 7 percent of the total U.S. budget, its fifth-largest expenditure (U.S. Budget, 2001a).

Medicaid also consumed a steadily expanding percentage of total state expenditures (including all sources of funds), averaging about 19 percent by 2000; proportions ranged from under 10 percent in Delaware and Hawaii to 25 percent and over in Maine, Missouri, New York, Pennsylvania, Rhode Island, and Tennessee (State of Vermont, 2002). Long-term care services became the fastest-growing segment of the program; with costs increasing by about 13 percent annually during the 1990s, they typically represented about 30 percent of a state's Medicaid budget (GAO, 1999h; Kane, Kane, and Ladd, 1998; SSCA, 1995b). Though there is considerable variation among them, most states devote the vast majority of their LTC funding to nursing homes, with some places, such as Arizona, Illinois, Louisiana, Mississippi, Ohio, and Tennessee, spending as much as 90 percent or more of this funding on skilled and intermediate care facilities (AARP, 1998).

Medicaid Cost Containment

Restrictions on Nursing Home Placement

From the beginning, the driving forces underlying Medicaid policy have been efforts to rein in its costs and reduce access to care through new regulations, less coverage, and more stringent eligibility requirements. The national government increasingly has accorded the states more responsibility for the program while steadily reducing their federal funding. Because institutional care had become the largest single expense, by the early 1980s state leaders focused on curbing its growth.

States are required to pay for every Medicaid-eligible person residing in a nursing home. Therefore, one of the earliest approaches was to control the supply of available openings. A majority of the states imposed certificate of need (CON) restrictions on additional Medicaid-certified beds as well as moratoriums on new construction of facilities beginning in the mid-1970s. Consequently, the number of nursing homes and available beds relative to the growth of the eighty-five and over population decreased steadily. In 1977 there were 19,500 Medicare- and Medicaid-certified nursing homes; by 2001 the number had been reduced to about 17,000, with 1.8 million beds.[17] One consequence has been inordinately high occupancy rates—averaging over 90 percent nationally by 1986—that have inflated charges and bolstered profits.[18]

States also have attempted to keep Medicaid beneficiaries out of nursing homes by establishing strict screening procedures; by 1989, thirty states had enacted such measures (Abel, 1991). For example, in order to enter a nursing home, Medicaid-eligible elders must show that they cannot remain at home, that institutional placement is medically necessary, or both (Meyer and Storbakken, 2000). Between 1990 and 2000, nursing home usage declined from 5.1 percent to 4.5 percent of the sixty-five and over population. The drop was most conspicuous among elders eighty-five and over, from 24.5 percent to 18.2 percent, despite the fact that their numbers had grown rapidly over the decade and this sector of older people is the most in need of care (U.S. Bureau of the Census, 2001g).

Despite their success in restraining the growth of the nursing home industry and the number of Medicaid beds, states have been less effective in curbing the annual cost of care per recipient; total public funding for institutional services continues to mount.[19]

Tinkering with Reimbursement Formulas

Another approach to controlling LTC expenditures has been through restructuring payment methods. Medicaid nursing homes' reimbursement rates are set by each state within general federal guidelines. In 1972, states were required to compensate facilities on a "reasonable cost-related basis," which included capital investments. As Vladeck holds, "Hospitals took the generosity of reimbursement formulas to construct opulent workshops in which physicians could employ the most esoteric scientific technologies; nursing homes took the money and ran" (1980, 131).

In 1980, Congress passed the Boren Amendment, which provided that states pay nursing facilities for Medicaid beneficiaries based on what is "reasonable and adequate to meet the costs incurred by efficiently and economically operated facilities in order to provide care and services in conformity with applicable state and federal laws, regulations, and quality and safety standards" (Wiener and Stevenson, 1998, 93). In some cases, when states attempted to cut their reimbursement rates, the nursing home industry used the Boren Amendment to resist them through actual or threatened lawsuits (Lee and Estes, 1981; Wiener and Stevenson, 1998). Proprietors further enhanced their interests by means of the Omnibus Budget Reconciliation Act (OBRA) of 1987, which specified that states must include the costs of meeting quality standards in their rates. At the time, 41 states were using a cost-based reimbursement approach, thus increasing outlays considerably (Cohen and Spector, 1996).[20]

Repeal of the Boren Amendment, effective in 1998, granted states more flexibility in setting nursing home rates. Most of them took advantage of the repeal by switching to new reimbursement mechanisms in order to lower payments: these included various forms of PPS and flat, per diem rates; a diminishing number of states continued to use cost-based (or retrospective) approaches (Clarette and Johnson, 1998). But they still must contend with the powerful nursing home industry. It is one of the most powerful health care interest groups, especially at the state level, rendering serious cost-cutting a formidable task (Wiener and Stevenson, 1998).

Access and Quality Problems

Since in many places demand exceeds supply and some institutions even have waiting lists, proprietors can discriminate against the lowest-paying elders, regardless of need. Although a few states have prohibited or limited differential charges for Medicaid and private-pay residents, in most places the disparity is substantial. Medicaid recipients, especially those requiring "heavy care," often have more difficulty finding a nursing home bed than higher-paying clients (Abel, 1991). A 1990 GAO study, for example, found that in over half of the states they studied, Medicaid recipients had to wait at least two to three times longer to find a placement than those who pay privately. In some places, they were denied access entirely (Meyer and Storbakken, 2000). This can be particularly problematic for older people who are forced out of hospitals prematurely; their families are forced to provide high levels of medical care at home. In 1998, Vencor, even attempted to evict all of its Medicaid patients en masse, leading to a federal law disallowing such actions.

Moreover, the mix of high occupancy rates and comparatively low payments per bed tends to relegate Medicaid patients to the most substandard facilities. The Institute of Medicine (1996), for instance, found a correlation between low service levels and high numbers of Medicaid recipients within an institution. From the earliest studies of the subject to more current ones, most researchers have concluded that there is a relationship between the socioeconomic status of residents (especially welfare recipients) and the caliber of services they receive (GAO 2002k; Holmberg and Anderson, 1968; Kosberg, 1973). Even in "preferable" nursing homes, elders on public assistance tend to receive inferior treatment. Wiener and Stevenson explain, "Few nursing homes can survive without Medicaid residents . . . which limits the extent to which facilities can reduce access" (1998, 94). Instead, they decrease services for their Medicaid patients, lowering the quality of their care. In his study of nursing homes, Diamond found that Medicaid recipients were invariably moved to less desirable wings or floors of a facility when management wanted to make room for new private-pay residents; the latter, in turn, were displaced as soon as they became Medicaid eligible: "Being in a nursing home is a journey from one place to another and a rapid journey through social class as well" (1992, 65). As states continue to reduce Medicaid outlays, nursing homes will maintain their profits by cutting back on their own expenses, especially staffing levels.

Community Care

Policymakers also have endeavored to curb the use of expensive nursing homes by promoting in-home assistance. By the 1970s, some analysts began calling for in-home and community services as a means of saving on Medicaid costs (Buhler-Wilkerson, 2001). In the 1980s, a more concerted effort was launched to contain nursing home payments by testing, on a limited basis, whether in-home formal services—including social-supportive care—would be a cheap substitute for institutionalization.

Home care has always appealed to the American populace, including the elderly. And it often has been used to foster specific political goals, such as spending cuts, under the guise of high-principled values. Deinstitutionalization of the mentally ill during the 1960s and 1970s, for example, was promoted in the name of compassion and justice; the process was accompanied by inadequate funding for community-based alternatives (Abel, 2000; Hooyman and Gonyea, 1995). Similarly, when budget-cutting and austerity policies emerged as dominant national goals in the 1980s, pressures began to build for providing aid to the elderly at home. As part of the new conservative rhetoric, in-home care was touted as a more humane, family-oriented substitute for institutional placement. It was also championed as a means of empowering states. The admixture of retrenchment, devolution, and institutional prevention policies, however, has meant that localities have greater flexibility in designing Medicaid community services but retain fewer resources with which to implement them.

Many states sought to provide cheaper care by using section 2176 waivers, initially authorized under the 1981 Omnibus Budget Reconciliation Act, to develop community and in-home services for Medicaid-eligible individuals whose nursing home placement is imminent.[21] These new options were particularly appealing since they could better control eligibility and utilization by targeting benefits to certain groups or specific localities; any attempt to experiment under the conventional Medicaid program had to be an open-ended entitlement for all eligible individuals.[22]

Taking advantage of the waivers, states increasingly developed and broadened diverse and innovative programs that included integrated health and supportive services, both for the younger disabled population and frail elderly. The clear intent was to ascertain whether such an approach would reduce Medicaid outlays by delaying or preventing institutionalization (Kane, Kane, and Ladd, 1998). Federal regulations reinforced that objective: states have to clearly demonstrate that their waiver initiatives do not cost Medicaid more than nursing home care; any new initiatives must be budget neutral.

The percentage of Medicaid expenditures for noninstitutional services grew steadily over the 1980s and 1990s, accounting for about 21 percent of the $51.3 billion devoted to long-term care by 1996 (AARP, 1998; SSCA, 1998c). Outlays for waivers alone rose 29 percent a year from 1988 to 1999, reaching $10 billion. In 1987, thirty-seven states had instituted waiver programs assisting 59,000 people nationally; as of 1998, there were over 200 programs with about 450,000 recipients (GAO, 2001c; Meiners, 1996). The assorted ventures included New York's Nursing Homes without Walls, Connecticut's Home Care Program for Elders, Wisconsin's Community Options Program, and Ohio's Passport program. Based on the On Loc Senior Health Services in California, Program for All-inclusive Care for the Elderly (PACE) projects, which pool Medicaid and Medicare funds using a managed care approach, have been created in several states since 1983. The Medicare/Medicaid Integration Program (MMIP), under the auspices of the Robert Wood Johnson Foundation, also has been instituted in a number of places.

Despite the increase in costs for in-home and community services, they continue to be dwarfed by institutional care: the large number of such programs conceals the reality of the situation. The numerous state waiver programs, which represent over half of all home-based care under Medicaid, are quite restricted in scope. They tend to be available only in scattered areas within each state and limited to very few Medicaid-eligible clients relative to need (Kane, Kane and Ladd, 1998). In order to qualify for in-home services, frail elders must not only meet strict income/asset eligibility criteria but also must be medically eligible for placement in an institutional facility. Individuals requiring only limited homemaker services can not receive assistance under the waiver programs (SSCA, 2001a). Elders also are at a disadvantage; most beneficiaries are mentally or physically disabled children and young adults (Meiners, 1996; Wiener and Stevenson, 1998). In many states, there is a per diem dollar cap on allowable services for each client and long waiting lists, forcing large numbers of frail older people into nursing homes or continued dependency on already overburdened family caregivers.[23] Moreover, Medicaid only covers about one-third of the aged poor, leaving most indigent and low-income people to fend for themselves.

Total funding for supportive services per se has remained sorely limited. In 1996, of the $10.5 billion in Medicaid outlays for home- and community-based care, only $2.9 billion was used for personal assistance services. Such spending is concentrated in only a few states: New York, California, and Texas account for fully 74 percent. With slightly over 7 percent of the nation's elderly, New York alone spent $1.6 billion or about half of the total. In fact, the state funded nearly one-third of all Medicaid home- and community-based services in the nation. Since most of its services are covered through the general Medicaid plan and not through a waiver, all of New York's Medicaid-eligible frail elders are entitled to the full range of services offered (GAO, 2002b).[24] On the other hand, twenty states have no PAS programs and some, including Illinois, Indiana, and Mississippi, provide only limited types of home care (AARP, 1998). Moreover, as states increasingly are forced to cut their home and community care budgets, the main targets tend to be social and supportive services rather than the more medicalized forms of assistance (Hooyman and Gonyea, 1995).

Though nearly all of the states strongly support the development of alternatives to nursing homes, only a few have made any significant strides in reducing their reliance on them. Oregon, for example, spends a significant percentage of its Medicaid money on in-home care, respite services, adult day care, and residential options such as assisted living facilities, adult foster care, and boarding homes. The overwhelming majority of states, however, continue to spend most of the program's long-term care funds on institutional facilities, partly because of the difficulty in surmounting federal eligibility restrictions.

Only a few states have initiated or expanded home- and community-based programs that are fully or partially funded through their own general revenues, and these efforts generally are targeted toward older people who meet the states' requirements for nursing home placement. California, Florida,

Massachusetts, and Wisconsin, for instance, have modest state-funded programs for low-income frail elders. However, most states, particularly the poorest ones with the greatest need, have established few, if any, such programs. The vast majority of all public money spent on long-term care—over 90 percent—comes through Medicaid. In 1996, all of the states together spent barely $1.2 billion on home and community services for non-Medicaid-eligible older people (Wiener and Stevenson, 1998).

Since the primary impetus for care in community settings is to generate savings rather than to enhance the well-being of frail elders and their caregivers, the debates over home-based services have centered on how well they delay, prevent, or replace entry into nursing homes. The Long-Term Care Channeling Demonstration projects, completed in the mid-1980s, set out to show whether or not the government provision of in-home services would, in fact, be cost-effective. The results suggest that such benefits tend to be add-on costs; despite recipients' risk of institutionalization, many of them would not have ended up in a nursing home (*Journal of Health Services Research,* 1988). Weissert and Hedrich (1994), in their review of thirty-seven studies, report that home- and community-based services are not lower-cost substitutes for institutional care. Similar outcomes have been found by a number of policy analysts (Abel, 1991; Garber, 1995; Kane, 1994; Weissert, 1991; Williams and Temkin-Greener, 1996).

Kane, Kane, and Ladd (1998), on the other hand, have pointed out that most of these investigations are based on small-scale projects; the evidence suggests that formal in-home services are cost-effective in the few states that have seriously endeavored to expand them. Although their conclusions have been confirmed by others, state officials continue to be wary of promoting home-based care aggressively. One of their foremost concerns is that such public assistance, if not held in check, will substitute for free family care, thereby increasing overall use of services—and state budgets. Therefore, states tend to impose strict criteria on eligibility for home aid and spending limits per client that are generally equivalent to the cost of institutionalization (Wiener and Stevenson, 1998). Under New York's Nursing Homes without Walls, for example, the total cost of each patient's care is capped at 75 percent of the average annual cost of institutional care in the resident's locality. HCFA is especially cautious about approving certain waivers because of apprehension over runaway costs (Abel, 1991).

The narrow discussion over the cost-effectiveness of formal care disregards the actual needs and preferences of elders and their caregivers. According to Weissert and Hedrich, the popularity of in-home services "suggests that life satisfaction improvements and consumer preference may be the most appropriate rationales for offering it, if costs can be kept reasonable" (1994, 52).

Even if they are not substitutes for nursing home care, they benefit frail elders and their families considerably.

Cost Shifting

Since the 1980s, the national government has attempted to abdicate responsibility for social programs, particularly those serving the poor, through devolution of authority and reduced allocations to the states. However, as their budgets tightened, the states devised strategies for shifting expenditures back to the central government. For instance, since they only have to put up a part of the cost to secure federal dollars, some states have saved money by transferring parts or all of their self-funded home care programs to Medicaid through the waivers.[25] Another tack has been to ferret out dually eligible beneficiaries—those elders with coverage under both Medicaid and Medicare—and maximize usage of the fully national program (Wiener and Stevenson, 1998). Institutional costs became a particular target since nearly one-fourth of such recipients live in nursing homes (HGRO, 1997). For example, Massachusetts and New York pressed facilities to charge Medicare for services to public assistance patients whenever feasible. In areas where Medicaid reimbursement rates were particularly low relative to Medicare, proprietors did this on their own. States also adopted policies that integrated the two programs, including PACE and social HMOs; though they lowered overall costs, the states claimed most of the savings for Medicaid. And when Medicare's home health benefits were liberalized, the states diverted as many of these services as they could from their budgets to the national government (Wiener and Stevenson, 1998). Nursing homes also saved money for themselves—and Medicaid—by sending patients to the hospital for an acute episode, paid for by Medicare, rather than provide the expensive care on site (HGRO, 1997).

Elaborate schemes also have been devised for maximizing federal and minimizing state shares of Medicaid spending. In a number of states, intergovernmental transfers are used not only to augment national matching funds for Medicaid services but also to attain federal funds for other purposes. Though Congress and HCFA have attempted to limit gimmicks that exploit the federal share of the Medicaid program, other schemes invariably emerge (SF, 2000). In fact, many states have become financially dependent on such contrivances, thus rendering it difficult for the national government to eliminate them suddenly or even completely (SF, 2000).

Recent audits and reports by the Office of the Inspector General (OIG) have analyzed a number of these ploys, including the manipulation of "enhanced" state payments to nursing homes and hospitals owned and operated by local governments. In order to better serve the financially needy population, the federal government will match these higher contributions. However, in many cases, the facilities return the "excess" state share to the state, which puts the money in its general fund. As a case in point, over the last nine years, Pennsylvania has garnered $3.1 billion in federal Medicaid matching funds for its county-administered nursing homes, which it used to substitute for state money instead of to increase services. And since 1998, the state has used about 20 percent of the national share for non-Medicaid purposes (OIG, 2001a, February). By 2000, about twenty-eight states were taking advantage of the enhanced payments to reduce their share of Medicaid payments, costing the program $5.8 billion in that year alone (GAO, 2001d).

Another method has been to use supplemental federal reimbursements to hospitals that serve a disproportionate number of low-income patients (disproportionate share hospital payments, or DSH) as the source of the state match. In effect, this practice enables states to use federal Medicaid money to engender even more federal money (OIG, 2001, July). For instance, North Carolina received $412 million (from 1996 to 1999) and Alabama $302 million (from 1996 to 2000), allowing them to provide enhanced public funding to their hospitals at little or no cost to the states (OIG, 2001, May, July).

The OIG also found that several states were using a portion of the voluntary contributions under Older American Act (OAA) programs in lieu of state matching funds; these contributions should have been spent on expanded services such as congregate meals and in-home care. Misused donations amounted to $155 million in 1996 and 1999 (OIG, 2001, February).

Although benefiting different levels of government and proprietors, cost shifting obviously does not increase the overall supply of services or improve the quality of care. Instead, public officials are vying with each other for ways to reduce their social responsibilities, efforts that will only impair the well-being of the frail elderly and their caregivers.

Individualism and Privatization

Policymakers have renewed and invigorated their commitment to individualism, self-reliance, and privatization. For long-term care, this is played out in a number of ways. First and foremost, in the United States privatization implies self-reliance and familism. The needs of the frail elderly are defined as personal problems to be dealt with by individuals and their families instead of as a social concern requiring collective decisions and supportive structures (Hooyman, 1999).

Privatization also signifies a movement from the public sector to profit-making or, to a lesser extent, nonprofit enterprises. When public benefits are privatized, they tend to undermine support for broader social programs. The assumption is that our pressing long-term care problems can be substantially alleviated through private sector solutions such as long-term care insurance, tax incentives, and medical savings accounts (MSAs), initiatives that shift benefits to better-off groups while rendering public outlays less visible.

LTC insurance initially became available in the mid-1980s. Since premiums are costly and can be deducted from federal income taxes, LTC insurance provides a public subsidy for the rich; about 5 to 6 percent of the wealthiest elderly currently have policies, and only 10 to 20 percent of the top earners can even afford to purchase them (Brody, 1995; Montgomery, 1995; Schwartz, 1994). Moreover, many of the policies have low levels of coverage, lifetime maximums, lack of inflation protection, rigid health exclusions, and few government regulations or protections (Mellor, 2000). And some premiums that are relatively low in the earlier years are raised sharply later on (AARP, 2001d).

Despite these problems, by the 1990s tax subsidies and private sector financing dominated the national discussion over long-term care. In an attempt to promote private insurance, the Health Insurance Portability and Accountability Act (HIPAA) of 1996 allowed special tax treatment for some individuals and employers purchasing LTC insurance policies. Four years later, President George W. Bush proposed legislation to expand individual tax deductions for them at an estimated cost of $5.1 billion to the national government over five years.

There also have been attempts to encourage the purchase of LTC insurance at the state level. California, Connecticut, Indiana, and New York, for example, participate in public/private partnership programs allowing individuals who buy state-approved private policies to apply for Medicaid after exhausting their insurance benefits; they also can protect a certain level of their personal assets, depending on the state. However, the number of people participating in these programs has been minuscule, particularly since the OBRA 1993 legislation that exposes Medicaid benefits to mandatory estate recovery (Wiener and Stevenson, 1998). As one observer concludes, "Despite the prospect of continued growth, private insurance is unlikely to provide the majority of financing for LTC in the near future" (Garber, 1995, 19). Certainly, it won't meet the needs of low-income, high-risk individuals.[26] Both Presidents Clinton and Bush also initiated various forms of individual tax breaks for long-term care expenses, policies that foster high public costs but provide no assistance to low-income families and vastly inadequate help to the middle class. The poorest 20 percent or so of the American population who pay no federal income tax—but high payroll taxes—would receive no benefits at all.

The $3,000 tax credit "to provide support for Americans who care for a disabled or elderly relative" included in the 2001 federal budget is estimated to cost the public treasury $175 million over the next five years (U.S. Budget, 2001a, 117).

Familism and Estate Recovery

Through various forms of estate planning, enterprising middle-class elders divested themselves of their assets through gifts to their children or, more commonly, by establishing trusts in order to become eligible for Medicaid. To curb this practice, Congress enacted OBRA 1993. At the time, twenty-six states already had their own Medicaid recovery laws, many since the 1970s, though the ease of sheltering assets varied across the nation.

The intent of the new federal legislation was to make it more difficult for elders to qualify for Medicaid, recoup public money, save costs, discourage dependence on government, and encourage long-term care insurance. The act increased the waiting period to five years for sheltering assets through trusts and to three years for transferring money to relatives before an elder could apply for Medicaid. It also mandated estate recovery, forcing the states to reclaim Medicaid costs from the estate or property of beneficiaries age fifty-five and over who lived in nursing homes or received home and community services. In addition, states could now consider jointly owned property, including homes and bank accounts, as part of the estate. A lien would be placed on the holdings, recoverable after the death of the recipient and his or her spouse (Schwartz, 1994).

In effect, OBRA 1993 forces even more elders to deplete their lifetime savings before receiving any publicly supported benefits. In addition, elders who want to retain the title to their home or leave a modest legacy to their children may forgo needed services entirely. Schwartz argues that the act "picks the bones" of the low-income aged in need of long-term care; it essentially converts their public benefits into loans to be paid back by family members. Even adult children and siblings, including those who provided intensive care for their elderly kin, can find themselves impoverished, forced out of their homes, or both (Schwartz, 1994). At the same time, the New Republicans and President George W. Bush are clamoring for elimination of inheritance taxes on the rich.

Private Costs of Care

The current structure of public programs and the lack of universal long-term care benefits simultaneously serve to generate a deep cleavage between the rich and poor dependent elderly and to level those in the middle. Despite the huge and growing federal and state budgets for Medicare and Medicaid, these programs are sorely inadequate to meet the needs of the overwhelming majority of frail elders and their families. Community-based care in the United States tends to be reliant on the marketplace; the bulk of services are privately owned and privately paid for. Most functionally impaired older people cannot afford the high costs of formal care but do not qualify for assistance under Medicaid; there are few publicly supported in-home services available for those who are "merely" low-income elderly. Middle-class elders who can buy in-home help often steadily deplete their resources and eventually are forced into Medicaid-funded nursing homes (Wiener, Sullivan, and Skaggs, 1996).

Some minimal federal assistance for the low-income elderly is available through the Social Services Block Grants (formally title XX of the Social Security Act). Under the program, states have the option to provide a wide range of services, including long-term care, for all age groups. However, these resources already have been sharply cut back over the years. For example, under OBRA 1981, federal block grants to the states were reduced by 20 percent (Hooyman and Gonyea, 1995). By 1993, they amounted to only $2.8 billion and steadily decreased to $2.3 billion in 1998, $1.9 billion in 1999, and $1.6 billion in 2000 (GAO, 1995a; U.S. Budget, 2001a, 2001b).

Though funding under the Older Americans Act has been targeted increasingly toward the low-income, functionally impaired elderly, only limited amounts of its outlays have been used for actual in-home care. Even these scarce resources have diminished considerably in recent years: the program was capped at $800 million in 1997 and 1998, with only 1 percent devoted to home-based formal services for the frail elderly.[27] For 2001, Clinton proposed a slightly higher funding level of $1.1 billion; included are $125 million to assist families caring for disabled elders (under the new National Family Caregiver Support Program)[28] and $325 million for supportive services. As Cohen (1997) puts it, the funding stream has been a trickle in the face of overall need among chronically ill and dependent older people.

Consequently, the vast majority of the elderly who do receive formal help must pay a large part of the charges themselves; a significant percentage rely entirely on their own resources. Overall, older people and their families pay about 55 percent of the total long-term care bill in the nation. For a large number of low-income and middle-class dependent elders, these services represent their highest out-of-pocket health care costs and, for some, chronic frailty could "come to mean living the life of a pauper" (Diamond, 1992).

Institutional care is the major cause of catastrophic out-of-pocket health care expenditures for low- and middle-class older people who are suddenly confronted with medical problems (Wiener, 1996). Annual costs, which continue to grow at rates higher than inflation, averaged about $55,000 nationally in 2000 (GAO, 2001c). Since about one-fourth of the total nursing home bill is paid by the elderly themselves, one or several stays can lead to financial ruin.

Under current arrangements, sickness and poverty become inextricably linked: the longer one stays in a nursing home, the more one dissipates his or her life savings. About 14 to 18 percent of people entering institutional facilities as private-pay patients deplete their assets, many within six months, and are forced to depend on Medicaid for the rest of their stay (Garber, 1995). Consequently, a significant percentage of elders who return to the community have few remaining resources; others may find themselves impoverished. Moreover, about half of private-pay patients who remain permanently in the institution eventually exhaust their own funds (SSCA, 1998c; Wiener, Sullivan, and Skaggs, 1996). Even then, they must contribute all of their monthly income, including Social Security and other pension benefits, leaving them with only a small personal allowance (about $30 or slightly higher, depending on the state).

Spouses of institutionalized elders also face economic disaster. Though there are some federal protections since 1989—they can keep the couple's house, about half of the assets up to a state-defined amount, and a certain amount of their income—community partners can be stripped of most of their life savings; many suffer serious economic hardship.

Elders not eligible for Medicaid also may be heavily burdened by high medical costs because of enormous out-of-pocket Medicare expenses, such as premiums, coinsurance, copayments, and deductibles, as well as unprotected services (routine checkups, dental care and dentures, prescription drugs, eye and ear examinations, eyeglasses and hearing aids, and most routine foot care); the program does not cap personal beneficiary payments. Coinsurance amounts for skilled nursing care alone, applicable after twenty days, reached $102 per day in 2002. The hospital deductible for the first 60 days cost beneficiaries $812, with daily coinsurance charges of $203 for days 61 to 90, and $406 for days 91 to 100 (HWM, 2002).

About 17 percent of Medicare beneficiaries receive assistance from Medicaid for some or, to a lesser extent, all of these personal expenses; certain low-income older people with incomes at 120 percent of the poverty level—about 1.3 million elders—receive help with cost-sharing requirements if the state participates in a qualified Medicare beneficiary program. However, BBA 1997 reduced the federal share of such assistance by $2 billion, thereby forcing states to reduce even further access to health services for those who can least afford them.

About one-third of the Medicare population is assisted by employer-sponsored supplementary assistance. Those with sufficient income, about 25 percent of recipients, also may purchase expensive and escalating supplementary Medigap insurance premiums costing more than $1,300 annually in 1999; fully 20 percent is for administrative expenses rather than actual benefits (GAO, 2001g). These policies do not protect beneficiaries from catastrophic medical expenses or long-term care costs. Even those beneficiaries purchasing the higher-cost plans that include pharmaceutical coverage must pay most of their prescription drug costs themselves (HWM, 2002).

According to a recent GAO report, despite public programs, elders financed about 45 percent of their health care bill themselves in 2000. On average, they paid $3,100 or about 22 percent of their income; older people in poor health and with no Medicaid or supplementary insurance spent about 44 percent. Low-income single women aged eighty-five or over who are not eligible for Medicaid were liable for over half of their income on health care (GAO, 2001g). Clearly, out-of-pocket health care expenses "act differentially on rich and poor persons and may cause the latter to forgo needed care" (Kane, 1993, 106). These exorbitant costs also can impoverish low- and middle-class elders and drive them into nursing homes.

Conclusion

The enormously expensive but sparse publicly supported long-term care in the United States is enmeshed in the broader context of government retrenchment, fiscal austerity, and devolution as well as a strengthening of familism, individualism, and privatization. Supportive services, largely residual, contain a medical and institutional bias with access strictly controlled. The types of assistance that people do receive are mainly based upon the interests of providers: the long-term care industry prioritizes services according to payment amounts rather than need, seeks low-cost clients with the highest reimbursement levels, and favors elders paying privately.

Medicaid, which currently funds over one-third of the nation's long-term care costs—mostly for nursing homes—is grounded in a welfare mentality that fosters impoverishment and indignities. Its programs are based on individual state policies and support, fostering nationwide inequities and lack of uniformity. Decision making tends to be dominated by powerful nursing home chains that feed on the program.

Medicare focuses on acute medical services and provides only carefully circumscribed supportive aid. Efforts to contain its escalating hospital costs have led to greater outlays for long-term care settings, enriching home care and institutional providers. More recent attempts to control these subacute expenditures have generated access problems for elders with heavy service needs while exacerbating the already problematic quality of in-home and institutional care. Moreover, the program's expensive out-of-pocket costs are increasingly burdensome, particularly for low-income, frail older people.

Clearly, our misguided and paltry publicly supported elder care services disproportionately affect females and represent a form of gender discrimination (Browne, 1998). Medicaid has a particularly female face for younger and older people alike. At the more advanced ages, women are more likely than men both to be poor and to require paid help. They comprise the bulk of nursing home patients as well as those elders in need of community-based care. Medicare, too, has a female stamp; women represent about two-thirds of its home health care users (GAO, 2001c). They also are the main providers of care: the overwhelming majority of chronically ill, dependent older people are forced to rely on their spouses and adult children, most of whom are wives and daughters.

Yet, as suggested above, long-term care services under both programs are severely circumscribed. And even these insufficient efforts have been vulnerable to deep budget cuts at the various levels of government. Most state legislatures currently are addressing a myriad of new proposals for further restricting such services; in 1998 alone, over 100 bills on the subject had passed at least one of their chambers (Clarette and Johnson, 1998). They also have convened countless commissions and study groups to assess additional means for moderating spending. Greater cost-cutting will continue to shift caregiving obligations to already overburdened families.

In reaction to rising concerns about long-term care, the short-lived Long-Term Care Campaign was formed in 1989. A broad-based coalition of 140 senior and disabled advocacy groups, it called for federally funded LTC services available to all those in need, regardless of income or age. The following year, the U.S. Bipartisan Commission on Comprehensive Health Care (the Pepper Commission) released its report, concluding that unless we change our policies, increasing numbers of people with severe disabilities will have difficulty in obtaining the care they require. It recommended an expansion of Medicare to include home and institutional services for seriously disabled individuals of all ages. And in 1993, as part of his doomed health care reform package, President Clinton proposed a comprehensive, national long-term care plan that also included the frail young and old alike; its cost was estimated at $45 billion over five years.

By the following year, however, the New Republicans had grabbed the political agenda. Since then, their views—which reject intergenerational connectiveness and collective responsibility for human needs—have been bolstered with the election of President George W. Bush in 2000. Though there is a conspicuous and growing demand for some type of universal long-term care coverage, the new political climate has prevented the emergence—or even discussion—of any such measures.

Climbing public costs for health services, an ideological climate opposed to social welfare programs generally, and a growing anti-entitlement mentality in the nation have precluded serious consideration of enlarging elder services at collective expense. Debates regarding Social Security, Medicare, and Medicaid are infused with hyperbole, obfuscating rhetoric, and crisis politics, as well as accusations of budget busting aimed at specific generations. At the same time, because of growing public outlays for older people under these programs, federal mandates for budget-neutral program improvements, and large tax refunds benefiting those who need them the least, it is unlikely that Congress will enact any kind of national long-term care program in the near future.

Notes

1. From 1990 to 2000, total expenditures on nursing homes, both private and public, rose from $53 billion to $92 billion (GAO, 2000c).

2. The frail elderly are defined as individuals experiencing one or more ADL or IADL needs.

3. Fully 25 percent of the elderly live in California (3.5 million), Florida (2.8 million), or New York (2.4 million). About 938,000, or nearly 40 percent, of New York state's older population live in New York City (U.S. Bureau of the Census, 2001g).

4. This was a slight decline from 5.1 percent in 1990.

5. During FY 2001, Medicare spending grew by 10.3 percent (GAO, 2002g).

6. The actual fee varies by metropolitan area, region, and whether the facility is a teaching hospital.

7. From 2001 to 2002, fees were reduced by 5.4 percent (SA, 2002).

8. In the early 1960s, nearly all of the home health agencies were nonprofit VNAs, other voluntary organizations, or government agencies (mostly affiliated with public health departments); only about 8 percent were proprietary agencies (Buhler-Wilkerson, 2001). According to the latest estimate by the GAO, about 50 percent of HHAs in mid-2001 are for-profit entities (GAO, 2002e).

9. After the OBRA 1997 cuts, the number of agencies decreased to about 7,099 in 2000 and 6,900 by mid-2001. There also are another 2,600 branch offices serving beneficiaries. About 2.5 million elders receive home health assistance under Medicare, which cost $9.2 billion in 2000 (GAO, 2002e; OIG, 2002b).

10. In 2002, the industries again engaged in a multimillion-dollar campaign to extend the supplementary payments that were set to expire in October (Schmitt, 2002).

11. As of September 2001, 5.6 million elders or 14 percent of Medicare beneficiaries were enrolled in M+C plans. Though most were able to enroll in another MCO, in nine states they had no choice as to which one (AARP 2001c; GAO, 2001j).

12. In 2000, Medicaid funded 45 percent of all long-term care costs in the nation, or $62 billion (GAO, 2002a).

13. In 1999, about 800,000 Medicaid recipients were served by HHAs, costing about $2.2 billion nationally (GAO, 2002e).

14. About 46 percent of all nursing home beds are in ten states: California, Colorado, Florida, Illinois, Massachusetts, Missouri, New York, Pennsylvania, Texas, and Washington (GAO, 1999l).

15. Another 10 percent of nursing home residents rely on Medicare for their nursing home services.

16. Costs for Medicaid grew by 14 percent in 2001 (AARP, 2001c).

17. Currently, about 77 percent of nursing homes are dually certified for Medicare and Medicaid (GAO, 1999j).

18. Though still high, the average occupancy rate has declined since 1995 to 87 percent by 2000.

19. Though there are wide variations across the states, in 1992 the national average Medicaid payment per resident per day was $71.03, rising to $83.72 in 1995 and to slightly over $100 in 2000. Connecticut gives $150; Texas, $81; Florida, $110; and New Hampshire, $221 (Collins, 2001; Gren, 2001; Harrington, Carillo, and Mullan, 1998; HGR, 2000b).

20. Another 18 percent were using flat-rate approaches.

21. These initiatives expanded on the more limited and earlier Medicaid demonstration projects under section 1115 of the 1965 Social Security amendments. At the same time, the National Long-Term Care Channeling Demonstrations were authorized in ten states, beginning in 1979.

22. Though home care became a mandatory service under the 1967 amendments to the Social Security Act, the majority of the states restricted its use in practice (Benjamin, 1993).

23. In 2002, for example, Louisiana's waiting list for its Medicaid-covered home- and community-based services was three times the number of people actually receiving assistance. There also was a per diem cap of $55 for each beneficiary (GAO, 2002b).

24. Nevertheless, nursing home care represented 68 percent of New York's long-term care expenditures in 1999.

25. According to AARP, as states were struggling to balance their budgets without increasing taxes, some began cutting back home- and community-based services. But these reductions tend to focus on programs supported exclusively by the states rather than by Medicaid-funded efforts "that bring in significant federal matching dollars" (AARP, 2001c).

26. Though the number of long-term care insurance policies increased threefold after the 1980s, by the beginning of the twenty-first century they totaled only about 6 million. Moreover, the average annual premium rose 11 percent from 1995, reaching $1,607 by 2000 (AARP, 2001d).

27. In the 1990s, OAA faced a reauthorization battle. Though its programs continued to be funded, the act itself was not officially sanctioned by Congress until 2000.

28. The national Family Caregiver Support Program also assists grandparents caring for children (NCC, 2001a).

3

THE DOMESTIC SPHERE: FAMILY CAREGIVERS

Giving help eventually embitters us, unless we are compensated at least by appreciation; accepting help degrades us, unless we are convinced that our helpers are getting something in return.

—Wendy Lustbader, from *Counting on Kindness*, 18

ELDER CARE POLICIES AND PROGRAMS grounded on government retrenchment, extreme individualism, residualism, and privatization have led to greater burdens on individual households generally and women in particular. The massive discharge of patients—including the elderly—from mental institutions in the 1960s and 1970s, along with the limited community resources available for their care, was predicated on the assumption that families would take on any unmet needs (Abel, 2000). Similarly, ongoing efforts to control Medicaid costs by discouraging entrance into nursing homes have occurred without sufficient affordable home-based services. The curbing of Medicare outlays also has had dire impacts on women caregivers. As suggested in the last chapter, both the introduction of PPS for hospitals and the more recent growth of managed care organizations have led to the discharge of elders "quicker and sicker." Though some patients are sent to nursing homes, most go directly home, where they require substantial care. Home care services under Medicare, as shown, are limited and carefully controlled. Moreover, the newly enacted PPS provisions for home health agencies are likely to restrict the availability of formal services even further.

The centerpiece of these strategies, strengthened since the 1980s, has been familism, which purposely does not take into account the gendered division of labor. Familism, along with privatization, glorifies personal care for relatives while downgrading services at collective expense. Consequently, policymakers have aimed to economize by thrusting unpaid care work increasingly on wives and daughters while celebrating and enshrining family values and virtues. Caregivers are applauded as "everyday heroes" as Congress calls for even greater family responsibility for their elders (SSCA, 1998f). Such appeals for filial and spousal obligations have been reinforced with economic incentives and sanctions.

Critically, according to Stoller,

> Implicit in this emphasis on the cost effectiveness of care within the community is the assumption that informal care is somehow free, an orientation reflecting conventional accounting systems in which unpaid domestic labor is privatized and not counted in estimates of economic production. (1993, 161)

Expenses are not reduced; they merely are shifted to spouses, adult children, and other kin. Although essential to the successful functioning of the American political economy, care labor is largely unappreciated and unrewarded by the larger society. Nor is it respected. Its invisible nature, behind closed doors in private households, allows policymakers to gloss over the substantial personal costs in caring for dependent elders, a price that is being shifted increasingly onto women. It is these "hidden" costs, borne by private households, that are at the core of long-term care policy. The market value of unpaid elder care services is estimated at over $194 billion a year (SSCA, 1999c).

Publicly supported elder care services, then, are driven by policies to safeguard against any reductions in family care; contain demand as much as possible; deny or reduce benefits to those with kin supports; and intervene only when the caregiver is absolutely exhausted and institutionalization is imminent. Yet, the reality is that despite the hardships and sometimes devastating economic, social, and psychological consequences, caregivers tend to assist their relatives until it is no longer feasible. Most disabled elders who have families move into a nursing home only during the later stages of their serious, chronic diseases (SSCA, 1998f). Institutionalization, for the most part, is a last resort, and even then with much hesitation: it generally occurs after years of backbreaking labor and only after the carer is totally exhausted, too ill, or too frail to continue her assistance; the burden becomes psychologically unbearable or physically unmanageable; the family must relocate; or the condition of the frail elder becomes too burdensome for care at home. On the whole, families make the choice to place their kin in a facility with great anguish and trepidation and only after years of personal sacrifice and attention. Even in these cases there tends to be a sense of guilt, especially when they subsequently observe the low quality of care that is provided to their spouse or parents (Greene and Coleman, 1995; O'Brien, 1989).

The evidence also indicates that women do not slack off in their duties when formal services are available. Nor do they clamor for paid care or replace their own efforts when they don't actually need help. In short, the assumptions underlying substitution theory, upon which much of elder care policy is based, are not supported by the actual dynamics of family caregiving (Brody, 1995; Kane, Kane, and Ladd, 1998). As Lee and Estes write, "The relationship between formal and informal care appears to be more one of complementarity rather than substitutability" (1981, 182). Overall, paid long-term care services are utilized mostly by older people with insufficient or no family assistance. Moreover, service substitution, when it does occur, frequently is based on a temporary need, such as when the caregiver becomes sick (Wiener, 1996).

The Gendered Nature of Care

Beginning in the nineteenth century, with the growth of large-scale markets and industrialization, social, political, and economic life was steadily separated into private and public spheres. Women became solely responsible for reproductive labor; for White middle- and upper-class families, it was assumed that female nurturing within individual households would allow men to compete and achieve economically in the outside commercial and political worlds (Coontz, 1992).

Social reproduction entailed wide-ranging duties and caring labor. In addition to bearing, nurturing, and socializing children and providing general housekeeping chores, women were responsible for kin keeping, maintaining social relationships, and the hands-on care and emotional support of ill, disabled, and dying neighbors and relatives, both young and old. When they became sick, most people were nursed at home by their mothers, spouses, and sisters. Indeed, since there were few public services, hospitals, or doctors, unpaid caring labor—including health services and birthing assistance—became a major occupation for many women throughout the 1800s (Abel, 2000; Glenn, 1992).

According to Abel (2000), women developed close bonds of interdependence in their communities, often helping each other when in need. Such responsibilities fell on females of all ages, sometimes beginning in adolescence. The care of sick family members—cousins, brothers, sisters, aunts, and uncles—could be unremitting and all-consuming, especially for single women who generally did not have any opportunities for achieving economic independence. The care of functionally impaired elders, however, was not one of their primary caregiving tasks, since few people reached old age, especially their more advanced years.[1]

By the early twentieth century, White, middle-class households became more isolated, extended kinship and community bonds had weakened, and fewer women benefited from mutually supportive networks of family and friends. After the introduction of the telephone, people were more apt to express their concerns through calls rather than offer hands-on assistance (Buhler-Wilkerson, 2001). Furthermore, the emergence of the powerful health care industry considerably reduced the need for at-home medical services. Home care increasingly was replaced by hospital-based care: "For caregivers, the hospital was becoming an acceptable solution to the endless obligations of caring for the sick at home. [They were] recast from a place of last resort for the urban poor into a medical center for everyone" (Buhler-Wilkerson, 2001). Concurrently, because of demographic changes, especially rising longevity, at-home care of frail older people was becoming more common. As elder care responsibilities mounted, women were increasingly on their own to fulfill them.

Today, families provide from 80 to 90 percent of all long-term care in the nation. Only about 5 percent of older people living in the community rely exclusively on paid help and another 21 percent combine, to varying degrees, both formal and informal assistance. All other community-based frail and vulnerable older people depend entirely on family and friends to tend to their daily needs (Brody, 1995).

Despite growing expectations that women participate in the paid labor force and economically support their households either partially or fully, elder care has remained highly gendered: fully three-quarters of unpaid caregivers are females (SSCA, 1998f). For older White couples, the wife tends to have primary, and often the entire, responsibility. Since, on average, men marry individuals younger than themselves as well as have higher remarriage rates at older ages and experience lower longevity than women, they are far more likely to have an available mate for their care: wives constitute over 64 percent of spousal assistants (Cantor and Brennan, 2000). Female relatives and friends provide the bulk of aid to unmarried frail elders living in the community. Adult daughters, who comprise over 37 percent of all informal caregivers, also are most likely to help out when one parent—or both—can no longer fully or partially take care of the other (Abel, 1991).

Studies show that in families with mixed-gender siblings, sisters provide markedly more hours of help to their frail mothers and fathers. In these cases, sons may assist occasionally, as needed. Their contributions, by and large, center on transportation services, financial guidance and support, and home repairs; daughters more often provide whatever is required, especially hands-on personal care, housekeeping, and kitchen chores (Dwyer and Coward, 1992).

However, sons can take on substantial responsibilities for all aspects of care labor when there is no daughter available. When they do so, however, they tend to rely on their spouse both for hands-on assistance and emotional support, thereby relieving some of the stress (Abel, 1991; Hooyman, 1999). In fact, daughters-in-law can be a significant source of informal assistance whereas daughters frequently keep their husbands as uninvolved as possible (Mui, 1992). Male caregivers also can experience less burden and depression than women because they tend to receive more help from other family members, neighbors, and friends (Calasanti and Slevin, 2001). And since they are not "expected" to become primary carers, they may be accorded more respect and esteem. In addition, given the income inequalities between the genders, sons are more likely to afford—and hire—paid help for their frail parents.

Because of an admixture of population aging and social policies, elder care has been increasing among women and is becoming, as Brody (1995) puts it, a "normative" experience. About 45 percent of females born between 1907 and 1917 had assisted an older relative compared to over 64 percent of those born between 1927 and 1934 (Gannon, 1999). Over the last ten years alone unpaid elder care has grown nearly threefold (SSCA, 1998f). A national caregiving survey, supported by the nonprofit National Alliance for Caregiving (NAC) and the American Association of Retired Persons (1997), found that more than 22 million households, or 25 percent of the U.S. total, were responsible for some form of informal aid to their aged kin within the last year. The evidence suggests that approximately 60 percent of all middle-aged and older women will provide care for a chronically disabled elder at some point in their lives (Mellor, 2000).

Furthermore, as Hooyman and Gonyea explain, "In most instances, *family caregiver* is a euphemism for one primary caregiver, typically female" (1995, 3). And she is mostly on her own: about 65 percent of such carers don't receive meaningful assistance from anyone. In other words, though other family members, neighbors, and friends may help out intermittently, the wife—or designated daughter—commonly supplies the bulk of the care, some assisting their relatives full-time for long periods of time. According to the NAC/AARP survey (1997), about 20 percent of caregivers provide "constant care," defined as at least forty hours per week; the average length of time is 4.5 years.

Care labor also has intensified over the last several decades. For every seriously disabled person living in a nursing home, there are currently two or more equally debilitated elders requiring help at home (Hooyman and Gonyea, 1995). For instance, approximately 75 to 80 percent of the nearly 4 million people afflicted with Alzheimer's disease or related disorders live in community settings (SSCA, 1999c). Their numbers will continue to increase commensurately with the expansion of the very old population as a whole: though the lifetime risk of dementia is 15 percent, the chances increase to a whopping 40 percent by age eighty-five (Gaines, 1999). Mentally impaired older people, who require assistance with most activities of daily living, often demand round-the-clock attention. Others are in need of increasingly complex medical care. As suggested earlier, many elders released from the hospital require ongoing, hands-on care and complicated services involving sophisticated technical equipment installed in the home: some are on "dialysis, ventilators, cardiac and apnea monitors, feeding tubes and infusion pumps for administering narcotics, antibiotics, and chemotherapy. These instruments require constant supervision" (Abel, 2000, 257). Therefore, a significant number of caregivers bear heavy responsibilities and have considerable demands on their time, energy, and well-being.

The Dynamics of the Family

Since families in American society are expected to look after their dependents—including frail older people—without seeking any public aid, full-time kin work actually requires a two-adult unit with differentiated gender roles. Therefore, as Fineman (1995) points out, in making care labor a private household responsibility, we socially create derivative dependencies—female caregivers who require a spouse (or some other private means of financial support) to meet their economic needs. These unpaid helpers, of course, cannot uphold our idealistic notions of individualism, independence, and autonomy.

Nor are families themselves self-sufficient. According to Coontz, most of us fiercely retain the myth that the gendered division of labor within traditional families created a unit that worked coactively and succeeded on its own: "The self-reliant family is the moral centerpiece of both liberal capitalism and the ideology of separate spheres for men and women" (1992, 67). However, despite the political jargon, families have always relied on others, especially government, for their well-being. The American political economy continues to support and advantage middle- and upper-class traditional family units through tax legislation, inheritance laws, health care rules, Social Security benefits, and other private and public measures (Fineman, 1995).

Just as significantly, the functions assigned to traditional families are clearly incompatible with social realities today. Our public policies have been enacted and sustained based on mythical notions of what actually exists. Despite the renewed emphasis on "natural" patriarchal families by the New Right and others, over the last three decades American society increasingly has generated new family types that are becoming more common than conventional households. By 2000, only a quarter of all households in the United States consisted of "traditional" families—married couples with dependent children or married couples living alone (28 percent)—down from a total of 55 percent in 1990. Female-headed families account for another 12 percent, 60 percent of them with children aged eighteen or younger. Nonfamily households—which increased faster than those with families over the last ten years—rose 23 percent from 27.4 million to 33.7 million. Fully a quarter of all households are composed of individuals, mostly women, living by themselves. There also are 6.5 million unrelated people living together; 5.5 million unmarried partners, of which 0.6 million are documented as being of the same sex; and 3.9 million multigenerational households (U.S. Bureau of the Census, 2001b).[2] Although the family is not deteriorating, just transforming (Hooyman and Gonyea, 1995), social policies have not adjusted accordingly.

The array of family structures prevalent today has had a severe impact on women's role as unpaid care workers. Because of divorce, early widowhood (averaging at about age fifty-seven), or choice, a large percentage of adult females, nearly 38 percent, are not married, forcing many daughters both to earn a living and care for their frail parents by themselves (Browne, 1998; SSCA, 1999c). Furthermore, growing numbers of single parents, many of whom are choosing to have children later in life, are caught between the needs of their young offspring and those of their frail kin.

Additionally, new family constellations resulting from remarriage have disrupted the established notions of family obligation and the gender division of labor. In "blended" households, for instance, is the stepdaughter responsible for her chronically ill stepparent when there are two available biological sons? What is her duty if she is the only adult child? Does it matter if the parents had remarried during her childhood or later, when she was out of the house? Should it be incumbent on stepsiblings to physically care for each other in their old age? What are the obligations of older wives in the increasing number of late-life marriages? As a case in point, my grandfather's elderly spouse, whom he married in his seventies, absolved herself of all responsibility when he became incapable of caring for himself, dropping the task onto my mother, her step daughter-in-law. In divorced families, are daughters expected to provide assistance to their estranged fathers? What about their former in-laws? Are domestic partners, regardless of sexual orientation, liable for each other? How do we protect their "spousal" rights?

The number of dependent elderly per carer also is growing steadily due to declining family size, greater life spans, and more living generations. As it increasingly consists of more older than younger members, the family is becoming top-heavy: for the first time ever, the typical married couple has more parents than children, and many middle-aged people may have two or more parents or parents-in-law—and even grandparents—in need of care (Cantor and Brennan, 2000). According to the NAC/AARP survey (1997), about 5.2 million people are caring for at least two older people and 1.8 million are caring for three or more. In another study, Brody (1995) reports that about one-fifth of her respondents were caring for more than one older person at the same time, a situation that is likely to become even more prevalent over the next several decades.

Duty or Choice?

Unlike men who can choose to retire from their life's work, women have caring roles that tend to be ongoing and often continuous throughout their life span. In fact, a significant number of females begin their elder care responsibilities simultaneous with or soon after rearing their children. Fully 40 percent are between thirty-five and forty-nine, and the vast majority have children under the age of eighteen (NAC/AARP, 1997; SSCA, 1999c). Others embark on their new duties later in life, when they are elderly and vulnerable themselves: about half of all primary caregivers are over the age of sixty-five.

Assistance to frail parents can continue for years since the very old, as a rule, are afflicted with chronic diseases that can last for long periods of time. Today, some women spend more years caring for their older relatives than raising children (Abel, 1991). Some analysts estimate that this situation will worsen: baby boomers probably will put in, on average, 18 years assisting elders as compared to 17 raising their children (Cantor and Brennan, 2000).

Nor do women seem to have a meaningful choice about whether or when to provide care for their spouse or parents. Although modern technology and scientific advances have allowed them greater control over some aspects of their life, such as the decision of whether to have children or not and the timing of their pregnancies, elder care responsibilities generally are unpredictable, unplanned, and expected of them (Abel, 1991).

Though it is widely accepted that wives and daughters will serve as primary caregivers for their frail kin, their motivations for acceding to the role are much less understood. After analyzing several perspectives on the question, Stoller concludes that their "decision" to give hands-on care stems from a complicated interplay of "structural realities and ideological forces" (1993, 159). In other words, there is a confluence of socialization (i.e., women's internalized need to care for others, even at the expense of the self, as well as their considerable capacity for empathy, intimacy, and connectedness); patriarchal power relations that not only define women's roles and obligations but also devalue females and their own needs; the gendered workplace, which relegates women to low-paid work; pressures by relatives, service providers, and other outside forces; and especially the paucity of any viable alternatives. According to Aronson (1992), for most women there are few options, both real and perceived, whether from the community or the men in their lives.[3] As she aptly sums it up in her subtitle: "But Who Else Is Going to Do It?"

However, elder care can simultaneously be based on love and affection, the desire to care for a parent or spouse with whom one has developed a deep, enduring bond. Or, for some, the caregiving "decision" is rooted in a desire to pay a parent back for the sacrifices and care provided to them. The reality is that people serve as caregivers either because they want to or because they have to, though even here the distinction can be murky. In caring for her husband, Cohen (1996: 147) is at times unsure: "A very big piece of my dilemma was, am I doing this by choice or by coercion?" Regardless, under existent conditions many women who otherwise would elect to assist their relatives can't do so whereas others are forced to provide assistance under intolerable circumstances. Still others are forced to serve because they have no place else to turn: they and their parents either can't pay for or find a satisfactory alternative. Indeed, the absence of decent, affordable paid services restricts women's options measurably. Browne (1998), for one, insists that this lack of government assistance is a form of gender discrimination.

Women also are being pressed into care labor particularly because of the dearth of quality—or even acceptable—nursing homes. In her study, Abel (1991) found that many caregivers refuse to place even their severely debilitated elders in institutions mostly because of the notoriously abusive conditions or their own firsthand observations of the facilities during their search for a home. Others who reluctantly accede to institutionalize their spouse or parents in many instances encounter a dearth of nursing homes in their area that accept elders with severe cognitive and other disabilities and, if they are Medicaid-eligible, also encounter long waiting lists, especially for the better places.

Though it is assumed that caring labor is the natural and appropriate role for women, even conservative politicians have conceded that at least some government programs must be available if we are to delay or keep chronically ill older people out of expensive nursing homes. For most political leaders, however, the emphasis is on cost shifting rather than actual concern for the well-being of the caregiver per se. The goal of current approaches to long-term care is to maintain and reinforce the status quo by helping women cope with what are generally viewed as their inescapable, uncompensated elder care duties.

Not only is public funding for in-home and community services severely circumscribed, but whatever support is available centers on reducing caregiver stress: the programs seek to provide assistance to women so that they can better manage their myriad and growing responsibilities at work and in the home. Although helpful to some individuals, such tactics deflect attention from fundamental societal issues. The newly enacted Family Caregiver Support Program, for example, primarily offers information and referral, individual counseling, peer support groups, and stress management and family training. Such programs typically encourage women to accept and accommodate themselves to their situation rather than promote a more accommodating society for frail people and their families (Abel, 1991).

In one of the more poignant accounts of the caregiving experience, *Dirty Details: The Days and Nights of a Well Spouse,* Marion Deutsche Cohen shares her agonizing years of caring for her husband who is afflicted with multiple sclerosis. She points out that well spouses and other caregivers "don't suffer ordinary stress; we do not need stress-management workshops" (1996, 32). Nothing, she writes, could make a dent in all of the work she had to do for her husband "but they kept calling it stress" (44). Cohen forcefully argues that carers suffer from what she calls "dire straits," which require long-range, lasting help.

Clearly, "the overriding issue is not how to relieve stress but how to organize society to make care for the dependent population more just and humane" (Abel, 1991, 66). Although existing government programs can help individual women adjust to their particular situation, the focus on personal responsibility diverts attention from our collective obligation for dependent older people. In addition, this societal commitment should be concerned not only about those who are chronically ill but also with those spouses and adult children who are pushing the wheelchairs; lifting their kin in and out of beds and chairs; operating their ventilators or dialysis machines; feeding them slowly, spoonful by spoonful, so that they will get the proper nutrition; and otherwise tending to their constant and sometimes overwhelming everyday needs.

Even respite services currently designed to "shore up families" with temporary, intermittent help facilitate and "encourage their uncompensated labor" (Kane and Penrod, 1995). Caregivers of those few elders who are eligible for assistance rarely are provided with sufficient relief from what can be twenty-four-hour days, especially if the relative is afflicted with dementia. Cohen plaintively asks, "Why did everyone seem to think that respite care was enough? Every time I came back from a respite I'd . . . need more respite. No amount of time off was enough" (1996, 148–49). She wanted full-time attendants so as to eliminate "as completely as humanly possible" the dependency relationship, thus allowing her to provide greater emotional support and care as a wife.

Universal entitlement to personal and instrumental services, as well as an option for day care, would free women from the obligation to provide full-time hands-on care and ease their burden if they choose to do so. Likewise, families could better meet the affective and psychosocial needs of their frail relatives. Such entitlements also would ensure that those who do care for their highly dependent kin don't have to quit their jobs or forgo employment opportunities.

The Caring Burden: Economic Costs

Despite the persistence of unpaid child and elder care as their special tasks, the vast majority of women today also work outside the home. One of the most staggering changes affecting families and family life since the mid-1960s has been the steady flow of women, especially those with young children, into the labor force.[4] Whether married or single, most are employed out of economic necessity; for many, their income is the sole means of support for themselves and their families. The vast majority, however, are employed in low-wage jobs in the service, clerical, or retail sectors, a pattern that has persisted among female baby boomers despite some gains in the labor market (Dailey, 1998).

For most females, their public and private roles have become blurred: regardless of their employment status, women continue to take on care duties, whether for young children, frail parents, or increasingly both. According to the NAC/AARP survey (1997), fully 64 percent of caregivers are employed, with 52 percent working full-time and 12 percent part-time. The percentage of working women who will provide such care in the coming years is expected to increase steadily (Cantor and Brennan, 2000).

As several researchers have reported, there doesn't even seem to be a difference in the amount or type of care provided by employed and unemployed daughters: both provide substantial aid to their functionally impaired parents when circumstances require it (Cantor and Brennan, 2000; Hooyman, 1999; Stoller, 1993). However, many of these working caregivers are disadvantaged at their jobs as they struggle to balance their occupations with assistance to their older relatives. The NAC/AARP survey (1997) shows that about half of the women have to make at least some adjustments at work in order to meet their elder care obligations.

Because of conflicts between the requirements of their job and the needs of their frail kin, large numbers of working caregivers report working fewer than normal hours, regularly rearranging their work schedules, taking long lunches and unpaid leaves of absence, and using up sick leave and vacation time. Some women must refuse overtime, promotions, training, vocational openings, more lucrative assignments, jobs requiring travel, and other challenging but time-consuming opportunities. Others experience unanticipated workday interruptions, a deterioration in their performance, reduced productivity, absenteeism and tardiness. Nearly everyone faces more than her share of stress (Metlife, 1997; SSCA, 1999c).

Caring labor can become so burdensome that a substantial number of women are forced to quit. Data from the NAC/AARP survey (1997) indicate that 11 percent of the women had to take a temporary leave of absence, about 10 percent gave up their employment permanently (4 percent accepted early retirement and 6 percent quit), and another 7 percent moved either from full- to part-time work or assumed less demanding jobs. Additionally, unemployed women, including those on welfare, may have to turn down jobs; others do not have the time to look for work. According to one estimate, adult children lose nearly $5 billion in earnings each year because they are caring for a chronically ill parent (Spalter-Roth, 1988). Projections indicate that at least two-thirds of all baby boomer women will, at some point in their working career, be forced to drop out of the labor force or abridge their hours to care for children, frail parents, or both (Dailey, 1998).

Caregiving evidently has a significant impact on the financial situation of most women. The consequences for those who quit their jobs, are temporarily unemployed, or shift into part-time work can be devastating. For some, taking care of one's parents or spouse full-time can mean impoverishment. This is especially true for widowed, divorced, and single women who rely exclusively on their own income for support. Moreover, married female caregivers may suddenly lose their economic independence.

Unemployed, unpaid care workers not only face immediate financial hardship, but they also commonly lose their health insurance protection, encounter difficulties in reentering the labor force, and compromise their retirement security. For instance, Social Security benefit levels are tied both to wages and length of employment. In the computation of their average lifetime earnings over a thirty-five-year work history, women who leave the labor market for elder care duties are rewarded with zero-income years, thus lowering their future benefits measurably. Unpaid caring labor negatively affects overall wage levels as well, further depressing future pension amounts: childcare and increasingly elder care responsibilities account for slightly over 10 percent of the pay differential between the genders (Hooyman and Gonyea, 1995). By the same token, private pension income, vacation pay, and other fringe benefits may be jeopardized. One study estimates that individuals could lose up to $659,000 over a lifetime because of lost wages ($566,500), private pensions ($67,000), and Social Security benefits ($25,500) (Metlife, 1997; Wisensale, 2001). Thus, women who care for their relatives are seriously disadvantaged both as workers and as retirees.

Out-of-pocket outlays on behalf of their older kin also can be substantial and burdensome, especially for low-income carers. For instance, adult children may have to pay for their parent's expensive cost-sharing charges under

Medicare and any formal personal care required. Surveys show that relatives spend an average of $2,052 annually for expenses related to elder care, including food, transportation, and medicine (SSCA, 1999c). Such costs could erode any current savings or prevent further accumulation of assets for retirement.

The Class-Based Divide

As with most aspects of American society, there is a sharp class-based divide in the caregiving experience: clearly, female carers confront divergent realities based on their socioeconomic situation. Though professional workers must contend with many of the work conflicts and financial burdens described above, including barriers to their career advancement, they have significantly more advantages and privileges than low-income employees. In a recent study, Deitch and Huffman (2001) found that, on the whole, family-responsive supports in the workplace mostly accrue to a professional elite and are even more class-based than conventional fringe benefits. Top wage earners are more likely to have dependent care assistance, flexible work options, family leave, and greater job autonomy.

Low-income earners, who tend to have more rigid schedules, risk being fired if they are late or take any time off from work. Their employers generally offer only limited, if any, sick or vacation days. In fact, most low-income women would lose their jobs if their performance flagged as a result of family obligations. Thus, because of less and in many cases no flexibility, such caregivers are the most likely to quit or be discharged.[5]

Moreover, low-income women also are the least able to afford a leave of absence, even if they could obtain one from their employers. In 1993, then-President Clinton signed the Family and Medical Leave Act (FMLA), which grants twelve weeks of unpaid leave and job security for employees to care for a family member, including their chronically ill spouse or parents. Of the 15 million people using the act's provisions from 1993 to 1995, about 2.3 million individuals did so to care for an ill or disabled adult. However, recent studies of FMLA have found that low-income caregivers who might have benefited from a leave were much less likely than those with higher incomes to take advantage of the legislation, because they couldn't afford to give up their salary, even for a short while. This is especially true for women who rely on their own wage alone (Deitch and Huffman, 2001; Wisensale, 2001). Moreover, the working class are less likely to have jobs in companies with fifty or more employees, the minimum number covered under FMLA.

Furthermore, although the vast majority of families do not neglect their frail elders, middle- and upper-class daughters and spouses have more financial resources, and thus options, for resolving the conflicts between their work and elder care responsibilities. Specifically, they can purchase private help to provide some—or all—of the hands-on care. Their frail older relatives also may have amassed substantial assets, private pensions, and high Social Security benefits, enabling them to hire full-time assistance themselves.

Middle- and upper-class families, of course, have always relied on low-income workers, especially Blacks and other minorities, to service their needs. The gendered division of labor among White households in the nineteenth century was highly reliant on the exploitation of African Americans (including slaves), immigrants, and other working-class people "with very different age and gender roles" (Coontz, 1992). As the next chapter will discuss, such dependence has continued into the twenty-first century, albeit in altered forms. The steady movement of White women into the labor force over the last five decades, with growing numbers achieving professional status, has coincided with their growing elder care obligations, generating an ever increasing demand for domestic help. Today, poorly paid Blacks, Latinos, and immigrants provide the bulk of household chores, childcare, and elder care for a significant percentage of White middle- and upper-class females.

Nevertheless, as the myriad studies and personal narratives bring to light, these privileged caregivers still hold considerable responsibility, confront innumerable obstacles, and experience substantial pressures, anxious concern, and sometimes exhaustion as they struggle to meet the needs of their dependent elders. Among other duties, they tend to be in charge of hiring and coordinating aides and negotiating their wages, hours, and working conditions, sometimes at a considerable geographic distance. The high turnover in attendants, as well as those who fail to show up, are habitually late, or are sick, adds to the stress and time commitment. On occasion, the search for reliable aides—and constantly training new ones—can be as stressful as the work itself (Cohen, 1996).

Kate Millett (2001), in *Mother Millett,* and Alix Kates Shulman (1999), in *A Good Enough Daughter,* provide personal accounts of women's elder care obligations from the perspective of daughters with well-off parents who can afford relatively decent living quarters. Millett takes us through the inevitable range of painful emotions: watching her mother deteriorate, fear of becoming an orphan, the obliteration of her roots and childhood, apprehension at leaving her mother alone, the terror of her mother falling, and the horror of watching her mother's harsh and insensitive treatment in the nursing home. After obtaining a copy of the nursing notes and realizing how close her mother is to being physically restrained and drugged, she decides to rescue her mother from the facility, despite the resistance of her siblings and the nursing home and the difficulties of caring for her at home. Though her mother eventually is situated in a respectable housing complex, Millett must deal with the incessant, demanding tasks of finding, hiring, and coordinating acceptable live-in help. She also discovers that because even sorely inadequate nursing homes have long waiting lists, she will have no alternative if the home care situation she has cobbled together does not work out.

Shulman is pulled back to suburban Cleveland where she, too, is confronted by steady decline—in her case, of both parents. Her narrative provides a wrenching account of emotional upheavals, including guilt, warmth, and anger. She, too, is responsible for hiring round-the-clock practical nurses until her parents move into their assisted living quarters. She is one of the luckier caregivers: she and her parents are mostly satisfied with the facility, Judson Park, an expensive place with "airy rooms" and "caring people."

In *Elder Rage: or Take My Father . . . Please!*, Jacqueline Marcell (2000) tells her story of caring for her mother and father at home. Her father had always had a bad temper and was a controlling, dominating, explosive, and verbally abusive husband and father. Now eighty-three and afflicted with Alzheimer's disease, he constantly raged and cursed at her and his wife, threatened physical violence, and refused to take his medications. She was torn between the horror of placing her parents in a nursing home ("I cringed to think of my mother in one of those places," 18) and the inordinate difficulties in finding a paid in-home attendant who could cope with the situation. She was forced to provide the personal care herself, moving in with her parents for nearly ten months. After finally finding help, she still was "consumed with their care every single day of [her] life long-distance" (240). At one point she writes, "It had been over a year already that my life had been totally absorbed with my parents, not to mention the eleven years before that. I wanted my freedom from all the responsibility and emotional torture before my life was over" (215).

Paying Family Carers

There is considerable debate about compensating families for home care through cash grants and vouchers. Contemporary conservatives assume that such payments would not only inappropriately increase government involvement in private matters and raise public costs, but would also undermine traditional familial obligations. Consequently, current rules are quite restrictive and any remuneration available generally is limited to those elders poor enough to qualify for Medicaid, SSI, or state income supplements. Though about three-fourths of the states allow some funding for personal care by family members under Medicaid waivers, Social Services Block Grants, state programs, or all of the above, the vast majority exclude spouses, many disallow adult children, about one-fourth force the carers to quit their jobs, most wait until institutionalization is imminent, and all are insufficiently funded and provide low reimbursement levels (Barusch, 1995). Keigher (1999) puts it well: "Concern for community care appears to be focused on government providing only what it cannot get families to do for free."

Many feminists argue that society will recognize the importance of caring for dependent kin only if relatives are paid—and adequately so—for these services (Abel, 1991; Fraser, 1994; Hooyman and Gonyea, 1995). Such compensation would ease some of the economic burden of providing care, raise the household income for those who life with their frail relative(s), allow caregivers greater options in their lives, and provide them with a sense that society views such work as valuable. However, payments must be high enough to enable the adult child or spouse to leave her job and support herself and her family (Barusch, 1995; Fraser, 1994).

However, although concurring that rewarding women financially could be a gender-responsive policy, Browne (1998, 190) cautions that it also "reaffirms gender-role stereotypes and prevents long term structural change." For instance, cash payments to a particular person would reinforce the notion that she alone has the responsibility for her kin (Ungerson, 2000). Japanese women, in their successful fight for universal long-term care legislation in 1997, fought against family compensation, fearful that it would reinforce and perpetuate traditional filial and spousal responsibilities (Eto, 2001).

On the whole, the most advantageous approach is to provide publicly supported funding for a wide range of supportive services to all chronically impaired people in need of help. In many cases, attendant allowances could be paid directly to elders, allowing them to hire family members or not. Nearly all European and other developed nations entitle disabled elders to purchase and manage at least some in-home services in this way (Linsk and Keigher, 1995). In the United States, a number of states, especially Oregon, are experimenting with limited amounts of money for client-employed in-home services, including some payments to relatives (except spouses), through their Medicaid waiver programs (Tilly and Wiener, 2001). Consumer-directed programs would allow frail older people to reciprocate for their care, thus easing some of the tensions inherent in the informal caregiving relationship. It would also render the frail elderly less dependent on their family (Gibson, 1998; Ungerson, 2000). At the same time, however, we must change "the structural arrangements which generate both the division of domestic labor and women's experience of obligation" (Stoller, 1993, 165).

The Caregiving Burden: Emotional and Psychosocial Consequences

Elder care responsibilities affect all aspects of women's lives and well-being since they are labor intensive, physically exhausting, and emotionally stressful.

Despite some positive benefits, social isolation, strain, guilt, feelings of help-lessness and hopelessness, frustration, anger, conflict, and deteriorating health are common among family caregivers of frail elders: fully one-third report medical problems, mental problems, or both (Gould, 1999; Loucks, 2000; SSCA, 1999c). Substantial numbers are prone to depression, with estimates ranging from one-third to as high as 46 percent of the total. In one study, the female caregivers reported numerous somatic symptoms, including weight loss, physical weakness, sleeplessness, exhaustion, nervousness, and ulcers (Calderon and Tennstedt, 1998).

Assisting elders with dementia can be particularly demanding, especially if they are seriously impaired, completely immobile, and dependent on others for all of their needs. Moving, lifting, and transferring such patients, who have to be helped continuously to and from bed, on and off the toilet, and into and out of the bath or shower, is enormously strenuous. Providing fully for their care can be a daunting task, one that takes an extraordinary physical and emotional toll; sometimes it goes on for years. Such carers may even be at a greater risk for cardiovascular diseases (Vitaliano, Dougherty, and Siegler, 1994).

One of the largest problems is the emotional devastation of watching one's spouse or parent deteriorate, become depressed, or engage in inappropriate behaviors. In addition to impairments in cognition, Alzheimer's disease and other mental disorders can cause disconcerting vacillations in mood and behavior, loss of impulse control, and extreme agitation. In the case of older couples, the caregiver steadily loses the companionship and comfort of her lifelong partner as well. Adult children tend to experience a traumatic, disorienting role reversal, prevalent in cases of serious disability, that few families are prepared for (O'Brien, 1989; Schiff, 1996). Cynthia Loucks (2000), in a personal account of her caregiving experience in *But This Is My Mother!*, is anguished as she watches her mother transform from a vital woman to a frail old lady with dementia.

Barbara Boyd, a state representative from Ohio, describes her experience to the Senate Special Committee on Aging:

> My mother, Sarah Hamlet, was diagnosed with Alzheimer's Disease. . . . Her progression was rapid: Agitation and behavior swings, pacing from one room to another, pouching of food, destruction of jewelry, clothing twisted and tied in knots, paper shredded, a packed suitcase—for home was never where she was. She literally destroyed the chair she sat in, thread by thread. She became proficient in profanity. . . . She started wailing as she lost the ability to converse and forgot how to hold a glass in order to drink. As she progressed, feeding her took up to 30 to 40 minutes. Incontinence and the use of Depends (diapering your parents as they are still walking is a quick adjustment!). She was incontinent within a year and a half of diagnosis. (SSCA, 1999c, 39)

Caregiving can take over every spare moment, making it difficult for well spouses and adult children to attend to their own needs: in many instances it curtails leisure, limits outside relationships, and restricts freedom in other respects as well; in some cases, carers do not have any personal life at all (Loucks, 2000). Studies show that employed women, instead of slacking on either their elder care duties or work, often sacrifice their own relaxation, extracurricular activities, intimacies, and friendships (Mui, 1992). Many feel invisible as they labor alone, mostly without help from anybody else. As one spouse who took care of her husband for ten years remarked, "It can be very, very lonely" (Dribben, 2001, 14).

The requirements of some elders can go beyond what an individual—or even a family—can provide, eventually engendering burnout. Many caregivers become totally overwhelmed, exhausted, and fatigued, with stress levels at the breaking point. After trying to keep her mother at home by rotating care among all of the children, Loucks realizes that they just can't do it any longer and reluctantly places her in a nursing home: "The cold reality is that many families find themselves with no other viable choice" (2000, 46).

Cohen, who also ultimately has to institutionalize her husband, writes, "If someone were to ask me, 'what's it like to be a well spouse?' I would answer, 'nights, lifting, and toilet'" (1996, 26). She describes the emotionally and physically arduous, tedious labor involved in her tasks, such as adjusting his respirator and providing therapy for his spasms throughout the night, hoisting him on and off the toilet and monitoring his feeding tube. Constantly on call, including interrupted meals and broken sleep, she often feels imprisoned in her own home, controlled by his needs and schedule, and alienated from the outside world. Though much of the time she tends to him lovingly, she notes, "There's no question that anger, however expressed or repressed, is a huge part of the well-spouse experience" (17). Notwithstanding, she often feels ineffectual, inadequate, ashamed, and guilt-ridden. By the time she decides to put him in a nursing home, she is at her wits' end:

> It was untenable. I had a right to call for help. I had a right to be rescued. I had a right to rescue myself. I am not the only solution. I had the right to burn out. . . . I was, in short, fighting for my life. (165)

Families continue to suffer caregiver burdens even after the spouse or parent is placed in a facility. Because of the poor quality of care in most places, they must constantly intercede on behalf of their kin, especially since they tend to have more influence than the residents themselves (Shield, 1988). On balance, however, family members are kept uninformed and have very little power to affect the frail elder's overall situation. Moreover, they generally are afraid to complain or demand better care because the staff could retaliate with even worse treatment (Foner, 1994a).

Loucks (2000) experiences a sense of devastation, as though she is abandoning her mother by placing her in an institution. Her distress and workload are exacerbated by the poor care her mother receives at the facility, one that is ranked as "average" for the Indianapolis area. She is forced to sustain "unmitigated vigilance" (184) pertaining to almost every aspect of her mother's care, including ensuring that the staff adheres to her mother's dietary requirements, feeds and washes her properly, provides sufficient fluids, and includes her in at least some recreational activities. Loucks has to make sure that her mother is not drugged unnecessarily, check that she receives appropriate medical attention, watch out for bedsores and other skin problems, and replace personal items that are inevitably missing every time she visits.

She is mostly saddened by having to witness the indifference, unkindness, and detached manner in which most of the care is provided as well as the unexplained deep cuts and broken bones.[6] Though she frequently has to fight battles to protect her mother—most of which she loses—Loucks has to temper her complaints, afraid that the staff will take it out on her mother when she is not present. She tells us that she is "continually exhausted and distressed from having to put out one fire after another" (168) from "the constant struggle of getting Mama adequate daily treatment" (178). "There was never any question of giving up, even though overseeing Mama's care in that nursing home was truly the most demanding, frustrating, and disheartening job I have ever had" (142).

A Labor of Love

Despite the often grueling nature of care work, for many it can also be a labor of love, at times outweighing the hardships. Various investigations indicate that carers can experience a range of personal benefits, including enhanced self-esteem and the opportunity to feel proud of themselves, capable, and useful. Even the arduous work of tending to elders afflicted with dementia can be rewarded with the sense that one is giving tender, loving care to a parent or spouse and, for adult children, may afford an opportunity to reciprocate for earlier parental attentiveness to their own needs. In some cases, mothers may have provided significant money, childcare, and comfort to an adult daughter, especially during difficult times such as divorce (Fingerman, 2001; Lim, Luna, and Cromwell, 1996).

In his study of ninety-four caregivers, Scharlach (1994) found that one-fifth experienced a sense of satisfaction that they could assist their frail family member. Over 10 percent also reported gratification in repaying the recipient for what he or she had done for them in the past; peace of mind in knowing that their kin was receiving the best care possible; and feeling closer to their spouse or parent than ever before. Nearly two-thirds, in fact, rated their caring labor years as mostly positive and only one-third as mostly negative. He concludes: "Like many other challenging life situations, caregiving apparently can be a source of great stress as well as substantial satisfaction and personal growth."

For Shulman, her "dad's tenderness seemed to grow with his frailty" as "she sat in his room, holding hands and smiling" (1996, 11). She "relished being needed," enjoying the "fulfillment of giving of [herself]," and "the sweet caress of her parents' gratitude" (105). Loucks, despite the many difficulties in caring for a mother afflicted with dementia, writes, "Mostly, though, I treasured our relationship, standing by her and thriving on the love we shared" (2000, 106).

In reality, emotional reactions often are mixed. As Millett cares for her mother, she finds herself "deeply loving this small creature with an over-mastering tenderness, a closeness I would never have believed possible, so that these days are a miracle and a grace, a gift" (2001, 298). At the same time, she tells us, "There are moments I hate her, moments I feel enslaved, interspersed with moments of infinite tenderness, compassion and pity. Finally and always there is simply her need, that she cannot do without me" (198). Marcell, too, despite the grief and anger at her situation, writes, "[I] embraced the enormous pride I felt in my determined will and perseverance—and I treasured my own authentic power . . . that had made their lives so much better at the end" (2000, 266).

For adult children and their parents, interpersonal dynamics, even before the elder needs care, are as varied as early family relationships, ranging from warm, loving settings to angry, abusive ones. Although elder care can, indeed, derive from a deep bond with one's parents, as Abel (1991) discovers in her study, or from relatives willing and able to forgive past transgressions, it also can be thrust upon reluctant spouses or daughters who can't afford or find alternative forms of care. In her analysis of the mid-1980s Channeling Demonstration Project data, Mui (1992) reports that adult daughters, at least those who are White, feel more strain when the relationship with their frail parent has always been inharmonious. She further found that though the vast majority of family care workers suffer from emotional stress, their actual overall well-being tends to be related to the nature of their relationship with the recipient and the auxiliary resources available rather than to the condition of the frail elder per se.

Elder Abuse

Unquestionably, the early family experience influences one's attitude and responses to elder care obligations, with some relatives abusing (psychological or physical violence), financially exploiting, or neglecting (i.e., failing to provide basic care such as water, clothing, personal hygiene, medicine, and safety) their frail elders. Intergenerational transmission of violence, for example, is common: abusers of the aged often have themselves been abused as children or have observed such behavior between their parents or other family members over many years. Abuse and neglect also can occur when the caregiver has "unresolved and long-standing anger regarding the victim, especially when the latter is the abuser's parent" (Young, 2000, 58).

For some adult children and spouses, the physical and emotional pain as well as time commitment can become so overpowering that they lash out at their dependents. Caregivers who are forced into the role with no possible alternatives or supplementary help are particularly prone to mistreat their charges, as are those who don't know how to deal with a person with severe mental and physical impairments. In fact, in a comprehensive study of elder abuse, Suzanne Steinmetz (1988) found that those caregivers perceiving themselves as particularly stressed and burdened were the most likely to hurt their frail kin. Moreover, she observed that large numbers of otherwise "caring, thoughtful, loving children who were duty bound to provide the best possible care for their elderly parents" at times slapped, restrained, threatened, force-fed, or jammed medicine into their older dependents, mostly out of frustration rather than ill intent. Studies show that because of the overwhelming emotional and physical demands of severely cognitively impaired elders and their tendency to manifest aggressive behavior, they are particularly at risk for abusive treatment (Fulmer and Ramirez, 1999).

It is difficult to ascertain precisely the incidence of elder abuse in the family setting: estimates from available data range from 1 to 10 percent of the sixty-five and over population (Costa, 1993). According to the National Elder Abuse Incidence Study (NEAIS), there were about 450,000 cases of elder abuse and neglect by relatives in 1996 (Fulmer and Ramirez, 1999). However, the number is probably somewhat higher since victims tend to be reluctant to report mistreatment because of shame, embarrassment, fear of reprisal, and guilt (Costa, 1993). In addition, individuals in the later stages of dementia generally are unable to convey their experiences verbally. Another inquiry, which closely observed clients in New York state's adult day health care programs, reported that about 3.6 percent of the sample most likely were victims of some form of abuse (Fulmer and Ramirez, 1999). And investigators warn that the prevalence rate is rising as frustrated adult children, weighed down with inordinate responsibilities, increasingly "cross the line" and abuse or neglect their older wards.

NEAIS data suggest that the vast majority of victims are women over the age of eighty, most of whom are highly dependent on their carers and have only limited financial resources. Whites comprised 79 percent of the total, compared to 17.2 percent for Blacks,[7] 2.7 percent for Latinos, and 0.3 percent for Asian Americans (Fulmer and Ramirez, 1999). Nearly half of family abusers are adult children, followed by the victim's spouse and grandchildren. Men are the main perpetrators, accounting for fully 60 percent of all cases, a particularly high percentage given their relatively low level of caregiving responsibilities (Young, 2000).

Conclusion

The admixture of declining family size, increased longevity, alternative household structures, rapidly changing lifestyles, high levels of labor force participation, geographic mobility, and greater in-home medical treatments has intensified elder care duties for a significant number of women. Though females have traditionally assumed a disproportionate share of care labor, the costs and sacrifices are rising considerably today while women's ability to discharge their multiple obligations is decreasing. Exhaustion, isolation, physical and emotional illness, and financial drain are common. As caregivers struggle to balance their work and family roles, they often forgo time for their own needs. Current demographic, social, economic, and political trends portend even larger burdens for them in coming decades. After relating her ordeal, Loucks (2000) questions whether anyone should have to make that sort of sacrifice. She writes, "Trading the well-being of one person for another surely is not the answer" (45). Similarly, Cohen firmly declares, "One person, one family cannot do this alone" (1996, 38).

Clearly, women must be afforded greater control over their lives and not have to relinquish their autonomy and selfhood in order to care for their elders. As a society, we must provide greater options through affordable, high-quality community supports so that individuals can choose whether to provide personal care, the extent to which they can do so, and the amount of extrafamilial resources they require. Furthermore, the services provided must be sufficient to meet people's needs: as some feminists warn, the funding of limited, ineffectual assistance to carers actually can serve to reinforce women's hands-on familial obligations (Hooyman, 1999). They also can serve to patch up and mask the systemic structural, ideological, and gender-based problems that underpin long-term care in the United States.

Frail, chronically ill people—indeed, any people who are in need of care—should be viewed as a societal rather than as an individual responsibility. At the same time, individuals who are providing the care, usually at a great cost to themselves, merit more attention and regard. Certainly, services must be made available before the older person is on the brink of institutionalization and his or her caregiver at the point of collapse. Not only does our current strategy ignore the needs of our female kin keepers, but it isn't even effective: by the time help is offered, the carer is already too exhausted to go on assisting her spouse or parent (Montgomery, 1995).

It also is necessary to ensure that women are not penalized financially when they do assume their various caregiving roles, whether at earlier or later stages in their life cycle. Nor should they have to suffer economic devastation and even poverty as a price for taking care of their frail relatives. Many lower- and middle-class families and their older dependents struggle to pay for private services when needed, as well as out-of-pocket Medicare costs, medicine, transportation, and other essential expenses. Many full-time kin keepers confront a loss of earnings, health care coverage, and retirement security as well.

The work site also must become a more accommodating place so as to conform to the realities faced by single mothers and dual-income couples who are raising children or taking on elder care duties. Just as important, men should begin to shoulder their share of kin work, taking equal responsibility with women for both children and frail older people.

Finally, greater emphasis has to be placed on the affective aspects of care. As many feminist researchers recognize, spouses and adult children can care about, without physically having to care for, their frail kin: emotional closeness does not necessitate hands-on assistance, and in some cases actually can interfere with family bonds (Baines, Evans, and Neysmith, 1998). Certainly, parents need emotional care at least as much as physical assistance: studies show that older people view affection and love from their children as one of their highest priorities (Cantor and Brennan, 2000; Hooyman, 1999; Schiff, 1996). Besides, because of other family and work requirements, many adult children must—and do—"care" from afar. Regardless of distance, nearly 70 percent of all adult children talk to their parents on the phone at least once a week (Coontz, 1992).

Despite its gendered subtext, the current push toward home- and community-based care is not inherently detrimental to women. The fundamental issues are the lack of social responsibility for chronically impaired elders as well as the shortage of affordable housing alternatives, decent nursing homes, and readily available, accessible, and quality publicly funded programs to help them and their carers with personal care, day-to-day living, and household chores.

Notes

1. Prior to and through the nineteenth century, there was a particularly high mortality rate among women in childbirth.

2. Sixty-five percent of multigenerational households (2.6 million) consist of a householder and their grandchildren; another one-third (1.3 million) include a house-

holder, their parent or in-law, and children; and the rest, 78,000, contain four generations (U.S. Bureau of the Census, 2001b).

3. he also notes that as part of the internal pressures to provide elder care, some
women view the acceptance of outside help as an inability or failure to cope. Thus,
those women who set limits on what they provided often suffered from a sense of in-
adequacy, disloyalty, and/or guilt and were reluctant to ask for help (Aronson, 1992).

4. Today, 57 percent of all women work full-time and another 23 percent part-time.
Among married couples, 49 percent of Blacks, 64 percent of the working class, and
nearly half of the middle class include two full-time earners. About 58 percent of all
single mothers are full-time earners (Waite and Nielsen, 2001).

5. Obviously, then, since most women are employed in low-wage occupations, as a
whole they not only take on the vast majority of care work but also confront greater
hurdles than men in the workplace.

6. Her mother had received a cut on her arm that was more than two inches long
and required stitches. The aide in charge of her mother said she had no idea how it
happened. Loucks forced an investigation, but the nursing home and the Indiana state
Department of Health both accepted the aide's account of the matter. A week after the
cut, her mother's paralyzed leg was broken. Again, the staff claimed that they didn't
know what had happened and the matter was dropped after a brief investigation.

7. Studies show that the physical abuse of older people is particularly unacceptable
among Blacks. However, as with other groups, they may abuse their elders financially,
neglect them, or both (Fulmer, 1995).

4

THE WORKPLACE
ENVIRONMENT: PAID CAREGIVERS

K IN KEEPING—ONCE THE SOLE role of wives and mothers—has become increasingly institutionalized and commodified as ever-growing portions of
the work are shifted to the marketplace (Glenn, 1992). Though families, particularly wives, daughters, and daughters-in-law, continue to shoulder the major burden of caring for frail elders, workers in nursing homes, assisted living facilities,
and private households now assume a growing share of the responsibility.

The valuation of elder care skills in the marketplace closely parallels that of
informal care work in the home. For the most part, women involved in the provision of paid care are invisible, devalued, and disregarded. They comprise a
large segment of the generally low-wage female labor force and are among the
poorest paid. Their cheap labor absorbs much of the private and social costs of
providing for frail older people and, as such, links the family sphere with the
public domains of production and the state (Stoller, 1993). Their work also is
enmeshed in the complex relationships among the imperatives of capital, national and global labor markets, and social welfare provision for the aged. The
mix of social and private policies affecting formal caregivers—and the gendered construct that underpins them—reinforces patriarchal norms, serves the
needs of business enterprises, and contributes to women's inequality, oppression, and impoverishment both nationally and internationally.

Paid care work remains within the context of the gendered division of
labor, but it is also highly stratified by race/ethnicity and class: both institutional and home-based personal care attendants are, to a large extent,
women of color, Latinas, and female immigrants, especially in cities and the
urban fringes. In rural areas, small towns, and the suburbs, many of the

nursing assistants are low-income White women (Mercer, Heacock, and Beck, 1994; Tellis-Nayek and Tellis-Nayek, 1989). However, the evidence indicates that long-term care increasingly will depend on minorities and especially imported labor in the future.

Although there is substantial and growing documentation—if not action—on the issues faced by frail older people and their informal caregivers, relatively few studies have centered on the personal lives and experiences of their hired help. Most of the congressional hearings, government reports, and scholarly research delineating the inadequacies of long-term care and the serious problems with nursing homes and home care agencies focus on the elderly and their families. Even studies that do address worker issues, such as staffing and training inadequacies, tend to stress their effects on the quality of patient care rather than on the aides themselves.

In recent years, investigators have begun to examine the barriers to meeting the long-term care needs of ethnic groups such as people of color, Latinos, and Asians. However, even in these studies only limited attention has been devoted to the ethnic/minority formal caregivers who have many cultural, language, economic, and social problems of their own. Overall, there has been relatively little concern by nursing facilities, home care agencies, government regulators, the American public at large, or even individual household employers with the plight of the aides or with their rights. Savishinsky writes,

> If older Americans often feel neglected or overlooked, our work led us to suspect that the same is true of those who work with and care for them . . . At times, they seemed to be supportive players in a theater whose central characters were the elderly. (1991, 143)

He notes that direct-care staff are observable everywhere in nursing homes—and are indispensable elements of patient care—yet they appear as inconsequential, shadowy figures to visitors and outsiders (Savishinsky, 1991).

The vast majority of the frail elderly and their families who require formal in-home assistance must fund these services out of pocket. According to Kane and Penrod (1995), employed baby boomers seem more inclined to rely on privately paid help to care for their frail parents than previous generations. Obviously, a willingness to utilize formal services to substitute for, or more likely supplement, informal care tends to be directly related to an ability to pay. Although many feminists have advocated greater publicly supported, community-based elder care, they have not paid adequate attention to those who do the work and the conditions under which they labor (Neysmith and Aronson, 1997). Similar to nursing homes and home care agencies, under current circumstances privately purchased care depends on taking advantage of the nurturing labor of others. Better-off White women tend to ignore the deplorable conditions and inadequate wages of in-home attendants—along with the racial and class issues entailed—because they rely so extensively on their services (Glenn, 1992).

In her study of informal caregivers, Abel (1991) notes that a significant number hired personal assistants to relieve them at least some of the time. She pointedly tells us, however, "Although many women complained about the financial burden on their parents, only one questioned whether the wages were sufficient to permit aides and attendants to maintain a decent standard of living" (143). In fact, several feminist observers have suggested that the availability of a low-paid, exploitable female labor force has been instrumental in the career and income advancement of more privileged White women; it is likely that they will have an even greater need for their cheap labor in the future. Clearly, the experiences and situations of personal care employees and middle-class White America are worlds apart (Tellis-Nayek and Tellis-Nayek, 1989).

Since the late 1980s, a few researchers have singled out the attitudes, realities, and working conditions of those who provide formal care. One of the more important of these studies is Nancy Foner's (1994a) *The Caregiving Dilemma*, in which she assesses conditions in a nonprofit New York City facility from the perspective of the aides. Another is *Making Gray Gold*, by Timothy Diamond (1992), who worked as a certified nursing aide in the role of participant-observer in four Chicago nursing homes. Although his investigation includes the residents and their plight, he is most interested in the specific situation of the nursing assistants themselves. Joel Savishinsky (1991), Evelyn Nakano Glenn (1992), the Tellis-Nayeks (1989), Jane Aronson and Sheila Neysmith (1996, 1997), and some others also have concentrated their research on the circumstances of these frontline workers.

The Global Economy: Immigrant Labor

The demand for elder care workers has exploded over the last several decades. In fact, nursing aides and home care attendants are two of the fastest-growing occupations in the United States. From 1988 to 1998, there was a 40 percent increase in jobs for nurse's aides, reaching over 2.1 million positions; work opportunities in the home health care field, the most rapidly expanding industry in the United States, climbed from 244,000 to 636,000, an increase of 161 percent. The Bureau of Labor Statistics named nursing homes, personal care facilities, and in-home services among the top twenty industries gaining the most employment during the 1990s; for nursing and personal care establishments, the number of jobs overall rose from 1.4 to 1.8 million, an increase of about 30 percent. It is projected that these trends will continue over the next several decades; at least 800,000 more nursing assistants alone will be needed by 2008 (GAO, 2001k; Hatch and Clinton, 2000). However, it has become increasingly difficult to recruit and retain native-born American workers as nursing aides or as other low-level staff. Nursing homes, home care agencies, and private households are experiencing perennial shortages of elder care workers and, consequently, have come to rely on foreigners, both legal and illegal.[1]

Since the nineteenth century, U.S. immigration policy has encouraged contract labor, predominantly men, who were recruited for specific purposes; after their projects were completed, they were sent back to their homeland (Hondagneu-Sotelo, 2000; Kasinitz, 1992). The large inflow of immigrants at the turn of the twentieth century consisted primarily of White men, many of whom initially came without their families (Foner, 1997). However, the restructuring of American society from an industrial to a service economy has changed the nature of transnational employment. Because of a growing need for domestic and service workers over the last several decades, the demand for low-cost immigrant labor has shifted to women; a large majority of the post-1965 wave of immigrants has been females, mostly from Latin America, the Caribbean, and Asia (Hondagneu-Sotelo, 2000; Kasinitz, 1992; Waters, 1999). Moreover, First World nations, including the United States, Canada, Western European countries, Japan, Australia, and New Zealand, are experiencing rapid population aging and increasingly use immigrants to care for their elderly.[2]

Concomitantly, global workers are fleeing countries experiencing civil wars, economic turmoil, and onerous external debt. Indeed, beginning in the mid-1980s, the outflow of women swelled as a result of new lending strategies forced on Third World countries; many of them had borrowed heavily from commercial banks and international financial institutions after 1948, becoming burdened by debts that they couldn't repay. Faced with a looming large-scale default by borrowing nations, the World Bank and International Monetary Fund (IMF), in collaboration with the United States and Western European countries, imposed structural adjustment policies (SAPs) on them. In order to receive additional loans, countries that owed money—in Latin America, the Caribbean, Africa, and parts of Asia—had to meet certain conditions: emphasize imports over domestic production, encourage foreign investment, privatize industry (including health care), reduce or eliminate government subsidies for locally produced products, and sharply cut wages as well as spending for social programs (Epstein, 2001; Gershman and Irwin, 2000).

A primary goal was to ensure that lending institutions recouped their money. To that end, the World Bank and IMF encouraged Third World nations to increase their foreign exchange, promote economic growth, and encourage big business and large-scale agriculture, especially multinational companies, all at the expense of the poorest sectors of society. Although SAPs did not significantly cut overall debt, they led to the destruction of local industries and small farms, along with the livelihood they provided to the vast majority of the population. Over the next two decades, wages and per capita income fell, food prices rose, average living standards declined, and poverty spread in Third World nations subjected to these policies. In many places, there were food shortages and fewer services such as health care and education (Epstein, 2001; Gershman and Irwin, 2000).

Grace Chang (2000), Rhacel Parrenas (2001), Barbara Ehrenreich and Arlie Hochschild (2003), and others show how these economic policies have had a particularly deleterious effect on the situation of Third World women, forcing many to migrate in order to support their families. Female workers have become a highly important component of a debtor nation's economy and, as such, are viewed as essential raw material for export; both their families and the national economy depend on the wages female emigrants send back. For many Third World countries, the flow of remittances and savings homeward is a major source of foreign currency; for some, such as the Dominican Republic, it is their most important one (Wichterich, 2000).

In the Philippines, the government actively promotes the export of labor as a means of servicing its external debt. Though Filipinos have immigrated to countries such as the United States for decades, "Contemporary migration is a central component of the export-led development strategy implemented in the Philippines through the intervention of the International Monetary Fund and World Bank" (Parrenas, 2001). Under earlier initiatives set up under the Ferdinand Marcos regime in the mid-1970s, male workers predominated. However, as the demand for manual labor decreased and the worldwide need for domestics, nurses, and nurse's aides increased, by the mid-1980s women gradually took their place; care work currently is the nation's leading product (Parrenas, 2002).[3]

There are about 3.5 million Filipinos working abroad; 2.1 million of them are women, representing nearly 8.6 percent of the nation's females aged fifteen to sixty-four. Approximately 750,000 are employed in the United States, most of whom work as nurses, nurse's aides, child and elder care workers, or at other domestic services (Wichterich, 2000).[4] In some cities, such as Los Angeles, migrant Filipinas are the principal source of elder care workers, primarily serving as live-in home help (Parrenas, 2001). Most of their wages are sent back home: in 1994, according to official calculations, the country's overseas nationals sent back $2.9 billion in earnings, the Philippines' greatest source of foreign currency after electronics manufacturing. Some researchers estimate that the amount may be as high as $7 billion if informal channels are taken into account. From one-third to half of the population rely on this outside money (Chang, 2000).[5]

The feminization of the international labor force has fostered a new transnational form of family life. Today, most female immigrants are mothers, many of whom leave their children behind, sometimes for long periods of time—even years (Hondagneu-Sotelo, 2000). In the main, female immigrants have been relegated to low-wage domestic jobs that lack occupational advancement. Because of their poor earnings, most domestics cannot afford to raise their children in the United States. Caribbeans tend to practice serial migration: they come here by themselves, handing over their children to spouses, parents, siblings, or aunts. The rest of the family generally arrives later, sometimes one by one (Waters, 1999). Others, such as Mexicans living in the United States near the border, visit with their families on weekends or when they are able (Wichterich, 2000).

U.S. policies facilitate the importation of cheap female domestic and service workers while also perpetuating their status as an underclass (Kasinitz, 1992). Immigrants are viewed as commodities to be used without any concern for their rights, needs, or personal well-being. Moreover, as Chang (2000) points out, the government also attempts to extract their labor at the least cost to American society, whether economic or social. California's Proposition 187, the Illegal Immigration Reform and Immigrant Responsibility Act of 1996, the Personal Responsibility and Work Opportunity Reconciliation Act of 1996 (PRWORA), and new Medicaid rules all were attempts, among other objectives, to limit childbearing, keep children in the home nation, and cut the costs of immigrants generally by reinforcing restrictions on tax-supported benefits and services. Children who are left behind do not require expensive schooling, medical care, or other services. Moreover, as chapter 6 will discuss, before it was amended PRWORA specifically denied food stamps and welfare benefits to both legal and illegal immigrants and their families. At the same time, a five-year maximum limit was placed on all welfare recipients, thereby ensuring a large pool of inexpensive workers as well.

Employers take advantage of immigrant labor. For instance, hospitals and nursing homes have been recruiting and importing low-wage Filipina nurses since the 1960s.[6] Not only do the employers get cheap labor, but these women are also exploitable in additional ways; they can be and sometimes are threatened with deportation if they react against low wages or poor working conditions (Chang, 2000). Likewise, Diamond (1992) found that many nurse's aides work under contract, with their home country providing the initial funds for travel. Since they owe large sums of money, they are afraid of losing their jobs. Therefore, "The corporate arrangements under which they worked supplied the ownership hierarchy with more than just cheap labor; they provided a mechanism of social control as well" (189). He calls this a cross between paid work and bonded labor. When privately hired, new immigrants often are beholden to their employers: in order to obtain a green card, the workers must stay with their sponsoring families for two or more years, rendering many of them subject to the whims, power, and even abusive behavior of their employers (Parrenas, 2001).

Foreigners who enter the country illegally are even more vulnerable, including the substantial number of low-level nursing home staff without official papers (SSCA, 1998b). The Tellis-Nayeks (1989) have observed that they may be actively recruited by some facility owners who have a direct pipeline to these sources of labor, often paying them below the minimum wage. Such workers employed in private households may confront additional problems. Many of them are forced to labor long hours without a break, sometimes earning wages well below the going rate. They also are susceptible to abuse, including sexual harassment, by the care recipient and his or her family. As Chang (2000) puts it, they are like indentured servants; some are threatened with exposure of their illegal status if they complain. Others are taken advantage of because they are imbued with cultural values that hold the elderly in high esteem, thereby obligating them to put in additional, unpaid hours to satisfy any unmet needs of their clients.

Dominance and Power: The Nursing Home Hierarchy

Within the nursing home, there are distinct social, educational, and cultural divisions among the personnel that are reflected in sharp differences in status, salaries, authority, and privilege. These cleavages mirror the racial and class inequities in society at large. At the bottom of the nursing home chain, low-paid staff predominate—disproportionately women of color and Latinas—accounting for about 80 to 90 percent of direct patient services (IOM, 1996). In addition to certified nursing assistants (CNAs), other low-level jobs, including housekeeping, laundry, supplies, and food service, also include sizeable numbers of female minority workers, though Black and Latino men can be found in some positions such as maintenance.[7]

At the next level are floor nurses. Among them, licensed practical nurses (LPNs)—also disproportionately minority women—are the most marginalized and provide the least skilled medical treatments, such as changing bandages, cleaning open wounds, and distributing drugs. They also are delegated administrative tasks as needed. Registered nurses (RNs), who are higher up on the ladder, tend to be immersed in paperwork and supervision; in recent years, they have provided little actual patient care (Mercer, Heacock, and Beck, 1994). Charge nurses are responsible for overseeing the frontline staff, including CNAs and LPNs; devising and meeting the goals of resident care plans; dispensing drugs; rendering certain medical procedures; and coordinating care activities on their ward (Daly, 1998). According to a 2000 study by the Health Resources and Services Administration, out of the 2.7 million employed licensed RNs in the United States, 82 percent work in nursing homes. Nearly all of them are women (94 percent) and most are White (88 percent) (*Aging Research and Training News*, 2001).

Above floor nurses are professionals such as social workers; the director of nursing; physical, occupational, and speech therapists; dietitians; and the activities director. These positions are held disproportionately by White women and generally comprise less than 7 percent of the total nursing home staff (Tellis-Nayek and Tellis-Nayek, 1989). The home's administrator, any assistant managers, various department heads, and the medical director, most of whom are White and generally—though not always—male, are at the upper end of the pecking order and have most of the policy-making and administrative power. They tend to have limited contact with patients and almost none with nursing aides and other low-level personnel. In fact, in the nursing home in which Foner (1994a) conducted her study, administrators and professional staff failed even to acknowledge nursing aides when they did run into them. Top staff are, of course, the highest paid, usually receiving an array of benefits as well.

Even personal space reflects the stark cleavages among personnel. Administrators, department heads, and many of the professional employees have their own offices and usually a separate dining area. Moreover, charge nurses tend to view the workstation on each floor as their own private domain. Nursing assistants, however, generally do not have any specific place of their own. In many facilities, nurses, especially RNs, have little social interaction with them at all (Foner, 1994a; O'Brien, 1989). Moreover, socializing among the frontline workers themselves commonly is based along the lines of race and ethnicity (Tellis-Nayek and Tellis-Nayek, 1989). Because of network hiring in some nursing homes—direct-care workers who are recruited from family and friends of current employees—ethnic enclaves can be established within the workplace, especially at mealtime (Foner, 1994a; Waters, 1999).

Overburdened, Understaffed

Compared to the medical industry, long-term care enterprises do not employ a sizeable number of highly trained technical or professional personnel (Kane, 1994). In hospitals, registered nurses provide the vast majority of direct patient care, whereas in nursing homes, residents are served primarily by low-level aides whose formal technical training is sorely lacking (IOM, 1996). Under OBRA 1987, the federal government requires only seventy-five hours of classroom instruction and clinical experience for certified nursing aides, testing within four months of employment, and some limited subsequent in-service training per year.

Yet, since the implementation of the PPS in 1983, hospitals have discharged patients to institutions, families, and their own homes both "quicker and sicker." Compared to earlier decades, by the 1990s nursing home residents were older, frailer, sicker, and more likely to stay for longer periods of time than in earlier years—probably for the remainder of their lives. In many ways, nursing homes have become "minihospitals," a situation that nursing aides are not adequately prepared for.

The case mix now includes patients suffering from diabetes, heart ailments, strokes, fractured hips, arthritis, and complex, multiple physical and psychological disorders. Some are on nasogastric tubes, ventilators, and dialysis machines; others require intensive rehabilitation therapies, oncology treatments, infusion services, and wound and ostomy care (SEIU, 1997). Moreover, growing numbers of patients are afflicted with various forms of dementia—as high as 50 percent or more in some facilities—and require specialized treatment and management. Thus, although nursing assistants have limited education, training, and medical expertise, they are increasingly required to take care of severely ill and disabled patients, and perform some highly technical tasks, frequently with insufficient staffing, supervision, or backup help (Glenn, 1992; IOM, 1996). There has been no increase in nursing aide-to-resident ratios despite the greater medical, social, and psychological needs of patients.

The long-term care industry is labor intensive, with payrolls representing about two-thirds of total operating costs. Therefore, in order to enhance profits, providers have kept wages low, prompting serious staff shortages across the nation that have worsened with increased competition for low-wage workers in recent years. Raises also tend to be minuscule—fifteen to twenty-five cents an hour—providing little incentive for employees to continue at the same workplace (Diamond, 1992). To save money, some nursing home owners have purposely cut personnel.

As chapter 7 will discuss, nursing homes tend to be short-staffed most of the time and have difficulty recruiting and retaining workers. Many facilities have an insufficient number of nurses and nursing assistants to meet even basic care needs. As a result, aides have severely unrealistic workloads, with some of them struggling at times to assist as many as fifteen to twenty patients—sometimes more—during the day shift (Zielbauer, 2001). In order to promote greater efficiency, providers actually have quickened the pace in nursing homes over the years. On average, nursing assistants spend less than two hours a day per patient (HCFA, 2000a). Frequent, unplanned absences add to the problem: rigid schedules, outside family responsibilities, transportation difficulties, and the like regularly force aides to call in "sick" (O'Brien, 1989).

Not surprisingly, turnover of direct-care workers is inordinately high, as much as 100 or even 200 percent annually in some nursing homes, with an average of between 80 and 90 percent nationally (*Aging Research and Training News,* 2001; SSCA, 1999a).[8] An admixture of low wages, inadequate benefits, few opportunities for advancement, lack of respect, overly burdensome workloads, harsh working conditions, and an inability to provide decent care foster dissatisfaction, stress, and burnout even among the most committed aides. For similar reasons, the turnover rate of nurses also is considerable: 28 to 59 percent for RNs and 27 to 61 percent for LPNs (National Citizen's Coalition, 2001a). As a result, most nursing homes are and will continue to be perpetually short-staffed.

Multiple Demands, Stresses, and Abuse of Workers

Nursing assistants perform a wide range of instrumental and technical tasks related to all aspects of patient care. They are responsible for the not-so-pleasant bowel work: frequent cleaning and washing of incontinent residents and those with diarrhea and other disorders, wiping linen, emptying bedpans, giving laxatives and enemas, keeping account of bowel movements, and continual toileting (Diamond, 1992; Foner, 1994a; Gubrium, 1975). They also are expected to accomplish a strict regimen of daily meals and snacks, grooming, showering, and dressing. They change bedding, sort clothing, fill out patient charts, check rooms for wanderers, transport residents to various activities and therapies, take them for walks, and supervise games or show movies. At the same time, nursing assistants regularly measure and record vital signs, including temperature, blood pressure, pulse, and respiration.

These frontline workers also confront innumerable pressures and demands from a variety of sources within the institution—immediate supervisors, family and friends of the patients, and the residents themselves (Foner, 1994a). They struggle under grueling conditions with little control over their environment. Studies show that nearly every aspect of their working lives is highly regimented and strictly enforced, even their clothing, mealtimes, coffee breaks, and arrival and departure times (Foner, 1994a). In one of the nursing homes studied by Diamond (1992), aides were docked a day's pay if they clocked in two minutes late more than twice. At some places, shifts are determined solely by supervisors, thereby generating potential conflicts with an aide's outside obligations, including childcare. By and large, they have no control over their daily schedules and, according to one observer, "No attendant knew where she was going to be from one day to the next" (Laird, 1982, 60).

Even though they are responsible for the bulk of patient care, nursing aides have no say in how it is to be provided and usually are reprimanded for making independent decisions. They are expected to follow a steady stream of orders from supervisors and not deviate from daily routines without prior approval (Foner, 1994a). Analysts have noted that frontline workers routinely are subject to arbitrary rules and regulations from above, have few rights and privileges, and are expected to behave deferentially toward their superiors (Foner, 1994a; Glenn, 1992). Overall, they tend to receive poor treatment from and are given little respect by supervisors and administrators who "frequently devalue and manage them as non-entities" (Mercer, Heacock, and Beck, 1994, 110). Their powerless situation not only impairs their well-being and sense of self but it also negatively affects patient care (IOM, 1996).

Patients themselves can be particularly needy or irritating, with insistent and unremitting demands; some are simply lonely and want attention (Foner, 1994a). Aides also must watch out for residents with dementia disorders, many of whom wander aimlessly through the halls, sometimes straying outside the facilities—the needs and reactions of these patients are unpredictable. Patients with cognitive impairments also can slip into other patient's rooms and mess up or steal their belongings, thereby provoking anger and agitation among those whose rooms have been invaded (Savishinsky, 1991). At times, nursing assistants have to referee between patients, particularly roommates who don't get along (Savishinsky, 1991).

Aides frequently confront resistant patients, some of whom mistreat them. One worker asserted, "It's been eight hours of non-stop activity and sometimes unpleasant interactions with patients. I've earned my money. It's hard labor, sometimes along with verbal and physical abuse" (Daly, 1998, 33). Certain residents refuse to eat, get dressed, have their nails cut, or take their medicine; shouting, shrieking, ranting, and sniveling are common. Others strike out at aides in anger, unhappiness, or frustration by hitting, biting, and scratching them (Foner, 1994a). Many residents are bitter because they are dependent, isolated, and institutionalized—their rage can be projected onto the staff (Daly, 1998). Patients who are forced to wait unduly for meals, baths, or other basic needs eventually may throw a tantrum (Gubrium, 1975). Aides also can be ill-treated by clientele who are "domineering or patronizing, either ordering them about as servants or treating them condescendingly" (O'Brien, 1989, 167). Such behavior can take its toll on worker morale.

At the facility studied by Joel Savishinsky, 10 percent of the patients were formally classified as abusive. The assistant administrator told him, "The abuse that some residents inflict on caregivers [is] the hidden side of nursing home life—the dimension that families, the media, and the muckrakers miss" (1991, 169). According to a Bureau of Labor Statistics report, caregivers in nursing home and hospital settings represent a significant percentage of all victims of nonfatal workplace assaults in the nation (U.S. Bureau of Labor Statistics, 1996). In 1994, 20,438 workers were injured in such attacks; 24 percent of them were employed in nursing homes. About 20 percent of those hurt had to stay three or more weeks away from their job (SEIU, 1997).

Given their situation, lashing out at aides is one of the few weapons institutionalized clientele have. As one nurse contends, even insignificant matters can be blown all out of proportion by older people who have so little left in their lives and such limited control over their circumstances (Savishinsky, 1991). To illustrate, a patient, unhappy with the whole wheat bread on his tray, exploded that he had asked for rye: "That said, he picked the tray up and hurled it at [the aide], splattering [her] dress and [the] nearby floor with meatloaf, gravy, peas, whole wheat crumbs, and smears of butter" (Savishinsky, 1991, 96). In another nursing home, two residents regularly expressed their discontent with their situation by defecating just as their aide was about to finish her shift (Diamond, 1992). Laird describes a patient who continuously spat at the aides—"and he could spit a long way" (1982, 109).

Nursing aides also can experience racial problems (O'Brien, 1989; SSCA, 1999a). Usually, there is a sharp racial and cultural divide between caregivers and recipients. Residents, who are mostly White, sometimes bring their life-long prejudices with them and resent being dependent on women of color and immigrants, particularly if the latter do not speak English sufficiently. The atmosphere can become highly contentious at times, especially when aides must deal with racial or ethnic slurs directed at them. Diamond (1992), for example, found that certain residents "expressed anger and confusion at having people taking care of them who were from a different race, country, or culture" (41). Several patients interviewed by Gubrium openly expressed their racial hostility, some using pejorative language when referring to aides of color (Gubrium, 1993). Direct-care workers may have to endure sexual harassment from male patients or similar assaults on their dignity (Mercer, Heacock, and Beck, 1994).

For some aides, the invariable death of patients, especially those whom they had become fond of, can be a source of anxiety (Savishinsky, 1991). An intrinsic aspect of their working environment is regularly observing and taking care of people with visible signs of decline and dying and who may be suffering for long periods of time (Gubrium, 1975). Though it may become routine after a while, "caregivers generally did find some residents' deaths difficult" (O'Brien, 1989, 129).

Residents' families, who are a constant presence at most nursing homes, are an additional source of stress for nursing aides. They can be helpful, sometimes feeding, dressing, or even calming their spouses or parents. At times, they even assist other patients who don't have any visitors, and a few relatives establish good relationships with the staff (O'Brien, 1989). A significant number, however, are unreasonable and demanding, throwing off orders, instructions, and grievances; some expect the aide to drop her other obligations to attend to their family member's every need, an impossibility given the constraints on the worker's time (Foner, 1994a; Mercer, Heacock, and Beck, 1994). Nursing assistants tend to be guarded when dealing with these families, who can take their complaints directly to top management. As one aide put it, "You just do what they want and get 'em off your back" (Gubrium, 1975, 143). Even relatives who are generally considerate may blame aides for the rushed, perfunctory care—and even neglect—of their frail parents when staff shortages are particularly acute. For others, a lifetime of family animosities, compounded by guilt at placing their parent in an institution, can be taken out on the staff (Savishinsky, 1991). As with patients, race/ethnicity and class differences intensify any issues between families and those who provide the care (Foner, 1994). Many visitors view the aides as little more than hired help and as such give them little respect. Families rarely express gratitude or take an interest in their lives, workplace struggles, or personal needs (Savishinsky, 1991). And they too can express racist attitudes and behaviors that aides must deal with on their own.

In addition, an Institute of Medicine study (1996) found that care work is particularly hazardous. Though injury and illness among workers in the private sector have decreased since 1980, the rate for nursing aides has actually increased by 62 percent. The report noted that such work generates high levels of stress and a great risk of being hurt. In fact, according to a Service Employees International Union special report (1997), the occupational illness and injury rates of nursing aides are even greater than those of workers in the mining, steel, paper mill, warehouse, and construction industries. Nearly 20 percent of all aides become sick or are hurt on the job annually, a rate more than double that of private sector workers overall. Only hospitals and eating and drinking establishments report a higher number of injuries.

These frontline workers are most at risk for back ailments, which account for nearly half of their total injuries (SEIU, 1997). The Occupational Safety and Health Review Commission (OSHRC), in a case against Beverly Enterprises by SEIU, recently determined that the manual lifting of residents by nursing aides is a recognized hazardous work practice engendering lower-back pain and as such is in violation of the Occupational Safety and Health Act of 1970 (section 5 (a) (1); see www.oshrc.gov/decisions/pdf_2000/91-3344.pdf, October 27, 2000,

52–53). Much of the labor is physically demanding—lifting, turning, transferring, dressing, and cleaning heavy, sometimes immobile patients. Bedridden clientele have to be moved from one position to another every two hours in order to avoid bedsores. Others—who can be quite heavy—have to be regularly transferred from their bed, wheelchair, bath, and toilet, often without their cooperation (Gubrium, 1993).

In 1992, Occupational Safety and Health Administration (OSHA) inspections of several nursing home chains in Pennsylvania found that staff shortages have increased the prevalence of physical impairment, particularly back injuries and strains, since aides are forced to lift and transfer patients by themselves (SSCA, 1998b). Moreover, because of high injury rates and lost days of work, there is an even greater turnover and scarcity of aides. Hazardous working conditions also are costly financially; institutional facilities pay nearly a billion dollars annually in worker's compensation insurance, of which over half is funded by the government (SEIU, 1997).

The most obvious injury prevention strategy would be to increase staffing, an approach nursing home operators have been unwilling to take on their own. There also are a wide range of affordable mechanical and other patient-handling devices that could reduce back injuries. This, too, has met with resistence from providers whose first priority is to keep costs down. One study, which analyzed the effect of ergonomic interventions in two nursing homes for a period of twelve months, found that back injuries were reduced by as much as 50 percent. In an Erie, Pennsylvania, nursing home, the operator instituted a no-lift policy in 1992 and provided mechanical equipment and training. Since then, it has had only one back injury due to lifting and transfers (SEIU, 1997). In general, however, nursing home owners have disregarded the perilous working conditions of its direct care staff.

In 2000, OSHA finally promulgated federal ergonomic standards that were to take effect in January 2001. Three months later, Congress, at the initiative of President Bush, canceled the regulations and precluded any further OSHA action on the issue, at least for the immediate future (U.S. Department of Labor, 2000).

Affective Care: The Discounted Tasks

Within the logic of business practices and commercialization, not only elders but also their paid caregivers are viewed as commodities. Nursing assistants have become cost-accountable units and as such are expected to work as quickly and methodically as possible. They are increasingly subject to more rigid schedules and greater productivity goals, thus allowing fewer workers to accomplish basic tasks; as the pace quickens, there is less time for individual patient needs. The nursing home workplace has become an assembly line with a prescribed set of instrumental tasks. The job, based on an industrial model, is organizationally produced as "menial and mechanical" (Diamond, 1992, 166). One worker sadly notes, "You wipe a bottom, move on to the next one. You don't have time to spend talking to them" (Diamond, 1992, 166).

Because corporate values and needs are mostly at odds with quality care, government has had to issue ever increasing rules, regulations, and procedures, along with the massive paperwork these mandates entail. Most nursing home administrators are concerned about meeting national and state minimal requirements rather than with providing quality care. Today, nurses spend much of their time charting and recording; when dealing directly with patients, they have been reduced to technicians (Savishinsky, 1991).

Nursing assistants are expected to provide only services that can be quantified and written down, the concrete, reimbursable components of care; nursing home owners and administrators only value care that can be "measured and priced" (Diamond, 1992) or what Gubrium (1975) calls "bed and body work." Therefore, aides are judged based only on physical and health care tasks and how efficiently they are performed. They are expected to note fluctuations in their patients' health, functional capacity, and bodily systems (such as eating, excreting, and urinating) and are accountable for specific physical services rendered.

Affective care, which often is invisible and difficult to code, is mostly unrecognized, devalued, and unrewarded (Cancian, 2000). As noted by Gubrium,

> Chart entries typically do not describe social features of the daily routines of clientele even though they are often quite noticeable, and even though a good share of what floor staff deals with on the floor involves the social aspects of patents' and residents' everyday lives in the home. (1975, 59–60)

Although many aides view communication with residents as one of their most important tasks, conversation and relationship building are not viewed as real work by owners and administrators. Getting to know patients, listening to their comments, and answering their questions; encouraging stories about their families, friends, and past life; talking with those who are depressed or lonely; helping residents cope with their losses; and calming agitated patients or just holding and soothing them are not part of an aide's formal responsibilities. Many institutions actually penalize frontline workers for such time-consuming emotional work. Even the limited training of nursing aides focuses on instrumental tasks—mostly biological and technical—to the exclusion of the expressive aspects of care. Furthermore, their schooling promotes emotional detachment and lack of involvement with patients, though some aides view a certain level of attachment as necessary for decent care (Diamond, 1992; Foner, 1994a; Stone, 2000).

Despite official assumptions, directives, and formal job descriptions, most of the actual work in nursing homes is, in fact, emotional and relational. Aides provide a wide array of psychological, social, and emotional tasks when they can—what Diamond calls the "physically and emotionally draining moments of non-work" (1992, 162). To illustrate, he describes a late evening when an aide attended to an agitated patient: she went off "to calm and cajole, clean, cuddle, and comfort Arthur, and he went back to sleep"—but the official record contained only the notation "patient had been cleaned" (163).

Occasionally, ties can develop between aides and particular residents. According to Gubrium and others, when this occurs nursing assistants can "give quite generously of their time and services with 'their favorites'" (Gubrium, 1975, 118). They can perform special favors and buy them assorted treats. Moreover, in order to relieve aches, pain, and suffering among patients, some workers bring in various health remedies, including aspirin, laxatives, lotions, and other items, at their own expense, when they are not available at the facility. Even though these supplies are scarce in many nursing homes, such solicitous acts tend to be discouraged or even prohibited by management (Diamond, 1992).

Nursing assistants are painfully aware of how rushed they are and of the limited nature of the care they can provide, a situation that can frustrate and demoralize them. Many aides view institutional care itself as a sorely inadequate and unacceptable means for dealing with old age and frailty (Savishinsky, 1991). Some immigrants come from places where such facilities are not an option. One aide flatly stated, "In my country we don't even have nursing homes. Our families take care of their old" (Diamond, 1992, 70).

In her study of these frontline workers, Stone (2000) found that, for a significant number, their actual standards of care conform to an image of loving family relationships. They mostly "struggle to sustain the meaning and value of care as they know it in their more intimate relations" (90). Since many patients are lonely, isolated, and frightened, the workers feel that it is important to build relationships to gain their trust, treat them with compassion, and provide company and friendship. In fact, many of the nursing assistants she surveyed regarded such "social contact as the most essential human need" (90).

Caring work is not only invisible, but the considerable abilities "required to do it are not recognized as real skills" (Glenn, 1992, 30). Indeed, these frontline workers need a vast array of interpersonal skills and practical knowledge. For instance, dressing people who can't do it by themselves calls for delicacy as well as strength (Diamond, 1992). Aides need patience when dealing with dependent elders, sometimes having to wheedle them into eating or bathing. Certain clientele, "feeders" and partial feeders, have to be gently and slowly spoon-fed or coaxed into consuming each bite (Laird, 1982). In fact, in one study, workers "rated patience as the most valued component of good caregiving" (Mercer, Heacock, and Beck, 1994, 117). The job also demands self-control, particularly when faced with physically and/or psychologically abusive residents. It also takes "a certain kind of just being there," an undefinable aspect of care that requires empathy and compassion (Diamond, 1992, 18). Quality caregiving requires "attention, intimate touching of residents, physical labor, anticipatory thinking, and problem solving," as well as "being a good listener . . . and having a 'gentle touch'" (Mercer, Heacock, and Beck, 1994, 118–19).

It takes a certain know-how, concern, and tenacity to reach unresponsive patients. Many of the aides surveyed by Stone (2000) believe that it is both possible and necessary to connect with clientele afflicted with dementia, mostly through facial expressions and body language. Some residents are unable to speak, or their words are slurred because of a stroke or other medical conditions. They, along with the hard of hearing, pose additional communication challenges for caregivers. Many of these residents are "nonetheless alert, ambulatory, and available for interaction" (Gubrium, 1993, 117). Moreover, without adequate communication it is difficult to know what patients want, when they are ill, if something hurts, or whether they are responding to or adversely affected by their medication (Gubrium, 1975; O'Brien, 1989; Savishinsky, 1991).

The Social and Economic Circumstances of Nursing Home Aides

Inadequate take-home salaries leave most full-time aides in dire economic circumstances; about 18 percent have incomes at or below the official poverty level.[9] Nationally, the average wage for nursing assistants in 1999 was $6.94 an hour (SSCA, 1999e), amounting to only $14,435 in gross annual income for a full-time worker; to reach the poverty level, aides would have to earn at least $8.00 an hour. Kane, Kane, and Ladd (1998) maintain that nursing homes spend too much money on supervisors and administrators and should shift some of their financial resources into higher wages for those who provide direct patient care.

Overall, nursing aides earn 35 percent less than their counterparts in hospitals (SSCA, 1999e).[10] Salaries vary across the nation: in 2001, the mean hourly rate in California was $7.00 an hour; in Massachusetts, it was $10.50 (Crummy, 2001a). Direct-care staff covered by a collective bargaining agreement, only about 17 percent of the total, receive slightly higher wages (Rhoades, 1998). In Pennsylvania, such workers averaged $9.00 an hour, compared to $8.00 for the state overall (Rotstein, 2001). In Connecticut, the forty unionized homes start their care workers at $11.00 to $13.00 an hour (Zielbauer, 2001).

For the most part, nursing assistants who are the heads of households, whether single or married, struggle to support themselves and their families. A significant number must work double shifts or take second jobs to provide for their basic needs. Moreover, most nursing homes do not offer health care benefits. Even when such coverage is available, aides are burdened with high deductibles, coinsurance, and other out-of-pocket costs that they can't afford (National Citizen's Coalition, 2001a; SSCA, 1998b). Their children often lack preventive care or early treatment of disease; a significant percentage depend on emergency rooms for meeting urgent medical needs. Because of cutbacks in social programs, especially for immigrants, these frontline workers receive limited, if any, assistance from the state.

Low pay and general lack of opportunities for promotion or advancement within the nursing home suggest that the vast majority of nursing assistants will continue to be part of the low-income working class throughout their life. Their major prospect for furthering themselves is to acquire an LPN or RN degree, an educational achievement most aides do not have the time or money to pursue. And because of a general absence of private retirement pensions, combined with Social Security benefits based on depressed wages, they face even greater economic deprivation during their older years. Illegal immigrants who fall outside of Social Security entirely may have no means of financial support when they reach an advanced age.

In addition, there is little distinction between the public domain of work and private household obligations for these female caregivers. A large percentage are single parents who are responsible for the needs of their own family after a long, arduous day assisting frail elders (Foner, 1994a). Lack of schedule flexibility and sometimes very early morning hours (which can start at 7:00 A.M.) or late evening shifts make childcare arrangements difficult and complicated. Some mothers are forced to leave their children unattended at home, often in poor inner-city neighborhoods, where they worry about deplorable schools, crime, drugs, and the general safety of their families. Most aides do not have easy access to a telephone, making it difficult to keep in contact with their family or even check up on a sick child.

Commuting to work also can be arduous; many nursing home workers depend on high-cost and inconvenient public transportation, sometimes traveling long distances by bus or train. The journey is especially problematic in inclement weather. Yet, O'Brien attests, "Some staff make heroic efforts to [get to] work, trudging through several feet of snow" (1989, 124).

As suggested earlier, foreign aides struggle to maintain ties with families in their homeland. In addition to children, some workers may leave behind frail relatives; while they attend to other people's parents, they are not available to care for their own mothers and fathers. This can cause guilt and sadness, particularly among women who have been culturally socialized to assume filial obligations.

In-Home Care

Home care workers tend to earn even lower pay and obtain fewer benefits than aides in nursing homes. Most start at the federal minimum wage—$5.15 an hour—though in a few states it is slightly higher. Salaries vary somewhat, depending on the geographic area and whether caregivers have joined organized labor. For example, personal attendants in San Francisco are unionized and average $9.00 an hour, just above the poverty level for full-time workers; the city also offers medical and dental benefits (*San Francisco Chronicle,* 2000). In 1999, the city of Chicago raised the minimum wage for home care assistants to $7.60 an hour; state employees in Illinois, doing the same work and sometimes employed by the same company, earn only $5.70 (Knowles, 2000).

Personal care attendants are more vulnerable and harder to organize than employees in general; only about 8 percent are unionized (*St. Louis Post Dispatch,* 1999). However, labor organizations have begun to target low-wage minority and immigrant workers in recent years. After eleven years and at a cost of $1 million, the 1.4 million-member SEIU won its largest victory in six decades when 74,000 Los Angeles County in-home aides, about half of whom are immigrants, finally voted to join the union in 1999. Even so, a year and a half later they received only a fifty-cent raise—to an average $6.75 an hour—an amount still under the poverty level (Greenhouse, 1999; Martin, 2002).

Similarly to those in nursing homes, home care attendants normally lack decent—or any—health care benefits, pensions, or paid vacations. In a 2001 study of state and private agency workers in Illinois, Metro Chicago Information Center found that half had no health insurance at all and the rest were covered mostly by Medicare and Medicaid. Nearly 50 percent of the survey respondents had to choose between buying food and paying utility bills (Rotzoll, 2001). It is also a dead-end job with no advancement opportunities. Even more than in nursing homes, the workforce is disproportionately represented by ethnic and racial minority women, many of whom are immigrants.[11]

Employment tends to be less stable and work schedules more chaotic than in nursing homes. Some personal attendants have to string together short assignments in order to get full-time work, generally relying on unde-pendable public transportation. Others are forced to spend fifty or sixty hours a week at the job. In a study of New York City Caribbean caregivers, Mary Wa-ters (1999) reported that a large number worked long shifts, often into the late evening; many of them had more than one job; and some provided full-time live-in care, even when they had children. Many times, teenage offspring attended to the worker's own household, including the care of younger brothers and sisters.

In order to reduce costs, the home care industry increasingly has deperson-alized home-based assistance by accelerating the tempo of work and focusing more on concrete tasks and less on the relational aspects of care (Aronson and Neysmith, 1996). Though serving more complex cases over the years, the agencies also tend to require their aides, most of whom have low levels of ed-ucation and technical skills, to act on their own without adequate supervision (IOM, 1996). Moreover, although nursing home aides are constrained by strict regulations and fixed duties, personal attendants often encounter ill-defined boundaries, informal settings, confusing rules and lines of authority, little su-pervision, and extensive, sometimes overwhelming responsibilities (Foner, 1994a; Glenn, 1992; Neysmith and Aronson, 1997). For those who are pri-vately hired, there are even fewer fixed standards as to wages, working condi-tions, job descriptions, or living situations.

Some employees may get attached to their clients, many of whom have no kin or other support system, and sometimes develop close personal ties. Re-becca Donovan documents, "Home care workers often provide the primary, and occasionally the only, human contact elderly clients receive. In addition to performing instrumental tasks, attendants become friends, companions, and confidantes" (1989, 60). In her study, Keigher (1999) found this to be espe-cially true when the elder was paying for the services privately. She reported that aides often enjoy one-on-one relationships but are less likely to develop them when employed by an agency: independently employed aides more often have "a strong sense of personal investment in the work and reliance on their own personal standards for giving good care," as well as "compassion, af-fection and identification with their clients."

However, these conditions can set the stage for exploitation of the atten-dants: since they recognize that the client relies so heavily on them, sometimes as a last resort for meeting basic needs, they can feel an intense moral pressure to provide more care than they are paid for. It also renders it awkward to ne-gotiate for fair wages or even to leave (Parrenas, 2001). The workers also are vulnerable to patient, family, and agency demands because many of them have few other marketable skills or occupational choices and they can't afford to lose their job (Aronson and Neysmith, 1996). The potential for victimization is furthered by the isolation of their workplace.

Many in-home aides are not treated with dignity or respect by the agencies, relatives, or even the elderly themselves. In one study, workers complained that they were viewed by many care recipients as "cleaning women" (Neysmith and Aronson, 1997). One disgruntled aide who now prefers nursing home work complained that one client expected her to scrub the floors (Diamond, 1992). Furthermore, they labor alone, without the sociability and support of coworkers. Tension and anxiety are common among personal attendants: a study in New York City found that a large percentage have stress-related illnesses, including hypertension, asthma, arthritis, and frequent headaches. Over half experience high levels of emotional strain (Donovan, 1989).

As chapter 2 discussed, states and localities increasingly are creating home-based alternatives to nursing home care for frail older people eligible for Medicaid. New York, for instance, has substantially shifted its Medicaid funding from institutional facilities to in-home services. It now has the largest number of home care workers in the nation, most of whom are employed in New York City's Personal Care Program. The considerable savings in government costs, however, have been on the backs of the underpaid, overworked aides.

Donovan (1989) describes the conditions these workers encounter. Many of the apartments, which are situated in crime- and drug-ridden neighborhoods, are infested with mice and rats, lack heat and hot water, have leaky faucets and noxious odors, and require long stairway climbs to reach. The attendants provide a vast range of personal, household, and medical tasks at poverty-level wages. Despite their lack of education and technical training, a significant percentage are caring for seriously ill clients and have little supervision. As temporary workers, they suffer periods of unemployment when clients no longer require their services because of death, institutionalization, hospitalization, vacations, or simply rejection of the worker herself. Virtually all of the aides are Black or Latino females (96 percent); nearly half are immigrants, mostly from Jamaica, the Dominican Republic, and Haiti. About 86 percent have children, and, whether single or married, over three-quarters are the primary breadwinners. Some have three or four children to support.

In California, workers employed by the state-funded In-Home Support Services (IHSS) do housecleaning; help with the everyday activities of daily living such as eating, bathing, and toileting; and even perform some medical functions. About 40 percent of the 170,000 attendants are immigrants. For their efforts, they earned $4.50 an hour in the 1990s, with no benefits. Similarly to New York and other Medicaid-funded programs, the clients themselves are quite poor, often living in unhealthy environments (Chang, 2000).

Conclusion

Diamond (1992) incisively sums up the situation of nursing home aides as both backbreaking physically and emotionally heartbreaking. Aides are caring for a population of older people who are frail and dependent, many requiring help in meeting their basic needs. In their daily work, they confront large numbers of residents who are angry, demanding, resistant, tyrannizing, and generally abusive. Undoubtedly, the mistreatment that is accepted as "part of the job" in nursing homes would not be allowed or tolerated in the outside world or even at other workplaces (Savishinsky, 1991). And, as Foner (1994a) argues, the various forms of violence suffered by aides are not even part of the official record.

Although some aides can and do react meanly and spitefully when they encounter difficult patients, and others are callous and disrespectful to patients generally, the vast majority

> are neither saints nor monsters. Only a very small minority is consistently cruel or consistently warm and supportive. Most aides are generally kind and helpful to residents, although at times they lose their tempers and behave in ways that come across as mean. (Foner, 1994b, 245)

Similarly, the majority of aides try to be as supportive as possible to residents, but "a few occasionally lost control, paying back patients with some of the same behavior they had received" (Savishinsky, 1991, 166).

Some nursing assistants even find personal fulfillment in caring for frail elders; they value assisting others, especially those who are old and dependent. Although a significant number regard their job merely as a paycheck and feel angry and bitter about their low salaries and the way they are treated, others feel that "their jobs [are] important and caring ones, even if they [are] insufficiently rewarded or poorly appreciated by the people 'on the outside'" (Savishinsky, 1991, 185). In a study of aides in three nursing homes in Arkansas, Mercer, Heacock, and Beck (1994) observe that most came to the job with an interest in helping people, especially the elderly. The vast majority enjoy their work, despite the fact that they are dissatisfied with the low regard in which they were held by administrators and supervisors and with what they view as inadequate facilities, pay, and benefits.

Other studies have a somewhat less positive view of how aides generally behave toward their patients. Gubrium (1975) submits that some aides can be particularly harsh when residents disrupt or slow down their "bed and body" work or bruise their personal sensibilities. Sometimes they ignore their urgent needs; shove them aside; wheel them into a corner of the room where they can sit for hours by themselves; herd them through meals, showers, treatments, and activities; and fail to recognize their individuality. Kayser-Jones (1981) similarly records the ongoing callousness with which many aides at Pacific Manor react to residents: she encountered authoritarianism, indifference, infantilization, depersonalization, and verbal abuse in their dealings with patients, with little concern for their dignity or property.

Regardless of perspective, however, nearly every analysis of nursing home work points out that it is the exploitation of aides that fosters their resentment and therefore much of the insensitive treatment suffered by patients. These studies all acknowledge that it would be impossible even for the most conscientious workers to provide quality care, given their harsh working conditions, staff shortages, inadequate wages, and poor training and the economic imperatives of the long-term care industry overall. Nursing home operators are narrowly focused on augmenting profits, improving market share, and meeting minimum government requirements rather than ameliorating the situation of aides or enhancing patient care. Deborah Stone aptly explains,

> When care "goes public," worlds clash. The values, feelings, and interactions that make up the relational essence of care in the private sphere are sometimes devalued, discouraged, and even forbidden in the public world. Care givers and the people they care for are pressured by the norms, rules, and policies of the public world to make care conform to the image of work that predominates in the public world. (2000, 90)

She adds that "this conflict between private ideals and public practices is part of the stress that is so endemic to caring jobs" (111). Despite the constraints, at least some nursing home and home care workers manage to develop good relationships with their patients.

Clearly, current government rules and regulations are sorely inadequate to improve the fundamental, longstanding concerns regarding the long-term care industries in the United States. They fail to address the root causes of deplorable elder care both in institutions and at home. As several observers insist, public policies, such as those under the several Omnibus Budget Reconciliation Acts, are based on the assumption that low-quality care is caused primarily by deficiencies among the aides, especially their lack of skill, training, education, and experience (Mercer, Heacock, and Beck, 1994). As later chapters will show, these remedies leave undisturbed the "structural incongruities while proposing solutions of more training and stricter rules for the people who have the very least to do with the source of the problems in the first place" (Diamond, 1992, 231).

Notes

1. After the enactment of the 1990 Immigration Act, which will be discussed in chapter 6, more than 13 million immigrants entered the United States legally, and well over 3 million came here illegally. There are approximately 7 to 10 million people with undocumented status currently residing in the United States.

2. During the 1970s and 1980s, for example, there was a significant influx of women from the Caribbean region into New York City, most of whom found work in domestic household services, childcare, and the health and home care industries. Nearly a third were employed as nurses and even more as nursing assistants (Kasinitz, 1992). Today, the majority of female Caribbean newcomers to the city continue to work in these fields (Waters, 1999). Similarly, a 1991 study of the San Francisco Bay Area found that 58 percent of undocumented Latinas are house cleaners, childcare workers, or aides to the frail elderly (Chang, 2000).

3. In Los Angeles, Parrenas (2001) found that the Filipino migrant community has significant gender and class cleavages: professionals, semiprofessionals, and low-wage workers.

4. Though Filipino workers go to nearly 130 nations, Italy and the United States are the most popular destinations.

5. Parrenas (2002) observed that the IMF and World Bank policies have had a negative impact on the lifestyle of middle-class as well as low-income families. Thus, many middle-income women leave in order to avoid downward mobility in the socio-economic status of their households. She found, for instance, that a large number of the migrants in Los Angeles had a high level of education, including a college degree. However, as domestics in the United States, they were earning over twice the pay they received as professionals in their homeland. Though they experience a sharp decline in their occupational and social status, their remittances provide their children with health care, education, and material benefits they could not otherwise afford in the Philippines.

6. Under the H-1 nursing visa program, they can obtain permanent residency after five years.

7. According to the GAO (2001k), females comprise 90.9 percent of nursing home aides. About 57 percent are White, 32 percent are Black, and 12 percent are Latina and other minorities. Among all U.S. workers, the corresponding percentages are 74 percent, 12 percent, and 15 percent.

8. An American Health Care Association survey of twelve nursing home chains in 1997 found an average turnover rate of 94 percent (GAO, 2001b).

9. The poverty level was $16,700 for a family of four in 1999 and $17,650 in 2001 (U.S. Bureau of the Census, 2001e).

10. Overall, the average annual earnings of RNs working full time in 1992 was 14 percent lower in nursing homes than in hospitals. The average pay of staff nurses was 17 percent lower. Benefits, if provided, also were more sparse (Harrington, 1996).

11. According to the GAO (2001k), about 49 percent are White; 34 percent, Black; and 18 percent, Latina and other ethnicities.

5

THE FRAIL ELDERLY:
HOW THEY EXPERIENCE CARE

THOUGH POLICYMAKERS MUST ADDRESS the problems faced by those who assist frail people, they equally must be concerned with the needs, rights, and preferences of dependent elders themselves and the quality of their care. Similarly to the feminized worlds of both informal and formal caregivers, the population of the very old is highly gendered: women increasingly predominate at more advanced years. In 2000, there were 83 males per 100 females aged 65–74 but a ratio of only 65:100 for those aged 75–84. Among elders over the age of 85, the male–female ratio drops even more steeply to 41:100, (U.S. Bureau of the Census, 2001g). Currently, the life expectancy for women is 79.3 years compared to 73.7 for men.

Feminists argue that lack of control over one's body and vulnerability to violence are primary locations of women's victimization. Thus, they struggle for abortion rights, protection against domestic abuse and rape, freedom from sexual harassment, and economic security. However, for the frail elderly these sites of oppression engender additional hardships that adversely affect their life and well-being. The vast majority are widowed, divorced, or never-married women whose low or poverty-level incomes are compounded by functional impairments and physical dependency: a majority of the oldest old require ongoing help with at least some activities of daily living and will never be entirely self-sufficient (Baines, Evans, and Neysmith, 1998). Their situation is clearly at odds with the prevailing individualistic norms and expectations of self-reliance and financial independence in the United States, leaving them open to additional forces of exploitation and violence as well as a deprivation of their rights, liberty, power, and choices. Increased emphasis on privatization, extreme individualism, government retrenchment, and familism have put a significant and growing percentage of older females at the mercy of others.

Government officials generally view the growing dependent older population with alarm, especially because of the large number of women with inadequate resources to meet their own needs. However, as a number of feminists astutely point out, in stressing the difficulties these females pose for society, the government has failed to address the problems that society poses for them (Browne, 1998; Gibson, 1998). The structure of social provision for the elderly continues to rely on male experiences and patterns of aging, assume a patriarchal family structure, privilege men over women in terms of social benefits and rewards, and penalize women who have accepted traditional gender roles throughout their lives. Overall, current policies related to long-term care do not serve the interests of older women, many of whom have experienced multiple inequities and disadvantages during their earlier years and are now subjected to additional oppressive forces at the final stage of their lives.

Relying on Others: The Care Recipients

Women are particularly vulnerable when they reach extreme old age; despite a lifetime of expectations that they provide care to others, they are more at risk than men of lacking any care for themselves (Hooyman, 1999). Because older men are more likely than women to be married and even to remarry in their later years, when they become chronically ill they generally receive hands-on assistance from their wives. Only 14 percent of older men aged sixty-five to seventy-four, and 22 percent aged seventy-four and over, live by themselves. In contrast, there has been a steady increase over the decades in the number of older women who are single, especially among those at more advanced ages: only 41 percent of the sixty-five and over female population reside with a spouse. Approximately one-third of women aged sixty-five to seventy-four live alone, with the percentage climbing to slightly over 50 percent for those aged seventy-five and over (Federal Interagency Forum, 2000).

When unmarried older women become frail and dependent, they have difficulty remaining in the community unless they can rely on an adult child for support. The evidence indicates that women's prospects for spousal care will be even dimmer in the future. Female baby boomers who have married are likely to be widowed at about age sixty-seven, and only one in ten will remarry (Dailey, 1998). The growing percentage of never-married and divorced women among their ranks—19 percent and 16 percent, respectively—suggests that even fewer of them will have a spouse during their older years (U.S. Bureau of the Census, 1997). At the same time, since women are having fewer children—and are having them later—there will be increasingly fewer and older caregivers for them, many of whom will be physically unable to provide sustained, intensive care.

Moreover, extended kin tend to maintain strong family bonds but sometimes at a distance. With greater occupational mobility and geographic dispersal of families, grown children are not always readily available to provide hands-on care. Though at least half of all parents live in relatively close proximity to at least one child, about one-fourth are more than an hour's drive away, and some are in other areas of the country (Fingerman, 2001; Kane and Penrod, 1995). Elders also may have sons or daughters who are ill, incapacitated, otherwise incapable of providing care, or simply unwilling to do so. Some of the aged are estranged from their family altogether, a situation more often faced by divorced fathers. Widowed, divorced, separated, or never-married older women who have outlived their children, or those who did not have any offspring, are at a particular disadvantage. About one-fifth of all older people, mostly women, have no children on whom they can rely for assistance, and nearly 10 percent are without any living kin (Abel, 1991; Brody, 1995). They often are viewed "as surplus, extra, a public burden" when they can't take care of themselves any longer (Browne, 1998).

Female Elders: Their Financial and Health Status

As a group, women not only live in a material world that differs significantly from men's, but they also experience cumulative disadvantages over their life cycle: economic inequality between the genders tends to intensify and broaden at older ages. Income distribution among the elderly is highly concentrated at the top: the uppermost 20 percent receive about 46 percent of the total resources; the bottom 20 percent, composed mostly of unmarried women, racial/ethnic minorities, and the disabled, take in only 5.5 percent (Hendricks, Hatch, and Cutler, 1999).

Mostly because of inequities in the labor market and childcare responsibilities, younger females, especially those who are single parents, often suffer from insufficient income: they are more likely than men to work in poorly paid jobs, many of which fail to lift them out of poverty. Sorely inadequate welfare payments (averaging approximately $3,000 annually in 2000) also contribute significantly to the dire economic situation of those who are forced to rely on public assistance (U.S. Bureau of the Census, 2000c). And since the Personal Responsibility and Work Opportunity Reconciliation Act of 1996, young and middle-aged women have become more dependent on low-wage employment. In 2000, only 4.7 percent of married-couple families lived in poverty, as compared to 25 percent (or 3.1 million) households headed by women, including many who work full time.[1] Female-headed households represent 17 percent of all families, and yet 50 percent of those who are poor (U.S. Bureau of the Census, 2000a).

Since one of the leading indicators of poverty among younger adult females is single motherhood, many policymakers erroneously construe it as the cause of their destitution. Fineman (1995, 109–10) explains, "The socially and economically based deprivations that poor children and their mothers suffer are thereby transformed into deprivations attributable to and based upon their deviant family form." Though alternative household forms among single elderly women are as common as, and at the oldest ages more widespread than, the conventional patriarchal types, their living arrangements are not labeled as aberrant nor are they blamed for their unmarried status as are younger women. Yet, they are penalized by the state nonetheless.

Many social policies affecting the aged, notably the Social Security system, disproportionately disadvantage unmarried women. Social Security is based on a traditional patriarchal family structure with adequate benefits accruing primarily to two-adult older households. Upon the death of or divorce from their spouse, many elderly females—similarly to young mothers without husbands—tend to be relegated to a life of poverty. Specifically, the surviving spouse loses one-third and the divorced spouse two-thirds of the couple's original benefit, leaving many newly single women with insufficient income. Significantly, over 50 percent of all elderly women living in poverty were not poor before the loss of their husband (Browne, 1998). Women also tend to have inadequate Social Security pensions in their own right because of their concentration in low-wage employment—in 2000, women averaged 63 percent of the earnings of men, or $18,978 annually— and the penalties imposed on individuals taking time out of the labor force to care for their children or elders (U.S. Bureau of the Census, 2000c). In fact, by retirement age, fully 60 percent of the female baby boomer workforce will suffer the negative impact of some zero years calculated in their lifetime earning average.

Furthermore, females are more likely to work in jobs that are not covered by private pensions; when they do participate in such plans, their benefits generally are low. If widowed or divorced, they can lose all or a portion of their husband's stipend. Projections indicate that gendered differences will be sharp even among the baby boomer generation: though women have experienced increased coverage over the years, their actual receipt of benefits as well as pension amounts will continue to be suppressed by their low wages, part-time and intermittent employment, and disadvantageous vesting schedules. And many working women can't afford to contribute to a 401(k) or other type of individual retirement account. Although some retirees will receive high private pension income, the vast majority of women will receive little or none (Dailey, 1998).

Unmarried female elders also are less likely than men to possess any savings or assets other than a house, and, as Dailey (1998) warns, given the high and growing rate of divorce, even that is increasingly at risk. Only a minority of women have accumulated enough money to sufficiently meet their financial needs during their later years. At the same time, the Supplementary Security Income program, whose beneficiaries are mostly female, doesn't even lift elders out of poverty: in 2000, the mean annual SSI stipend was $6,233.[2] In addition, the benefits are decreased by one-third if elders move in with family members; they can lose their Medicaid eligibility as well.

Not surprisingly, nearly a third of all single older women had incomes at or below 125 percent of the official poverty threshold (the poverty threshold for an individual aged sixty-five or over was $8,259, and 125 percent of that was $10,323, in 2000) (U.S. Bureau of the Census, 2001f). Studies show that under current structural arrangements, baby boomer women will fare just as badly: only about 20 percent will have an adequate income during their older years (Dailey, 1998).

Women's relatively lower socioeconomic status is associated with women's higher incidence of chronic diseases and disabilities, a relationship that increases with age. Because of the cumulative negative health effects both of inadequate income and lack of medical coverage, disparities in health, which run across the life course, are not always visible prior to old age.[3] Even when they become eligible for Medicare, many older women do not have full access to program benefits since they can't afford the expensive cost-sharing charges or Medigap policies. Nor can the vast majority meet Medicaid's stringent eligibility requirements for medical services.

Certain disorders disproportionately threaten the aged female population with disability and a loss of independence, including osteoporosis,[4] Alzheimer's disease, arthritis, and diabetes (Scharlach, 1994). High blood pressure, which can lead to disabling strokes, also is more common among females, though the condition is a major cause of disability for both sexes. And because of their greater longevity, women are more likely to experience functional impairments at some point in their lives.[5]

Medicaid and Medicare: Stripping Women Bare

The ability of elders to maximize independence, choice, and control over their lives, particularly at the oldest ages, depends considerably on their income and other economic resources. In order to remain in their own home, chronically ill individuals who require outside help must finance it themselves. Currently, well over half of all noninstitutional formal assistance is paid for out-of-pocket, whether by the client or his or her family (Cantor and

Brennan, 2000). Those who need round-the-clock attendants are in a particularly precarious financial situation. Since most single elderly women have very low incomes, they cannot afford to purchase services privately, nor, in this country, do they have legitimate claims on the resources of society to meet their needs. Most simply must manage on their own in the community or with the support of relatives.[6] A significant percentage of frail older people without available kin and who are eligible for Medicaid are banished into nursing homes where they are hidden away from public view.

As suggested in chapter 2, many middle-class elders spend down their life savings on at-home and nursing home services before becoming eligible for public aid. Medicare does not fund long-term care, only temporary, skilled nursing services.[7] Thus, frail elders requiring just custodial care, such as those with mental incapacities, must pay the entire amount of their stay privately until they run out of money.[8] Slightly over half of self-funded nursing home residents become eligible for Medicaid within a year. They not only lose nearly all of their possessions—and usually their home—but they also become paupers who are dependent on public aid for the rest of their lives. Frequently, spouses and children who pay some or all of the bills for their kin may find themselves living in seriously reduced conditions as well.[9]

Some elders are caught in a vicious cycle: after they run out of money, they can't ever leave the facility because of their financial dependence on the government (Zebrak, 1998). Moreover, once on Medicaid, all of the resident's benefits and income are sent directly to the nursing home, whether from Medicaid, Medicare, Supplementary Security Income, Social Security, or a private retirement fund. Under SSI, patients are only allowed to keep from $30 to $50 a month, depending on the state, as a personal needs allowance (PNA), though in a few areas the amount is slightly higher (NCC, 2001b). These meager funds must cover such everyday items as stamps, writing paper, phone calls, cigarettes, glasses, dental care, dentures, treats, clothing, haircuts, and toiletries. The PNA itself is held, managed, and disbursed, as needed, by the facility, thereby further reducing the autonomy of patients. Though the money must be placed in an interest-bearing account, much of it can disappear into the facilities' own till as they legally and often illegally charge patients for various "extras," lotions, "upgraded" laundry services, and the like.

Frail Elders in the Community: Housing and Living Arrangements

Even in the early years of the nation, older people tended to live separately from their adult children, preferring "intimacy at a distance." They normally lived nearby, often on the same landsite in rural localities or in the same neighborhood within urban areas. In the case of serious disability, the parent(s) would move in with the adult child's family; if the daughter was single, she would live in the parents' household (Cantor and Brennan, 2000).

Beginning in the 1950s, adult children and their parents became increasingly more geographically dispersed. There also was a growing demarcation between the nuclear family and extended kin, especially among the White population. Over the next several decades, a trend toward greater independent living was further fueled both by the growing preference of elders, mostly because of the renewed stress on independence and self-reliance in American society overall, and their improved financial resources. In particular, the availability of Social Security, Medicare, Medicaid, and later SSI benefits allowed more elders to maintain their own households, however meager.

Most female elders today, especially in their more advanced years, live by themselves, whether in a house, apartment, senior citizens' complex, assisted living facility, or retirement community. About one-third of all White women aged sixty-five to seventy-four, 52 percent aged seventy-five to eighty-four, and 59 percent aged eighty-five and over live on their own as compared to only 12 percent, 18 percent, and 28 percent, respectively, of White men (SSCA, 1998e). As suggested in an earlier chapter, men are more likely to live with a spouse and therefore have readily available in-home care, if needed.

Currently, well over two-thirds of the noninstitutionalized older population own their home, the vast majority mortgage-free (U.S. Bureau of the Census, 2001c). For most of the aged, this is their major and sometimes only asset. Yet, single women and other economically disadvantaged elders in many instances are forced out since they cannot afford to pay rising property taxes, repair their dwelling, modify it structurally or buy special equipment to make it suitable for a person with disabilities. Moreover, the number of affordable rental units for the aged is steadily declining and has been at a crisis level for some time. Government-subsidized housing for the poor (section 202 and section 8: rental assistance and public housing, respectively) has conspicuously failed to meet growing demand.

Only about 7 percent of older men and 17 percent of older women live with their adult children (Federal Interagency Forum, 2000). However, at the oldest ages, growing numbers—mostly women—seek joint residency; about one-fourth of elders aged eighty-five and over live with a relative (Linsk and Keigher, 1995). The evidence seems to indicate that, given the preference of the elderly to live on their own, many move in with a family member only after they become so severely impaired that constant supervision is required, they can't afford to maintain their own dwelling or hire sufficient outside care, or their kin are in financial need themselves. The older person, then, can contribute whatever financial resources she has toward household expenses.

Clearly, the vast majority of elders would choose to stay on their own for as long as possible: most don't want to be a burden on anyone, especially their children. In account after account on family elder care experiences, frail parents insist that they do not want to intrude on their children's lives or saddle them with onerous kin work. Baby boomers seem even less willing to impose on their family than did previous generations. According to the 1997 National Caregiving Survey, 72 percent of Whites, 68 percent of Blacks, 60 percent of Latinos, and 49 percent of Asian American baby boomers stated that their children shouldn't have to care for them (AARP, 2001e).

Nor do older people want to be institutionalized; not surprisingly, an overwhelming majority dread the prospect of entering a nursing facility. In a survey of 3,000 seriously ill hospitalized patients, 26 percent said they were unwilling to and 30 percent said they would rather die than live in a nursing home—only 2 percent said they would do so voluntarily (Kane, Kane, and Ladd, 1998). In other words, frail elders want to live as independently as possible, preferably in a community setting and without overwhelming their family members, whether a spouse or adult children. However, their actual choices depend on their financial situation: there is a decided lack of possibilities for the vast majority of the dependent population with low or poverty-level incomes. On the other hand, a growing mix of private sector facilities and services are attainable for those elders with the ability to pay. Thus, the two-class system in long-term care, which allows some of the aged to pay for full- or part-time assistance in their own homes, increasingly has been broadened to include a wide variety of housing options for them as well. Consequently, demand for nursing home care among higher-income older people has been decreasing steadily.

Community Care for Elders Who Can Pay: Assisted Living

Over a million elders currently reside in assisted living facilities (ALFs), though estimates vary widely ranging from 400,000 to as high as 1.5 million people (AARP, 2000a; GAO, 2002a; Hawes, Rose, and Phillips, 1999; Zebrak, 1998). Most residents (about 70 percent) are unmarried women, with an average age of eighty-two (SSCA, 1998g). ALFs generally are targeted toward frail older people who can maintain at least some independence in their daily activities but cannot live on their own, including those with dementia; one study found that about one-third of the residents had some cognitive impairments (Hawes, Rose, and Phillips, 1999).

Variously called board and care homes, residential care facilities, homes for the aged, adult family homes, personal care homes, domiciliary care, adult foster homes, or rest homes, depending on the state, ALFs by and large offer meals, housekeeping, personal care assistance and supervision, aid with medications, transportation, recreational activities, and some health-related services. Individuals pay for room and board, which may come with a few basic services, and buy additional assistance, as needed; prices vary considerably according to location, type of room, and support package purchased.

On average, ALFs accommodate about fifty-three people each, though they range from small, independently owned homes with a few beds to large, corporate facilities housing over 1,500 elders; nearly two-thirds are for-profit companies (GAO, 1999a; Hawes, Rose, and Phillips, 1999; SSCA, 1999a). Since the mid-1990s, they have been the fastest-growing housing option with supportive services for older people. Expanding at the rate of 15 to 20 percent a year, they became a $20 billion industry by the beginning of the twenty-first century (AARP, 2000a). As demand swelled, nursing home firms as well as some other large companies followed the money, including Marriott, Kensington, Sunrise, Manor Care, Standish, and Alternative Living Services (SSCA, 1998g). One study found that much of the increase in ALFs was attributed to their high profits: by the late 1990s, they comprised seven of the ten top stocks in elder care. They also were viewed as one of the three strongest potential growth industries in the nation (Hawes, Rose, and Phillips, 1999). Moreover, unlike nursing homes, in many states ALFs are not subject to certificate of need restrictions.

Currently, 90 percent of all assisted living accommodations and services are paid for privately (SSCA, 1998g). Thus, even this relatively modest housing option is not affordable for most elders; two-thirds of older people can't even pay the usual basic price. Averaging over $25,000 a year for a private room in 2001, annual costs range from $18,000 to $48,000 and even higher (AARP, 2000a; GAO, 1999a). Residents also have numerous additional expenses such as health care, medicines, dentures, glasses, snacks, general supplies, clothing, haircuts, toiletries, phone, stamps, other personal items, and any additional assistance that they require.

Given the growing costs of nursing homes and the ongoing expansion of the oldest-old population, states have cautiously begun to investigate the inclusion of these relatively less expensive residential settings for Medicaid-eligible frail elders. By 2000, thirty-nine states used Medicaid home- and community-based waivers to fund some limited assisted living services for the very poor under their state programs. Most of these efforts, however, do not cover room and board, expenses that recipients or their families must pay themselves; a few states fund that portion of the AFL costs through a supplement to the beneficiary's SSI benefit—SSPs. Overall, less than 9 percent of assisted living residents are covered under Medicaid and only a minuscule number (about 250,000 in 1998) receive an SSP (SSCA, 1998g). In some states such as California and Pennsylvania, which have the second- and third-highest number of licensed beds in the nation, respectively, no Medicaid money is allowed to fund ALFs. On the other hand, in Oregon about 75 percent of long-term care residents on public aid reside in assisted living or other community-based alternatives to nursing homes. In Nebraska, state leaders are seeking to help nursing home owners build or convert their current institutions into ALFs (AARP, 2000a; SSCA, 1998b).

Compared to nursing home residents, ALF residents tend to have greater privacy, autonomy, and control over their lives. The facilities also offer them a less medical environment. But the extent of such advantages depends on one's ability to pay. For instance, though most units are private, about a fourth of them are semiprivate rooms and a small number are wards. Not surprisingly, elders with more limited income—and those on public assistance—reside in the more crowded dwellings and receive fewer supportive services (Hawes, Rose, and Phillips, 1999).

Since ALFs are not subject to federal regulation and oversight and there are no uniform or even minimum national standards, quality of care has become a growing concern. They are the sole responsibility of the states, which only recently have begun to issue any controls.[10] On the whole, licensing standards and regulations, when they exist, are sorely inadequate, and in some cases such as in Pennsylvania, facilities may be circumventing the rules (Casey, 1998a). Consequently, ALFs have the potential to become a variation of substandard nursing homes, especially for the poor.

A GAO (1999a) study of four states in 1996 and 1997 reported that one-fourth of the 753 facilities in its sample had five or more quality care/consumer protection violations, and 11 percent were cited for ten or more infractions. These included inadequate care; lack of access to physicians and other necessary medical treatment; insufficient, unqualified, and untrained staff; improper use of medications; and the inappropriate eviction of elders for health or financial reasons. Abuse is a serious problem as well: in Oregon, there were forty-eight verified cases in about 25 percent of the state's facilities during those two years; and Florida had thirty-nine verified instances of abuse, along with 103 cases of neglect.

In many places, elders must leave either voluntarily or involuntarily when their condition deteriorates and they require higher levels of care (Kane, Kane, and Ladd, 1998). In some states, the allowable levels of nursing care or amount of supervision required are set by the state; however, ALFs generally can choose whether or not to admit and discharge elders with cognitive problems (GAO, 1999a; SSCA, 1999a). Hawes, Rose, and Phillips (1999) determined that slightly over 70 percent of the facilities don't admit residents with behavioral problems, and 53 percent eschew those with moderate to severe cognitive impairments. Over half of the ALFs wouldn't keep residents who eventually needed nursing care, needed help with transfers, or became afflicted with cognitive impairments.

In a 1998 national survey, researchers found that between 20 and 43 percent of all residents eventually must leave; about one-fourth are forced out, mostly because they require greater care (Phillips and Spry, 2000). Other elders who exhaust their assets (about 8 percent during the study year) and become eligible for public assistance find that Medicaid will not pay the bill for ALFs. Most "discharged" residents move to a nursing home, though some go to another ALF that is willing to serve their higher level of care needs. About one-third of all elders living in ALFs ultimately wind up in a nursing home.

Contracts, marketing materials, and other written information are sometimes vague and misleading. The 1998 survey, for example, showed that 98 percent of people living in ALFs expected to stay as long as they wanted (Phillips and Spry, 2000). Less than half of the companies actually apprise elders and their families about their criteria for eviction. A similar percentage fail to provide written information about what services are not included in their fees or are unavailable at the facility (SSCA, 1999a).

Community Care for Those Who Can Pay Even More: Continuing Care Retirement Communities

The sharpest housing divide between the rich and poor is found in the life care or continuing care retirement communities (CCRCs), where entrance fees alone can cost well over $100,000. Monthly costs, which depend on the type of accommodations and level of services, also can be substantial. Some places, for example, offer a choice of small houses, apartments, or studios. In one facility, Willow Valley Manor North in Pennsylvania, the nonrefundable entrance fee for a one-bedroom apartment in 2002 was $117,200, along with a monthly rent of $1,427, adjusted upward on an annual basis. Individuals are required to have twice the entrance fee in assets and twice the rent in income in order to be accepted into the facility.

These luxurious dwellings attract a relatively wealthy and healthy population of elders who are investing not only in a residence but also in their future long-term care needs: CCRCs, which as a rule guarantee "care for life," allow elders to "age in place" with a continuum of care including assisted living and nursing home services, the latter sometimes part of or in addition to the monthly fee (Williams and Temkin-Greener, 1996). They offer a wide array of options and services such as fine dining facilities serving a broad variety of food and desserts; recreational activities (including exercise programs, massage therapy, croquet, card games, tai chi, and numerous other types of classes); entertainment, lectures, reading groups, and educational seminars; a library (books, newspapers, journals, and magazines); stores (bank, gift shop, beauty salon and barber shop); trips (to museums, ballets and orchestras, and for shopping); and investment counseling. Most CCRCs are situated on relatively large acres of land, and some include one or more pools, tennis courts, and the like.

There has been some concern, however, that the resident's money may be at risk. Although some states require an escrow account for at least part of the entrance fees, in other places the protections, where they exist, are rather limited. As with other corporate entities, "The CCRC's ability to meet its contractual obligations depends on its financial performance. There are no guarantees" (Connecticut Human Services Committee, 1998). A CCRC's bankruptcy in particular could threaten the well-being of residents, many of whom may have invested their life savings in the facility.

Nursing Homes: The Last Resort

By 2000, there were over 1.6 million chronically ill and disabled older people residing in nearly 17,000 nursing homes in the United States.[11] At more advanced ages, the chances of nursing home placement rise dramatically: though only about 1 percent of individuals aged sixty-five to seventy-four and 5 percent of those aged seventy-five to eighty-four are institutionalized, the proportion increases to 18 percent for the eighty-five and over sector of the population (U.S. Bureau of the Census, 2000a).[12] Moreover, about 43 percent of all older people eventually will spend at least some time in a nursing home.

Women, the vast majority of whom are single, represent over 70 percent of all nursing home residents (NCHS, 1985). A number of factors, discussed above, converge to push frail widows, divorcees, and never-married women into institutional facilities: as compared to men, they tend to live to more advanced ages, be more economically disadvantaged, experience greater health problems, and reside alone. Their precarious situation is exacerbated by the fact that Medicaid primarily funds institutional rather than home- and community-based care.

The nursing home population, most of whom suffer from multiple and complex social, cognitive, and physical problems, has become increasingly sick, disabled, and older over the last several decades. At least half of the patients are afflicted with Alzheimer's disease or some other type of cognitive impairment and typically require only custodial care (SSCA, 1998g).[13] Most residents initially enter an institution straight from the hospital. Once admitted, a large percentage of the very old remain institutionalized for the rest of their lives, mostly because they have run out of money for alternative forms of care or available caretakers.

Despite their mental and physical limitations, elders should have the opportunity to maximize their well-being and maintain their basic rights. American culture esteems independence and self-reliance, values that are consistently and extensively violated by most aspects of the nursing home experience. Nursing homes are warehouses for unmarried women, whether they were always poor, suddenly impoverished, or in the process of becoming so. For the most part, residents are robbed of their power, freedom of choice, rights as individuals, dignity, and self-respect. They lose their sense of self-efficacy and competence as their lives are devalued and their preferences ignored.

Even the "decision" to live in an institution can be forced upon a person without his or her permission. And because nursing homes that have a good reputation have long waiting lists, chronically disabled elders released from hospitals commonly must accept the first facility with an opening, regardless of its quality; discharge workers tend to have only limited time, sometimes less than a day, to find a placement (Kane, Kane, and Ladd, 1998). Elders on Medicaid generally have the fewest options.

Formal long-term care takes place primarily within the context of business priorities, especially profit maximization. The organizational needs, practices, norms, and rules of long-term care enterprises shape the work environment, fostering efficient, methodical, technical, and impersonal care at the expense both of residents and their aides. The primary goals in private, for-profit institutions are cost-effectiveness, financial performance, and profits rather than concern for the patient's desires, well-being, psychological needs, or the quality of their care. As the Tellis-Nayeks tell us, for nursing home owners, "The pious platitudes about 'commitment' and 'caring' seem only a thin mask for what they really want: productivity and efficiency" (1989, 311). The vast majority of nursing homes have become big business, primarily accountable to individual owners or stockholders. As such, they are driven by balance sheets, bottom lines, and short-term investments. Thus, there are substantial structural forces that militate against humane, sympathetic, and attentive care (Foner, 1994a). For elders relying on Medicaid, their situation can be the most appalling.

Nursing homes also are based on a bureaucratic, medical model: they adhere to the structure, routines, strict rules, and regulations common within hospitals. However, the type of medical treatment required for those with acute illnesses is not suitable for places serving long-term residents suffering from chronic disabling diseases, conditions that will never be "cured." At the same time, "The most bitter irony in this situation is that, despite the 'medical model' of life, nursing home residents receive some of the worst acute care in the country" (Kane, Kane, and Ladd, 1998, 216). They have only limited access to physicians, who tend to prescribe and monitor medications over the phone and provide standing orders for patient care. Actual examinations, if they take place at all, are most often hurried, perfunctory, and superficial. Individuals seldom obtain adequate medical attention or hands-on care from RNs, either. Nor do they receive proper rehabilitation in most places. Aides recognize that the completion of daily routines—making beds, feeding and washing patients—must take precedence over time-consuming efforts to improve residents' functional abilities, such as regular range-of-motion or walking exercises (Gubrium, 1975; Kane, Kane and Ladd, 1998; Shield, 1988).

Emotional Neglect: Residents' Psychosocial Needs

Clearly, nursing home residents have psychological, emotional, and social needs in addition to their physical debilities and medical problems. For most, entry into an institutional facility is an indication of their social situation, particularly their lack of an available caregiver (Savishinsky, 1991). As suggested earlier, many institutionalized elders either have outlived or exhausted their children, other relatives, and friends or are estranged from their kin; a large percentage are childless or do not have any family at all. Others have relatives who live far away. Once they go into the nursing home, they are cut off from any neighbors, remaining friends, or other previous associates and may even lose a longtime pet. At the same time, they have been stripped of their home and lifetime belongings, allowed to keep only what fits into their half (or one-third and sometimes one-fourth) of a tiny room. They have left everything behind and may need help in coping with their overwhelming losses.

In nearly all places, residents are separated from the outside world entirely: nursing home routines do not generally entail interaction with the community in which it is situated. The inhabitants "become isolated within the institution and lose contact with the real world" (Kayser-Jones, 1981, 31–32). Many are lonely and frightened. Their emotional well-being, especially for those without family, depends on the aides who play a major role in their day-to-day existence, sometimes as their only contact: about 75 percent do not have anyone visiting them regularly (SSCA, 1995a). Consequently, residents tend to view good nursing aides as the most important aspect of their nursing home experience, sometime. And studies show that it is the human qualities in staff that they value most—kindness, compassion, listening, chatting, gentleness, and responsiveness to their problems and needs (Foner, 1994a; O'Brien, 1989; Tellis-Nayek and Tellis-Nayek, 1989).

In his work as a nursing home aide, Savishinsky (1991) noticed that the residents had an "emotional hunger" stemming from their isolation. He insisted that it was essential to build a relationship with them to gain their trust as well as to provide company, warmth, and friendship: "Depending on their needs and abilities, they desired to be seen, spoken to, heard, and held" (241). For some patients, sharing pieces of their past lives allows them to maintain a sense of identity, a reminder of where they came from. Others merely need sufficient time to make clear their real needs, especially if they are afflicted with cognitive impairments. Dementia patients should have tactile stimulation as well: "holding hands, embracing a person's arm or shoulder"; some form of regular physical contact is essential for their well-being (Savishinsky, 1991, 133).

Within the corporate model, care work has been made into a commodity and as such discounts any tasks that cannot be "counted, coded, externally controlled, inspected and sold" (Diamond, 1992, 206). As one nurse explains, "If it wasn't charted, it didn't happen, but much more happened than got charted" (Diamond, 1992, 137). Client records include details about their food intake, bowel movements, sleeping habits, and bathing schedule as well as physical problems and medical attention they received, but they rarely contain any personal histories or comments about their emotional needs or current relationships.

Since nurse's aides are rated by what is quantifiable and therefore reimbursable, their ability to provide emotional tasks is seriously curtailed (Foner, 1994a). For those aides who enjoy helping others, there is insufficient opportunity to learn about individual patient concerns, personal background, religious values, and family circumstances. As one such assistant commented, "I don't have enough time to do little personal things for the patients" (Daly, 1998, 67). Even in one of the better, nonprofit homes, an aide lamented, "You don't have any time to socialize with the patients. You don't have any time for one-to-one contact. You just whip in and whip out. They don't get any companionship, really" (Tisdale, 1987, 50).

A survey of nursing assistants indicated that a large percentage view "social contact as the most essential human need" (Stone, 2000). Some pointed out that although friendship, personal engagement, and mutual sharing of their lives can help preserve an elder's dignity, nursing home rules and professional norms strongly militate against doing so. Aides frequently "are castigated for spending too much time on 'emotional work' with residents. Those who take the initiative in trying to improve patient care and respond to their patients' special needs can find themselves punished rather than rewarded" (Foner, 1994a, 59). Thus, meeting the frail elder's psychosocial needs and even forming any bonds with them are strongly discouraged. Kayser-Jones (1981) noted that most of the staff in the nursing home she examined communicated only minimally with the residents and were mostly distant with them.

Staff shortages also preclude attention to the affective aspects of care. According to Dr. John F. Schnelle (SSCA, 2000c), who conducted a time motion simulation for HCFA, current staffing levels are inadequate for either humane or effective care. Moreover, since the turnover of employees is inordinately high, the inhabitants have little continuity in their lives; they repeatedly complain that they don't get to know their aides (O'Brien, 1989; Tellis-Nayek and Tellis-Nayek, 1989). In a personal account of her mother's ordeal in a nursing home, Loucks writes, "Between staff rotations and people quitting, Mama never had the same caregivers for long, which deprived her of the comfort and reassurance that familiarity and continuity could have provided" (2000, 143). The paucity and turnover of personnel and the accelerating pace of institutional life not only allow limited time for emotional and relational labor, but they also engender harsh, often inhumane conditions.

Warehousing the Frail: Life in American Nursing Facilities

There are relatively few accounts that depict the nursing home experience through the eyes of the residents themselves. In one of the more prominent studies, Jaber Gubrium (1993) examines several Florida nursing homes, allowing the inhabitants to give us their perspectives directly. Through individual narratives, the elders make clear to him that they bring lives along as well as ills and disabilities. Gubrium discovers that despite the multitude of personal violations and insensitivities, certain individuals adjust, settle in, and make the best of things. A few take comfort in religion, especially those who seek meaning in the afterlife. Others, however, feel shortchanged, useless, a burden on their families, abandoned, angry, and disappointed. Some of the residents who are particularly affronted by the regimented life, loss of dignity, and impersonal treatment are consumed with rage over their poor treatment. One woman described her life as living in a prison. In another study, involving 130 ambulatory patients in a nonprofit, church-related facility ("Murray Manor"), Gubrium finds that many residents "virtually pine for a tie with the freedom they used to have before" (1975, 87). He hears testimony after testimony of people who feel lonely and abandoned, wondering how they could end up in a place like this.

Carobeth Laird (1982), in her memoir, *Limbo*, writes about her degrading circumstances as a resident in an Arizona nursing home. She makes clear the helplessness that dependent older people feel when they have limited resources and no available relatives to care for them. After reaching the Medicare limits for hospital care following gallbladder surgery, and unable to walk, she is forced into a nursing home (Golden Mesa Nursing and Convalescent Home) where she shares a room with three other people. She describes the "timeless monotony of institutional life" and the numerous indignities confronting her daily.

Joyce Horner (1982) chronicles her experiences in *That Time of Year: A Chronicle of Life in a Nursing Home*. A retired professor with no children, she is discharged to a nursing home when she can't take care of herself after a hospitalization for several broken bones. Though less critical of her care than Laird, Horner notes the boredom, poor food, and lack of medical attention that may prevent her from gaining her independence again. She, too, has a sense of vulnerability and desolation because of her financial situation: as her money is steadily depleted, she is caught between an inability to function on her own at home and a paucity of funds for her future care. She tells us,

> I go back to the small sums of money which won't add up to the cost of staying where I don't want to be, "living and partially living." . . . It isn't even any good resigning myself to staying here—one needs not only resignation but cash. (53)

Participant-observers have provided detailed investigations of nursing homes as well. For her study, Kayser-Jones (1981) chose one of the best facilities in California, "Pacific Manor," which only admits private-pay clients. Even in that place, however, she reports that on the whole residents receive dehumanizing and depersonalizing treatment. Their lives are severely restricted, with limited choices, freedom, or independence.

Mary Elizabeth O'Brien (1989), who spent two years observing and interviewing residents, family, and caregivers in a religious-affiliated, nonprofit institution ("Bethany Manor"), also found inhumane treatment, insensitivity, and violations of patients' basic rights. Similarly, Renee Rose Shield, in her inquiry— which included 200 elders in a nonprofit, northeast facility ("Franklin Nursing Home")—maintains: "Residents are generally treated alike. . . . Non person treatment . . . is a standard of resident care at Franklin" (1988, 5).

Indeed, in nearly all explorations of life in nursing homes, both participants and researchers state that the social structure and bureaucratic routines rule residents' lives, depriving them of any semblance of autonomy, power, and control over their environment; they have no impact whatsoever on major— or even minor—policies and decisions affecting their lives.[14] They must eat, sleep, nap, bathe, and take medications on rigid schedules and at specific times, allowing for little individuality in needs and preferences. Showers, for example, are highly routinized: in some places, even if the water temperature is cold the baths continue nonetheless. Washing up can become an ordeal for patients who at times have to suffer through both cold water and long waits (Diamond, 1992; Kayser-Jones, 1981).

In most places, patients must rise at 7:00 A.M. or earlier, regardless of their own inclinations. As one resident complained, "I worked all my life waiting for retirement, and now I can't even sleep in the mornings" (Diamond, 1992, 77).

Everyone is forced to bed at the same time as well, when the lights are turned off. In the nursing home where Lynne Daly (1998) worked as an RN, described in *A Certain Light: Nursing Home Experiences,* everyone had to get up at 6:30 A.M. and go to sleep at 8:30 P.M. sharp. At "Murray Manor," Gubrium (1975) observes that the night shift is responsible for waking up residents, and they begin dressing them for breakfast as early as 5:30 A.M. In their efforts to keep down their workload, aides would forbid residents to mess up their beds by napping under the sheets during the day. Laird's nursing assistants tell her firmly, "When I make that bed there's no getting back into it. Is that perfectly clear?" (1982, 51).

Meals, mostly institutional fare, tend to be unappetizing, uninviting, tasteless, without texture, and occasionally inedible. At times, hot meals or coffee are served cold. The inhabitants are forced to eat what is handed out, with no choice over their diet or any catering to personal tastes. Moreover, at least one observer submits that although the meals are "all scientifically designed for adequate nutrition . . . the result was often hunger": government regulations merely call for minimum levels of calories and nutrients (Diamond, 1992, 81). Residents as a rule cannot get food between meals, except for scheduled snacks, or keep a refrigerator in their room. In interviews, patients complained to Kayser-Jones (1981) about both the quantity and quality of the food and their lack of menu choices. Laird (1982) records how the facility not only skimped unmercifully on meals but also served the cheapest sort of dishes that were frequently watery, overcooked, and cold.

Even the residents' personal habits and leisure activities are circumscribed and carefully managed. Alcohol and cigarettes may be prohibited entirely. In a few places residents are allowed to smoke and less often have a nightly cocktail under heavily controlled conditions; these substances, purchased by the residents themselves, are always under lock and key. Where Laird (1982) resided, she was allowed one cigarette, twice a day, at specified times. At "Harvest Moon," the client's cigarettes were parceled out one at a time, exactly at the half hour (Tisdale, 1987).

The few social functions available tend to be based on low costs, ease, and the ability to carry them out en masse rather than on the interests of individual elders. Residents commonly have difficulty filling in their time; they spend most of the day sitting around, staring vacantly, napping, or silently waiting for their next meal (Gubrium, 1975). When asked if he was willing to be interviewed, one resident wryly remarked to Savishinsky, "That will be hard. . . . I have a full schedule. We are very busy here doing nothing" (1991, 740). Similarly to other observers, Shield (1988) points out that the activities tend to be childish—including Disney films and monthly birthday parties—or what the late Maggie Kuhn disdainfully referred to as "playpens." In describing the programs at her facility,

Horner (1982, 17) tells us, "A number of people are there just because they're put in chairs and taken—those who go to sleep, those who have to be fed, those who don't even know they are there."

Kayser-Jones (1981), in comparing an American nursing home, "Pacific Manor," with one in Scotland, relates that the latter offers full-length films and readings; provides a voluminous library; allows unlimited visiting hours; regularly takes residents on excursions into the community for dinners and social events; encourages time at home with their family, when feasible; and holds periodic socials that involve staff at all levels of the institution, including the director. The in-house functions, which are mostly planned by the residents themselves, are more interesting, productive, and meaningful. Overall, their lives are equivalent to those of similarly situated elders living in the community.

In contrast, at "Pacific Manor" the quality of the activities, which are put together by the social director without any input from participants, is much lower. The inhabitants are apathetic, bored, and uninvolved; they rarely, if ever, leave the facility. Moreover, there are no books, current magazines, or materials for creative work. She states that the inhabitants sit around doing nothing or "aimlessly pace the hallways." Nonambulatory patients are wheeled into the lounge after breakfast, where they remain for the entire day.

In fact, waiting is part and parcel of the resident's nursing home experience, whether to eat, snack, get dressed, make a telephone call, shower, or go to an activity. Before every meal, elders must mark time until everyone is seated in the dining room—sometimes for up to an hour—and then again until the food is served, another half hour or so. According to Gubrium, patients regularly scream "in rage about undue waiting" or "throw dishes or trays on the floor" (1975, 130). As Lustbader (1991, 7) puts it, "Waiting emphasizes the inferior status of the person who is being helped."

According to many accounts, calls for help are routinely ignored, including for such necessities of life as going to the bathroom. Dependent residents can relieve themselves only when an aide is available and willing to help, regardless of bodily urges; sometimes they must wait long periods of time to get on and off the toilet. Laird (1982) notes that although her own requests "might or might not bring assistance," those who can't reach the call button or don't have the mental capacity to do so are completely disregarded. Similarly, in *Mother Millett*, Kate Millett (2001: 154) sadly observes that when she is not at the facility to assist, for her mother going to the bathroom is "a privilege she must lie in wait and beg for, ring and pray for, call out uselessly and dream of. . . . Even to urinate one must be privileged by a captor." Patients sometimes remain soaked in their own waste for hours if they don't make it to the toilet in time.

Even self-reliance is discouraged, especially if it interferes with the usual fast pace of the institution. Since the hurried rhythm is in conflict with the condition of residents, many of whom either walk or wheel themselves at a crawl, they are often shoved or pulled along (Diamond, 1992; Gubrium, 1975). Others need to eat slowly but instead have meals force-fed into their mouths (Kayser-Jones, 1981). Furthermore, many nursing homes expect obedience from their patients, punishing those exhibiting independence. Loucks finds that her mother is "chastised for any behavior but submission" (2000, 145), and Millett's (2001) mother is labeled a "behavioral problem" because she is insistent on going to the bathroom when she needs to do so and refuses to accept her objectionable situation. In general, when the resident doesn't adjust to institutional life or actively rebels against it through angry behavior, both staff and administrators assume that there is something wrong with the resident rather than with the practices of the institution.

Nor do residents have the means, capacity, or obligation to pay back anything to the staff for their care: in nearly all places, even small, inexpensive gifts are prohibited. In social relations, it is crucial to have at least some balance between giving and receiving; the nursing home patient's inability to participate in reciprocal relationships adds to her demeaned status, loss of dignity, vulnerability, and extreme dependency (Gannon, 1999; Savishinsky, 1991; Shield, 1988). When an individual doesn't have even a limited means of repayment, compliance becomes the only resource that can be exchanged for assistance (Lustbader, 1991). Shield, for instance, found that because residents can't contribute anything, their control over their situation is reduced while their dependency is increased: "They are . . . reduced to nonhuman physical neediness" (1988, 158).

Residents thus are transformed from acting beings to beings acted-upon (Diamond, 1992). They are given few, if any, responsibilities. For the most part, the inhabitants become passive recipients of services that are organized for the private profit of others. Many of them suffer a loss of identity, sense of self, and even personhood as they are treated as objects rather than as the unique beings they are and have always been. As Savishinsky (1991) puts it, people in nursing homes are handled rather than held. Observers describe how residents are herded and shoved, en masse, to their daily activities, including meals and showers; packed into elevators; pushed aside; left in the corner of a room for hours on end; and otherwise neglected (Gubrium, 1975). After noting the appalling treatment of her mother, Millett (2001) comes to the conclusion that it is more than dehumanization and depersonalization—it is physical bondage and psychological toxicity.

Residents endure innumerable other indignities as well. They frequently are forced to wear wrist identification bracelets; one elder complained that he felt "branded like a prisoner" (Gubrium, 1975, 103). In one of the nursing homes where Diamond (1992) worked, all residents were forced to wear bibs at every meal. Sometimes individuals are put in diapers, whether they need them or not, for the sake of efficiency. By and large, the inhabitants also lose their freedom of movement, unable to come and go as they please.

Their right to privacy is violated as a matter of course, despite the fact that the facilities are the residents' de facto homes and many will be there until their death. Elders can be found lying naked, with the room doors wide open, as the nursing assistants perform their duties (Foner, 1994a). Gubrium (1975: 139) reports, "Aides gossip among one another and run in and out of the toilet where a patient is urinating." Since you can't shut your door in some nursing homes or lock it in nearly all of them, disoriented patients can wander into anyone's room and rummage through their drawers. Even well-meaning aides infringe on residents' small spaces, using their radio, television, and other items whenever they choose without permission (Gubrium, 1975). Savishinsky (1991: 117) sums up: "Patients had difficulty controlling their doors, drawers, clothing, belongings, and the surface of their bodies—all of which were exposed, at one time or another, to others who lived in or worked at the home."

Nor is gender taken into consideration when giving showers, to the extreme embarrassment of many residents: "Little attention is given to patient modesty at bath time; while waiting for a shower, patients are clothed only in short hospital gowns, and men and women are bathed simultaneously in the same shower room" (Kayser-Jones, 1981, 33). Laird (1982) found herself wheeled through the hall half-naked, as did everyone else in her facility.

Infantilizing and patronizing behaviors by the staff are common, further taking away the dignity of the individual (Diamond, 1992; Kayser-Jones, 1981; O'Brien, 1989). Elders tend to be treated like children: scolded, threatened, and babbled at in baby talk. Savishinsky (1991) argues that dementia patients, too, are adversely affected by such conduct, which can actually exacerbate their condition. Residents also face various forms of meanness by some of the aides: taunting and teasing, cold stares and withering looks, jokes at their expense, and other forms of psychological mistreatment (Foner, 1994a).

They are victimized in other ways. Stealing is common, whether by aides, nurses, or other residents. Therefore, people can't keep any personal belongings, money, or snacks in their room. Even their glasses and false teeth can "disappear" if left unattended. Clothing, including inexpensive items, can be "lost" in the laundry room. Overall, administrators take no responsibility for theft and do little to stop it (Kayser-Jones, 1981). Thus, residents experience an endless process of loss.

In many instances, patients can even have difficulty in keeping up their appearance, especially those who can't dress on their own. Therefore, "aide-dependent patients are likely to appear tastelessly dressed, wan, uncombed, gray and toothless" (Gubrium, 1975, 140). Kayser-Jones (1981) found a look of "sameness" about patients—no jewelry; ill-fitting, unpressed clothing; some patients in robes and slippers; and hair unkempt.

Moreover, some facilities deny clients basic amenities, such as toothpaste, lotions, and aspirin, if they are not directly reimbursable by the government (Diamond, 1992). Towels, washcloths, and sheets often are in short supply as well. Loucks (2000: 216) notes

> the loss of comfort and dignity when a helpless elder must lie on dirty sheets, do without a top sheet or blanket, or even lie in his or her own waste because the meager supply of linens is used up faster than the laundry workers can replace them.

Nursing home buildings themselves are normally clean, but for both workers and residents alike the milieu can be an assault on their senses: the smells are an admixture of stale urine, feces, decay, disinfectant, bleach, and deodorant. The ceaseless cacophony of groaning, babbling, wailing, muttering, screaming, and chanting greets them daily: "Some of the residents emit wheezing, coughing, choking and spitting sounds, depending on their physical conditions, while others stare vacantly and/or sit hunched over, head hanging half asleep" (Shield, 1988, 136). Horner (1982: 5) writes, "But I was never anywhere before where so many cried out . . . and at times I have felt almost annihilated by it."

The actual living conditions tend to be cold and impersonal—often antiseptic. Patient rooms are stark, with sparse furnishings and bare walls. Without their familiar belongings, many of which have long histories, family associations, and other reminders of their past lives, elders can feel alienated and disconnected from their environment. Their isolation is compounded when they can't contact family, friends, or neighbors at will: some places don't allow private phones in the room, and when they do, many people can't afford to pay the additional cost. Individuals must have permission to use the public telephone, which can be difficult to operate: it requires change, something the inhabitants generally don't have, and can be too high to reach from a wheelchair (Gubrium, 1975).

There also is compulsory coexistence: nearly everyone must live with one and sometimes as many as three or four strangers in their room, a situation that elders are unaccustomed to. Most older people today fiercely guard their privacy and abhor the idea of sharing a room with anyone. Though they are forced to accept it, "they do not 'adapt' or come to like it" (Kane, Kane, and Ladd, 1998, 181). Nor do they get to choose whom they live with. Moreover, roommates are reassigned periodically, without notice, destroying any relationship or friendship that may have developed (Gubrium, 1975).

Overall, residents have little—or no—power and tend to be afraid to complain out of fear of retaliation (Foner, 1994a). O'Brien (1989) observes that the elders she interviewed at "Bethany Manor" were wary of criticizing any of the staff to her. Only the inhabitants with family nearby, who are constantly vigilant and willing to advocate for them and confront the workers or administration, have any leverage at all. According to Savishinsky (1991), those with engaging and well-liked kin tend to receive more attentive care. Though relatives can be used to affect patient treatment somewhat, most families are afraid to complain because they, too, fear reprisals against their loved ones and use whatever influence they may have sparingly.

At least some measure of self-determination, empowerment, and regard as an individual is essential to the human condition. O'Brien suggests,

> Indeed, being respected as persons and being allowed at least some small measure of control over life are among the most significant desires of the majority of the elderly. . . . They understood their dependency upon the home for physical security and care, yet at the same time they desperately clung to the wish for as much personal autonomy as possible given the circumstances of their condition. (1989, 88–89)

And psychological health often deteriorates for individuals who lose nearly all personal control over their well-being, rendering them helpless, depressed, and more vulnerable to physical illness. Because of the dehumanizing treatment, many patients suffer a downward spiral in their health. The evidence suggests that among institutionalized elders with Alzheimer's disease, "Dramatic improvements in functioning and reductions in mortality result from increasing the sense of control that these elders have over certain aspects of their lives" (Robertson, 1999, 143). Indeed, the most trivial gains in self-determination can improve a nursing home resident's spirits, alertness, and communicativeness (Gannon, 1999).

Conclusion

Among the very oldest age group, some level of reliance on others for personal and instrumental care is common. To some degree, though many people are loath to acknowledge it, we are all dependent on one another in our everyday life. Nevertheless, frailty brings what Lustbader (1991) calls captive dependency, along with few options for many elders. Since females are less likely than males to have an available caregiver and more apt to lack adequate financial resources for hiring paid help, they must turn to the government for aid. Even large numbers of middle-class women who initially fund their own long-term care—whether in the community or an institution—eventually spend down their assets and must resort to public assistance, especially if they experience a long life span. Since Medicare does not pay for long-term services and Medicaid funds primarily nursing homes, these vulnerable elders can find themselves institutionalized.

Because of inadequate public support, the failure of long-term care policies overall, and their very low incomes, frail female elders often are "passive participants in care arrangements, as if the objects rather than the subjects of the circumstances of their aging" (Aronson, 1998, 118). Disabled older people who either never had a decent income or who deplete their lifetime savings on care often are subject to the preferences, needs, or capacities of their kin; adult children frequently control whether their parent can live in a community setting or must enter a nursing home. Such decisions sometimes are made without consulting the elders or independent of their wishes. Chronically ill individuals without any resources or available family generally have no alternative other than an institution.

American elders desire—and deserve—at least some degree of freedom, self-assertion, autonomy, and respect, despite any physical or financial dependencies. Many frail older people, even those remaining in the community, become subject to the whims and capacities of relatives and others. Those living in a nursing home often are stripped of their dignity, choices, basic rights, and, indeed, their humanity. As Diamond concludes, the industry's priorities, procedures, and practices, along with cost-cutting measures, do not allow staff to concern themselves with

> hunger in the night, or that stale, urine-soaked air might have accumulated all through the day, or that tomorrow the showers might be cold or the pancakes soggy or . . . puzzle about why this barren care cost so much. (1992, 206)

Clearly, single older women at advanced ages often have only limited control over their body, well-being, and life. Their real needs depend on reciprocity, interdependence, and mutuality, which are feasible only through improving their financial situation and promoting public responsibility for their care. As a nation, we have the ability to care for dependent, frail people; we must now come to see them as our collective responsibility. At the same time, we have to increase their agency by providing them with meaningful choices within the limits of their disabilities. The current system accords elders, especially women, neither options nor decent care. And, as chapter 7 will elaborate, the nursing home industry, with its underlying propensity toward structural violence, has led to even more serious patient abuses.

Notes

1. In 2000, 44.5 percent of all families living in poverty, mostly those headed by women, had at least one full-time worker (U.S. Bureau of the Census, 2001f).

2. Slightly over 4 million elders currently are receiving SSI; about 75 percent of them are women (Browne, 1998; HGR, 2000e).

3. About 75 percent of adults without medical insurance are women under the age of thirty-five (Gannon, 1999).

4. Osteoporosis increases the risk of bone fractures and accidents. Consequently, about one-sixth of White women will have a hip fracture at some point in their later years.

5. According to one source, only 11 percent of elders aged sixty-five to seventy-four report functional disabilities. This rises to 25 percent for individuals aged seventy-five to eighty-four and fully 60 percent for those aged eighty-five and over (Cantor and Brennan, 2000).

6. About two-thirds of older people with long-term care at home receive only unpaid services from their family and occasionally from neighbors, friends, or other informal sources.

7. Under Medicare, providers must regularly verify that patients are progressing in their rehabilitation.

8. About half of all institutional care in the United States is financed by the residents, their families, or both.

9. Currently, out-of-pocket expenses for long-term care are about $31 billion or 23 percent of the total costs. About 80 percent is spent on nursing home care (GAO, 2002a).

10. Currently, at least twenty-five states are attempting to initiate some regulations or strengthen existing ones, but little progress has been made to date (AARP, 2002a).

11. About 91 percent of the nursing home population are people aged sixty-five and over (U.S. Bureau of the Census, 2001g).

12. The percentage of elders eighty-five and over in nursing homes has declined somewhat from 24.5 percent in 1990 (U.S. Bureau of the Census, 2001g).

13. The *National Nursing Home Survey* (NCHS, 1985) found that 63 percent of the patients in nursing homes are disoriented or memory impaired.

14. In her study of "Harvest Moon," a generally decent nonprofit home run by a fraternal organization with an interest in caring for the frail elderly, Sallie Tisdale (1987) notes that the facility is concerned with stopping any stealing, has better staff-to-patient ratios than required by the state, provides monthly beer and wine for those residents allowed to drink, and provides activities that are more interesting than in most places. And, though they limit the number of Medicaid patients or those who will need public aid shortly, they do not throw out patients who eventually spend down their resources, nor do they provide different types of care to patients based on their method of payment.

6

MULTICULTURALISM:
RACE, ETHNICITY, AND CLASS

THE AMERICAN POPULATION overall and its elderly population specifically are steadily becoming more racially and ethnically diverse. Between 1990 and 2000, the White population[1] as a whole rose slightly over 3 percent to 198.2 million people. Vastly outpacing their growth, racial and ethnic minorities currently represent about one-third of the U.S. population.[2] Latinos, which are now the largest minority group, increased their overall numbers by 58 percent, reaching 12.5 percent or 35.3 million people.[3] They are mostly comprised of Mexicans, 20.6 million; Puerto Ricans, 3.4 million; Cubans, 1.2 million; and other Latinos from South and Central America, 10 million. The percentage of Blacks, the second in size, expanded by 21 percent over the decade to 12.4 percent of the population or 36.4 million people.[4] Asian Americans and Pacific Islanders have swelled by 48 percent, totaling 4.2 percent or 11.9 million people. Including over thirty ethnic groups, the vast majority are Japanese (slightly over a million); Chinese (2.4 million); Koreans (slightly over a million); Vietnamese (1.1 million); and Filipinos (1.9 million). American Indians and Alaska Natives (AI/ANs) amount to another 1.5 percent of the nation (U.S. Bureau of the Census, 2001g).

Although the majority of elders are White and of European descent (see table 6.1 for statistics on White ethnic groups in the United States), the percentage of older racial and ethnic minorities is enlarging steadily as well. By 2000, they represented slightly over 16 percent of the total aged in the United States: Blacks, 8 percent; Latinos, 5 percent; and Asian and Pacific Islanders, 2.5 percent. Few in number, about 138,000 people, the AI/AN aged also have

TABLE 6.1
Ancestry (Total Reported) among the
U.S. White Population, 2000 (in Millions)*

Ancestry (single or multiple)	Total Persons
Arab	1.2
Czech**	1.7
Danish	1.4
Dutch	4.5
English	24.5
French (except Basque)**	8.3
French Canadian**	2.4
German	42.9
Greek	1.2
Hungarian	1.4
Irish**	30.6
Italian	15.7
Lithuanian	0.7
Norwegian	4.5
Polish	9.0
Portuguese	1.2
Russian	2.7
Scotch-Irish	4.3
Scottish	4.9
Slovak	0.8
Sub-Saharan African	1.8
Swedish	4.0
Swiss	0.9
Ukrainian	0.9
United States or American***	20.6
Welsh	1.8
West Indian (excluding Latinos)	1.9

Source: U.S. Bureau of the Census, 2000d.
* Data represent self-classification by people according to the ancestry group or groups with which they most closely identify. The ancestry question on the census allowed respondents to report one or more ancestry groups: these data represent a combination of the top two ancestries reported.
** Czech includes Czechoslovakian; French includes Alsatian; French Canadian includes Acadian/Cajun; and Irish includes Celtic.
*** The Census Bureau accepted "American" as a unique ethnicity if it was given alone, with an ambiguous response, or with a state name. If the respondent listed any other ethnic identity, such as "Italian American," generally the "American" portion of the response was not coded.

multiplied more rapidly than the older population overall (U.S. Bureau of the Census, 2000b). And over the next thirty years, racial and ethnic minority elders are projected to increase their numbers considerably, reaching about one-fourth of all individuals aged sixty-five and over. Older Blacks are expected to grow by 134 percent, Latinos by 238 percent, Asians by 354 percent, and AI/ANs by 159 percent, as compared to only 79 percent for older Whites (Williams and Temkin-Greener, 1996).

Despite the fact that the number of elderly among certain groups is rapidly increasing, some of them, especially Blacks, Latinos, and AI/ANs, will remain younger than the overall population because of their higher rates of fertility: about one-third of their respective populations are under age eighteen, compared to 24 percent of Asians and 23 percent of Whites. For Blacks, their greater fertility is coupled with lower longevity than other sectors of society. Asian Americans, on the other hand, have relatively low birthrates (U.S. Bureau of the Census, 2000b).

Immigration

Over the last several decades, immigration has had a significant impact on the growth of racial and ethnic minorities overall and their older populations in particular. By 2000, about 11 percent of the total U.S. population was foreign-born, with nearly 44 percent arriving over the last decade (U.S. Bureau of the Census, 2000d).[5] Since the 1960s, immigration to the United States has come primarily from Asia and Latin America. Prior to that time, immigration law was biased in favor of newcomers from Northern and Western Europe: about 53 percent of all new arrivals came from Europe, only 6 percent were from Asia, and 28 percent were from North America (primarily Mexico) (Gimpel and Edwards, 1999). In 1965, Congress enacted major changes in the statutes that both increased the number of entrants and altered measurably their ethnic composition; the most significant change was opening the door widely to Asians for the first time.[6] As a result, from 1981 to 1990, fully 35 percent of the immigrant population came from Asia, 18 percent from North America (primarily Mexico), and only 18 percent from Europe. Moreover, under the Immigration Reform and Control Act (IRCA) of 1986 Congress awarded blanket amnesty to undocumented residents, granting legal status to another 2 million illegal residents, mostly Mexicans (Gimpel and Edwards, 1999).

Subsequent legislation in 1990 fostered an even greater influx of legal immigrants.[7] By the middle of the decade, over 915,900 legal and an estimated 300,000 illegal immigrants were entering the country annually: of the legal immigrants, slightly under a third were from Asia, one-third were from Latin America, 10 percent from the Caribbean, and fewer than 14 percent from Europe. During the 1990s alone, immigration added 13.3 million people legally. By 2000, 27 percent (30.5 million people) of our foreign-born population was from Asia, with slightly over half (50.8 percent) from Latin America and only 16 percent from Europe; about 60 percent of the total were noncitizens (U.S.

Bureau of the Census, 2000d). Additionally, we received well over 3 million people illegally, about one-third from Mexico and a significant percentage of the remainder from other Latino nations (Gimpel and Edwards, 1999).

The earlier 1965 law modified the per country quota approach to immigration policy by emphasizing (1) family reunification, (2) job skills that were in short supply in the labor market, and (3) humanitarian goals (i.e., allowing refugees to immigrate). A preference system, along with annual caps, was set for each of the three categories, though there was no upper limit on the allowable number of new entrants who were immediate family members of citizens. In other words, along with spouses and minor children, elderly parents of naturalized immigrants would be given top priority to enter the country. By the mid-1990s, nearly two-thirds of all immigrants came on the basis of family relationships, primarily from Asian and Latin American nations (Gimpel and Edwards, 1999).[8]

To be eligible for legal residency based on a family reunification visa, an immigrant must have a sponsor who pledges that he or she will provide full support, ensuring that the new arrival will not become a public charge. Nevertheless, a significant and growing percentage of public assistance benefits, such as Medicaid, food stamps, and Supplementary Security Income, were being consumed by foreign-born noncitizens, particularly the elderly and young refugees. In 1992, older immigrants represented 11 percent of SSI funding, up from 3 percent in 1982, mostly because of the growth of foreign elders in need (Tress, 1997).[9] Moreover, about 64 percent of them were covered under Medicaid either fully or partially (Friedland and Pankaj, 1997).[10]

Consequently, Congress enacted legislation mandating legally enforceable sponsor financial responsibility in 1996: the Illegal Immigration and Immigrant Responsibility Act of 1996 also requires that sponsors have an income of at least 125 percent of the poverty level. Concurrently, the 1996 Personal Responsibility and Work Opportunity Reconciliation Act reduced substantially a legal immigrant's access to means-tested programs. Furthermore, a sponsor's income must be taken into account before any benefits are granted.[11] Illegal aliens were barred from most means-tested programs entirely. Federal policymakers estimated that it could save nearly $24 billion over six years, half of the total gained from the 1996 welfare law, because of its alterations in program eligibility for immigrants (Friedland and Pankaj, 1997).

The bulk of all entrants since 1965 have been the working poor, many of whom eventually sponsored their older parents. These foreign-born elders, especially those entering the country later in life, tend to have far fewer financial resources than the aged born here. Most of them are single, unmarried women, many of whom have come to join their children and grandchildren after the death of or separation from their spouse (Friedland and Pankaj,

1997). They generally arrive without any income or assets and have no means for securing a livelihood on their own. Nor are they covered under Social Security or Medicare. Therefore, the vast majority have been supported by their adult children, public assistance, or both. However, now they must wait at least five years before they are eligible for most federal benefits. Since their sponsor's income, however low, is taken into account, many never qualify for aid at all, thereby becoming dependent on relatives for the rest of their lives (Angel, Angel, Lee, and Markides, 1999). Most also are precluded from obtaining needs-based long-term care services, including nursing home care.[12] Moreover, as with other groups with high levels of non-English-speaking populations, Mexican and Asian elders have a difficult time attaining citizenship, further perpetuating their lack of access to social welfare programs.

Clearly, although powerful sectors of the business community successfully achieved legislation encouraging greater low-wage immigrant labor, policymakers have been unwilling to sustain any heavy public costs for either the new workers or their families. And by pledging substantial government retrenchment, the Republican Right, endorsed by President Clinton, has been able to cut welfare costs by placing greater burdens on the foreign-born, most of whom now consist of the Latino and Asian working poor. Undoubtedly, for many Latino and Asian families, it is no longer economically feasible to have their older parents join them here.

Diversity and Elder Care

Scholars only recently have begun to devote particular attention to understanding differences among the various sectors of the elderly population. As the diversity of the nation continues to increase, many groups retain some distinctive characteristics and face unique problems. Frail racial and ethnic minority elders may have similar long-term care needs as the dominant sectors of society, but they tend to experience them disparately: the degree of incapacitation, vulnerability, and powerlessness rendered by the chronic conditions of old age is largely dependent on the social, cultural, economic, and political context in which older people and their families function rather than the aging process per se.

Regardless of background, families are the primary providers of assistance to functionally disabled older people in the United States. However, for some racial and ethnic minorities, because of cost and other barriers to paid care, as well as cultural or religious mandates, adult children may have an even greater responsibility. For Blacks, Latinos, and Asians, whose values emphasize collectivism, interdependence, and mutual assistance, the dependency of frail older people on their family is both expected and accepted as a predictable phase of the life cycle. These groups also tend to stress a particularly high sense of filial loyalty, thereby creating strong bonds within the extended family and a relatively high status for older kin. However, these values not only translate into an extensive support system for the aged but also impose considerable burdens on their caregivers. And, though a significant number of racial and ethnic minority elders reside in their own homes—even those with functional limitations—such cultures expect and encourage frail parents to move in with their adult children; many have no other choice financially. Multigenerational households are most common among immigrant families, especially for elders who first arrived in the United States in their older years.

There also are divergent attitudes toward social welfare, needs-determined public aid, and formal care itself. Although most elders enter a nursing home only when there is no other alternative, ethnic and racial minorities have particularly low levels of institutionalization. Older people from these cultures are reluctant to rely on outsiders for any assistance, whether privately paid or publicly supported, placing inordinate strain on their informal caregivers. In fact, an American Association of Retired Persons study (AARP 2001e), "In the Middle: A Report on Multicultural Boomers Coping with Family and Aging Issues," disclosed that among baby boomers caring for their parents and other older kin, racial and ethnic minorities tend to be more squeezed between their aging parents and children than Whites, and are the most pressured. Yet, it is difficult to measure their stress levels or coping mechanisms accurately or compare them with other sectors of society since the various cultures have their own way of expressing such hardship. For instance, researchers found that Blacks and Latinos, regardless of the caregiver burden imposed on them, tend to react with more resignation and acceptance than Whites but often manifest their anger, tension, and struggles through somatic symptoms (Calderon and Tennstedt, 1998). At the same time, racial and ethnic minority adult children who are expected to provide all of the hands-on care on their own, many while working full time at low-income jobs with limited flexibility, can become so encumbered with responsibilities that their dependent parents may forgo much—and sometimes the bulk—of the help they require (Harel, McKinney, and Williams, 1987). And the actual assistance itself may be perfunctory and ineffectual.

Cultural differences, however, can camouflage the considerable interplay of race and class, especially because of the widespread indigence among racial and ethnic minorities as well as their relatively lower income and educational attainment overall. Such disparities are perpetuated and even worsened during old age; Blacks, Latinos, AI/ANs, and their caregivers are particularly vulnerable. The material conditions of discrimination and racism are experienced most dramatically by women of color, Latinas, and AI/ANs throughout their life cycle. Facing persistent poverty as they age, such females are likely to be the neediest older people in the United States. With incomes one-third lower than similarly situated older Whites, about 66 percent of unmarried elderly Black women and 61 percent of unmarried elderly Latinas live in poverty (Kiyak and Hooyman, 1994).

Moreover, since low socioeconomic status and the concomitant barriers to medical services are associated with greater levels of poor health and chronic conditions, disadvantaged groups confront more and earlier levels of disability and functional dependency than their financially better-off White counterparts (Kane, Kane, and Ladd, 1998; Markides and Mindel, 1987). Clearly, minorities have a greater need for services but fewer resources through which to seek help. Thus, although they often "prefer" family care, even more so than Whites, in actuality they have fewer options. In fact, many of the different approaches to long-term care among the sectors of American society "reflect economic necessity and social class factors" (Angel and Angel, 1997).

The number and proportion of economically needy populations are rapidly growing at a period when public programs and services are steadily eroding. Thus, the government austerity measures of the last several decades with regard to means-tested programs are most acutely felt by racial and ethnic minorities. They have a disproportionately negative effect on the female members of these groups, as well. Lacking affordable private alternatives or adequate publicly supported assistance, such women are forced to take on full responsibility for their frail spouse or parents, regardless of their willingness or capacity to do so.

Insufficient attention has been paid to the impact of declining public resources on Americans with diverse ethnic and racial backgrounds: racial and ethnic minority elders and their families are facing increasing hardship and isolation along with decreased levels of care (Torres-Gil, 1987). And policymakers will be forced to confront their varied and often greater long-term care needs even more as we advance through the twenty-first century. Today's low-income racial and ethnic minority baby boomer generation, many of whom are caring for their chronically ill, economically deprived elderly kin, are rapidly approaching old age themselves.

Black Americans

Racism and Classism

Though Blacks, especially women, confront many similar issues as other groups relative to long-term care, their particular situation is exacerbated by racialized and class dimensions of the problems; clearly racial oppression and low socioeconomic status intersect with gender to inform the experiences of Black caregivers and care recipients alike. They also demarcate, to a large extent, how a person ages. Indeed, because of lifelong structural conditions, single older Black women tend to be the poorest among the elderly population as well as the least healthy, most functionally disabled, and most at risk for a low quality of life. Black women's lives are deeply rooted in the prevailing notions of gender, but they experience it in vastly different ways than do White females. Mediated through specific social and historical forces, their public and private domains have been somewhat more blurred. Specifically, because of a long history of workforce participation, they have always had to balance outside employment with their obligations at home.

Prior to World War II, nearly three-quarters of Blacks lived in southern agricultural areas where women, including those with young children, labored alongside men in the fields for meager wages. Beginning in the 1940s and accelerating over the next several decades, millions of Blacks migrated to northern center cities, where they faced overcrowding, crime, drugs, and oppressive discrimination. And as with their mothers and grandmothers before them, Black women were expected to seek employment in order to support themselves and their families.

As Coontz writes, "The June Cleaver and Donna Stone homemaker role was not available to the more than 40 percent of Black women with small children who worked outside the home" (1992, 30).

For one, they had greater single parenthood and divorce and a lower rate of remarriage than their White counterparts; during the postwar years, nearly 25 percent of working Black mothers headed their own households, a percentage that grew steadily over the decades. Even married females had to work since their husbands rarely earned a family wage. Blacks also suffered high unemployment, underemployment, and periodic layoffs, contributing substantially to the inability of the men to provide for their families (Coontz, 1992).

The expansion of the economy in the post–World War II years generated growing real wages, and some Black women found pink- and white-collar jobs for the first time. However, the vast majority worked in the lowest-paid sectors of the labor market, barely earning subsistence wages, many as domestics (Chang, 2000; Kaledin, 1984; Rowbotham, 1997). At the end of the 1960s, 55 percent of Black families lived in poverty, compared to 17 percent of Whites (U.S. Bureau of the Census, 2000c). A significant number of Black women through the rest of the twentieth century and into the twenty-first continued in low-wage employment, including cleaning other people's houses and caring for their children and increasingly their frail elders while maintaining full responsibility for their own family and home (Ungerson, 2000).

Today, about one-third of all Black households are headed by women; nearly 20 percent of the total include single mothers with children aged eighteen and younger. Black men and women alike suffer from inadequate income and poverty throughout their lives, mostly because of their low-wage jobs; high rates of unemployment and underemployment; poor health, particularly during middle age and later; and low, declining levels of public support for families in need. In 2000, 22 percent of Blacks lived at or below the official poverty threshold (6 percent of Black married couples but fully 35 percent of Black female-headed households). This contrasts sharply with Whites whose overall poverty level is 7.5 percent (3 percent of married couples and 17 percent of female-headed households) (U.S. Bureau of the Census, 2001f).

Racial disparities in socioeconomic status tend to increase even further at older ages. Despite growing and costly programs for the aged, older Blacks have about half the financial resources of older Whites and are three times as likely to be impoverished. Older Black women, who are even more likely than White women to be single—and at younger ages—suffer the greatest economic deprivation, a situation that is clearly linked to their earlier experiences; a significant percentage approach old age already in poverty.

Among other factors, the prevalence among younger Blacks of poorly paid, dead-end jobs, which generally do not provide private pensions; longer periods of unemployment; and a higher percentage of early retirement than Whites generate considerably lower Social Security benefits. The scheduled increase in the retirement age under the program will cut their already low pensions even further. Moreover, the vast majority of older Black women must rely on a single Social Security benefit, whether as a worker, widow, or divorcee; those who labored as domestics or caregivers most likely were not covered at all.[13]

Many unmarried Black elders depend on SSI, which amounted to only $6,500 annually in 2002 or $541 a month. If they move in with their children, even this paltry allowance is cut by one-third. Few older minorities have accumulated enough savings in their younger years for any meaningful income from assets. In fact, the median net worth for Black heads of households under age sixty-five in 1999 was $13,000 compared to $181,000 for Whites, a difference that has held relatively constant over the decades (AARP, 2000d; Mishel, Bernstein, and Schmitt, 2001).

Health Status

It is well documented that Blacks have poorer health and higher rates of disability and morbidity than Whites throughout their life span, with some individuals exhibiting the physical indications of "old age" as early as their mid- to late forties (Louie, 1999; Tripp-Reimer, 1999). Discriminatory practices in the larger society, such as an inadequate number of available health care practitioners and unequal medical attention within hospitals and other facilities, affect all generations of the Black population. Research has documented that treatment may vary according to race for a wide range of disorders, including heart conditions, kidney disease, and mental illnesses (Shea, Miles, and Hayward, 1996). Blacks confront class-based health risks as well—inadequate income and poverty, malnutrition, high levels of exposure to environmental and occupational hazards, stressful residential conditions, and relatively low levels of medical coverage and services (Angel and Angel, 1997; Edmonds, 1999; Yee and Weaver, 1994).

Among other factors, early medical intervention not only helps manage an illness, but it can also curtail its potential for becoming a disabling condition. Yet, large numbers of Blacks under the age of sixty-five do not have any health care coverage at all. They are less likely than Whites to participate in private medical plans, a situation that is worsening over time for the working poor; about 48 percent lack such coverage as compared to 22 percent of Whites (Angel and Angel, 1997). Fully one-fourth of the Black population depends on the sorely inadequate Medicaid program to meet their medical needs: it is often difficult to find a doctor or hospital that will treat them and they receive insufficient, low-quality care. Such problems have intensified with the reduction of Medicaid payments to providers.

Black elders, too, face serious obstacles to care. Despite the availability of Medicare, a significant percentage must limit regular visits to the doctor or forgo services entirely, due to growing out-of-pocket costs. Many older Blacks, including some living in poverty, do not receive supplementary Medicaid benefits; and relatively few can afford private Medigap policies, which pay for expenses not covered by Medicare. An increasing percentage of Medicare recipients with low incomes have been forced to enroll in managed care, an option that is particularly problematic for elders with multiple chronic conditions (Cantor and Brennan, 2000; GAO, 1999k; Watson, 1990). Domestic and care workers not covered under Social Security are not even eligible for the program.

Consequently, because of years of accumulated disadvantages, Black elders have one of the highest incidences of health problems, chronic diseases, and incapacitating conditions, twice that of Whites (Hooyman and Gonyea, 1995). Such disparities actually have grown in recent years as the rate of disability for older Whites has declined somewhat (Clark, 1997). Blacks are particularly susceptible to diabetes, a disease that needs to be controlled early in life; the incidence is 50 percent higher among Black women and 16 percent higher among Black men than among their White counterparts (Angel and Angel, 1997; Mutran and Sudha, 2000). As another case in point, hypertension among Blacks is more prevalent than among Whites, more severe, strikes at an earlier age, and is more likely to lead to stroke, cardiovascular disease, and death (Jones, 1999; Sudha and Mutran, 2001).[14]

National research shows a strong relationship between the low socioeconomic status of Blacks and their high levels of chronic diseases (McBarnette, 1996). For instance, in a multiyear study comparing disability among Blacks and Whites in the 1980s, Clark (1997, 440) notes:

> It is well known that older Blacks are three times as likely as older Whites to be in poverty and half as likely to have completed high school and that these socio-economic differences generally account for a significant portion of racial differences in health status.

And he found that "Black and White disparities in disability appear to have widened" (438). Other studies have found comparable levels of health status between Blacks and Whites at middle and older ages when their socioeconomic situation is taken into account (Cantor and Brennan, 2000). Not surprisingly, aged Black women, who suffer from inordinately high levels of poverty throughout their lives, have the most disabling conditions (McBarnette, 1996; Yee and Weaver, 1994).

Not only do more affluent groups have higher levels of functional capacity but they are also more likely to live to older ages. Clearly, the low socioeconomic status of Blacks contributes to their higher mortality rates. For instance, though their incidence of such diseases as lung, cervical, and prostate cancer is not necessarily higher than that of Whites, they are more likely to die of these illnesses and at younger ages (Barusch, Kiyak, and Hooyman, 1994). Death rates are also higher from stroke, heart diseases, diabetes, cirrhosis of the liver, accidents, and homicide (Yee and Weaver, 1994).

Life expectancy for all groups has grown. However, Blacks continue to lag behind Whites except at the very oldest ages. At birth, a White male and female can expect to live to age seventy-four and eighty, respectively, as compared to age sixty-five for Black men and seventy-four for Black women (SSCA, 1998a). The most significant disparities are during earlier periods of the life span: by age sixty-five, Blacks' life expectancy differ from Whites' by only about two years (Shea, Miles, and Hayward, 1996). And beginning at age seventy-five and especially after age eighty-five, there seems to be a "mortality cross-over effect" in which Blacks gain a slight advantage (Mutran and Sudha, 2000). It is uncertain whether this is due to the fact that only hardier Blacks reach extreme ages or that the survivors have escaped the disproportionately higher risks of younger Blacks, such as homicide and AIDS. Some research suggests that the oldest-old Blacks do indeed have better functional capacities than their White counterparts (Jackson, 1995).

Mutual Assistance

Several studies have found that Blacks tend to place less value on independence and self-reliance than Whites (Lim, Luna, and Cromwell, 1996; Stanford, 1999). Centuries of racial oppression, with its admixture of adverse social, political, and economic forces, including slavery, subsistence wages, high levels of unemployment, and destitution, have generated and reinforced a dynamic, extensive system of reciprocity within Black communities. Under slavery, for instance, Black families, nearly all of whom lived in deplorable conditions, were readily and often unpredictably broken up by their owners. Therefore, they were forced to rely on each other for support; few White owners felt obligations for slaves who became sick or debilitated (Abel, 2000). Such pooling of resources was reinforced by the scarce, sporadic stretches of time available for caregiving: Black women could assist their sick or frail kin only after a grueling day in the fields or serving the slaveholder's family. In the decades after the Civil War, Southern Black families still had to pool their resources as they struggled to meet their daily requirements with low—or no—income and insufficient government assistance.

As noted in chapter 3, White women worked interdependently to care for their sick and otherwise dependent relatives, friends, and neighbors during the 1800s. But they did not share mutual burdens with or even concern themselves with their Black compatriots (Abel, 2000). Moreover, fewer White, middle-class households profited from mutually supportive community networks by the early twentieth century, and, with the growth of hospitals, their need for at-home health care declined steadily. On the other hand, Black women, having less access than Whites to formal medical or other services, were forced to continue their hands-on care when their relatives became ill. And, because of their low income, greater historical need than White women to work outside the home, and lesser likelihood of having a spouse for assistance, Black women retained their collective means of caring for the sick and functionally disabled elderly. Their disadvantaged socioeconomic situation also engendered an ongoing, strengthened sense of filial obligation to their elderly parents (AARP, 2001c; Mui, 1992).

Today, Black women rely on an extended network of kin and friends for economic aid, material goods, domestic duties, and other supports. Family boundaries themselves tend to be fuzzy both within and among the generations. Many households negotiate an intergenerational division of labor, with younger members working for a wage and their mothers or grandmothers providing child care. When adult children are unemployed or otherwise in need, their mothers also help them out financially to the extent that they can. In turn, elders expect to be cared for when they become chronically ill and dependent. Such reciprocal obligations can be extended to neighbors and close friends as well, though to a lesser extent (Cole, 1986; Jackson, 1995; Stanford, 1999).

The exchange of mutual assistance often takes place within multigenerational households. Census data show that more than twice as many single older Black women live with their relatives than do Whites, over 36 percent compared to 18 percent (Federal Interagency Forum, 2000; SSCA, 1999b). Although some researchers note that Black culture and its strong mandate for mutual assistance and filial obligation foster shared housing arrangements, the evidence suggests that lack of an adequate income is the more significant factor; because of the group's persistently low earnings, coresidence is the only feasible alternative financially (Wilmoth, DeJong, and Himes, 1997). Since Blacks tend to move easily among households, commodities, services, and other resources are shared both within and across families, providing elders with a larger and more fluid supply of potential caregivers (Belgrave, Wykle, and Choi, 1993; Dilworth-Anderson, Williams, and Williams, 2001). In fact, because care of the Black elderly is a collective family enterprise, the older person is less likely to rely on only one primary caregiver (Dilworth-Anderson, Williams, and Williams, 2001).

Importantly, joint residency is not always due to the needs of the aged. The evidence suggests that older Black women often are heads of these units and are likely to be providing services and financial aid for their adult children (and grandchildren) rather than receiving care themselves (Belgrave, Wykle, and Choi, 1993; Gerace and Noelker, 1990).[15] For instance, in their study of older households in New York City from 1970 to 1990, Cantor and Brennan (2000) determined that the vast majority of the Black elderly living in multigenerational settings were the head of the household. Moreover, 36 percent of all the Black elders reported babysitting for their grandchildren or great-grandchildren; fully one-fifth of them were responsible for regular, ongoing care of a grandchild, sometimes serving as their primary caregiver. The researchers concluded, "The portion of Black grandparents caring for grandchildren was far greater than that found among their White and Latino peers" (226).

Most of the Black aged do not live in extended families. In fact, similarly to Whites, large and growing numbers live alone: in 2000, 40 percent of older Whites lived alone, compared to 38 percent of older Blacks. Likewise, more female than male Black elders reside by themselves, 41 percent and 25 percent, respectively. However, even when they do have their own dwellings, frail Black women tend to live in close proximity to or relatively near their adult children and receive high levels of assistance from them (Gerace and Noelker, 1990). On the other hand, Cantor and Brennan (2000) discovered that fully one-fourth of the New York City Black elders in their sample had no living children at all.

Outside Assistance: Nursing Homes,
Community-Based Services, and the Black Church

Black families are less likely than the majority of older Americans of Western European descent to institutionalize their elders, whether for short-term postacute services or long-term care. Researchers have found that the usage of nursing homes among Blacks, who represent less than 6 percent of the total nursing home population, is about half the rate of Whites (Belgrave, Wykle, and Choi, 1993). Blacks represent only a fraction of nursing home residents and public funding for institutional care despite their relatively high participation in Medicaid. One study found significant differences throughout racial lines even when the care would have been reimbursed by Medicare (Falcone and Broyles, 1994).

Their low level of institutionalization also is clearly at odds with their greater health problems and disproportionately higher levels of functional limitations than Whites. Some evidence suggests that Black families may have a strong cultural preference to care for their disabled members at home, thus rendering them more reluctant than Whites to institutionalize their frail spouses and parents. However, a number of researchers reject that argument as specious; rather, they point to (1) discrimination by nursing home owners, (2) segregation, (3) an understanding among Blacks that they receive the lowest-quality care, (4) an inability to pay the high costs, even for services covered under Medicare, and (5) a shortage of beds for Medicaid residents (Belgrave, Wykle, and Choi, 1993). As early as 1981, an Institute of Medicine report concluded that though cultural factors may play some role, racial discrimination is the major cause of low nursing home usage among Blacks (IOM, 1981).

Black elders have particularly serious access problems since their Medicaid status is compounded by discrimination. More likely than Whites to rely on public funding for long-term nursing home care from the start, they face obstacles at the admittance stage and poor-quality services on that basis alone: older people relying on Medicaid tend to have higher staff-to-resident ratios, tinier rooms, more roommates, and fewer services (Angel and Angel, 1997). Racism plays a significant role as well. In a study of hospital discharge delays for seventy-six North Carolina hospitals, it was observed that non-Whites experience greater and much longer holdups in nursing home placement than Whites, primarily because of the difficulty in finding facilities willing to accept them. The researchers point out that the problem exists "regardless of patients' ages, sex, condition(s) or special care requirement(s), the co-operativeness of their families, their behavioral state, how they will pay for long-term care, or whether there were financial preparedness problems involved in their discharges" (Falcone and Broyles, 1994: 591). In areas where Blacks have a larger number of beds available to them, such as in Detroit, their rate of institutionalization is closer to that of Whites generally (Smith, 1990).

Discrimination has always been pervasive in the health care industry, including purposeful separation of acute-care hospitals in the south and neighborhood segregation in the north. Through the 1960s, Black patients also encountered ceilings on the number of beds allotted to them and denial of care entirely in many northern White hospitals. At the same time, since Black physicians were refused training and staff privileges, they established their own hospitals. However, after the passage of Medicare and Medicaid in 1965, which disallowed the participation of segregated facilities, some level of integration proceeded rapidly: hospitals and doctors wanted to cash in on Medicare's lucrative cost-based reimbursements, expand their markets, and avoid the prospect of bankruptcy facing those without certification (Buhler-Wilkerson, 2001; Smith, 1990).

The nursing home industry, on the other hand, has not only been segregated from the beginning, but also had few beds available to Blacks overall, even for the limited number who could afford to pay. Despite the nondiscrimination clauses that are part of the certification requirements, the public programs did not spur them to integrate: unlike hospitals, nursing homes and their medical staff were not dependent on Medicare funding for their income, and most sought to avoid Medicaid patients. Because the majority of states had imposed severe restrictions on the numbers of new beds and facilities, which fostered extremely high occupancy rates, the facilities did not need to pursue Black clients. Indeed, they feared that if they desegregated their facilities they would lose their higher-paying White residents, most of whom considered the institution their home. And since greater access for minorities under Medicaid would mean greater public costs, the states did not pressure them to do so. Additionally, many of the previously all-Black hospitals, which closed down after the 1960s, were converted to nursing homes and continued to care for a predominantly Black population. For the most part, Blacks were placed in the most substandard dwellings, and, except for the modified neighborhood hospitals, further from their familes and previous homes than more affluent Whites (Kosberg, 1973; Smith, 1990).

Today, nearly all nursing homes still are racially segregated, with those of the very poorest quality serving the non-White clientele (Belgrave, Wykle, and Choi, 1993). Further, low-income minority areas tend to be underserved: nationwide, states with the most Black residents have fewer nursing homes and available beds; studies of specific states, such as Florida and Pennsylvania, have documented that facilities are clustered in the more affluent White communities (Abel, 1991; Han, Barrilleaux, and Quadagno, 1996; Smith, 1990).

Compared to Whites, then, a higher percentage of chronically ill Black elders reside in community settings. Not only do they tend to have greater and more severe functional disabilities, but a larger percentage also are totally disabled and completely dependent on others to meet their daily needs. Nevertheless, the evidence suggests that Black older people and their families benefit from far fewer home-based formal services than do Whites (Logan and Spitze, 1994; Mui, 1992). Their utilization rate is lower for a wide array of paid help, including personal care, homemaking, home health, skilled nursing, and rehabilitation services, even after controlling for need (Jones, 1999).

As with institutionalization, notions of filial responsibility and cultural "preference" among Blacks for hands-on care at home are best understood in the context of gender, class, and race. There is a strong preference for family assistance across racial lines. But Blacks are disadvantaged in their ability to access formal services when they are needed. Cantor and Brennan (2000) found that regardless of cultural mandates and strong intergenerational and friendship support networks among Blacks, fully one-fifth of the Black elders in their study—and 40 percent of those with low and poverty-level incomes—reported that they did not get enough help.

Affordability obviously is a primary factor in low usage of in-home paid services. There are other structural barriers typical of low socioeconomic groups as well, impediments that are exacerbated by discrimination and racism. In order for Blacks to take advantage of formal services, even those that are publicly subsidized, they must be available, accessible, and acceptable. Individuals also must be aware that the services exist. Yet, it can be difficult for Blacks to find assistance: their neighborhoods tend to have fewer health care practitioners and services overall than White communities, a problem recently confirmed by an American Medical Society (AMA) review commission (Gerace and Noelker, 1990; Sudha and Mutran, 2001). Their lack of transportation renders it particularly difficult for them to benefit from any assistance that is far from their home, such as day care facilities and community centers where hot meals and services may be offered. And the quality of the programs is generally much lower than in other areas. In two studies comparing the experience of older Blacks and Whites, investigators found that a number of Blacks viewed the level and quality of community services located in White neighborhoods as vastly superior to their own. Blacks also tended to distrust the staff and others providing assistance more than Whites (Miller and Stull, 1999).

The primary source of outside support, services, and social outlets for the Black community as a whole, including the elderly, traditionally has been the Black church (Dilworth-Anderson, Williams, and Williams, 2001; Gerace and Noelker, 1990). Although there is some evidence that it still assists a small number of older people in need of limited, temporary aid and that elders may more readily accept church services than those provided from other extrafamilial sources, most frail Black elders and their families are not receiving church-based help with hands-on caregiving tasks (Gerace and Noelker, 1990; Taylor, Ellison, Chatters, Levin, and Lincoln, 2000). Recent data suggest that slightly less than 10 percent of Black churches provide any help to the dependent aged population (Caldwell, Chatters, Billingsley, and Taylor, 1995).

Whatever resources the Black church devotes to the needy in urban communities increasingly has been focused on younger generations who face a host of problems, including high and growing levels of at-risk youths, AIDS, impoverished single mothers, and drug usage. Even those churches with vigorous programs for older people do not and cannot provide long-term care for their chronically ill and disabled parishioners. Nonetheless, because Blacks have high rates of church membership and attendance—especially among the elderly—along with high levels of spirituality, the church undoubtedly adds to their emotional and psychological well-being (Caldwell et al., 1995; Dilworth-Anderson, Williams, and Williams, 2001; Gerace and Noelker, 1990; Jackson, 1995).

Caregiver Burden and Stress

Since Black elderly women are even less likely than Whites to have a spouse to care for them, adult daughters generally have the bulk of the responsibility. Despite the integrated family system and kinship ties, they can experience overwhelming burdens. And reciprocal obligations of assistance among family and friends are becoming less viable as growing numbers of Black mothers and grandmothers live to very old ages and are dependent on others for assistance. In one nationwide study, the researchers determined that Black caregivers did more chores, spent more time, and reported greater financial, emotional, and physical strain than Whites (Calderon and Tennstedt, 1998). They also must put in more hours of care because their elders tend to have more multiple functional disabilities (Calderon and Tennstedt, 1998). With few supplementary formal services, even for elders requiring continuous, intensive care, Black spouses and adult daughters confront significant problems because of their low socioeconomic status and race, a situation that has become even more problematic as public programs are cut.

First, the material conditions of rich and poor female caregivers differ considerably. Low-income women of color not only have difficulty hiring assistance, but they also have less choice as to whether to provide care in the first place. With limited resources, they also are more likely than Whites to be burdened financially (AARP, 2001e; SSCA, 1999b). As a matter of fact, Mui (1992) found that despite the greater caregiving requirements and higher expectations of themselves, the Black daughters in her sample reported less strain than Whites when income was controlled.

Since Black daughters are more likely than White daughters to have low-paying jobs at which it is difficult to adjust schedules and other working conditions, balancing employment and kin work can be particularly challenging. And they generally can't afford to quit or cut their hours of employment because of caregiving responsibilities. Nor can they pay for home improvements or purchase special equipment to meet the needs of their incapacitated kin, and this adds to their physical labor. Certainly, publicly subsidized monetary compensation for caregiving would improve the condition of Black elders and their caregivers alike (Groger, 1998).

In addition, more Black caregivers than Whites are single mothers, juggling both children and elders simultaneously. Many Black middle-aged women are simultaneously raising their grandchildren, supporting and helping out their adult children, and caring for a frail elder (Cantor and Brennan, 2000). And, not only are they caring for elders with greater impairments than Whites but they are also more likely to be in poor health themselves.

Latino Americans

Latino Americans confront myriad problems that mirror those of Blacks: a significant number are impoverished, experience high unemployment and inadequate housing, lack any savings, and suffer from discrimination. In 2000, 21 percent of all Latinos lived in poverty: 14 percent of married-couple families but 34 percent of female-headed households (U.S. Bureau of the Census, 2001f). Nearly 70 percent of Latino workers have dead-end, low-wage jobs, mainly in the manual labor and service sectors, with few benefits; about one-third have no health coverage (DuBois, Yavno, and Stanford, 2001; Sotomayer, 1995; Torres, 1999). The medical situation is even worse among Mexican Americans—60 percent of couples and 70 percent of female-headed households lack insurance. And despite widespread poverty, less than 20 percent of younger Latinos participate in Medicaid, a figure even lower than that for the Black population (Angel and Angel, 1997). Latinos thus generally enter old age after lifelong poverty; crowded, unhealthy living conditions; and deficient medical care.

During the last several decades, the number of older Latino immigrants, especially from Mexico, has increased measurably both absolutely and in relationship to other groups (Sotomayer, 1995). Currently, about half of all Latino elders are foreign-born, and most of them are legal residents (Sudha and Mutran, 2001). The native-born tend to rely entirely on a small Social Security pension, sometimes supplemented by SSI; they are even less likely than either Whites or Blacks to receive a private pension or interest from assets (Applewhite, 1998). The situation of immigrants is even worse. Not surprisingly, the poverty rate of aged Latinos, 19 percent, is twice that of Whites (U.S. Bureau of the Census, 2001f). Nearly half of older Mexican Americans live at or below the poverty level, and the vast majority are single women.

Aged Latinos, then, are heavily dependent on others for financial support. Though most receive some help from their children, a large percentage rely on SSI, Medicaid, food stamps, and public housing to meet at least some of their basic needs: fully 44 percent of Latino elders receive SSI, more than any other group (Villa, Cuellar, Gamel, and Yeo, 1993). Since the passage of the Welfare Reform and Illegal Immigration and Immigrant Responsibility laws in 1996, increasing numbers of Latino families, despite their inadequate resources, must now bear the full monetary burden of their elderly kin. Noncitizens have been particularly likely to lose benefits, and this has mostly affected Mexicans; Puerto Ricans already are U.S. citizens and between 1959 and 1980, Cubans were automatically given permanent residency as political refugees under an open-ended policy (Gimpel and Edwards, 1999).

There are other intragroup differences among Latinos as well. Mexicans and Puerto Ricans, for instance, have relatively lower socioeconomic and educational status than their Cuban counterparts, suffer from more disabilities and other health problems associated with poverty, require greater levels of service, and have less health care coverage (Angel and Angel, 1997; Markides and Stroup-Benham, 1999; Torres, 1999). Yet, there is wide variation even among the Cubans: although a large percentage of the 1960s refugees came from middle- and upper-class backgrounds, those from the 1970s and the "Marielitos" of 1980 were of lower socioeconomic status.

Mortality and Morbidity

The mortality rate of Latinos as a group is equivalent to that of Whites, and after age sixty-five may be lower, especially because of their advantage with regard to deaths from heart disease and cancer (Angel and Angel, 1997; Markides and Stroup-Benham, 1999). Consequently, there is an even greater rise in Latinos reaching extreme ages than that of elders in general (Sotomayer, 1995). However, despite favorable mortality statistics, studies indicate that elderly Mexican Americans and Puerto Ricans may, on average, suffer from premature and greater functional disabilities than the overall aged population and require considerable medical care and personal assistance, sometimes beginning in their early sixties. There is some indication that they experience even higher levels of impairments and dependency rates than Blacks or Whites at the very oldest ages (Angel and Angel, 1997; Cantor and Brennan, 2000; Torres, 1999).

Certainly, inadequate health care coverage at younger ages and the consequent delay of medical intervention until an illness reaches crisis proportions prevent early diagnosis and treatment, fostering adverse long-range consequences for their health.[16] For example, the incidence of end-stage renal disease for Mexican Americans is six times greater than for Whites, mostly because of uncontrolled diabetes (DuBois, Yavno, and Stanford, 2001). Limited access to preventive care and rehabilitation services can worsen their medical conditions at all ages. Elderly Latinos covered under Medicare suffer from similar barriers to medical services as Blacks and other low-income groups. And restrictive eligibility requirements also limit their access to supplementary Medicaid benefits. Moreover, because a significant percentage of Mexican elders are noncitizens—and some are illegal entrants—a substantially greater proportion than other older people have no medical coverage at all.

Latino Culture and Elder Care

Nearly all frail Latino elders live in the community and are cared for by their family (Angel, Angel, McClellan, and Markides, 1996). As with other Americans, among married couples the spouse is the primary caregiver. However, when one partner dies, the parent is single, or her health deteriorates, an adult daughter is expected to take on the responsibility, especially for the hands-on tasks; such assistance is taken for granted (Lim, Luna, and Cromwell, 1996; Sanchez-Ayendez, 1998). And because of the large percentage of single older females—though fewer than Blacks—the burden on adult daughters can be considerable. The AARP study (2001e) on multicultural baby boomers revealed that fully one-third of Latinas, most of whom work full time, were taking care of their parents or other relatives, often at great sacrifice. As Sanchez (2001: 90) put it, "Elder care responsibilities are so common among Puerto Rican women that sometimes it appears to be a stressful but normal situation for them."

As a group, Latinos tend to deemphasize individual problem solving, viewing the needs of the family as a whole as taking precedence over individual wants. Interdependence, strong social bonds, and reciprocity within and among generations are basic to Latino culture, including a strong emphasis on respect for elders and filial responsibility: "Adult children are understood to have a responsibility toward their aged parents in exchange for the functions that parents performed for them throughout their upbringing" (Sanchez-Ayendez, 1986, 176). In their study of New York City elders, Cantor and Brennan (2000: 57) reported that "the strength of cultural expectations regarding the role of children (and other kin when children are not present) was clearly evident among Latino elderly respondents." However, mutual support and reciprocity also means that a significant number of aged Latinas provide substantial help to their children and grandchildren: as with Black elders, they may give them money and babysitting services, sometimes serving as the primary carer of their grandchildren (Angel et al., 1996; Cantor and Brennan, 2000; Sanchez-Ayendez, 1986).

Their large, informal networks also include siblings, aunts and uncles, cousins, in-laws, friends, and neighbors, "a network of ritual kinship whose members have a deep sense of obligation to each other for economic assistance, encouragement, support, and even personal correction" (Torres, 1999, 206). Since fictive kin[17] can offer emotional support, companionship, some instrumental tasks, and other help, they "alleviate the stress adult children often feel in assisting their aged mothers, particularly those who live by themselves" (Sanchez-Ayendez, 1986, 185). Though fictive kin can serve as a buffer, lessening the full burden of elder care on the primary caregiver, there is some indication that the amount of actual hands-on long-term care services by friends and relatives is relatively limited. For example, Cox and Monk (1993), in their study of Latinos taking care of a parent or spouse with dementia, found that the extended family provided emotional support but very limited instrumental help. Most of the primary caregivers "had sufficient confidants with whom they could discuss their problems" (96), but few could rely on them to take over the actual care, if necessary.

Older Latinos—Mexican Americans more so than Puerto Ricans or Cuban Americans—have a greater incidence of multigenerational households than do Whites (Angel and Angel, 1997). Females in particular, especially when they reach very old age, tend to move in with their kin. Approximately one-third and 15 percent of older Latino women and men, respectively, live with their children (Federal Interagency Forum, 2000). However, most research suggests that the prevalence of joint residency among Latinos is as much due to financial need as it is to filial obligation and reciprocity. The particularly large number of multigenerational households among Mexicans, for example, is associated with their considerable poverty as well as cultural imperatives (Angel and Angel, 1997). Lacking any resources of their own, foreign-born elders are particularly prone to coresidency; one study found that among Latino immigrants, fully 71 percent were residing in extended family households (Wilmoth, DeJong, and Himes, 1997). In Puerto Rico, where more than half of the Puerto Rican elders live in poverty, over 75 percent share housing with their kin (Sanchez, 2001). Clearly, immigration and other public policies play significant roles as well: as suggested earlier, given their financial situation and lack of government aid, most older immigrants have little alternative but to move in with their children.

Nevertheless, large numbers of elderly Latinos live alone, about one-third of the women and 14 percent of the men; the vast majority are poor. And there is evidence that independent living arrangements have not only grown but will also likely increase even further (Cantor and Brennan, 2000). For Mexican elders, for example, though living with their family "is still a desirable and viable option," many adult children cannot offer joint residency because of their own poverty and cramped housing situation (Angel et. al., 1996, 466). In her study of Puerto Ricans, Sanchez-Ayendez (1986) notes that the aged, when possible, actually prefer to live away from their kin. But they clearly value and receive substantial support from their children, including frequent phone calls and visits. Even more than Whites and Blacks, older Latinos report that they can rely on their adult children for personal assistance: they tend to live close by and are in regular contact with them; older Mexican Americans are the most likely to see their children on a daily basis (Angel and Angel, 1997; Calderon and Tennstedt, 1998). Moreover, the high fertility rate among Latinos and their larger-than-average family size provide more potential caregivers and thus greater opportunities for frail elders than some other groups both for shared living arrangements and for remaining in the community on their own (Angel and Angel, 1997; Tennstedt, Chang, and Delgado, 1998).

Despite early and high levels of disability and heavy demands on adult children for care, few Latino elders and their families utilize formal services. Low and poverty-level incomes and cultural and religious barriers, along with exclusionary and discriminatory practices, have limited their access to private and public sources of assistance, including health care, nursing homes, and community services. Though most Americans view nursing homes as a last resort, Latinos—similar to other racial and ethnic minorities—have particularly low levels of institutionalization, estimated at 2 to 3 percent of the older Latino population. Even elders with considerable care needs, such as those afflicted with Alzheimer's disease, are more likely than Whites to live in the community, and they live mostly with their children. For Latinos, placement in a nursing home is tantamount to abandonment. "When the Hispanic elder cannot be cared for at home by the family and is institutionalized, the elder is expected to suffer from intense feelings of isolation, anguish, and feelings of being betrayed by his or her loved ones" (Torres, 1999, 212). Ironically, in some facilities Latinos represent a significant percentage of the nurse's aides: in a sample of thirty-three long-term care facilities in San Diego, Mexican Americans alone comprised nearly one-third of the attendants (Saghri, 2000).

Although Latinos may have a strong aversion to nursing homes and "choose" to provide care at home, again we must be careful to differentiate between cultural imperatives and structural factors. Discrimination as well as a paucity of facilities in Latino communities, insensitivity to Latino customs, financial limitations, and other barriers restrict their access considerably (Angel and Angel, 1997; Torres, 1999). At-home services, too, tend to be underutilized because of socioeconomic inequities and societal constraints. Unquestionably, the most considerable barrier is cost: few Latino elders or their families can afford to hire paid help. Research data also reveal that many needed services are not located within Latino communities, are difficult to reach without adequate transportation, and are not sensitive to their cultural preferences, distinctive lifestyle, traditions, and beliefs. High levels of illiteracy and an inability to speak English pose significant problems since few public programs provide bilingual staff or translators. In fact, nearly 60 percent of elderly Latinos have limited or no facility with English (Kiyak and Hooyman, 1994). In many places, elders must negotiate a large-scale, complex bureaucracy—in an unfamiliar language—in order to receive assistance. A significant number of older Latinos don't know what services are available and can't fill out intake forms, read vital information about the programs, or communicate with agency staff. Therefore, they often must depend entirely on their informal network as a liaison to government assistance and service providers (DuBois, Yavno, and Stanford, 2001).

There is some evidence that Latinos are not averse to using supplementary services and will do so when structural barriers are reduced. Many Latino elders, for example, especially those who are the most acculturated, prefer not to overly burden their children and thus would be willing to take advantage of formal aid if they could (Cantor and Brennan, 2000; DuBois, Yavno, and Stanford, 2001). And caregivers seem equally willing to utilize supplementary services, when necessary. Many of the Puerto Rican adult children in one study indicated that they would readily accept outside help with their tasks, though they didn't want to give up their obligation to their frail parents entirely. Because of multiple demands, including young children and work, they couldn't devote as much time as either they or their care recipients wanted and needed. Yet, none of the households qualified for government services or could afford to pay for them on their own (Sanchez-Ayendez, 1998). Indeed, a number of researchers have found that regardless of the extensive network of care among Latinos and the considerable assistance by adult daughters, many frail older people do not receive all of the personal care that they require (Cantor and Brennan, 2000; DuBois, Yavno, and Stanford, 2001). The most serious deficiencies are suffered by elders with ongoing, heavy care needs, many requiring technically skilled services.

Asian Americans

The percentage of East Asian Americans—predominantly Koreans, Japanese, and Chinese—has increased rapidly since 1965, the population of the latter doubling between 1980 and 1990 alone, mostly because of immigration. Indeed, by 1980, the majority of the Chinese population and over 80 percent of its older members were foreign-born (Wong, 2001). There also are well over a million mainland Southeast Asians, most of whom have fled Vietnam, Cambodia, and Laos: in 1975 over 100,000 Vietnamese came to the United States, and since then the Vietnamese population has grown to about 1.1 million people (Tran, Ngo, and Sung, 2001; Yeo and Kikoyeda, 1995; U.S. Bureau of the Census, 2001d). Many of these refugees brought their aging parents either with them or at a later time; a large percentage are now middle-aged or elderly themselves. Moreover, there are nearly 2 million Filipinos, the largest Asian group, the majority of whom are immigrants; many of its aged are single men living alone. Though still relatively few in number, Asian American elders are the most rapidly growing percentage of older people in the nation. And their population continues to swell as elders continue to follow their children into this country: today there are more foreign-born than native Asian elders residing here (Yeo and Kikoyeda, 1995).

There are vast intragroup and intergroup variations within and among Asian Americans, dependent on such factors as socioeconomic status, gender, education, acculturation levels, and immigration experiences. In general, the Asian aged population tends to be healthier, experience fewer disabling conditions, and have a higher life expectancy than other older people, including those at the oldest ages (Yee and Weaver, 1994). Japanese and Chinese elderly, in particular, have a superior health status and life expectancy to all other sectors of American society. The mortality rate of Chinese Americans, for example, is about two-thirds to three-fourths that of older Whites (Yeo and Kikoyeda, 1995). On the other hand, poor health is prevalent among the foreign-born, who are also at a higher risk for mental health problems, especially depression, than the dominant population.

Though the poverty level of younger Asian Americans overall was 10.8 percent in 2000, only slightly above the 7.5 percent for Whites, nearly 20 percent of Asian female-headed households live at or below the poverty threshold.[18] Moreover, although some Asian American elders have acquired significant income and wealth, and as a group are more advantaged than Blacks and Latinos, others—about 10 percent—are impoverished (U.S. Bureau of the Census, 2001f). The Filipino aged, for example, experience disproportionately greater levels of poverty than other older people, especially among single men who were recruited as laborers in earlier years; their poverty rate is about 40 percent (Kiyak and Hooyman, 1994). Mainland Southeast Asians, too, are among the poorest subgroups. The older refugees tend to have particularly high levels of economic deprivation and service needs, many of them having suffered from disrupted families and relocation pressures (Yeo and Kikoyeda, 1995). Those who came at middle age or later often were unemployed for long periods of time or worked at minimum-wage jobs. Most of these elders today don't have a private pension or asset income, and many don't even meet the minimal work requirements to qualify for Social Security benefits. Because of the low income of their adult children—more than 25 percent of the Vietnamese population, for example, live in poverty—mainland Southeast Asian elders frequently do not have relatives who can afford to care for them (Tran, Ngo, and Sung, 2001).

Intragroup variations also occur between current immigrants and those coming to this country in earlier periods. For instance, young Chinese immigrants from the mid-1960s, many of whom have attained middle-class standing, are now in their sixties or older. For the most part, they are or will be self-sufficient when they retire, relying on Social Security pensions and other types of income. However, since 1980 the vast majority of Chinese are newcomers, struggling to support their nuclear families; they tend to have few remaining resources for their generally impoverished, older immigrant parents (Wong, 2001). In a similar vein, though many Korean native-born and immigrant elders can support themselves, the great majority of the aged, who have come more recently to join their adult children, do not possess sufficient resources of their own. In fact, the most economically deprived among the sixty-five and over Asian population are the "invited elderly," those who come to the United States late in life, mostly to follow their children. They are the least acculturated, have the fewest resources, receive low—or no—Social Security income or Medicare benefits, and are dependent for support on their children and public programs, including SSI, food stamps, Medicaid, and government-subsidized senior housing (Kim and Kim, 2001; Min, 1998).

On the whole, Japanese Americans are the most educated, acculturated, and assimilated of the Asian subgroups. They have the greatest percentage of native-born elders, longest life expectancy, highest socioeconomic status, and lowest level of poverty (Kiyak and Hooyman, 1994; Shibusawa, Lubben, and Kitano, 2001; Yeo and Kikoyeda, 1995). Nonetheless, a significant percentage of their immigrant parents also are vulnerable and economically dependent.

Cultural Mandates

Unlike the dominant American ideology that extols individualism and self-reliance, Asian culture views dependency in a positive light, as both basic to the human condition and a normal part of the aging process. Their ancient traditions of interdependence, filial piety, and high status of older people tend to govern relationships between and within the generations. The Japanese and Chinese, for instance, are subject to Confucian ethics, which includes obeying one's parents and fulfilling obligations to one's kin. Moreover, the family is viewed as more important than the individual, and any dishonor on oneself shames all of its members. Together, these values promote self-sacrifice, loyalty, and care of frail parents—according to prescribed roles based on gender, age, and birth order—without question or resentment (Shibusawa, Lubben, and Kitano, 2001; Wong, 2001). Filial piety, then, practiced within a patriarchal system, requires that women care for their elders at home, regardless of their situation or the intensity of the older person's needs. For many aged immigrants, the primary hands-on elder care duties reside with the wife of their eldest son, with whom they expect to live.

Many students of ethnicity point to the evolving nature of cultural values, attitudes, and practices as immigrant groups encounter the dominant American society and its views. Gelfand and Barresi (1987) call it the "emergent" nature of ethnicity. Traditional ethnic culture can become "Americanized," sometimes bearing little resemblance to the practices of either the home country or the United States. Filial duties, in some cases, have been substantially altered to better suit the situation of Americanized families. In the more recent Vietnamese family codes, for example, all children are expected to care for their dependent parents on a rotating basis (Tran, Ngo, and Sung, 2001). And, as Kim and Kim (2001) observe, among Koreans sole reliance on eldest sons and their wives assisting only the husband's relatives has, by necessity, given way to the care of parents of both genders as well as some shared filial responsibility among all offspring, regardless of birth order or gender. Researchers also note the declining expectations of filial piety overall among the current elderly Japanese Nisei who have adopted aspects of American self-reliance: though most of them had to care for their aged parents, they don't want to impose on or become dependent upon their own offspring. Likewise, given the choice and sufficient resources, growing numbers of other subgroups of Asian elders would not depend so heavily on their children (Shibusawa, Lubben, and Kitano, 2001; Tran, Ngo, and Sung, 2001).

Of all groups, Asian Americans have the highest percentage of elders living in multigenerational households, about 37 percent of women and 21 percent of men (Federal Interagency Forum, 2000). As with Latinos, Asian immigrants—especially single women—are the most likely to share a residency with their adult children. Furthermore, older Asians, including females, are slightly more likely to be married and sharing a household with a spouse than are other sectors of American society.[19] Thus, they have one of the lowest percentages of older people residing alone, about 21 percent.

However, increasing numbers of single Asian elders would prefer to live on their own. Even immigrants now want their own residence, especially when they confront some of the realities of American life. For one thing, those who stay with their adult children when first coming to the United States eventually move out if they can, choosing their autonomy over the myriad difficulties, tensions, and even sense of marginalization they can face in the homes of their Americanized families (Kim and Kim, 2001; Kiyak and Hooyman, 1994). Some resist a move to the suburbs, preferring to live independently in an urban ethnic enclave and relying on government services when they are available. A large number of Korean elders, for instance, prefer to live in government-subsidized senior housing rather than to depart from their central city neighborhoods with their adult children (Kim and Kim, 2001). Similarly, many Chinese immigrants elect to stay alone in Chinatown rather than leave their familiar surroundings (Wong, 2001). Ironically, many of these older people actually migrate to the United States reluctantly and only because of "the traditional value that children should take care of their older parents" (Wong, 2001, 21). Therefore, even though it may be a mutual decision for the parent to live by herself, such an arrangement still can be a serious source of embarrassment and shame both for the aged parents and their family (Wong, 2001).

Barriers to Informal Care

Because of such factors as greater longevity than other groups, smaller family size, and strong cultural mandates for hands-on care, many Asian American women are faced with growing numbers of surviving frail parents and parents-in-law that they must take care of on their own. The recent AARP report (2001e, 95) on multicultural baby boomers concluded that Asian caregivers are the most burdened among the groups they studied. It also found that they "express more guilt that they are not doing enough for their older relatives." Despite even the best of intentions, given the nature of U.S. society today, many of them simply cannot meet their cultural obligations. The reality is that cultural directives for elder care often conflict sharply with the actual situation of Americanized Asian females, most of whom work full time and many of whom have young children as well. For instance, most Korean American wives contribute equally to the family finances; many work with their husbands either as owners or employees in small businesses, laboring long hours, often six or seven days a week (Kim and Kim, 2001). Thus, they and other Asian American women are increasingly incapable of providing the intensity of care to their parents that traditional custom would dictate.

Fulfillment of traditional modes of elder care also may have diminished somewhat because adult children in the United States experience less social and community pressure than those living in Asian nations, may interpret their obligations differently than their more traditional parents, and confront American values that stress the autonomy of the nuclear family (Wong, 2001). High rates of interracial marriages also may seriously erode customary expectations; over 40 percent of Japanese American women and 20 percent of Japanese American men enter into interracial marriages (Shibusawa, Lubben, and Kitano, 2001). Thus, Asian American elders, despite a cultural mandate for filial responsibility, cannot always rely on their families for personal care, especially those frail older people with heavy service requirements.

Barriers to Formal Care

Of all groups in American society, Asian American women tend to have both the greatest prevalence of elder care duties and the least utilization of formal services (NAC/AARP, 1997). Institutionalization among Asian elders is one of the lowest in the nation, fewer than 2 percent. They also are less likely than other older people to reside in group residential housing or use community long-term care and medical services, regardless of their need or situation (Angel and Angel, 1997; Yee, 1999). As a result, frail older Asians move in with their children, overburden them with elder care demands, or do without much of the essential services they require.

As suggested earlier, there is some indication that Asian American elders increasingly would be willing to use formal assistance rather than impose on their children or jeopardize their close relationship by becoming dependent on them. Studies show that growing numbers of Japanese and Korean elderly, for instance, would accept paid formal services or placement in a nursing home, especially if they required intensive care (Kim and Kim, 2001; Shibusawa, Lubben, and Kitano, 2001). Thus, though certain cultural values and traditions impose considerable constraints against Asian elders and their families turning to outside help, a growing body of research on the subject suggests that substantial structural barriers to service come into play as well. First, as with other groups, most Asian elders and their families cannot afford to pay for ongoing, full-time services on their own. And, because of the strong mandates for filial piety and the consequent assumption among policymakers that Asian elders are well protected by their families, there tends to be relatively less concern about their needs than for other groups. In point of fact, adult children who can't provide sufficient care have difficulty finding publicly supported assistance even if they are willing to use it: in many Asian neighborhoods, there are few long-term care services overall and a paucity of low-income housing or other residential options, including public housing, assisted living facilities, and nursing homes.

Language is a significant problem as well: a large percentage of Asian elders are foreign-born, and the vast majority speak only their native language or have very limited English proficiency. Many are functionally illiterate; they cannot read or write at all (Louie, 1999). Thus, when they become ill or disabled, they face serious communication issues, including lack of adequate information on available services, difficulty navigating the social service and health care systems, and an inability to communicate with program providers. Overall, health and social service agencies outside of Asian ethnic enclaves require an ability to relate in English in order to access and use any available services; most require transportation as well (Tran, Ngo, and Sung, 2001).

As with other ethnic minority elders, they also suffer from an absence of culturally competent programs and culturally sensitive services. Older Asian immigrants tend to eschew assistance that is at variance with their belief system, including certain types of Western medical care and intervention. For example, the Chinese aged, many of whom have traditional views on the origins and nature of disease that differ substantially from American views, may prefer classic Chinese folk therapies, homemade health remedies, acupuncturists, and herbalists; they often mistrust American-style medical care (Wong, 2001).

Similar issues also serve to constrain their use of nursing homes; Asian American elders have a particularly difficult time adjusting to institutional care. For them, the already formidable problems encountered by frail older people in American nursing homes are compounded by social, emotional, cultural, and linguistic isolation (Tran, Ngo, and Sung, 2001). Among other factors, the facilities generally don't serve ethnically specific foods, observe their special holidays and other traditional customs, or provide bilingual staff who speak their native language. And many Asian elders fear discrimination and prejudicial treatment. Japanese elders tend to be particularly wary: the internment in relocation centers of close to 120,000 people of Japanese ancestry during World War II has had lingering effects on them (Shibusawa, Lubben, and Kitano, 2001).

In some urban Asian localities, there have been limited attempts to provide ethnic-oriented long-term care services, especially by nonprofit groups. In major cities, older Asians may be served by ethnic-specific agencies, such as the Vietnamese social service center in Boston (Tran, Ngo, and Sung, 2001). Most Japanese and Chinese communities offer some programs, such as congregate meals, recreational activities, and skilled nursing homes and a few, such as Little Tokyo in Los Angeles, even have senior citizen residential facilities. In areas where Japanese nursing homes are readily available, the rate of institutionalization among frail Japanese elders rises measurably. According to one source, "Most of the elderly in Little Tokyo plan to move to a Japanese American retirement home or nursing home in the event that they can no longer live on their own" (Shibusawa, Lubben, and Kitano, 2001, 41). Although such efforts are more responsive to Asian values and traditions, they are sorely inadequate to meet the growing needs of frail older Asians and their increasingly beleaguered caregivers. For example, nearly all Japanese nursing homes and residential housing for the elderly have long waiting lists, some for as long as four years.

Given the ongoing steep cuts in public funding for social needs over the last several decades and the steady increase in the number of frail Asian elders overall, it is likely that there will be even fewer ethnic-specific facilities and services commensurate to demand in the future. At the same time, "Community-based ethnic agencies face constant pressure to secure funding and donations from the private sector" (Shibusawa, Lubben, and Kitano, 2001, 44). And, although religious institutions, too, may serve Asian elders, they are more likely to provide spiritual sustenance, companionship, and ethnic culture and food rather than actual services for chronically ill older people (Kim and Kim, 2001).

Conclusion

Clearly, the United States is becoming more racially and ethnically diverse, both among the population at large and among the elderly specifically. The influx of Latino and Asian immigrants since the 1960s and especially during the 1990s, including the entrance of frail older parents under the family reunification provisions of the 1965 immigration law, has added measurably to the diversity mix.

Among the federally designated racial and ethnic minorities—Blacks, Latinos, Asians, and AI/ANs—a disproportionately greater percentage of elders experience low and poverty-level incomes as well as more chronic disabilities and dependency. Many of them enter old age after a lifetime of discrimination, deprived economic circumstances, and disadvantages in the various measures of health: morbidity, mortality, medical care, and insurance coverage. At the same time, they have lower utilization rates of community services and nursing homes, engendering considerable burdens on their caregivers.

The greater prevalence of multigenerational households among certain racial and ethnic minorities and their lower usage than Whites of formal services are generally attributed to cultural mandates but are at least as much due to financial and structural constraints. The evidence indicates that both caregivers and their parents would be willing to accept some supplementary aid if it were affordable, accessible, and available. An admixture of low socioeconomic status, discriminatory practices among practitioners and providers, and reductions in federal funding render it difficult for Blacks, Latinos, AI/ANs, and new immigrants, including Asians, to obtain outside help. Despite the network of family and fictive kin who provide extensive and often intensive personal care, such groups are heavily dependent on social welfare programs. At the same time, public policies in the 1990s have given more financial responsibility to families who want to bring their parents—generally widowed mothers—to this country. It would seem that most of the cuts in social welfare programs have been on the backs of already struggling working-class racial and ethnic minority households, including immigrants.

In addition to issues of class, race, and gender faced by ethnic and racial minorities, foreign-born elders, especially Latinos and Asians, confront additional problems related to language and culture. However, even the large number of Americans who are first-, second- and even third-generation immigrants from Western Europe, the Middle East, and elsewhere can retain distinctive characteristics that affect their aging and long-term care options (see table 6.1). Some sectors of American society confront specific issues tied to their culture, religion, experiences, and outsider status. The problems of vulnerable Jewish elders who are Holocaust survivors, for instance, are compounded by their past traumas, particularly for those who must enter a nursing home (Harel, 2001). Institutionalization also can be particularly stressful for AI/ANs who had been forcibly placed into government educational facilities during their youth (Polacca, 2001).

Researchers have become increasingly aware of how culturally sensitive care contributes to the well-being of older people, both enhancing their self-respect and the quality of their lives (Gelfand and Barresi, 1987; Gooloo, Sloan, and Davis, 1996). In fact, it has long been recognized that frail elders, whether at home or in an institution, value "emotional work" at least as much as help with the physical aspects of their care (Foner, 1994a). One undervalued component of this "emotional work" has been respect for the traditions and culture that often are an essential part of an older person's life. For nursing home residents, in particular, it provides a sense of continuity, allowing them to keep a piece of their identity intact (Gelfand and Barresi, 1987). By disregarding their racial, ethnic, and socioreligious backgrounds, we treat our vulnerable elders as objects rather than as individuals with special histories and concerns.

Consequently, if we want to meet the needs of ethnic and racial minority elders and their caregivers, programs must be adequate, available, accessible, affordable, and culturally sensitive. There is no "right" place for older people to live and receive care; the elderly and their families need to have options from which to choose, and these should take into account their varied cultures and traditions. Long-term care services should be provided in specific languages (and sometimes several dialects); be more plentiful in poorly served communities; include at-home assistance, nursing homes, assisted living facilities, and low-cost housing; and involve staff who are trained in the culturally appropriate values and customs of the people they serve. Social workers and others also must engage in aggressive outreach, targeting isolated ethnic and racial minority elders who may lack information and be apprehensive about government programs generally. Given their inadequate transportation and language difficulties, a significant number of Asian and Latino aged are not only living on their own but are also isolated from the mainstream of American society.

Although policymakers should respect diversity and devise government programs that are more responsive to racial and cultural needs, they must not let these issues override feminist concerns. Culturally sensitive policies and services can provide positive means for dealing with ethnic and minority elders but may risk reinforcing norms, behaviors, and strict patriarchal structures that seriously limit the opportunities and well-being of females throughout their life cycle (Cohen, Howard, and Nussbaum, 1999).

Certainly, filial obligations to provide personal care to one's disabled kin generally translate into women's work, whether for wives, daughters, or daughters-in-law. With rising longevity, these racial and ethnic minority females may have several generations and large numbers of relatives to care for, sometimes four generations living in the same household. Many of the caregivers also have only limited resources themselves. The vast majority, out of necessity, now participate in the paid labor force, often in low-wage, mostly exhausting jobs that do not offer flexible hours. And growing numbers of them are single parents. Total reliance on such adult daughters for elder care, even when they are willing to provide assistance, ignores the realities of their lives. Not only does it entail particularly burdensome financial, physical, social, and psychological costs for these caregivers, but also their charges cannot receive all of the help that they need.

Because of ongoing fundamental structural inequities across the life span that relegate a large percentage of ethnic and racial minorities to poverty at an early age, such groups will continue to face hardship as they age. As Groger points out, the elders of 2040 are now twenty-two and "many of them have already embarked upon careers of lifelong poverty. Many of them already have children living in poverty" (1998, 121). At the same time, middle-aged women in these economically deprived groups are forced to support and care fully for their frail elderly kin, lessening their ability to work full time, pay for their children's education, afford medical services, and accumulate assets for retirement, further perpetuating the cycle of poor health and poverty into their old age. The admixture of a growing number of racial and ethnic minority elders and the persistence of their disadvantaged socioeconomic and health status will engender a considerably greater need than the dominant population will have for publicly supported long-term care services in the future. If current austerity measures persist, their caregivers will be increasingly overwhelmed and incapable of providing sufficient care.

Notes

1. In this chapter, "White" will refer to the White non-Latino population.

2. This chapter will focus primarily on the four racial/ethnic minority groups officially designated by the federal government in the census: Blacks, Latinos, Asians, and American Indians and Alaskan Natives.

3. These figures include Latinos of any race.

4. The figures used throughout the chapter, when applicable, will be for "race alone or in combination with other races." Other combinations include people of two or more races. For example, in 2000 there were 34.7 million Blacks categorized by the Census bureau as one race and another 1.7 million categorized as "in combination with other races." Thus, there were 36.4 million Blacks in the category "race alone or in combination with other races."

5. About 12.2 million of the foreign-born in the United States are citizens, and another 18.2 million are legal residents (U.S. Bureau of the Census, 2000d).

6. The Immigration and Nationality Act Amendments of 1965 eliminated national origin quotas that favored Western Europeans; they also imposed numerical quotas on immigration from the Western Hemisphere (Tress, 1997).

7. The Immigration Act of 1990 allowed a 40 percent increase in the number of people who could enter the United States with permanent residency status.

8. Most legal immigrants who have entered the country after age sixty-five are parents of a U.S. citizen. Another 20 percent are refugees (Treas, 1997). More than half of elderly legal immigrants reside in three states: California, Florida, and New York. About one-third come from Asia or the Pacific Islands (Friedland and Panka, 1997).

9. About 70 percent of legal immigrants as compared to only 38 percent of U.S. citizens receiving SSI are the elderly; the rest of the recipients are the blind and disabled younger population (Tress, 1997).

10. About 16 percent of legal immigrants were covered entirely by Medicaid; the remaining 48 percent used Medicaid as a supplement to their Medicare benefits (Friedland and Pankaj, 1997).

11. Under the original legislation, most legal immigrants, current and future, were cut off from federal cash assistance programs and food stamps until they became citizens. The states had the option to stop Medicaid for current immigrants; new entrants were ineligible for the first five years and after that time period their sponsor's income could be taken into account when they applied for benefits. Moreover, sponsors were now responsible for their charges until immigrants had worked at least ten

years or became U.S. citizens. Subsequent legislation in 1997 allowed older legal residents to receive SSI benefits.

12. In 1995, about 80,000 to 90,000 nursing home residents were legal immigrants (Friedland and Pankaj, 1997).

13. In 1998, an older Black female beneficiary averaged $6,907 annually as compared to $7,879 for White women.

14. On the other hand, Black women have a lower risk (about half the incidence of White women) for osteoporosis and its related hip and other bone fractures (Edmonds, 1999; Gannon, 1999).

15. In fully 65 percent of all multigenerational households in 2000, the head of the family took in his or her adult children, grandchildren, or both rather than the other way around (U.S. Bureau of the Census, 2001b). Over 2.4 million grandparents not only have their grandchildren living with them but also are the primary person responsible for their welfare. Overall, there are 4.5 million children residing with their grandparents, an increase of 30 percent since 1990 (although the total number of children rose by only 14.3 percent over the decade).

Relative to their population, Blacks and Latinos are disproportionately represented among grandparents who are raising their grandchildren. They comprise 29 percent and 18 percent, respectively, of the total. One source found that possibly 12 percent of all Black children live with their grandparents, primarily grandmothers. Moreover, such households tend to be among the most economically disadvantaged in the United States (Olson, 2001; Calasanti and Slevin, 2001).

16. About 52 percent of Latinos under the age of sixty-five have no private health insurance. However, this varies considerably among subgroups: nearly 75 percent of Cubans under the age of sixty-five have such insurance, a percentage nearly equivalent to that of the White population (Angel and Angel, 1997).

17. According to Carmen Sanchez, fictive kin "are close friends and neighbors who, over the period of years, have proved willing to engage in family matters and events" (2001, 92).

18. However, this poverty rate, though substantial, is still lower than those of both Blacks and Latino female-headed households.

19. One reason for this is the lower female-to-male ratio among Asians after age seventy-five than among other groups. About 60 percent of Asians aged eighty-five and over are women as compared to 73 percent of Blacks, 67 percent of Latinos, and 71 percent of Whites (U.S. Bureau of the Census, 2000b).

7

NURSING HOMES: A SYSTEM RUN AMOK

[A trainer at a dog training school and kennel, "Cloud 9,"] was caught on videotape choking, dragging and striking a dog she was training. It was on the front page of the *Atlanta Journal/Constitution* and the leading story on the evening news of every television channel. The entire city of Atlanta was disgusted and outraged. By the end of the week, the owner of "Cloud 9" had publicly apologized for his staff's behavior and the evening news reported that "Cloud 9" was out of business. . . . I had to ask myself: Why is it that the tragedies we see in some of our nursing homes don't get the same response? . . . Why doesn't the mistreatment of our mothers and fathers cause the same outrage?

—Testimony of Becky A. Kurtz, Georgia State
Long-Term Care Ombudsman (SSCA, 1999e, 35)

The Emergence of the Modern-Day, Proprietary Nursing Home

ELDER CARE HAS ALWAYS BEEN the primary responsibility of the family. However, by the 1800s, an institutionalized system had developed for indigents who didn't have a relative to care for them: almshouses (or poor houses), public mental institutions, and later county homes.[1] Initially, almshouses contained the sick, orphans, the mentally insane, and the elderly; increasingly, however, the aged became their main residents. Meanwhile, there was mounting public outcry about the "cruel, inhumane and filthy" conditions, minimal care, brutality, and corruption, especially since the poor, disabled older population now was, by and large, regarded more sympathetically (Holstein and Cole, 1996; Kaffenberger, 2000; Vladeck, 1980).

By the turn of the twentieth century, reformers denounced both the conditions in the almshouses and encouraged the expansion of alternatives. At the time, these consisted mostly of nonprofit establishments, including homes that were operated by immigrant and religious groups for their own members. There also were some small, privately owned boarding homes, generally owned and run by individual licensed nurses. By 1920, their number, though few, equaled that of the poor houses (Kaffenberger, 2000).

Over the next several decades, however, state and national policies had a dramatic impact on the growth of nursing homes generally and large-scale, for-profit facilities specifically. In particular, the Social Security Act of 1935, with its earned pensions and Old Age Assistance Program, disbursed money to a large percentage of elders, allowing more of them to choose their own housing and purchase services. Just as importantly, the legislation prohibited the payment of benefits to individuals residing in public facilities, thus precluding its funding of poor houses. As a result, dependent older people steadily relocated from almshouses into private boarding homes, small convalescent homes, homes for the aged, and nursing homes (Holstein and Cole, 1996).

By the early 1950s, unsafe and deplorable living conditions prevalent in the boarding homes and nursing facilities again generated public concern. Consequently, in addition to licensing provisions, the states established some regulations that focused mostly on health concerns, building codes, and safety measures, including fire construction standards, sprinkler systems, and support bars (Kane, Kane, and Ladd, 1998; Vladeck, 1980). These limited but costly early rules eventually led to the gradual disappearance of smaller homes, whose owners couldn't afford to meet the new standards, as well as the eventual transformation of nursing facilities into medically designed institutional settings (Holstein and Cole, 1996; Kane, Kane, and Ladd, 1998; Kayser-Jones, 1981).

The spread of large-scale facilities after World War II was fostered by the passage of the 1960 Kerr-Mills legislation, which established a new category of "medically needy" aged. Its Medical Assistance to the Aged program also expanded the system of direct vendor payments, now assuring the nursing home industry an even greater, steady stream of income. By 1954, the Hill-Burton Act, too, allowed a limited amount of funds to support the development and modernization of nursing homes, though the money was restricted to nonprofit establishments. In 1959, proprietary institutions became eligible for direct loans and loan guarantees through the Federal Housing Administration (FHA) and Small Business Administration (SBA). With relatively low mortgage rates fueling profits, the number of facilities multiplied rapidly. According to several scholars, the advantageous loan program was available to them only because of the intense, forceful lobbying efforts of the newly formed (1950) American Association of Nursing Homes (Holstein and Cole, 1996; Kaffenberger, 2000).[2]

The most important stimulus to the proliferation of nursing homes, as suggested in chapter 2, was the 1965 enactment of Medicare and especially Medicaid. With no benefit caps on institutional services for covered individuals, potentially huge subsidies, and opportunities for enormous profits, Medicaid generated an expansive construction of proprietary facilities. Medicare, though of lesser importance to them financially, provided ample funding for 100 days of a resident's recuperative care following a hospital stay of at least 3 days. Thus, owners were now assured not only a patient's Social Security check but also her Medicaid or Medicare benefits, both paid directly to the institution. Billions of dollars in public money began pouring into their private coffers: about 80 percent of nursing home care was privately funded in 1960, but by the early 1970s, three-fourths of all patients were supported under public sources, primarily Medicaid.[3] At the end of the 1970s, fully 57 percent of all facility revenues came from government programs (Estes and Harrington, 1981; Rhoades, 1998).

In addition, the deinstitutionalization movement, which began in the mid-1950s, accelerated after the passage of Medicaid. In order to substitute federal for local dollars, the states began "dumping" frail elders with psychological disorders from their mental hospitals into nationally funded nursing homes, boarding houses, old hotels, and even the streets (Estes and Harrington, 1981; Holstein and Cole, 1996). From 1969 to 1974, the number of aged residing in state mental hospitals decreased by 56 percent (SSCA, 1995b). The relocation of such older people was facilitated in 1974 by the passage of the Supplementary Security Income program; as under the earlier Social Security legislation, inhabitants of public institutions were prohibited from receiving benefits.

From 1965 through the 1970s, the number of nursing homes mushroomed, from about 10,500 in 1960 and 18,000 in 1977 to 19,100 (1.5 million residents) in 1985, at which time their growth slowed down, mostly because of limits on construction in many states (Kayser-Jones, 1981; Vladeck, 1980).[4] As the percentage of for-profit facilities increased, reaching two-thirds of the total by the 1970s, they increasingly were formed into chains.[5] Moreover, in order to raise ever-growing capital requirements, firms began offering public stock. From the mid-1970s through the 1980s, the percentage of beds controlled by publicly held companies, especially chains, steadily expanded.[6]

Care of the frail elderly had become big business. Nursing homes were viewed as "gold mines," delivering high returns and stimulating new, resourceful methods of profiteering. For example, since Medicare and Medicaid reimbursed the owners for all capital costs, including construction, renovations, depreciation of property, and interest on mortgages, the value of their holdings increased at government expense. Such lucrative policies stimulated unfettered real estate speculation: homes were bought and sold on a regular basis. Proprietors also tended to extract the equity from their property, leaving the facilities with limited resources for patient care. By the end of the 1980s, sizable fortunes had been made, and many of the original speculators had moved on to other ventures.

Bilking Medicare in the 1990s: Ancillary Services

During the 1990s, Medicare spending on skilled nursing homes soared, rising 500 percent between 1990 and 1997. However, because of a confluence of ill-advised government policies, most of this growth in public money was expended on ancillary services, which rose by 19 percent annually during the period.[7] First, unlike hospitals, nursing home payments under Medicare were still cost based. And, though some financial limits had been placed on routine care, both ancillary services and capital-related costs remained uncapped. Second, the PPS increasingly cut the length of stay in hospitals, thus fostering greater demand for postacute care, especially rehabilitation services. Third, as will be shown later, after the Omnibus Budget Reconciliation Act of 1987 took effect in 1990, nursing homes had to assess and meet certain needs of their residents more extensively, including whether they needed physical, occupational, and speech therapy (SSCA, 2000a).

Quick to capitalize on the financial bonanza, large nursing home companies built up in-house capacity in the area of rehabilitation, postacute care centers, and other high-reimbursable ancillary services. Sun Healthcare, for one, invested heavily in equipment and staff for complex medical and rehabilitation care (GAO, 1999n). Many of the chains, such as Genesis Health Ventures, Integrated Health Services (IHS), Beverly Enterprises, and Extendicare Health Services, actually bought up pharmacy, therapy, medical equipment, and other related businesses (Peterson and Stanley, 1998; Salganik, 2001). Concomitantly, they immediately sought Medicare certification for their current and newly purchased facilities; during the 1990s, the number of such homes, mostly for-profit chains, grew by about 6 percent per year (GAO, 1999n). Proprietary institutions also shifted a substantial number of existing beds from Medicaid to Medicare patients in order to exploit the situation to the fullest extent. From 1997 to 1999 alone, Medicare-certified beds increased by 23 percent, mostly replacing Medicaid patients (SSCA, 2000a).

Since they could bill Medicare separately and directly for ancillary services and didn't have to specify exactly how much time was spent in providing them per patient, the facilities were able to charge exorbitant rates (GAO, 1996a). They took advantage of the situation by overusing the high-priced therapies and related services (SSCA, 2000a). In fact, it was difficult to prove whether the ancillary care had been provided at all when the nursing home and the services were owned by the same company (HGR, 1997).[8] Between 1990 and 1998, average per capita reimbursements increased by about 12 percent annually, as compared to only a 3 percent rise in facility costs for goods and services. And the nursing home chains became increasingly dependent on providing ancillary services at inflated charges. For example, Genesis's reliance on Medicare payments rose from 14 percent of its total revenues in 1993 to nearly 25 percent in 1997 (Smith, 1998a). Indeed, Beverly Enterprises boasted in the mid-1990s that because of such high-cost treatments, it would bring in the highest nursing home profits in years (Peterson and Stanley, 1998).

At the Financial Brink?

Medicaid, too, provided an ongoing, dependable flow of money during the 1990s, contributing over 60 percent of total nursing home revenues; between 1990 and 1997, their Medicaid reimbursements rose 87 percent (SSCA, 2000a). Because of the unremitting generosity of the government, nursing homes continued to be a lucrative business; stocks skyrocketed, enriching owners and investors alike. Vencor, Beverly Enterprises, Genesis Health, and IHS experienced operating net profits amounting to $83 million, $125 million, $127 million, and $97 million, respectively, in 1996; and they earned $224 million, $108 million, $185 million, and $224 million, respectively, in 1997 (SSCA, 1999e).

With the promise of boundless gains, new investors were attracted to the industry, including businesspeople who had "no interest in health care or the elderly" (Kaffenberger, 2000, 44). The influx of huge amounts of cash encouraged frequent mergers, acquisitions, and takeovers; big nursing home chains increasingly devoured smaller ones as well as independent homes, depleting the facilities of their assets and burdening them with debts. For instance, in 1997 and 1998, Genesis Health purchased Multicare ($1.4 billion); Extendicare Health Services, Inc., purchased Arbor ($450 million); InvestCorp purchased Harborside ($291 million); Vencor purchased Hillhaven, Thera Tx, and Transitional Hospital (over $2 billion); Mariner Post-Acute Network was established from the merger of Apollo Advisors—which had been created by the merger of Living Centers of America and Unifour in 1995—and Mariner Health Networks; and Health Care and Retirement (HCR) purchased Manor

Care (Peterson and Stanley, 1998; Smith, 1998a; SSCA, 2000a). By the end of 1998, the five largest megachains, with revenues of $14 billion, operated over 28 percent of all the nursing homes in the nation (SSCA, 2000a).[9] The most prominent among them were Genesis, IHS, Vencor, and Sun Healthcare (SSCA, 2000a).

As Medicare and Medicaid costs continued to escalate, policymakers focused on controlling them, paying little attention to the financial situation of the institutions or their financial manipulations. First, under the Balanced Budget Act of 1997, Congress repealed the Boren Amendment, thereby authorizing states to switch from cost-based reimbursement formulas under Medicaid to new mechanisms that would lower payments. Thus, though their exact approach differed, the states generally began offering less generous per capita payments to the facilities.[10] Second, and just as devastating to the industry, BBA 1997 also instituted PPS for nursing homes under Medicare. Using a case-mix approach, they would receive a daily flat rate, per capita, based on the average national cost of providing care to patients in specified classifications, adjusted for locality.[11] However, now the homes or outside vendors could not charge the government separately for certain ancillary and capital costs, expenses that would be built into the reimbursement fee schedules. Moreover, occupational, physical, and speech therapy were each capped at $1,500 per patient. After the implementation of BBA, average Medicare payments to nursing homes declined; instead of the exorbitant 30 percent annual increases expected by the industry, they were now closer to 10 percent (SSCA, 2000a). Third, as will be shown in the next chapter, national policymakers intensified their efforts against Medicare and Medicaid fraud, also threatening nursing home revenues.

Because of the aggressive acquisitions and mergers of the 1990s, the giant nursing home chains were highly leveraged, draining their cash surpluses and saddling them with excessive debt, amounting to an additional $5 billion over the decade for the industry as a whole (SSCA, 2000a). Interest payments alone could be 9 percent or higher of a company's total operating costs (Harrington, 1996). Thus, there was little equity in the facilities themselves, working capital was tight, and operating margins were small. At the same time, the facilities extracted huge sums of money for extravagant administrative costs, including excessive salaries and profits at the expense of patient care. According to a study by Charlene Harrington (1996), administrative costs accounted for 28 percent of all operating expenses.[12] A recent investigation of the financial statements of nursing homes by *U.S. News and World Report* found that "many nursing home operators steer big chunks of their revenues to themselves or related businesses before they calculate the bottom line" (Schmitt, 2002, 67). About one-fifth of the facilities it surveyed spent 20 percent or more of their revenues on administrative costs. Big-chain CEOs were—and are— paid millions in salary, benefits, bonuses, and other amenities (Hilzenrath, 1999). As a case in point, in addition to his multimillion-dollar annual salary and use of a corporate jet, Robert N. Elkin, the CEO of IHS, received a whopping $3.25 million bonus in 1997 (Salganik, 2001).[13]

U.S. News and World Report also determined that in one year alone, nursing homes spent fully $3.4 billion of their total revenues on often questionable related-party transactions that can hide nursing home profits. These self-dealing maneuvers, which are widespread in the industry, include bleeding profits from local nursing homes to their corporate parent, hiding some of the parent's costs among its local homes, and paying management or consulting fees to affiliated firms or relatives, some of which serves "to siphon money from a home, depriving patients of benefits" (Schmitt, 2002, 72). Moreover, in order to maximize profits, a few chains restructured their assets so as to milk some segments of their holdings at the expense of others (SSCA, 2000a). Specifically, in 1998 Vencor split into two separate, publicly held companies: Ventas, which acquired the real estate, would lease to Vencor, the actual operator of the nursing homes. Ventas immediately increased Vencor's rent 400 percent, from $42 million in 1997 to $171 million in 1999, generating an enormous rise in the latter's capital costs.[14] In fact, the rental of facilities from related firms is common (Schmitt, 2002).

The new Medicare and Medicaid cost-cutting policies hit the for-profit nursing home industry hard, especially since their high profits had depended both on elevated charges for ancillary services and coverage of their debts (SSCA, 2000a). As one newspaper account put it, "Nursing chains that had reaped huge profits under the old system saw their futures suddenly darken" (Malone, 2000). Beginning in 1999, although many facilities continued to be a strong investment, profits declined. And a growing number of firms, especially chains, were in financial distress, including Vencor, Sun Healthcare, Beverly Enterprises, Genesis, and Nova Care; on the other hand, few nonprofits experienced such problems (AARP, 2000c; SSCA, 2000a). Because the for-profit firms were so weighed down with debt and could no longer manage to discharge their interest payments, five of the ten largest chains declared bankruptcy; most of their homes were full and earning money (SSCA, 2000a).[15] Vencor was the first (1999), followed by Sun Healthcare (1999), IHS (2000), Genesis (2000), and Mariner Post-Acute Care Networks (2000).[16] By the beginning of the twenty-first century, at least 10 percent of all nursing homes were under the protection of Chapter 11 federal bankruptcy laws. In some states (e.g., Florida, Texas, West Virginia, and Massachusetts), over 20 percent of the beds were in bankruptcy proceedings, and in a few places the rates were even higher (e.g., New Mexico, 50 percent; Nevada, 30 percent) (Collins, 2001; SSCA, 2000a).

Mounting a multimillion-dollar public relations campaign, including widespread newspaper advertisements and intensive lobbying of Congress, the American Health Care Association blamed the financial problems facing nursing homes on the 1997 reductions in government reimbursements. The industry charge, however, was soon refuted by a General Accounting Office study (GAO, 2000f) of the issue documenting that aggregate Medicare payments to nursing homes actually were sufficient—and sometimes more than sufficient—to cover the costs of care. Moreover, it reported that about three-fourths of the nursing home chains in bankruptcy continued to be profitable; their losses stemmed primarily from the ancillary businesses that they purchased.[17] Indeed, the chains in financial trouble tended to be those most heavily in debt, more highly dependent on Medicare, or both, especially for ancillary services, than the industry as a whole. IHS, for example, not only had a debt of $3 billion, but it also depended on Medicare for one-third of its revenues. Sun Healthcare and Vencor received about one-fourth of their incomes from the program in 1998, though only 10 percent of the residents relied on it for funding (GAO, 1999n; Salganik, 2001; SSCA, 2000a).

Under Chapter 11's bankruptcy law, the nursing home chains ceased making debt payments, renegotiated their obligations, obtained special private financing to help them operate, and continued to function without interruption (SSCA, 2000a). In addition, the government backed down, restoring most of the 1997 Medicare cuts by paying the industry billions of extra dollars from 1999 to 2002 and promising more for the future. For example, under the Balanced Budget Refinement Act of 1999, nursing homes received a 20 percent upward adjustment in reimbursement for certain patients and a 4 percent rise in overall payments for 2001 and 2002. The following year, the Medicare, Medicaid, and SCHIP Benefits Improvement and Protection Act (BIPA) increased the nursing component of the Medicare rate by nearly 17 percent, thereby raising overall payments by 4 to 12 percent. Moreover, the $1,500 therapy caps were suspended beginning in 2000. With the inflow of additional public money, most nursing home chains eventually emerged from bankruptcy, albeit not always under the same name or company.[18]

Currently, any attempts by policymakers to reduce Medicare reimbursements are met with industry threats to go back into bankruptcy, such as during the industry's latest struggle to keep another $1.4 billion (2003) and $1 billion (2004) in supplementary funding intact. Moreover, operators argue that Medicaid rates are so low, covering only about 93 percent of patient costs, that they are steadily losing money from such patients; over the last several years, state nursing home associations have been threatening bankruptcy in order to raise Medicaid rates, and many states are succumbing (Powell, 2001a–b).[19] In the case of Alabama, where by 1997 rates had grown higher than the national average and the state was experiencing budget problems, the governor attempted to cut back the level of reimbursement; he was stopped by the nursing home lobby, which warned that facilities would have to close, throwing frail patients into the streets (Wiener and Stevenson, 1998).

Despite industry complaints, the *U.S. News and World Report* investigation found that Medicaid payments actually had little effect on profitability or losses: rather, it determined that there was no relationship between a facility's financial situation and the percentage of its patients participating in Medicaid (Schmitt, 2002). In fact, nursing homes remain a highly lucrative industry, with profit margins as high as 20 or 30 percent in some places. And, despite the stock market declines and generally poor U.S. economy in 2002, financial analysts note that many of the megachains, including those that have recently emerged from bankruptcy, are in excellent financial health (Schmitt, 2002).

Patient Abuse and Neglect

Exposés, Hearings, and Private Greed: The Early Years

Over the decades, residents in nursing homes have been at risk of poor care, abusive conditions, maltreatment, exploitation, and other serious harms to their well-being. As one expert on the subject tells us, "Probably no other type of health care organization has been demonstrated to have as many quality-of-care problems as nursing facilities"(Harrington, 1996, 457). A significant percentage of the institutions, particularly the for-profit ones, have proven themselves unconcerned with the type of care they provide; proprietors have focused almost entirely on improving their financial position and profits. Thus, not only has the government supported the nursing home industry economically, but it has also had to maintain constant vigilance over patient care.

This surveillance, although extremely costly, has been mostly lax and ineffective. Government interest in the problems, for the most part, has been scandal driven, with short-term damage control as the major goal. The politics and policies related to the neglect and mistreatment of nursing home residents have been a vicious cycle of "new" revelations, government studies, congressional hearings, additional rules and regulations, poor enforcement, and more disclosures. Decades of intermittent mass media exposés, voluminous documentation of the situation, and eruptions of short-lived public concern have generated only insufficient legislative fixes. Unwilling to address the underlying structural problems, policymakers have allowed poor quality care and abusive practices to persist.

Prior to the 1960s, the national government had taken relatively little interest in the subject of nursing homes and their treatment of patients. The states, most of which were woefully remiss, had full responsibility for their regulation.

Some federal standards eventually were imposed when Congress set up minimum requirements for participation in the Medicaid and Medicare programs.[20] But the limited measures not only were vague, but also had been steadily watered down by the Department of Health, Education, and Welfare (HEW), which regularly granted liberal waivers to the facilities. Moreover, state enforcement tended to be haphazard, ineffectual, and even nonexistent in some places (SSCA, 1995).

Beginning in 1959, hearings by the Senate Subcommittee on Problems of the Aged and Aging, followed by additional hearings in 1964 and 1965 by the newly established Senate Special Committee on Aging (SSCA), uncovered myriad shocking problems prevalent among the institutions.[21] During the early 1970s, the scandalous state of affairs was again dramatically unveiled through several tragic events highlighted by the press, including the death of some residents from food poisoning and hazardous living conditions, including a major fire. In 1974, the *New York Times* ran a series on its findings of fraud and abuse in New York nursing homes. In addition, the deplorable situation was publicized in three major works aptly titled *Tender Loving Greed,* by Mary Mendelson (1974); *Too Old, Too Sick, Too Bad: Nursing Homes in America,* by Frank Moss and Val Halamanderis (1977); and *Unloving Care: The Nursing Home Tragedy,* by Bruce Vladeck (1980). At the same time, government investigations, including a GAO audit in three states, at least twenty-seven hearings from 1969 to 1975 by Frank Moss's Senate Special Committee on Aging Subcommittee on Long-Term Care, and the ten comprehensive *Nursing Homes in the U.S.: Failure in Public Policy* reports, issued in 1975 and 1976, revealed even more horror stories, along with pervasive provider fraud and theft (SSCA, 1975, 1976a–i).

Jointly, the various revelations identified sweeping abuses, exploitation, unsanitary and hazardous conditions, malnutrition,[22] lack of basic medical care, routine overuse of antipsychotic drugs and physical restraints,[23] as well as injuries and deaths due to negligence. Indeed, over 40 percent of all residents were found to be tied down, mostly for the convenience of the staff (SSCA, 1975b). The facilities relied primarily on untrained, unlicensed, and overworked nurse's aides who labored without any meaningful assistance from registered nurses or physicians (SSCA, 1975e). As Medicare and Medicaid money flowed increasingly into their coffers, the nursing homes were failing to meet even basic minimal standards—about half of them were woefully substandard. The evidence showed that many patients were deteriorating soon after placement (SSCA, 1975b; Vladeck, 1980).

Though promising sweeping reform in the late 1970s, the federal government proved unwilling to enact tough measures; for the most part, despite their clear inability to improve the appalling situation, the states remained in charge

(SSCA, 1975, 1976a–j). The major national response to the nursing home disclosures was the Medicare–Medicaid Anti-fraud and Abuse Amendments of 1977, requiring states to establish Medicaid Fraud Control Units (MFCUs). These entities, where they existed, were charged with investigating provider fraud, along with patient abuse and neglect under the Medicaid program. In addition, in 1978 Congress required the states to establish an ombudsman program, under the Administration of Aging, to look into and resolve consumer complaints both in nursing facilities and board and care homes.

The Federal Government Rears Its Head: OBRA 1987

In 1982, responding to complaints by the nursing home industry that federal regulations under Medicare and Medicaid were overly rigid, HCFA attempted to ease them.[24] Supported by President Reagan (who favored private accreditation, deregulation of industry, and the reduction of national authority overall) but facing congressional and aging advocacy group opposition, HCFA requested an inquiry by the Institute of Medicine (IOM) on the conditions in nursing homes, the effectiveness of the regulatory system, and mechanisms for improving it. In its scathing 1986 report, *Improving the Quality of Care in Nursing Homes,* the IOM found that the horrendous conditions identified in the 1970s, including far-reaching abuse and neglect, poor quality of life, violation of residents' legal and civil rights, and sorely inadequate nursing and medical care, had not perceptibly improved. The work argued emphatically for a stronger federal role and concluded with a comprehensive set of recommendations for reform.

Incorporating most of its suggestions, Congress enacted the Omnibus Budget Reconciliation Act of 1987, which took effect in October 1990. The most rigorous set of national regulations to date, it contained, for the first time, standards for the quality of care, quality of life, and some basic patients' rights. Among other particulars, nursing homes had to accommodate patients' needs and preferences; provide services that would allow them to attain or maintain the highest practicable physical, mental, and psychological well-being; guarantee their freedom from physical and mental abuse, punishment, material and chemical restraints, and involuntary transfers or discharges; and secure their rights to dignity, privacy, and security.

OBRA 1987 also set minimum national training standards for nurse's aides (at least seventy-five hours, along with competency testing and regular in-service education) and required twenty-four-hour licensed nursing services, including a registered nurse for at least eight hours per day.[25] Furthermore, the act mandated the assessment of residents' capabilities and needs, using standardized formats (the Resident Assessment Instrument—RAI—and the Minimum

Data Set—MDS) and the development of an individualized care plan for each inhabitant.[26] Among the tougher federal inspection procedures, states now had to conduct a survey at least every fifteen months, unannounced; make them available to the public; and investigate all complaints in a timely fashion.

Prior to the new legislation, the only sanctions available to HCFA were to close down the facility, reject a home's participation in the Medicare and Medicaid programs, or deny federal payments for new admissions, all of which the agency was reluctant to execute. OBRA 1987 expanded the types of deficiencies that could invoke a denial of payment; provided for additional intermediate sanctions, most importantly the imposition of civil monetary payments;[27] and permitted corrective action plans, thereby letting nursing homes correct their deficiencies before any penalties would take effect. Moreover, the type of sanction imposed would take into account both the level of severity and scope of any infractions, both of which were clearly demarcated under the law (see table 7.1).[28] If a nursing home jeopardizes the health or safety of residents, immediate action would now have to be taken to correct the deficiencies, including temporary management of the facility by the state.

However, the enforcement measures did not take effect until July 1995, fully eight years after OBRA 1987 was enacted. Immediately the nursing home industry challenged them, again charging the government with overregulation. In response, scarcely three months later, the Senate Special Committee on Aging held hearings on the subject (SSCA, 1995a). Nearly all of the nonindustry observers agreed that strong federal mandates were imperative to ensure the health, safety, and well-being of nursing home residents. Among other concerns, they pointed to the ongoing, inferior care provided by at least 20 percent of the facilities and insufficient guidelines, protections, and enforcement efforts at the state level. A few witnesses identified some of the positive outcomes of OBRA 1987 regulations to date, such as a slight reduction in the use of antipsychotic drugs.[29] Nonetheless, Republicans in Congress attempted to dismantle the new national standards and controls. In its Medicaid block grant proposal, the House passed a requirement, eventually rejected by the Senate, that all regulatory power over nursing homes be turned back to the states.

Déjà Vu: The Neglect and Abuse Persist

A new round of congressional hearings on nursing homes was initiated in 1998. Fueled by reports of over 3,000 resident deaths in California facilities because of unacceptable care, the Senate Special Committee on Aging requested an investigation by the GAO and in July held two days of hearings based on its findings (SSCA, 1998b). In yet another serious indictment of the industry, *California Nursing Homes: Care Problems Persist despite Federal and State Oversight,* the GAO (1998) discovered that out of a sample of sixty-two case records of elders who allegedly died from poor treatment, at least half had encountered conditions that endangered their health and safety. Moreover, about one-third of the nursing home documentation it sorted through had such clear inconsistencies and omissions that the agency questioned the validity of the data per se.

In the second part of its probe, which sampled all of California's facilities, the GAO determined that "certain California nursing homes are not sufficiently monitored to guarantee the safety and welfare of their residents" (1998, 3): fully one-third of the institutions had "serious or potentially life-threatening care problems," including violations for conditions that caused death, seriously jeopardized residents' health and safety, or subjected them to substandard care; only about 2 percent of the facilities had minimal deficiencies or none at all. In what was and would continue to be consistent problems over the years, the study found:

1. A significant number of homes had repeated infractions that injured their residents or placed them in immediate jeopardy of harm.
2. Very few of the facilities, even if sanctions had been imposed, ever actually suffered any penalties. In what was to become known as a yo-yo pattern of noncompliance, nursing homes would "correct" their deficiencies within the grace period allowable under HCFA guidelines, only to resume their poor care in a short time. Even the few homes that had their funding terminated because of the most egregious actions were soon reinstated into the program, and again injured residents.
3. Rather than verify that a home had corrected its deficiencies, the state agencies frequently accepted the facilities' own documentation; these self-reports often turned out to be fallacious.
4. Conditions in the nursing homes most probably were even worse than those recorded in the state surveys: not only do inspectors miss some of the most serious care problems, but the timing of their surveys also tended to be predictable, thereby allowing the operators to cover up any problems. In calling for stronger enforcement of the OBRA 1987 regulations, the GAO warned that the numerous problems it discovered were not confined to California, but were prevalent nationwide.

Overall, the Senate Special Committee on Aging hearings (1998b) corroborated the GAO findings, further exposing the serious shortcomings of the federal regulations under OBRA 1987; for the most part, impotent state agencies and the nursing homes themselves were still in control. Harrington, for example, presented her study on the effects of the legislation (Harrington and Carrillo, 1999). She determined that the average number of deficiencies given out to nursing homes actually had declined by 42 percent between 1991 and 1996, a change more suggestive of weaker implementation of the rules than of improved care. Witnesses also contended that HCFA had informally watered down many of its enforcement procedures, similar to earlier years. For one, its new regulatory term "substantial compliance" now permitted nursing homes to evade full adherence to federal mandates.

Importantly, the mounting evidence presented during the proceedings brought out even more explicitly that the current system of inspections was understating the full extent of problems within the facilities. To illustrate, several nurse's aides, along with a physician affiliated with nursing homes in Sacramento, testified that patient charts were regularly falsified. The aides also pointed out that administrators could accurately predict when the inspectors were coming, at which time they would temporarily add more staff by plucking them from other nursing homes owned by the same company, schedule overtime, or hire part-timers during the survey period. In addition, a researcher who had studied the quality of care in two California homes simultaneous with state inspections reported that there were both greater and more severe facility-wide problems than those officially cited.

At the request of the Senate Special Committee on Aging, the GAO prepared two more studies in conjunction with the committee's second set of hearings in March 1999 on the implementation of OBRA 1987 and the quality of care in nursing homes (SSCA, 1999f). The first one, *Nursing Homes: Additional Steps Needed to Strengthen Enforcement of Federal Quality Standards,* focused on four states (California, Michigan, Pennsylvania, and Texas) that represented nearly 25 percent of all U.S. facilities. It found that, despite OBRA 1987, more than one-fourth of all nursing homes "had serious deficiencies that caused actual harm to residents or placed them at risk of death or serious injury" (GAO, 1999i, 3). The report, yet again, revealed an ongoing yo-yo pattern: after receiving a sanction, the homes would correct their deficiencies temporarily, but the problems would reappear by the next survey.

Critically, during the three-year time span under study, 40 percent of the facilities with the most severe deficiencies—those with actual or potential for death or serious injury and other actual harm—continued to have problems of equal or worse severity. These included the failures to prevent the development of bedsores, which can cause pain, infection, increased debilitation, and damage to muscles and bones; eliminate improper use of physical restraints and psychotropic drugs; provide appropriate treatment for incontinence; protect residents from serious accidents, such as hip fractures; meet patients' basic nutritional needs; supply appropriate services to wheelchair- or bed-bound patients; and maintain patients' dignity.

Nor had the states gained much ground in their enforcement efforts: there continued to be "few consequences to noncompliance": despite poor, sometimes seriously deleterious conditions, few proprietors ever paid civil monetary penalties, were denied payment for new admissions, or had their Medicare and Medicaid agreements revoked; a mere 5 percent of all facilities that were given notices of termination actually were dropped from the public programs. In the event that monetary penalties actually were assessed, the owners could and would delay payment and avoid fixing the problems for years while they appealed the sanctions. The GAO urged HCFA to act more aggressively against nursing homes that repeatedly neglected and mistreated residents.

The March 1999 hearings themselves (SSCA, 1999f) centered on the second GAO study (1999j), *Nursing Homes: Complaint Investigation Processes Often Inadequate to Protect Residents,* and one of six audit reports on nursing homes prepared by the Inspector General's Office (OIG, 1999), *Quality of Care in Nursing Homes: An Overview.*[30] Based on 1997 and 1998 data from the ten largest states and representing over half of all nursing home beds in the nation, the OIG probe found that although some deficiencies had declined, the more serious ones were increasing. Not surprisingly, it reported that neither the states' complaint investigative processes nor their enforcement procedures were effective in curbing the prevalence of chronically substandard care and abusive conditions. As with previous research, the agency held that the situation was most likely even worse than the data indicated since the predictability of surveys afforded nursing homes the opportunity to cover up their poor care.

The GAO report (1999j) delved more deeply into the question of resident, family, and staff complaints. After reviewing procedures in fourteen states, investigators discovered that even grievances about extremely hazardous conditions often were ignored by officials or put off for long periods of time. Though states are required to investigate within forty-eight hours problems that may immediately endanger a resident, they generally classified few complaints in such a high-priority category. Moreover, not only are states allowed to determine their own timeframe for responding to "less imminent" situations, including neglect, abuse, and significant risk of injury, but several places also put off their checks for months or sometimes until the next annual survey. In one case, a nurse became suspicious when there were twelve deaths within a two-week period at her Pennsylvania nursing home, including a resident who had received ten times the proper dosage of medicine. Her complaint was not investigated until the facility's usual inspection, months later. In another instance, a home with prior problems related to the treatment of diabetic residents was accused by family members of failing to manage the insulin injections of their mother, who later died; Michigan state inspectors waited until the next annual survey—eight months—before they investigated. The study concluded that "extensive delays in investigating serious complaints alleging harmful situations . . . can leave nursing home residents in poor care and unsafe conditions for extended periods" (22).

Under serious attack for its negligent oversight and drawing from the agency's own lengthy two-year study indicating widespread quality-of-care problems, HCFA officials acknowledged that there was an urgent need for more and stricter national controls (HCFA, 1998). Accordingly, beginning in July 1998, the Clinton administration advanced comprehensive, multifaceted proposals to crack down on ineffectual state inspections and regulation enforcement. Among other provisions, they included a call for more frequent scrutiny of nursing homes with repeated violations and poor compliance records; staggered annual reviews, including nighttime and weekend visits to make them less predictable; a targeting of enforcement efforts on chains that have particularly poor records;[31] the posting of inspection results on the Internet; the designation of "poorly performing facility" and an immediate penalty, without a grace period, for any nursing home cited for actual harm to residents—deficiencies at level H or higher—on two successive annual surveys (see table 7.1); and increased federal oversight of state processes overall, including the referral of facilities providing exceptionally poor care to the Department of Justice or other federal agency for possible civil or criminal action (SSCA, 1998b).[32] In addition, HCFA identified two nursing homes in each state with the worst compliance records as "special focus" facilities that would be subject to more intense monitoring (SSCA, 1999f).

After the March 1999 congressional hearings, HCFA responded by announcing yet more "corrective actions" to deal with the ongoing problems, including a Complaint Improvement Project (CIP), a requirement that states investigate any complaints involving harm to residents within ten working days and that they vigorously prosecute nursing homes with egregious violations. The federal agency also emphasized that any complaints involving immediate jeopardy must be investigated within two days (SSCA, 1999f). In addition, it enlarged the category of "poorly performing facility" to include level-G deficiencies (see table 7.1 for a list of the different levels of nursing home deficiencies), rendering about 15 percent more homes subject to immediate fines without a grace period. There were now thirty new federal initiatives attempting to upgrade nursing home care, including one that focused inspections specifically on bedsores, dehydration, and malnutrition.[33]

In June 1999, the Senate Special Committee on Aging held hearings to assess the effects of the government's cumulative efforts (SSCA, 1999d). As a major part of the proceedings, William Scanlon of the GAO discussed the findings of

TABLE 7.1
HCFA's Scope and Severity Grid for Nursing Homes Deficiencies

Severity Category	Scope			Sanctions	
	Isolated Harm	Pattern of Harm	Widespread Harm	Required	Optional
Actual or potential for death or serious injury (immediate jeopardy to resident health and safety)	J	K	L	***	* or **
Causing actual harm	G	H	I	**	
Potential for more than minimal harm	D	E	F	* (D and E) ** (F)	** (D and E) * (F)
Potential for minimal harm (substantial compliance)	A	B	C	none	none

Source: SSCA, 1999d.
* Sanctions include a directed plan of correction, directed in-service training, and/or state monitoring.
** Sanctions include a denial of payment for new admissions or all individuals, and/or civil monetary penalties.
*** Sanctions include the appointment of a temporary manager, termination from Medicare and Medicaid, and/or civil monetary penalties.

his agency's latest study. He observed that not only had HCFA neglected to make the vast majority of its directives operational, but also the states had not revised their practices appreciably, most citing high costs as justification.[34] For example, many states were not meeting the ten-day requirement for investigating complaints involving actual harm to residents. In fact, in his statement Scanlon warned that "HCFA is not well informed on what the states are doing with regard to these initiatives" (GAO, 1999k, 12). In another inquiry a few months later, the GAO (1999g) confirmed, yet again, that the states were not being held accountable to the national government for their persistently poor performance in protecting elderly residents in nursing homes.

The following year, the Senate Special Committee on Aging held yet more hearings (2000b), coupled with new studies by both the GAO (2000g) and HCFA (2000c), to assess the impact of the Clinton/HCFA initiatives on the situation in nursing homes. Again, the conclusions were not encouraging: the states had not made tangible progress in combating the problems, including the abuse, neglect, and exploitation of residents (SSCA, 2000b). Among its findings, the GAO (2000g) revealed that the percentage of homes with documented incidences of actual harm and/or immediate jeopardy actually had increased slightly, from 28 percent to 30 percent nationally, a change the agency attributed mostly to declining staffing levels;[35] over 2,000 facilities, nearly one-third of the total, had been cited over the previous two years for repeatedly harming residents; at least one-third of the states were not promptly investigating complaints involving actual or potential danger to residents; and state investigations continued to understate the severity of the problems.[36]

In March 2002, the Senate Special Committee on Aging documented more horror stories of mistreatment, spurred by a three-state (Georgia, Illinois, and Pennsylvania) GAO (2002j) review of physical and sexual abuse of residents by nursing home staff. The study revealed that nursing homes rarely report the attacks to the police and, indeed, are not required to do so under federal rules. If and when administrators tell state regulators, as required by law within twenty-four hours, the regulators generally delay the information for days or weeks, thus hindering investigations. According to the GAO, nursing homes often disregard such assaults on patients because they fear both bad publicity and state sanctions, while victims, relatives, and staff tend to be afraid of reprisals. At times, the crime is discovered only after a resident is taken to the hospital. Moreover, even when the facilities are charged with abuse or failure to look into the wrongdoings, state agencies frequently recommend "corrective action" rather than civil monetary penalties or criminal charges; relatively few cases involving abuse are prosecuted.

In reaction to the flurry of shocking government reports and expert testimony during the Senate hearings in the 1990s, some House members became more concerned. In 1999, a number of them requested the staff of the Committee on Government Reform to conduct special studies evaluating nursing homes in their district or state (HGR, 1999, 2000 b–d, 2001c–f). As expected, all of the inquiries revealed that few facilities "were in full or substantial compliance with federal standards during their most recent annual inspection" (HGR, 2000c, 1).[37] In other words, the overwhelming majority of homes "had at least one violation with the potential to cause more than minimal harm to residents" (HGR, 2000c, 2); many of them had a continuous history of such dangerous conditions. In Texas, 55 percent of the institutions "had violations that caused actual harm to residents or placed them at risk of death or serious injury" (HGR, 2000b, 2).[38] Documented injuries included untreated pressure sores, dropping residents on the floor; unsanitary and unsafe conditions; improper dispensing of medication; failure to administer required drugs (including pain medication and insulin) or monitor feeding tubes sufficiently; medical errors; lack of basic medical care; physical, sexual, and verbal abuse of patients; improper use of restraints; malnutrition; and dehydration.

The several special House reports also uncovered patient abuse, mistreatment, and neglect that were not classified as such. Nor were many of these instances documented in the state surveys. For example, when federal investigators independently visited a nursing home in New York just after an annual state evaluation they detected about "twice as many violations—and over three times as many serious violations—as the state inspectors" (HGR, 2001b, 1). Overall, the "federal inspectors found that New York inspectors committed 'egregious omissions' and missed 'overwhelming evidence of widespread quality of care problems'" (5). In some places, the federal inspectors discovered residents lying in feces and urine; elders stretched out naked and exposed to others; inoperative fire alarm systems; showers hot enough to produce first-degree burns; uncontrolled infections or contaminations by insects and other pests; lack of air conditioning, despite room temperatures of over 86 degrees; failure to maintain an alternate power supply for life-sustaining equipment; cold and inedible meals; poor sanitation in food preparation; a disregard of patients' dietary restrictions; unexplained bruises; limited—or no—basic dental hygiene; and residents who were choking on food (HGR, 2001b).

Moreover, it was revealed that the states were "losing" resident, family, and staff complaints of abuse and neglect; ignoring complaints; neglecting to conduct in-depth investigations; and not carrying investigations out in a timely manner. In the vast majority of cases, the states were not imposing penalties. Thus, though New York boasted a declining number of nursing home violations in recent years and its facilities appeared superior to those of other places, the congressional study suggested otherwise: the favorable state data were more reflective of poor enforcement efforts than enhanced conditions (HGR, 2001b).

In 2001, U.S. Congress Representative Henry A. Waxman commissioned a detailed study (HGR, 2001a) on abuse in nursing homes and in July held House committee hearings on the subject. The final report, which examined physical, sexual, and verbal abuse in American nursing homes from 1999 to 2001 utilizing a wider range of sources than some of the earlier Senate investigations, detailed patient injuries such as broken bones, lacerations, fractures, and choking. It documented that fully one-third of all nursing homes had been cited for physical or verbal abuse, sexual assault, corporal punishment, and involuntary seclusion of residents, a rate double that of 1996. Though some of the growth was possibly due to greater state oversight, most of it represented "an increase in the incidence of abuse" (7). The investigators, as usual, suggested that their assessment probably represented an underestimation of the problems since "abuse cases are especially likely to go undetected or unreported" (8). Subsequently, Waxman introduced his Nursing Home Quality Protection Act of 2001, which was cosponsored by numerous House members. As with other such bills, it languished in committee.

Inadequate Staffing, Criminals, and Poor Care

Numerous government studies and outside experts since the late 1970s have found a direct relationship between staffing and the quality of patient care, including a 1996 Institute of Medicine study (Harrington, Carrillo, and Mullan, 1998).[39] A noted authority in the field, Harrington also argues that the stressful conditions fostered by low staffing levels is a significant factor in the psychological and physical abuse that takes place (SSCA, 1999e). In addition, as shown in earlier chapters, the inordinately high ratio of patient to direct staff in the vast majority of homes renders it physically impossible to provide even basic levels of assistance. Many observers, including researchers, state long-term care ombudsmen, and nursing home personnel themselves, emphatically point to the correlation between a paucity of nurses and aides and such problems as hip fractures, greater urinary infections, pneumonia, pressure sores, dehydration, malnutrition, injury, and hospitalization (SSCA, 1997a, 1999e).

OBRA 1987 did not mandate any specific staffing requirements except that a registered nurse must be on duty for at least eight hours a day and a licensed nurse for twenty-four hours a day.[40] It also inserted the vague condition that nursing homes should have "sufficient staff to attain or maintain the highest practicable physical, mental and psychosocial well-being of each resident" (Nursing Home Reform Act, P.L. 100–203). In 1990, when the legislation was first implemented, Congress requested a two-year study by HCFA to determine whether minimums should be set. The agency did not even begin the task until 1997 and completed phase 1 of the study fully three years later.[41] Its three-state analysis confirmed, once again, the strong association between staff intensity and the quality of patient care. In particular, it found that nurse's aides, the primary direct caregivers, spend less than two hours a day assisting residents, a level detrimental to the latter's health, safety, and well-being. The inquiry revealed that fewer than half of all nursing homes have enough aides to avoid harm to residents (HCFA, 2000a).

Acknowledging the direct relationship between homes that met certain staffing levels and improved quality of care, the Department of Health and Human Services (HHS) established *guidelines* for "preferred minimum" staffing levels of 3.45 hours of nursing care for each resident per day (2.0 hours from nurse's aides; 1.0 hour, registered or licensed nurses; and 0.45, registered nurses). The agency also set "lower minimum" staffing levels of 2.95 hours of nursing care for each resident per day (2.0 hours, nurse's aides; 0.75, registered or licensed nurses; and 0.20 hours, registered nurses), below which the "quality of care in nursing homes may be 'seriously impaired'" (HGR, 2001e, 6). Using a time-motion analysis for HCFA, Dr. John F. Schnelle of the University of California, Los Angeles, determined that in order to provide "humane care," the amount of nursing aide assistance alone may have to be as high as 2.9 hours per person each day. Furthermore, in 1998 a panel of experts recommended a minimum of 4.13 hours of total personal care each day.

Despite ongoing, clearly documented interconnections between decent care and the number of available personnel, there still are no national standards, though some states have enacted their own requirements, generally below HHS's "preferred minimum."[42] Overall, the federal government permits the institutions themselves to decide how much direct nursing care and other assistance each resident will receive. Therefore, operators, for the most part, are free to cut back on staffing to enhance their profits with no penalty at all. Incredibly, the new prospective payment system for paying the facilities takes into account their greater staffing needs for complex cases but does not insist that the facilities meet these levels (SSCA, 1999e).

Indeed, the vast majority of homes do skimp on staff; more than 90 percent nationally have inadequate staffing levels. Over 93 percent of the institutions in Texas, 90 percent in Oklahoma, and 84 percent in Chicago, for instance, failed to meet the HHS "preferred minimum" (HGR, 2000b, 2001c, 2001 e–f). The majority of places do not even abide by the agency's "lower minimums," and very few have personnel levels as high as the recommendations suggested by the panel of experts. According to recent government data, nursing homes that do not meet the HHS "preferred minimums" are the most likely to be cited for serious health and safety violations (HGR, 2000d).

In her work, Harrington (1996) ascertained that the institutions averaged one nursing aide for every twelve residents, with for-profit facilities and those with a very high percentage of Medicaid patients having the most dangerously low levels.[43] At one home in Los Angeles, three assistants were responsible for as many as forty-two residents who were either totally dependent or needed considerable assistance. At another place, two licensed nurses and two aides were assigned to care for seventy-two elders (HGR, 1999).

National policymakers continue to study the question of staffing, searching for ways of "inducing" facilities to hire more help, including additional federal rules and standards, greater penalties, and especially more extensive training of aides, all of which have been successfully resisted by the nursing home industry over the decades. In 2000, Congress attempted to "encourage" additional staffing through monetary means: as suggested earlier, BIPA provided for a 17 percent raise in the staffing component of nursing home reimbursement rates for Medicare (about $1 billion annually) but did not require the facilities to expand their workforce. The GAO (2002l) found, however, that the extra money did not improve staffing ratios; instead, as usual, the funds were used to inflate profits.

States, too, have become concerned about staffing vacancies and shortages. According to a recent GAO study (2001k), over two-thirds of the states are actively seeking to address the issue of nursing aide recruitment and retention. Despite research that shows the lack of relationship between reimbursement and staffing levels (Harrington, Carrillo, and Mullan, 1998), the major approach has been to increase Medicaid payments to facility owners: as of 2002, about twenty-five states have enacted some form of wage-pass-through or wage/benefit supplement. For instance, under its Nursing Home Quality Initiative, in 2000 Massachusetts gave providers $42.1 million ($35 million targeted to wages);[44] the state pledged another $70 million the following year for a 4 percent increase in salaries (Crummy, 2001a).

In reality, the state increases are sorely inadequate relative to need, funding is tied to greater staffing levels in only a few states,[45] and there have not been adequate evaluations to see if the money actually reaches the direct-care staff (*Aging Research and Training News*, 2001; SSCA, 1999e). As a case in point, in 1999 California increased its Medi-Cal funding to nursing homes in order to give workers a 5 percent raise; many aides claim they never received the money. The state's 2000 budget included an additional 7.5 percent raise, again without adequate safeguards (Vogel, 2000). During 1999, nursing homes in Connecticut received an additional $200 million in Medicaid funding, an increase of 10 percent. Yet, both workers and the families of clients claimed that the money, which had no stipulations attached to it, had not generated staffing or salary increases (National Citizen's Coalition, 2001a; Zielbauer, 2001). The following year, the governor earmarked $180 million exclusively for improved staffing and wages but only after SEIU threatened a strike (Swoboda, 1999). It has become increasingly clear that nursing facilities will not put additional reimbursements into staffing unless they are forced to do so.

Both the government and proprietors continue to blame staffing problems primarily on growing vacancy rates, arguing that it is becoming increasingly difficult to find and retain help. In 2000, over 53 percent of private nursing homes (and 46 percent of HHAs) had vacancy rates higher than 10 percent, and in 19 percent of the facilities (and 25 percent of HHAs) they exceeded 20 percent (GAO, 2001k). However, as chapter 4 has shown, unless the government centers on the fundamental determinants of staff shortages—inordinately low wages, few fringe benefits, harsh, inflexible working conditions, heavy and stressful workloads, and profiteering proprietors—the situation will not be substantially ameliorated.

In fact, some states are now attempting to lower standards as a means of responding to the growing scarcity of nurses and nurse's aides, an approach that will only worsen the quality of care (NCC, 2001a). At the same time, Republicans in Congress and the nursing home industry, along with HHS Secretary Tommy Thompson, are seeking to deskill the nursing home workforce even further: they are advocating new regulations allowing the facilities to hire "single-task aides" for specific duties such as feeding residents; these part-time assistants not only would receive lower pay but also would be exempt from the usual training and state abuse registry requirements (NCC, 2001a–b).

In addition to obscuring the real staffing needs of residents, public officials have not even protected them against criminals; the federal government—and seventeen of the states—do not require the institutions to make any criminal background checks on potential employees.[46] Nor is there a federal registry to ensure against abusive personnel (OIG, 1998). Though nursing homes or other long-term care facilities are not allowed to hire direct-care staff with a history of elder abuse, the regulations do not cover nondirect staff, such as housekeepers and food service employees, or individuals committing other violent acts, including child abuse. And abusive aides who have been dismissed without being legally charged can easily slip through the net (GAO, 2002j; SSCA, 1998d).

The evidence suggests that a significant percentage of the people who have been prosecuted for abuse in nursing homes had prior convictions for other types of crimes. Moreover, studies show that about 5 percent of all nursing home employees have criminal records, and in some places it may be as high as 10 percent (OIG, 1998). In an audit of facilities in Missouri, the government discovered that there were nearly 600 workers on a central registry of child abuse and neglect and another 500 convicted or facing court action for mistreatment of the disabled or mentally ill (SSCA, 2000b). Similarly, 5 percent of the staff in eight Maryland institutions—fifty-one people—had criminal records, many of them for such offenses as assault, child abuse, theft, prostitution, and drug possession (Levine, 1998). In Illinois, about 90 percent of the criminals who applied for special waivers to work as aides in nursing homes received them (King, 1998). Consequently, some current and misguided approaches to ease staff shortages by relaxing the already scanty regulations will only increase further the potential for patient abuse.

The Evidence Streams In

Along with the federal studies, congressional hearings, and academic research, various state agencies and task forces periodically launched their own inquiries. In Indiana, for instance, the State Department of Health in 1998 disclosed severe nutritional problems and malnutrition among the elders in its facilities (Williams, 1999). The Colorado auditor reported in 2000 that the state's inspectors were neglecting to spot many threats to the life and well-being of its nursing home residents (*Denver Post,* 2000). Among other findings, the Missouri auditor uncovered an extensive number of nursing home employees in the state with criminal backgrounds (Shesgreen, 2000). In Atlanta, the Long-Term Care Ombudsman Group, which followed up on seventy verified complaints of neglect and abuse at twenty-three nursing homes, found that only five citations were dispensed by the state (*Atlanta Journal/ Constitution,* 2000). Similarly, a Louisiana legislative report noted that though nearly half of the state's facilities were not in substantial compliance with federal regulations, only three of them had been fined by Louisiana's Department of Health and Hospitals. Moreover, the agency collected only half of all monetary penalties due (Cox and Crummy, 2001).

In 1998, Robert Casey, auditor general of Pennsylvania, initiated a three-year audit of nursing homes in his state, with a follow-up inquiry in 2000, unmasking, as usual, a lack of timely investigations of complaints, including residents remaining in life-threatening situations, the downcoding of serious grievances to lower priority status, inadequate checks on criminal backgrounds, a decline in the number of state sanctions, the frequent reduction or elimination of civil monetary penalties as soon as facilities submit a "plan of correction" without adequate—or any—documentation that the deficiencies had been eradicated, and inadequate staffing levels (Casey, 1998a–c). The later audit showed that among the ten nursing homes with the most deficiencies, some actually injuring residents, only half received any sanctions at all—and these were "more lenient than reasonable standards would dictate" (Casey, 2000, 69). In response, the Pennsylvania Department of Health (PDH) issued regulations to improve its complaint investigative procedures. However, it failed to confront most of the foremost issues, including the absence of meaningful sanctions on nursing homes with egregious care problems; PDH continued to require only an unsubstantiated "plan of correction," or, in some cases, in-service training for the aides (Casey, 2000).

In recent years, horror stories also have made the front page of newspapers or have elicited the outrage of editorial writers. Generally incidents involving a particular elder or an entire nursing home, these accounts tend to focus on the most flagrant abuses, ranging from criminal aides, sexual and physical assaults, and improper staffing to health epidemics, fires, facility-related deaths, and substandard care. The press also intermittently has generated longer exposés, sometimes in reaction to the latest government revelations, at other times initiating their own investigations. In November 1998, a six-month investigation for the *Tampa Tribune* by Lindsay Peterson, Vickie Chachere, and Doug Stanley produced the series "Money or Mercy?" Based on inspection data and other information on Florida nursing homes, the reporters uncovered particularly high levels of mistreatment and neglect in facilities serving Medicaid patients and those owned by large chains.

The *St. Louis Post-Dispatch* embarked on a two-year study of institutions in Missouri. In its special August 2001 report, "Aging Dangerously: Inadequate Care in Missouri Nursing Homes," reporters detailed the decline and death of patients because of improper care in specific homes and the minor sanctions they received, concluding that the state Division of Aging either failed to fine the facilities or gave them a "regulatory slap on the wrist" (Young, 2001). Henry Davis and Dan Herbeck's year-long project on nursing homes in New York resulted in a four-day series, "Special Report: Nursing Homes," for the *Buffalo News* from December 9 to 12, 2001. In it, they explored such issues as understaffing, neglect of patients, and particularly the high profits accumulated by owners of the most substandard facilities.

Various other newspapers and magazines have run investigative stories, including the March 1998 *Philadelphia Inquirer*'s four-part series, "Life's Last Chapter: How Well Will We Care?" (Vitez, 1998); and *Time Magazine*'s "Fatal Neglect," in October 1997, exploring maltreatment and dereliction that led to the death of many residents. In 1998, Mike Berens of the *Chicago Tribune* presented a three-part series, "Warehousing the Mentally Ill in Nursing Homes," focusing on the role of Illinois in encouraging the warehousing of volatile, mentally ill younger people in nursing homes since 1995; they, in turn, assaulted elderly residents. In 2000, the *Detroit Free Press* published a three-part series exposing bed rail deaths that were not reported either to the state or the patient's family. In such cases, the patients died after becoming entangled in the rails or attempting to climb over them.

Recently, in 2002 the *Pittsburgh Post Gazette*, jointly with KDKA radio, presented the results of their survey on conditions in Pennsylvania homes; the series ran over the course of a week (Rotstein, 2002a–c). And, the *Atlanta Journal/ Constitution* ran a four-part series, "The Bottom Line of Care" (July 28–August 1), describing the results of their investigation and concluding that the current method of financing nursing homes promotes understaffing, neglect, abuse, and poor quality of care generally, as well as lack of accountability by the nursing home industry (Teegardin, 2002). That same year, the *New York Times*, after a four-month probe, found that since the early 1990s New York had been shifting mentally ill people from costly psychiatric hospitals paid for by the state to locked units in nursing homes partly funded by the federal government through Medicaid. Though saving the state millions of dollars, these special sites were not only unregulated, but they also offered few mental health services (Levy, 2002).

From time to time, these disclosures capture the attention of the public, provoking state legislators to act. For example, a new ombudsman in Indiana complained that she couldn't induce state investigators to take action against even the most seriously substandard homes. After an investigative series by the *Indianapolis Star* in 1998, "The Tarnished Years: Who Will Protect Our Seniors?" however, the Indiana General Assembly began addressing the issues related to poor nursing home conditions (Harris and Fahy, 1998).[47] Shortly after a three-part series by the *Daily News* in New York, Governor George Pataki offered a number of initiatives, including double fines for facilities with substandard care, an improved patient abuse hotline, and criminal background checks on nursing home staff (Calderone and Zambito, 2000).[48] A five-day investigative series in December 1999, "Throwaway People," by Eric Nalder and Kim Barker of the *Seattle Times* unveiled the lack of penalties for crimes against residents of nursing homes and other long-term care facilities. In response, Washington's governor ordered a review of the places cited by the reporters and, along with the state attorney general's office, supported some of their legislative recommendations.

The Industry Response: Some Myths and Realities

Over the decades, the AHCA has fought vigorously against any national or state attempts to impose controls over nursing homes, insisting that the government should work cooperatively with owners instead of penalizing them. The industry has resisted most aspects of the Clinton/HCFA initiatives as needlessly "punitive." More recently, it is actively calling for privatization of the regulatory process itself.

In hearing after hearing, the owners tend to blame ongoing problems on overzealous state regulators and burdensome, confusing rules and regulations. When HCFA expanded the definition of "poorly performing facilities" in 1998 to include those with G-level deficiencies, AHCA rejoined that it was "symptomatic of a regulatory system run amok." The group contended that many G-level citations are dispensed by "overzealous surveyors" and result from trivial deficiencies such as the "cancellation of a painting class" (GAO, 1999h, 1–2). Under pressure from the industry, Congress ordered the first of many studies on the issue. After surveying 107 nursing homes with repeated records of

G-level deficiencies, the GAO (1999l) found that in 98 percent of the cases, the effect on residents had been of a serious nature; two-thirds of the facilities had repeated violations resulting in actual harm to elders, including pressure sores, broken bones, severe weight loss, burns, and death. In the several subsequent government inquiries, investigators consistently debunked the notion that G-level citations were unmerited or trivial in nature; rather, they generally involved "serious neglect and mistreatment of residents" (GAO, 1999a, 1999h, 2000e–g).

Operators also argue that they are blamed for problems that are beyond their control; they maintain that many of the social and medical issues of the frail elderly, such as malnutrition, are complex and not easily prevented (SSCA, 1998b). Research shows, however, that understaffing is one of the major causes of inadequate food and caloric intake in nursing homes. In 1997, witnesses for the Senate Special Committee on Aging hearings on risk of malnutrition, testified that dietary deficiencies were killing thousands of residents who did not get the assistance they required in order to eat properly. Others were fed too quickly, too forcefully, or both. The evidence also suggested that food supplements often were not dispensed, even when ordered. Some other causes of malnutrition in nursing homes—poor basic dental care; improperly fitted dentures; unappealing, inedible meals; and a disregard of patients' food preferences, including ethnic fares—also are related to substandard care (SSCA, 1997a).

As in the case of nursing home bankruptcies, the industry places much of the blame for poor care on insufficient government payments, denouncing the reductions under OBRA 1997 and particularly the repeal of the Boren Amendment. The AHCA and state nursing home associations have lobbied strenuously against minimum staffing regulations, claiming that personnel problems are mostly because of a shortage of workers and low, inadequate Medicare and Medicaid reimbursement levels.[49] They make clear that any mandate for lower worker-to-resident ratios must include greater government payments to them (HCFA, 2000a; SSCA, 1998b, 447) And although they don't oppose criminal background checks per se, they want the government to pick up these costs as well (Calderone, 2001). In some places, such as Missouri, the state nursing home lobby forced the legislature to back down on both new staffing requirements and greater protections against criminals, convincing them that the state would have to bear the extra costs (*Arizona Republic*, 2000). Similarly, the latest nursing home bill in California, aimed at curtailing elder abuse, purposely avoided a mandate for increased staffing levels (Vogel, 2000).

Another major industry battle is over lawsuits, along with the growing cost of liability insurance; about two-thirds of the states now have a patient's bill of rights with provisions permitting elders and their families to sue facilities. In some areas, such as Florida, contingency-fee lawyers are initiating a growing number of legal actions (Smith, 1998b). State nursing home associations in Florida and Texas have been particularly forceful in opposing consumer protection laws, arguing that they encourage unnecessary lawsuits and unreasonable financial awards, draining money from patient care and bankrupting the industry (AARP, 2001a). However, the nineteen-member Florida Task Force on the Availability and Affordability of Long-Term Care, appointed by the state legislature, "found that tort litigation in Florida is not frivolous. Lawsuits involve . . . serious failure-of-care issues" (NCC, 2000, 4). It also determined that much of the liability insurance increases are a result of an unregulated, greedy insurance industry with little competition for its business (NCC, 2000).

Nevertheless, nursing home proprietors threaten that unless such litigation is curtailed, they will close their facilities or leave the state. And some firms have made good on their warning: Extendicare Health Services (EHS) moved out of Florida in 2001 after one of its homes was found guilty of negligence and the patient's family was awarded $20 million. Moreover, the insurance companies have used similar tactics, warning legislators that they will stop offering nursing home liability policies if "burdensome" controls are imposed on them (Peterson, 2000). Consequently, rather than address the underlying issue—negligent, profiteering owners—many states are buckling under to nursing home and insurance industry demands by imposing monetary caps on liabilities, weakening patient's bills of rights, and making it more difficult to take legal action against the facilities.

Though Florida enacted legislation requiring all nursing homes to have liability insurance, effective in January 2002, it also eased their insurance requirements and limited the ability of residents and families to sue them. In particular, it raised the standard of proof "by requiring the plaintiff to prove a conscious disregard of life, health or safety. Before, plaintiffs only had to show that the nursing home had violated the resident's right to adequate care." As a result, lawsuits dropped dramatically (Kay, 2003). Now nursing homes are demanding that caps be placed on lawsuits for noneconomic damages; however, a Republican-led bill to enact the caps was defeated in 1993. Governor Jeb Bush currently is campaigning for the caps while a group of trial lawyers is attempting to place a constitutional amendment on the November 2004 ballot aiming, among other issues, to ensure the rights of nursing home residents to sue for negligence (Dorschner and Wallsten, 2003). In Ohio, a new law enacted in 2002 curtails the type of evidence that can be used against nursing homes, including the results of state surveys. The bill also "shortens the statute of limitations [from two years to one year], dictates who can bring a suit on behalf of a resident, and requires juries to consider homes' ability to pay punitive damages" (Martin, 2002, 1).

The AHCA also has challenged implementation of the HCFA initiative that would focus on chains, maintaining that each home must be judged on its own merit. To date, the United States still does not even have a national database for tracking violations by common ownership. And most states do not systematically collect such information, rendering it difficult to detect large companies with a history of poor care either within a state or nationally.[50] Yet studies indicate that large for-profit corporations tend to have higher than average rates of neglect and abuse.[51] Among four of the six major chains in Florida—Beverly Enterprises, IHS, Vencor, and Mariner Health Group—from 32 to 40 percent of their homes were on the state's substandard list in 1998 (Peterson and Stanley, 1998). In a study of Genesis that year, the fifth-largest nursing home chain at the time, the Service Employees International Union determined that fully one-third of its facilities had been substandard over the prior three years (SEIU, 1998). Sun Healthcare, too, has a poor history: in 1999, nearly 40 percent of the facilities nationwide "had harmed or threatened immediate harm or death to its patients" (Cox and Crummy, 2001, 1). Though the firm owns less than 7 percent of the homes in Massachusetts, nearly one-third of the attacks on residents by other residents in the state—over 350 cases—occurred in its facilities (Crummy, 2001b).

A recent joint investigation of the 761 nursing homes in Pennsylvania by Gary Rotstein (2002a) of the *Pittsburgh Post-Gazette* found that out of thirty-three nursing homes with the worst records of patient care, twenty-four were for-profit facilities. HCR Manor Care, the largest operator in the state, had "serious deficiencies" among its homes 4.5 times more commonly than the state average; 19 percent of its homes fell into that category compared with 4 percent of facilities statewide. An earlier study in 1994 by William Anderson, then a professor at Temple University, Philadelphia, indicated that one contributing factor is the higher staffing levels in the state's nonprofit homes.

Moreover, the level of care often declines after a takeover by a megachain. For example, after a nursing home in Florida was bought out by IHS, there was more staff turnover, fewer supplies, and greater neglect and mistreatment of residents. When Genesis sought to take over homes from the Multicare chain, state officials in Rhode Island were so alarmed about its general record of care that they insisted on an independent third party to monitor the newly purchased institutions (SEIU, 1998). Similar concerns were expressed when Vencor attempted to secure more facilities for itself (Peterson and Stanley, 1998).

Civil monetary penalties have been a major point of contention for the nursing home industry as well; proprietors have been particularly concerned about the provision allowing the government to fine them for each instance of a violation (HGR, 2001a; SSCA, 1999d). In point of fact, as suggested earlier, they receive relatively few fines; penalties are small, especially in relation both to their misdeeds and overall revenues; and when they are imposed, the owners usually negotiate huge reductions.[52] The primary sanction appears to be a "correction plan," with much of the focus on "educating" the aides. Thus, owners who have skimped on staff, seriously endangering the lives and well-being of vulnerable elders, for the most part simply promise to do better.[53] And, as shown, they may dutifully "fix" the problems, but only temporarily.

Moreover, before federal fines can be collected, proprietors have the right to appeal, a process that can take weeks, months, or even years. If they waive their right to a hearing, they automatically receive a 35 percent reduction in their fines. And according to the GAO (2001a), in 1999 and 2000, the government often settled for even greater discounts, sometimes as high as 69 percent, thereby losing millions of dollars. Policymakers argue that "it may be in CMS' best interests to settle for less," given the cost of litigation and the risk of not collecting anything (GAO, 2001a, 3). Some states such as California allow a 50 percent discount on state fines that are not appealed. During 1996, the state collected only about 20 percent of the $2.4 million owed (Thompson, 1997).

The ultimate sanction, closure of a nursing home, is rarely imposed, as nursing home owners are fully aware. Despite ongoing mistreatment and abuse, many facilities are kept open because state officials simply "don't know what to do with the residents" (SSCA, 1999f). Due to a lack of available beds and alternative long-term care options, especially for Medicaid patients, state agencies are reluctant to cut off new admissions to facilities with a history of poor care. And hospitals continue sending patients to these substandard places. In addition, the legal process is time consuming: the state must give the facility a three-week notice that it will lose its license; again, the home can appeal, dragging out the process for long periods. As a result, there were only thirty-seven terminations in 1996, thirty-one in 1997, thirty-three in 1998, and sixteen in the first half of 1999 (SSCA, 1999f).

Conclusion

For the most part, the nursing home industry has had—and continues to have—its way: it has been politically influential from the start. In fact, some politicians in the early years were major nursing home investors themselves.[54] By the late 1960s, the American Association of Nursing Homes—now AHCA—had become a powerful lobby, both at the state and national levels (Holstein and Cole, 1996). A federation of fifty state associations representing over 12,000 nursing homes, assisted living providers, and other subacute providers nationwide, it currently has a strong presence in each state as well as in Washington, D.C. (Wiener and Stevenson, 1998). Along with other groups, such as the Alliance for Quality Nursing Home Care (a coalition of the largest eleven nursing home chains and an umbrella organization of AHCA), the for-profits have spent huge sums on advertisement campaigns and political contributions to protect their interests.

The industry is considered the strongest lobby on Medicaid issues.[55] Since nursing home owners are the most financially dependent on Medicaid, they center their lobbying efforts on state Medicaid policies more than any other group. Kane, Kane, and Ladd observe, "Indeed, nursing homes contribute handsomely to state candidates in absolute terms, as well as in proportion to other long-term care providers" (1998, 63). They have the money to purchase high-priced lobbyists and contribute millions to the campaigns of governors and legislators who support their positions. In California, Florida, New York, and Texas alone, the state associations spent nearly $638,000 in 1996 (Wiener and Stevenson, 1998).

Individuals, too, have contributed heavily: the then-CEO of Integrated Health Services, Robert N. Elkins, paid out over half a million dollars to the Democratic party in 1996 and was invited to three White House coffees with Clinton and one with Gore (Salganik, 2001). Similarly, Alan Solomont, chief executive of ADS group (one of the largest nursing homes in Massachusetts) and a former president of the state's nursing home association, along with his relatives, gave over $187,000 to the Democratic National Committee and Clinton's 1996 presidential campaign. When he was chair of the Democratic Business Council in 1996 and finance chair of the Democratic National Committee in 1997, Solomont met with national political leaders about nursing home industry complaints, particularly its grievances over civil monetary penalties (Pear, 1997).

Industry leaders also serve in top administrative positions, promulgating regulations and advising policymakers on long-term care issues, both at the national and state levels.[56] At other times, operators may work their will through key state officials. Nursing home inspectors, for instance, have testified at congressional hearings that state licensing and enforcement agencies are sometimes run by political appointees who seek to bend over backwards to help out the owners. A representative in the provider's district sometimes interferes directly if the regulators attempt stricter enforcement, overruling their decision to sanction a home (SSCA, 1998b).[57] In at least one state (Missouri), when the Senate repeatedly thwarted a law opposed by the nursing home lobby, consumer groups launched an initiative petition to get around the usual political process. The ill-fated initiative would have provided new regulations for seriously understaffed homes and protected residents against elder abuse (Young, 2002). In addition, as suggested above, when nursing home owners lose out politically, they either sue in court or appeal their sanctions.[58]

In reality, national and state rules more often protect the proprietors rather than the residents themselves. As shown throughout this chapter, such policies range from the safeguard of industry profits, advantageous monetary regulations, and a favorable environment for mergers and takeovers to economic support and a beneficial legal system, including the appeals process. The government also rescues nursing homes when they are in financial trouble as well as allows them a "fresh start" when taken over by a new owner, changeovers that occur frequently. This is particularly the case for facilities with a history of serious deficiencies; the "new entity" no longer bears any of the stigma, or responsibilities, of the previous proprietor (SSCA, 2000b). Moreover, the government often ignores the past record of operators who purchase new nursing homes, no matter how poorly they have treated residents in the past (SSCA, 1998b).[59] Sometimes chains and facilities simply change their names: Columbia/HCA Health Care Corporation became Healthcare Company and, in 1996, Tenet Healthcare; and Vencor became Kindred Healthcare.

Since the beginning of the George W. Bush administration and its even greater emphasis on privatization, devolution of power to the states, and deregulation, protections for the nursing home industry have strengthened. Under recently proposed legislation, the Medicare Education and Regulatory Fairness Act (MERFA) of 2001, facilities would have additional assistance from the government: states would be prevented from requiring proprietors to fix problems or impose any sanctions, including temporary management or a denial of Medicare payments for new admissions, until after the appeals process is exhausted, even if residents were in immediate danger (GAO, 2001l). The act also would broaden the ability of nursing home owners to contest any government regulations in court.

Four years after the first HCFA initiatives, fifteen years after OBRA 1987, and twenty-eight years after the alarming Senate *Failure in Public Policy* reports, policymakers have made little headway in checking the mistreatment, neglect, and abuse of nursing home residents. As Medicare and Medicaid funds continue to flow steadily into the pockets of profiteering and politically influential nursing home owners, there has been a downright (and unconscionable) failure by the national and state governments and the proprietors themselves to protect the vulnerable population they are supposed to care for. Large sums in public money (e.g., $58 billion in 2001) are handed over to the facilities without any assurance that it will be spent appropriately. On the whole, the government has shirked its responsibility for chronically ill elders who are regularly neglected, mistreated, and abused in our nation's nursing homes.

Periodically scandals erupt, drawing attention to the issues, followed by a flurry of government reports and committee hearings. Under the misguided assumption that nursing homes are reformable under current arrangements, some policymakers promulgate new regulations, encourage stronger enforcement, and disburse more money, only to discover that the problems continue unabated. Both at the national and state levels, political leaders investigate and experiment with alternative reimbursement methods and incentives for inducing owners to provide better care.[60] These efforts, however, deflect from the larger issues, primarily that the entire approach to nursing home care in the United States is fundamentally flawed.

Notes

1. Alongside these "charity" institutions, state-run veterans' homes, subsidized by the federal government in 1888, were established in twenty-eight states. According to Skocpol (1995), they were viewed as rewards for honorable service to the nation rather than as shameful places. By 1910, about 5 percent of all Union veterans still alive were residing in such institutions.

2. In 1975, the organization was renamed the American Health Care Association (AHCA).

3. For example, in 1974 Medicaid paid 50 percent of the nation's $7.5 billion nursing home costs; Medicare funded another 3 percent. At the time, there were 1.2 million beds in 23,000 facilities (SSCA, 1995b).

4. As a result of these restrictions, the number of beds per thousand people aged sixty-five and over steadily declined nationally and average occupancy soared to 92 percent (Cohen and Spector, 1996; Minkler and Estes, 1991).

5. Another 20 percent and 10 percent of the facilities were nonprofit or government owned, respectively (Kayser-Jones, 1981).

6. In 1974, 106 publicly held firms owned about 18 percent of the nursing home beds nationwide (SSCA, 1995b).

7. These include such services as laboratories, radiology, drugs, various therapies, and other items and services.

8. For example, in one Oklahoma nursing home, the records showed that seventy-nine residents had received rehabilitation therapy five times a week, but the facility had only two aides available to do the work. Aides testified that they had been told to falsify the records (HGR, 2001c).

9. In 2002, chains owned about 60 percent of all nursing homes in the nation. Overall, about two-thirds of all facilities were proprietary, 28 percent nonprofit, and 5 percent government owned (AHCA, 2002).

10. In retaliation, one nursing home giant, Vencor, began evicting its Medicaid patients in nine states, claiming it was withdrawing from the Medicaid program (Smith, 1998b). The following year, Congress passed a law disallowing the "dumping" of

Medicaid patients unless they had been warned beforehand. Though forced to keep the residents, at least six of Vencor's Florida facilities had their Medicaid funding cut off in October 2000; inordinately low staffing levels had fostered repeated abuse, mistreatment, and neglect of the facilities' inhabitants (*Tampa Tribune*, 2000).

11. These rates were dependent on the relatively high 1995 reimbursable nursing home costs, which would be updated for inflation thereafter. The government set forty-four different payment groups (RUGs).

12. According to Harrington (1996), only 54 percent of nursing home income finances direct and indirect patient care. Depreciation and interest represent another 9 percent; for-profit margins, 9 percent; and ancillary services, 2 percent. In a recent study of three states (Mississippi, Ohio, and Washington) by the GAO (2002k), it was estimated that about 50 percent of nursing home costs were devoted to patient care.

13. After the company went into bankruptcy, he received a court-approved severance package of approximately $55 million (Salganik, 2001).

14. Ventas is a real estate trust (REIT) that owns 215 nursing homes, forty-four hospitals, and eight personal care facilities. The company has been financially strong since its inception. In 2001, it ranked as the fourth-best-performing equity REIT (shares returning 121.11 percent) and in the top 4 percent of all companies traded on the New York Stock Exchange. Ventas receives 98.6 of its revenues—$187 million in 2002—through rent from its primary tenant, Kindred Healthcare, formerly Vencor.

15. HCR Manor Care was one of the only megachains that avoided bankruptcy; it also admits the fewest patients covered under Medicaid, about one-third of its total compared to 68 percent for the industry as a whole (Rotstein, 2002a).

16. At the time of their bankruptcies, Genesis and Sun Healthcare owned approximately 319 and 247 homes, respectively.

17. For example, though Vencor declared bankruptcy, its nursing home operations continued to be profitable; the chain's losses accrued from some of its other investments (GAO, 1999n).

18. For example, Vencor was bought by Kindred Healthcare, a company that now has about 294 nursing homes in thirty-two states. The company received millions in extra public funds in 2001 and 2002 under BBRA 1999 and BIPA. Revenues rose steadily, fully 8 percent in the first quarter of 2002. As of June 2002, IHS, with 300 facilities, is considering whether to sell its assets or emerge from bankruptcy; Kindred Healthcare is the most likely potential buyer.

19. Pennsylvania nursing homes received a $12 per person increase in Medicaid payments beginning on October 1, 2002; they now total $158 daily (Rotstein, 2002b).

20. Accordingly, the Health Care Finance Administration contracts with the states to certify that any facilities under its jurisdiction receiving federal money are in compliance with the national regulations. In addition to licensing nursing homes, the states must conduct annual inspections and investigate any complaints by staff, residents, or their families.

21. The Senate Special Committee on Aging was established in 1961 as a temporary committee but achieved permanent status in 1977.

22. Malnutrition can engender a decreased ability to fight infections and an increased risk of bedsores, confusion, memory loss, hospitalization, drug-induced side effects, and death (SSCA, 1997a).

23. Nursing homes generally use physical and chemical restraints as a means for controlling and taking care of patients with fewer staff. Patients who get in the way of routines, become agitated, have numerous needs, or are labeled as "troublemakers" are likely to be drugged and tied down.

24. HCFA was renamed the Centers for Medicare and Medicaid Services (CMS) on June 14, 2001. However, this book will continue to refer to the agency by its former name.

25. There are no national training, testing, and certification requirements for home health aides; these are left entirely up to the states. In 1996, only eleven states required competency tests; eight states (Alabama, Iowa, Massachusetts, Michigan, Ohio, South Dakota, Vermont, and West Virginia) had no regulations at all.

26. The MDS is an assessment and screening tool used to determine the patient's cognitive, communication, hearing, mood, and behavioral patterns; physical abilities and structural problems related primarily to his or her activities of daily living; any underlying disease conditions; oral and nutritional status; skin condition; activity interests; medication and rehabilitation needs; and discharge potential (GAO, 2002i; Stahl, 2000).

27. A civil monetary penalty can now be imposed for either each day ($50 to $10,000 per day) or each instance ($1,000 to $10,000 per deficiency) when a nursing home is not in substantial compliance.

28. States now determine whether to refer nursing homes to HCFA for sanctions based on twelve deficiency categories from A to L. They are classified by both scope (the number of residents potentially or actually affected) and severity (minimal harm, actual harm, or serious injury or death). If none of the deficiencies are past level C the home is considered in "substantial compliance" or as providing "acceptable care." Levels D to L represent actual harm or potential for harm.

For deficiencies D to I, most homes receive a grace period of thirty to sixty days to correct them; the homes are not referred for sanctions unless they fail to fix the deficiencies. Those facilities at the highest level of severity (J, K, and L) and "poorly performing facilities" (those who have committed repeat serious deficiencies) receive immediate sanctions. However, they have a fifteen-day grace period before any sanction takes effect, and if the institution comes into compliance during this timeframe the penalty is waived. Homes with deficiencies at J, K, or L levels may, at HCFA's option, receive only a two-day notice period (GAO, 1999l).

29. The use of antipsychotic drugs, though still high, decreased from 34 percent of all patients in 1954 to 16 percent in 1998. The percentage of residents in physical restraints declined from 38 percent in 1987 to 11 percent by 1999 (SSCA, 2000b).

30. The other OIG reports are *Nursing Home Survey and Certification: Deficiency Trends* (March 1999); *Nursing Home Survey and Certification: Overall Capacity* (March 1999); *Long Term Ombudsman Program: Complaints Trends* (March 1999); *Long Term Ombudsman Program: Overall Capacity* (March 1999); and *Public Access to Nursing Home Survey and Certification Results* (March 1999).

31. To date, HCFA still can't track problems with specific nursing home chains since it still hasn't developed nationwide ownership data.

32. Overall, the government has pursued money fraud more aggressively than cases involving patient abuses. In the former, expenditures of public money are "justified" by highlighting the financial gains of a suit relative to the costs. And there are no statutes allowing the DOJ (Department of Justice) to litigate human rights abuses by private nursing homes, thus limiting the agency to problems involving financial fraud under the Federal False Claims Act (Smith, 1998a). In 1996, DOJ litigated its first such case, accusing a nursing home (Geri-Med) of defrauding the government by using Medicare and Medicaid funds for inadequate care.

33. In 1999 and 2000, the federal government allocated, under Medicare, an extra $8 million and $23.5 million, respectively, for the nursing home initiatives (GAO, 2000g).

34. Only six of the thirty initiatives were actually implemented at that point.

35. The GAO argued that though the slightly greater incidence of actual harm and immediate jeopardy could be due to more rigorous enforcement, in its estimation staff shortages were the most likely cause (GAO, 2000g).

36. For instance, though Missouri homes were deemed "deficiency-free" by state inspectors in their annual surveys from 1999 to 2000, they had received 605 complaints against them, of which a significant number were later substantiated (GAO, 2000g).

37. The figures for nursing homes in full or substantial compliance were 3 percent in Los Angeles, 16 percent in Texas, 6 percent in the San Francisco Bay Area, and 14 percent in Oklahoma (HGR, 1999a, 2000a, 2000c, 2001b).

38. The corresponding figures for Los Angeles was 19 percent; for the San Francisco Bay Area, 41 percent; and for Oklahoma, 17 percent (HGR, 1999a, 2000c, 20001b).

39. In their national study of Medicaid-reliant nursing homes, Cohen and Spector (1996) observed that RN-to-patient and LPN-to-patient ratios have a significant impact on both resident outcomes (mortality, functional changes, and bedsores) and quality of care. Their study showed that the intensity of professional staff was even more critical than that of nurse's aides.

40. The Institute of Medicine (1996) cautions that not only do we need greater RN-to-resident ratios, but also because nursing home residents are now sicker, the facilities should hire geriatric nurse specialists and practitioners to take care of their more complex medical needs.

41. In 1996, however, HCFA sketched out an interim report on staffing issues.

42. For example, California, Oklahoma, and Pennsylvania nursing homes must provide 3.2, 2.44, and 2.7 hours, respectively, of care each day per resident. In Illinois, the requirements range from 1.7 to 2.5 hours and in Florida from 1.7 to 2.3 hours, depending on the type of facility (HGR, 2000d; NCC, 2001a; Rotstein, 2002c).

43. Harrington, Carrillo, and Mullan (1998) show that there tends to be a relationship between high numbers of Medicaid patients and poor RN and LPN staffing levels.

44. $5 million was aimed at career advancement programs and another $2.1 million for scholarships, education, and job supports for welfare recipients interested in becoming nurse's aides.

45. Oklahoma, for instance, increased its Medicaid reimbursements to offset greater state staffing requirements (GAO, 2002l).

46. *USA Today* investigated 150 instances across the nation involving abuse by home health aides. In a special report, Peter Eisler (1996) found that in 10 percent of the cases these caregivers moved into home care after being excluded from nursing home work because of serious wrongdoing. In fact, most states do not require home health care agencies to conduct background checks, thus paving the way for misconduct by crooks, including theft and abuse. Because there isn't a national registry, criminal aides can move to another state if they are fired. And they generally are not reported by the victimized elder, who may fear retaliation, living on their own without any help, or being placed into a nursing home.

47. The following year, the *Indianapolis Star* ran a four-part update on the series documenting the prevalence of malnutrition and aspiration pneumonia in Indiana homes serving Blacks (Harris and Williams, 1999).

48. Over a three-year period, the *Daily News* annually juxtaposed the excessively high publicly funded salaries and profits of New York City's nursing home owners against the inordinately low staffing and ongoing pattern of substandard care prevalent in their facilities: in 1998, the city's eighty-seven proprietary nursing home owners paid themselves $24 million in salary and earned another $140 million in profits, mostly from Medicaid, and profits grew to $158 million the following year (Calderone and Zambito, 2000; Zambito, 2000; Zambito and Calderone, 2001).

49. Proprietors also argue that caring for the variety of patient needs is too complex for universal staffing levels.

50. Thus, although Missouri and Texas had documented extensive care problems within Chartwell Healthcare homes in the mid-1990s, kicking the owners out of certain facilities and/or fining them hundreds of thousands of dollars, Florida was issuing the company new operating licenses. Soon after, two elders died of dehydration and others were hospitalized because of poor care (De Lollis and Rogers, 1998).

51. In a national study, Harrington, Carrillo, and Mullan (1998) found that for-profit nursing homes overall had 47 percent greater deficiencies than nonprofit facilities and 43 percent greater than government-run institutions.

52. For example, a newspaper investigation of nursing homes in Illinois found that some facilities in the state were not fined or disciplined at all, even for severe, life-threatening infractions (Berens, 1998). Journalists detected a similar situation in Georgia. In some cases, fines that were levied had never been paid. In New York, one home cited for seriously endangering its patients, including the death of one person, did not have to pay anything after it "corrected" its problems (Steinhaver, 2000). Moreover, for many nursing home chains declaring bankruptcy beginning in the late 1990s, civil monetary fines had been slashed considerably under their reorganization plans.

53. Among voluminous examples, residents in the Tampa, Florida, Ybor City Health Care and Rehabilitation Center were soaked in urine and had dried feces on their body; flies were buzzing around them; their clothing was torn and stained with food and drool; many patients were in poor health; and the place was seriously understaffed. State regulators merely imposed a "plan of corrections" on the proprietor

(Chachere, 1998). Another place, which had been banned from new Medicare and Medicaid patients for confining its residents to the basement for twelve hours a day while it was under renovation, was cleared as soon as it submitted its "plan of correction" (Steinhaver, 2000). The examples go on, ad nauseam, throughout the nation.

54. Many nursing home owners and lobbyists are or have been state office holders. For instance, George N. Leader, governor of Pennsylvania from 1955 to 1959, owned the Leader Healthcare Organization, a chain of nursing homes in his state. (After selling the company in 1981, the influential Leader, along with his wife and three children, established Country Meadows, which currently operates ten assisted living facilities and is planning three retirement communities in Pennsylvania.)

55. Because of their financial interests, home health agencies generally have a greater stake in Medicare policies than in Medicaid policies. Therefore, though they have strong state organizations, especially in places such as New York, they are more likely to exert their power at the national level (Wiener and Stevenson, 1998). Their major national trade organizations include the National Association for Home Care (founded in 1982, it represents just under one-third of the HHAs, including nonprofit, for-profit, hospital-based, and freestanding agencies); the American Association for Homecare (AA Homecare); and the Visiting Nurses Association of America.

56. Some current examples at the national level include Tom Scully (former president and CEO of the Federation of American Hospitals), the current head of CMS; and Thomas Grissom (a former employee of Vencor), a key player in CMS. Moreover, there also tends to be a revolving door: in two states studied by Wiener and Stevenson (1998), high-level government officials ultimately moved into high-paid positions in the state's lobby group or one of its nursing home chains. At the national level, Paul R. Willing, executive vice president of AHCA in 1997, had been deputy administrator of HCFA under President Reagan (Pear, 1997).

57. According to Catherine Hawes, political science director of the Program on Aging and Long-Term Care in North Carolina,

> I have seen health departments where legislators get a call from the nursing home operator in their community that they have just been given this exit interview and they are going to get all of these deficiencies and, "By God, it is just not right. Fred, you have been down here on a Sunday and seen what a good job we do." (SSCA, 1997b, 31)

58. The industry even litigated against the 1987 OBRA law itself.

59. In one particularly egregious case, an operator in Indiana with well-documented incidents of abuse and neglect resulting in at least one patient death was forced to close two of his facilities. However, he was given a license to operate two new nursing homes the following year, which were also forced to shut down because of life-threatening conditions (Williams and Fahy, 1999).

60. From 1995 to 2000, for instance, Colorado gave nursing homes $19 million to encourage them to provide decent care. Yet despite the "incentives," payments went to fifty-five places that had ongoing deficiencies.

8

BECAUSE THAT'S WHERE THE MONEY IS

When asked why he robbed banks, Willie Sutton famously replied, "Because that's where the money is."

ONE PERSISTENT DRIVING FORCE behind excessive and growing Medicare and Medicaid costs has been the problem of uncontrolled fraud. With billions of dollars in public money steadily flowing into nearly one million private coffers, the medical and long-term care funds are an irresistible target for legitimate providers and criminals alike. Profiteering, cheating, and scams are rampant—and getting worse. The health care programs are particularly vulnerable because of inadequate government oversight and controls and few criminal indictments, convictions, or appreciable financial penalties.

Exploitation of Medicare and Medicaid was evident from the beginning. In order to ensure maximum provider participation in and compliance with the programs, policymakers were reluctant to set restrictive rules and regulations. At the same time, doctors and hospitals were generally viewed as responding to a higher ethic, one that did not require myriad outside constraints. Yet, as early as 1969, Frank Moss's Senate investigations and hearings unmasked significant provider abuse and fraud, including gang visits by physicians to nursing homes and hospitals. The first in-depth exposés on Medicaid fraud centered on "Medicaid mills," where doctors would treat hundreds of patients a day in their office, obviously providing perfunctory care. By 1976, it was estimated that such mills accounted for about 70 percent of all program reimbursements in New York City (Jesilow, Pontell, and Geis, 1993).

Congress responded with a series of statutes, including the Medicare–Medicaid Anti-fraud and Abuse Amendments of 1977, referred to in the last chapter. Among the provisions related to fraud, the measures prohibited kickbacks; stipulated that any providers convicted of crimes against Medicare or Medicaid would be barred from further participation in the programs; and expanded the powers of the Office of the Inspector General, established in 1976 to protect the financial integrity, efficiency, and effectiveness of the health care systems as well as to audit them for possible criminal activities (HGR, 1997). It was generally assumed among policymakers that the new laws would reduce the plundering to a manageable level (Vladeck, 1980).

Medicare costs continued to escalate. Alarmed policymakers increasingly focused attention on fraud-related activities. Numerous congressional hearings, some investigating specific industries such as nursing homes, home health care, and medical equipment and supplies, concluded that national controls and enforcement mechanisms were sorely inadequate against sophisticated profiteers stealing from the health care systems. In 1992, Medicare was officially added to the list of programs at high risk for fraud; by the end of 1994, the U.S. attorney general labeled health care corruption as its second most critical concern, with only violent crime ranked higher (DOJ, 1994). The GAO warned that oversight by the Health Care Financing Administration had been lax, inefficient, and ineffective (HGR, 1995). In his book, *License to Steal: Why Fraud Plagues the American Health Care System*, Malcolm Sparrow (1996) maintained that the problems were worsening every year. He found that key government officials viewed the situation as out of control and few believed that sufficient remedies were at hand.

One government response to the growing financial abuses was Operation Restore Trust, launched by the Clinton administration in 1995. The joint national and state program originally concentrated on the billing practices of home health care agencies, nursing homes, and medical equipment and supply firms in five states with the highest Medicare and Medicaid outlays: California, Florida, Illinois, New York, and Texas; by 1997 the initiative was expanded to include six additional states. Congress also enacted the Health Insurance Portability and Accountability Act of 1996. The legislation established the Medicare Integrity Program (MIP) that allows HCFA to contract with new program safeguard contractors (PSCs) to perform specialized fraud prevention tasks, as needed; earmarked Medicare trust fund money specifically for antifraud efforts ($440 million in 1997, with increasing amounts thereafter, reaching $720 million in 2003); provided additional funding to the OIG and Department of Justice for investigating and prosecuting health care crimes, most of which was to be designated for expanding Operation Restore Trust; mandated the creation of a national database that would coordinate information on providers convicted of health care crimes or other adverse actions; and rendered any health care fraud a criminal offense. Though Medicaid has benefited from these efforts, the primary focus has been on Medicare (GAO, 2001e).

Additional legislation followed throughout the late 1990s, especially payment reforms in the Balanced Budget Act of 1997 and the Medicare Fraud Prevention Enforcement Act of 1999. President Clinton proposed (though it was not implemented) even more rigorous measures in his FY 2001 budget, including a team of "fraud fighters" (federal agents who would be placed in every Medicare contractor's office) and greater funding for new technologies to pursue false claims. However, despite intensified and ongoing national strategies to control misuse of the health care trust funds, the large-scale looting of Medicare and Medicaid has not abated to a significant degree and in some industries has risen.

The Financial Dimensions of the Problem

Nobody really knows the entire magnitude of health care financial fraud and abuse or its full costs. Though it did not have hard data, in 1992 the General Accounting Office (GAO) approximated the economic loss within the American health care system overall at 10 percent of total expenditures, or $100 billion (Sparrow, 1996). A full audit of Medicare did not commence until 1996, at which time the OIG estimated an "error" rate of approximately 14 percent of all fee-for-service reimbursements, or $23.2 billion (U.S. Government Budget, 2001b). "Improper" payments were subsequently tallied at 6.9 percent ($12.6 billion) in 1998, 7.97 percent ($13.5 billion) in 1999, 6.8 percent ($11.9 billion) in 2000, and 6.3 percent ($12.1 billion) in 2001.[1] Undoubtedly, these figures obscure the picture considerably since the OIG calculations primarily take into account billing "mistakes," insufficient documentation, medically unnecessary claims, inflated prices and other "erroneous" payments. The agency does not measure the total monetary losses to Medicare due to fraud, scams, and other unlawful behavior.

The full magnitude of financial exploitation of Medicaid has not been determined, though a few states—Illinois, Kansas, and Texas—have attempted to quantify the percentage of unwarranted payments (GAO, 2001e). Nevertheless, fraud and financial abuse are pervasive among the fifty state Medicaid programs, with estimates as high as 25 percent of total program costs (Jesilow, Pontell, and Geis, 1993).

The Medicare Contractors: The First Line of Defense

Dereliction of Duty

Appointed by the Department of Health and Human Services (HHS), Medicare contractors are responsible for all aspects of the claims administration process, including processing and paying bills, identifying fraud, and recovering overpayments. Intermediaries handle claims submitted by institutional providers (hospitals, nursing homes, and hospices), and carriers act on those from physicians, other practitioners, labs, and some suppliers. By 2002, about fifty of these operators were processing nearly 900 million fee-for-service claims (GAO, 2002c). In addition, durable medical equipment regional carriers (DMERCs) and regional home health intermediaries (RHHIs) were established to work specifically with medical suppliers and home care services, respectively.

Under Medicare, all patients receive an explanation of Medicare benefits (EOMB) statement for any services that they receive. If there are discrepancies between the EOMB and the actual services provided, beneficiaries are urged to call their local contractor at the number printed on the notice. Such problems could include services not rendered, unnecessary supplies, or undue charges. In turn, the operators, each of which must establish a fraud control unit, are expected to investigate these complaints for possible fraud. Approximately 90 percent of all allegations related to wrongful billings are from the beneficiaries themselves, fully 75 percent of whom assert that they pay close attention to their statements (GAO, 1991).

For the most part, however, contractors do not take beneficiary complaints seriously. In some cases, seniors reporting an unwarranted payment have been told by the telephone staff to ignore the claim since "It's not coming out of your pocket" or "It's too small. Don't worry about it" (HGR, 1995; SJ, 1994). In an examination of five Medicare carriers, the GAO (1991) monitored the trajectory of beneficiary complaints, most of which pertained to services and supplies that they did not need and/or had not received. Among other problems, it found that over half of the phone calls, including complaints related to potentially criminal misconduct, were not referred to fraud units. Instead, the elders were encouraged to submit their concerns in writing or work it out with providers on their own. The GAO further noted that such negligent behavior was not taken into account during HCFA's evaluation of its contractors' performance.

In March 2001, I called a local contractor, complaining that my mother-in-law had received an EOMB statement with Medicare charges for flu shots allegedly provided to her long-deceased husband. I was told that the contractor didn't have a fraud unit. When I spoke to a supervisor, insisting that her company had a large investigative department, she informed me that I couldn't contact them directly because they didn't have any phones![2] Finally, after repeated communication with HCFA over several weeks, I was able to initiate an "investigation." Six months later, again after repeated phone calls both to HCFA and the contractor, I was advised that the wrongful billing was due to a clerical "error."

Placing too much reliance on challenges by clients also is highly problematic since providers can submit fraudulent claims for elders who are not capable of acting on their own behalf. For instance, mentally impaired recipients in nursing homes obviously cannot effectively monitor their own EOMB statements. Moreover, beneficiaries often must navigate automated telephone systems with complicated menus (HGR, 1995).

The contractors have an obligation to catch questionable invoices through prepayment and postpayment safeguard procedures as well. Such reviews include computerized screening processes to identify and reject claims that are not billed properly, are duplicates, or do not meet Medicare guidelines. Special computer software also earmarks particular types of billings for routine manual review. Additionally, complex or focused medical review, in which trained specialists evaluate actual medical records and other documentation secured from providers, can be performed either prior to or following reimbursement. Contractors are supposed to target providers with particularly high levels of billing irregularities as well as those providing services known to be associated with excessive charges. They also are responsible for performing interim rate reviews and cost report audits of all providers who are paid on a cost-plus reimbursement method so as to assure the legitimacy of their expenses and confirm that Medicare has served as the payer of last resort, as required by law.

Despite concern by policymakers over billions of dollars in unwarranted payments and fraudulent activities, the actual percentage of claims reviewed by hand declined from 17 to 9 percent from 1989 to 1996 and the number of cost-report audits of hospitals, home health agencies, and nursing homes fell to 8 percent (GAO, 1997b). By 2000, fiscal intermediaries were expected to manually assess only 2 percent of claims prior to and .04 percent following payment (GAO, 2001l). According to the GAO, "This [meant], for example, that a home health provider has only a slim chance of having its claims, its year-end cost reports, or actual provision of services carefully scrutinized by Medicare" (1997b, 1).

Furthermore, compared to private insurers, the electronic claims processing systems used by many Medicare carriers are seriously antiquated. In fact, as of 1995, twenty contractors had technically advanced equipment that they used only for their private-sector clients (SA, 1995). Most of the operators do not even have screening procedures for some expensive procedures such as echocardiology, chest X-rays, and colonoscopies. Nor are the computers programmed to search for highly questionable situations such as a sudden escalation in the level of a provider's charges or an implausible amount of services rendered in a given period (GAO, 1997b). "Even claims that are patently absurd will be paid, unless, of course, they happen to contain one of the specific procedural billing violations that trigger rejection" (Sparrow, 1996, 167). For example, durable medical equipment regional carriers "pay many high-dollar, high-volume claims without review" (GAO, 1995c, 7). In one case, a contractor, which had paid a supplier $211,900 for surgical dressing claims over a three-month period, reimbursed the same provider $6 million the following year without triggering any of the automated screening devices (GAO, 1997b). Moreover, computer programs are incapable of detecting certain types of corruption such as kickbacks, forgeries, or services not rendered (GAO, 2001l; HB, 2000b).

If improper payments are uncovered, contractors must attempt to recover the money. On the other hand, whenever fraud is suspected, they are supposed to develop the facts and, if appropriate, refer the case to the IOG for further investigation. However, such endeavors entail significant staff time and money and require accurate and detailed documentation, data analysis, an examination of medical records, and even, at times, interviews with beneficiaries (GAO, 1997b). Thus, in order to enhance their profits, the contractors tend to dispose of problems as quickly, effortlessly, and inexpensively as possible: they emphasize billing "errors" and the collection of "overpayments" rather than ferret out patterns of criminal behavior. And they often just give unscrupulous providers a warning or refer them for education and training.

Even beneficiary complaints that are sent to fraud units generally are treated as isolated events and are not fully examined; in about three-fourths of the cases that involved "substantial indicators of potential fraud and abuse," contractor personnel opted merely to recoup the "overpayments." In one instance, a case against a provider with twenty-three similar complaints against him was dismissed as due to clerical "errors"; he only had to refund the money (GAO, 2001e). In its recent evaluation of contractors, the OIG testified before an HEC subcommittee that "allegations of fraud were being lost during the overpayment adjustment process," fewer than 50 percent of the carriers were pursuing any cases for fraud, and less than half were concerned with "program vulnerabilities" HEC, 2001, 5).

In addition, the growth of electronic claims processing per se has created easier and faster means of plundering the health care programs. Though the reimbursement system has become more efficient now, dishonest providers can engage in rapid, wholesale theft. They can bill Medicare exclusively through numerical codes identifying themselves, beneficiaries, procedures, and other required information. Unless specifically requested, participating companies do not submit any supporting documents, thus significantly reducing close inspections and eliminating signatures and other visual material. Because the computer screening procedures are routine and predictable, they can be circumvented by technically skilled scam artists. In essence, as long as the coding is correct and perpetrators avoid statistical extremes, their claims will be paid automatically. "Only excessively greedy or stupid" criminals get caught at this level. The speed of the electronic system also enables them to use a shotgun approach on any weaknesses they discover in the system and quickly disappear with the money (Sparrow, 1996).

Consequently, prepayment review, during which problems can be detected before any money is disbursed, tends to be more effective and efficient than postpayment methods. It also guards against the necessity of "pay and chase" activities, which can be particularly difficult when the ill-gotten gains are sent overseas before the crooked activities are substantiated (GAO, 1999m). Moreover, though contractors can offset debts against future payments, as will be shown later, many providers owing millions to the government drop out of the public health care programs, close down, declare bankruptcy, or become embroiled in litigation. Specifically, fifteen home health agencies that ceased operations between 1997 and 1999 owed $73 million, of which only $5.3 million was ever collected (GAO, 2000c).

The contractors also tend to be slack in their attempts to recover disallowed charges. In 1999 alone, $7.3 billion or 54 percent of the total had not been recouped. That year, HCFA engaged a private accounting firm to audit account receivables at fifteen carriers and intermediaries. Among other findings, it uncovered $290,000 that a contractor's own private business had not repaid Medicare. If the operators fail to recover overdue money, they are supposed to forward the delinquent accounts to HCFA; HCFA's record, too, tends to be seriously lacking both in vigor and success rates. At one intermediary, where providers owed $59.8 million in 1998, HCFA had only collected $2.1 million, or 3.5 percent, two years later. The agency's efforts are further hampered since many contractors do not promptly hand over their documents, many of them delaying for years (GAO, 2000c).

Outright Fraud

For part B Medicare services, HCFA is obligated to select its carriers from among health insurance companies. The main contractor for part A services is the Blue Cross/Blue Shield Association, chosen by the home health care agencies, nursing homes, hospitals, and other provider groups. The national "Blues" organization, in turn, subcontracts with its local affiliates, which serve as the fiscal intermediaries; their contracts are renewed each year automatically. This noncompetitive selection process raises questions of effectiveness, impartiality, and conflict of interest, accounting for some of the unwillingness and inability of contractors to effectively combat financial fraud and abuse in the Medicare program. Profiteering plays a part in their poor performance as well; a substantial number of them have engaged in questionable and fraudulent activities themselves.

Though they are evaluated annually by HCFA, the contractors themselves provide the information and performance data as well as certify their own internal systems. As a result, inadequate management controls, fabricated materials, and manipulated data have become widespread among the carriers and intermediaries, with little effective oversight by anyone (SA, 2000b). Since 1990, fully 25 percent of the contractors have been accused of dishonest activities, mostly by whistleblowers filing qui tam suits[3] (GAO, 1999d). In one study of twelve contractors in 2000, the OIG testified to the House Budget Committee that many of them had misused government funds, falsified their accounts, and "altered, removed, concealed and destroyed documents to improve their ratings on Medicare performance evaluations" (HB, 2000a, 4).

According to recent testimony by the inspector general, there are continuous investigations of contractors; in 2001 alone, there were twenty-four intermediaries or carriers under review for fraudulent practices. Since 1993, such probes have resulted in over $350 million in settlements with fourteen contractors, two of them pleading guilty for interfering with an audit of their activities. In one case, Anthem Blue Cross/Blue Shield of Connecticut admitted that it falsified hospital cost reports, thereby permitting the institutions to overcharge Medicare while improving its own performance record. Though the company is no longer an intermediary, it continues to function as a certified Medicare HMO, with some restrictions. Blue Cross/Blue Shield of Michigan ignored significant overpayments to hospitals, tampered with audit reports, and illegally reimbursed providers with Medicare funds in lieu of its own funds in cases of dual coverage. XACT Medicare Services of Pennsylvania similarly violated the Medicare secondary-payer regulations, pocketing the money instead. Moreover, it did not recoup millions of dollars in wrongful payments, it manipulated samples for audits, and it turned off its automated screening software when processing part B claims (HEC, 2001).

The contractors, which receive cost-based reimbursements for their services, also have claimed excessive (and unlawful) sums for the Medicare share of their business. An OIG audit of Independent Blue Cross of Philadelphia, for example, discovered over $4 million in questionable administrative expenses from 1995 to 1997 (OIG, 2001a, September). Blue Cross and Blue Shield of Montana was found to have exorbitant executive salaries and insufficient documentation of its indirect expenses, amounting to over $211,000 from 1997 to 1999. Trigon Blue Cross and Blue Shield had "overpayments" of $3.5 million for charges that were "unallowable, unreasonable . . . or unapproved by [HCFA]" (OIG, 2001). And in 1998 and 1999, AdminaStar of Indianapolis, overcharged Medicare nearly $5 million in administrative costs that included exorbitant salary increases, erroneous employee benefits, cost overstatements, and numerous clerical "errors" (OIG, 2002a).

In fact, the contractors exploit whatever payment scheme HCFA adopts. In one experiment with fixed-price contracts, in which the government allowed them to keep any savings, they engaged in rigid cost-cutting activities that boosted profits while fostering even more negligence in their duties. Under another method, incentive payments, the contractors increased their earnings by misrepresenting their performance results (GAO, 1999d). Despite these conspicuous failures, HCFA continues to propose allowing greater "flexibility" in payment methods as a means of improving contractor performance and accountability (GAO, 2001f).

Medicaid

As already indicated, Medicaid is administered separately by the fifty states through their respective agencies, generally located within health or welfare departments. Each state has its own rules, procedures, and methods for assuring the financial integrity of its programs. There are only a few national requirements (e.g., Medicaid agencies must verify that providers have a valid professional license before providing them with a pin number). HCFA also directs them to enter basic information into the central Medicaid Management Information System (MMIS), a charge ignored entirely or only partially adhered to by half of the states (OIG, 2001b).

These state agencies have the primary responsibility for all aspects of the Medicaid program: they enroll and credential providers, ensure the accuracy of claims, recover wrongful payments, protect the quality of services, and exclude incompetent providers or perpetrators of health care crimes from further participation in their state's program. Similar to Medicare, most states use automated computer screening software to conduct prepayment and postpayment claim reviews, though their degree of effectiveness varies, particularly since many of them do not have highly sophisticated fraud detection software packages (GAO, 1999b). Most of the Medicaid agencies also have surveillance and utilization review subsystem (SURS) units to identify aberrant billing patterns and corrupt providers.

State Medicaid Fraud Control Units (MFCUs), most of which are part of their state attorney general's office, pursue criminal investigations and prosecutions both for financial fraud and patient abuse and neglect in nursing homes, hospices, and other Medicaid-certified residential facilities. In 1999, Congress expanded their charge, allowing them to pursue Medicare cases that are associated with Medicaid. The agency that processes the claims and its SURS unit are supposed to refer questionable cases to the MFCU. However, as with Medicare contractors, the SURS unit must painstakingly develop them first, an effort they often eschew because of insufficient personnel and funding. Moreover, since they receive more credit for recovering money than for developing and referring potential fraud cases, the units generally prefer to classify wrongful activities as overpayments (GAO, 1999b). At the same time, the MFCUs may not even pursue cases forwarded to them, because of their considerable backlogs, among other factors (GAO, 1999b). In a major study of state Medicaid agencies and MFCUs from 1999 to 2001, the GAO found that they tended to be severely underfunded and understaffed (GAO, 2001e).

State Medicaid agencies tend to be lax in their enrollment and credentialing duties, as well. In fact, because their payments are commonly lower than those of both private insurance companies and Medicare, there can be a shortage of Medicaid providers, fostering a reluctance to establish stringent rules and restrictions that might discourage current or future participation in their programs (GAO, 1999b). Indeed, only a few of the agencies thoroughly check the credentials and qualifications of providers or engage in other essential activities aimed at excluding fraudulent firms (GAO, 2000b). In 2000, the OIG determined that only one state does criminal background checks on all, and nine states on some, of their Medicaid-certified providers; ten states conduct onsite office visits to verify that providers have a bona fide business; and eight states authenticate telephone numbers. Nineteen states do not independently check provider enrollment information, a practice mandated under Medicare rules (OIG, 2001l). And many states do not provide explanation-of-benefit statements to beneficiaries, rendering it difficult to know if services were even provided (GAO, 2001e).

The overall performance record among the states is quite uneven. For example, Kentucky, Texas, and Washington have pursued improper claims energetically, using enhanced computer technology systems (GAO, 2001e). And, Connecticut, Georgia, Florida, and New Jersey have tightened their operations or eligibility rules over the last several years (GAO, 2000b). However, few states are actively engaged in preventing, seeking, or catching fraudulent providers. Most of their endeavors are extremely limited, particularly given the scope of the problem (Sparrow, 1996).

Gaming Multiple Systems

Criminal health care providers can have multistate operations, move from state to state with impunity, and exploit both Medicare and Medicaid. Yet, there is a conspicuous lack of coordination between Medicaid fraud offices and Medicare contractors as well as among the state entities themselves. In many places, Medicaid agencies and their own MFCUs have experienced difficulty in sharing information, and some even have outright rivalry between them (Sparrow, 1996). Thirty-five state Medicaid agencies do not regularly contact the Medicare contractors in their area for past or current problems, nineteen fail to adequately communicate with their fraud units, and forty-eight ignore private insurance companies (OIG, 2001b). As a result, corrupt providers can defraud multiple systems either simultaneously or sequentially (SSCA, 1994). In 1997, HCFA instituted the National Medicaid Fraud and Abuse Initiative Partnership to encourage greater information sharing and training; its efforts, however, are dwarfed by the enormity of the issues (OIG, 2001b).

Furthermore, state Medicaid offices and MFCUs are supposed to report to the OIG providers who have been removed from their programs so that the agency can assess whether they should be banned nationally. In actuality, states often fail to forward the required information to the OIG; files sent to it are either lost or not processed expeditiously—sometimes for over a year; most states do not cross-check national lists against their own rosters; federal and state data often are incompatible; and there aren't universal identifiers, rendering it difficult to detect and track dishonest providers across states and programs (GAO, 1997a). Furthermore, companies suspended by Medicare and Medicaid can shift their fraudulent practices to private insurance plans. Thus, providers excluded in one state generally can continue their financially abusive practices in other states as well as receive reimbursements from the Medicare program and commercial companies.

Punishing the Perpetrators: Mistakes, Financial Abuse, and Fraud

At the national level, the OIG has a number of responsibilities related to the health care programs. First, it initiates audits and evaluations of the Medicare program and when it uncovers problems, forwards proposals for reform to HCFA. Second, the agency oversees the MFCUs, including issuing an annual certification that they are in compliance with federal regulations. Third, it investigates health care crimes for possible indictment and prosecution by the DOJ, which applies sanctions, if warranted. Cases are referred to the OIG from the Medicare contractors or they can initiate probes on their own. The OIG also develops specific MFCU cases, including those that are multistate (GAO, 2001e). Fourth, the OIG has the authority to impose civil monetary penalties for false or improper claims against Medicare or Medicaid and exclude individuals or entities committing unlawful or abusive acts from further participation in the programs.

The government defines "health care fraud" as purposeful misconduct that requires proof of intent to cheat the federal and state programs. All other provider practices that violate billing rules and policies, ranging from coding errors to misrepresentation and deceit, are considered "financial abuse" (GAO, 1991, 1997b). Though policymakers may attempt to differentiate between the two, in many circumstances the demarcation between fraud and abuse under Medicare and Medicaid is fuzzy at best. For instance, when Congress cuts reimbursement levels, some legitimate providers seek to maintain what they view as their rightful income levels. They basically push the envelope in order to gain maximum revenue, with at least some of their activities bordering on fraud.

Both the health care industries and public officials exploit the thin line between "oversights" and criminal activities to downplay questionable practices. When providers are challenged, they claim that a clerical error was made, blaming it on the complexity of the rules and regulations. The OIG identifies "incorrect" coding as the third-highest cause of improper payments, accounting for $1.7 billion in Medicare funds during 2000. Notably, the vast majority of providers receive a higher—not lower—reimbursement rate than warranted by the documentation (SF, 2001b). Though it is difficult to distinguish among such factors as ignorance, sloppiness, and duplicity, the "mistakes" rarely favor the government health care systems (Jesilow, Pontell, and Geis, 1993).

Investigators, too, argue that it is difficult to separate fraud from other conduct. When investigating a particular case, they ask such questions such as "Was there a genuine, isolated mistake? Was it part of a persistent pattern of mistakes resulting from a genuine misunderstanding of the regulations? Was it reckless disregard for the rules? Or was it a deliberate attempt to steal? (Sparrow, 1996, 140). Yet, growing numbers of "legitimate" providers are hiring new types of billing consultants—accountants, attorneys, and other business advisors—who may recommend that firms not report or even pay back any overcharges after they are discovered; advocate reimbursement maximization techniques that are illegal and difficult to detect; and offer ways to disguise claims for services that are unnecessary or double billed. (SF, 2001a)

Though Medicare contractors, MFCUs, the OIG, and the DOJ struggle with complex definitions, terminology, and intent in health care cases, government agencies and law enforcement departments generally do not anguish over such ambiguities in other, similar situations. For example, if a bank customer spends the $100,000 that was inadvertently credited to his or her account, nobody would assume that it was done "in error." Nor would anyone question the intent of individuals using credit cards that are not their own.

DOJ prosecutors, who have considerable leeway in which cases they will pursue as fraud, tend to avoid white-collar infractions such as cheating the health care systems (Jesilow, Pontell, and Geis, 1993). For one, health care fraud is time consuming, typically taking from two to four years to develop a case sufficiently (Sparrow, 1996). It is also hard to prove. There are two main statutes for litigating civil health care fraud cases. The primary one, the Civil False Claims Act (FCA), covers "offenses that are committed with actual knowledge of the falsity of the claim, reckless disregard of the truth or falsity of the claim, or deliberate ignorance of the truth or falsity of the claim" (Civil False Claims Act, U.S.C.C., Title 31, subtitle III, chapter 38, section 3803). The standard of proof is a "preponderance of the evidence" (i.e., it must be proven that the charge is more likely to be true than not) (Civil False Claims Act, U.S.C.C., Title 31, subtitle III, chapter 37, subchapter III, section 3731). The same standard of proof is required under the Civil Monetary Penalties Law. Such actions as mistakes, negligence, oversights, or disregard of the rules are not covered under either act. Criminal convictions are even more challenging, calling not only for the willful intent to commit a crime but also a standard of proof that is "beyond a reasonable doubt." Given the need to prove specific intent in criminal cases, considerable evidence is required before the DOJ even agrees to indict. For the most part, prosecutors accept only large-scale ($100,000 or more in 1996) and foolproof cases (HGR, 1996; Jesilow, Pontell, and Geis, 1993).

Consequently, at all levels—from contractors and MFCUs to the OIG and DOJ—whenever possible, health care crimes tend to be referred to as "inappropriate," "improper," or "erroneous" claims that are due to "carelessness," "inaccuracies," "omissions," and "misunderstandings." The responsible agencies, then, recommend recovery of "overpayments."

And even when accused of financial fraud, firms are likely to receive relatively lenient fines. Under FCA, the DOJ is allowed to impose damages of up to three times the amount of illegally obtained funds and a penalty—from $5,000 to $10,000—for each false claim (Rosenthal, 2000). The OIG and U.S. attorneys also have the power to negotiate deals, their preferred approach to resolving health care offenses. These settlements tend to be woefully insufficient in relation to both the crime committed and the amount of money stolen, sometimes because the perpetrator threatens to go out of business. Even when repayments are agreed upon or judgments imposed, it is often difficult to collect the full amount due. As a case in point, Rehability Health Services (RHS), which had defrauded the government of $5 million in 1998 by submitting claims for which they had no documentation and for services provided in facilities that lacked certification, evaded repayment by filing for Chapter 11 bankruptcy (OIG, 2001a, August). Firms also can appeal any fines or demands for restitution; in 2000, about half of these actions were decided in favor of providers, mostly at the Medicare contractor level (GAO, 2001l).

Companies that settle with the government are now allowed to continue their participation in the federal health care programs simply by signing a corporate integrity agreement (CIA), in effect from three to five years, that pledges compliance with Medicare and Medicaid rules in the future (HB, 2000a).[4] Though the specific terms of the agreement are negotiated between the firm and the OIG, most providers, among other stipulations, must hire a compliance officer, initiate training programs for their employees, submit to annual audits and reviews by an independent organization, summarize their compliance efforts annually, and establish an organizational code of conduct.

Financially abusive Medicare contractors, too, have been allowed to continue their work by using CIAs; from 1993 to 2001, eight CIAs were imposed on them. In one case, XACT Medicare Services of Pennsylvania had engaged in unscrupulous behavior for at least eight years—from 1988 to 1996—including rigging samples for HCFA audits, failing to recover overpayments, and turning off electronic edits and audits when processing claims. Rather than lose its government contract, the firm continued to administer Medicare money but now under the conditions of a CIA (HEC, 2001).

According to the OIG, "CIAs are imposed on companies to help reorient a corporate culture that may have previously been prone to fraud and abuse" (HCC, 2000b, 21). The underlying assumptions, of course, are that providers who have defrauded the government health care programs do not have to be harshly punished and deserve a second chance, their "mistakes" can be rectified by educating and training their employees, and they can acquire a sense of business integrity through proper coaching and supervision.

In the case of a criminal conviction, Congress has mandated that providers be barred from all federal health care programs for at least five years. Otherwise, the OIG has some discretion in whether to suspend them. In these instances, companies tend to be excluded only in the very worst cases. Moreover, terminations are temporary. Nursing home proprietors convicted of fraud, for example, can resume their participation in Medicaid after five years (Jesilow, Pontell, and Geis, 1993). Perpetrators also can easily circumvent the system; they often have several identification numbers that can be used if their original operation is suspended (GAO, 2001e).

Types of Fraud

There is a vast array of opportunities for defrauding Medicare and Medicaid. System abuse, viewed as a white-collar crime, is committed by otherwise legitimate providers who steadily steal from the federal health programs over a number of years. Their methods include overutilization of services (unnecessary or inappropriate tests and procedures), billing for services and equipment not rendered, code manipulation or upcoding (providing a less expensive service than the one billed for), paying and receiving kickbacks, self-referrals and other antitrust violations, unbundling (billing for individual stages of services that actually should be included in one lesser, overall charge), double billing (submitting the same bill to two or more places), and billing for professional services provided by unlicensed or inadequately trained personnel (e.g., physician assistants in lieu of MDs).

At the same time, new and highly sophisticated types of illicit schemes have emerged. In recent years, criminals with no medical background or interest in health care whatsoever are exploiting the federal health care programs for billions of dollars with a variety of get-rich methods (GAO, 1999m; HGR, 2000a). In a study of seven cases between 1992 and 1998, the GAO (1999m) found that career gangsters were implicated in Medicare, Medicaid, and private insurance fraud throughout the nation.

In the "hit and run" ploys, for example, an individual sets up a bogus operation (or simply a mailbox), obtains a provider identification and lists of beneficiaries, and bills one or both of the health care programs for millions of dollars over several months before moving on, using a new PIN. Data can be stolen from legitimate providers, acquired on the black market, or even bought from program recipients themselves (Sparrow, 1996). Others defraud the government by using people who are in jail or dead: from 1997 to 1999, $32 million was illegally paid by Medicare for 7,438 prisoners; in one state alone, Medicaid disbursed $82 million to 4,000 different providers over six years for services allegedly rendered to deceased beneficiaries (SF, 2001b).

Swindlers often prey on the vulnerable; in rent-a-patient schemes, recruiters are paid a fee to bring clients to clinics for unnecessary tests, treatments, and supplies. The enlisted "patients," the vast majority of whom are poor, mentally ill, homeless, or have language difficulties, are enticed by the money (GAO, 1999m; SSCA, 1994). Hustlers also lure unsuspecting customers by offering free medical goods and equipment through telemarketing (DOJ, 1994). Some of the wide variety of scams, deceitful activities, and questionable practices are detailed below.

The Profiteers

Everyone is cashing in on Medicare and Medicaid. The scope of criminal misconduct is enormous, encompassing nursing homes, home health care agencies, hospitals, physicians, psychiatrists and psychologists, durable medical equipment (DME) suppliers, transportation services, laboratories, dialysis firms, drug companies, pharmacists, community mental health facilities, substance abuse centers, and transportation companies.

Nursing Homes

Clearly, nursing homes loom large among unscrupulous health and long-term care businesses. One of the specific targets of Operation Restore Trust, they serve as a breeding ground for fraud.[5] In addition to the financial and patient abusive practices discussed in chapter 7, the facilities and their suppliers utilize numerous other methods of looting the public programs. Moreover, because their ploys can be executed in volume and large numbers of residents are cognitively and physically impaired, the swindlers not only can easily defraud the government, but they also can reap thousands of dollars in one fell swoop. Such crimes are difficult to prove given the state of beneficiaries who generally are unaware of what is being billed in their name. I will briefly sketch only a few additional issues here, since nursing homes have already been covered in the previous chapter.

First, facilities frequently bill for unnecessary services or for services never rendered. One such scheme uses Medicare case-mix adjustment formulas to swell their revenues: institutions receive a per person payment for daily care that is augmented for more complex cases; however, funding is based on consumption rather than on actual patient need. "Thus, a facility could increase a patient's reported service use merely to increase payments" (SA, 2000a, 6). They also claim reimbursement for patients already discharged or deceased, overcount the number of Medicaid patients, and "misrepresent" services by charging for more complex care than that actually delivered (HGR, 1997).

Second, some places bill twice for the same items or services, presenting claims to both Medicare and Medicaid for dually eligible patients; such unsavory practices tend to be difficult to detect since there is a lack of coordination between the two programs.[6] In addition, nursing homes that receive funding for a patient's full care under Medicaid's per diem rate also can surreptitiously bill both health care programs separately for particular items. For instance, several facilities required to provide nonemergency transportation to dialysis centers as part of their set rates billed Medicare or Medicaid additional amounts for the ambulances. Another fraudulent "double dipping" practice is to inflate cost reports by shifting already paid Medicare part B services to Medicaid cost reports, thus augmenting overall expenses and future reimbursements (HGR, 1997).[7]

Third, owners often inflate administrative expenses, sometimes filing false cost reports that include personal and family expenses such as trips, entertainment, and home improvements (HGR, 1997). In one case, the U.S. Attorney's Office charged a proprietor of nineteen homes in Pennsylvania with billing Medicare and Medicaid for management functions that were not performed, fictitious staff, and personal expenses. The proprietor also drained the facilities financially (Bauer, 1999). Many nursing homes routinely embezzle patients' assets, despite express legal prohibitions against such practices. Even the tiny monthly personal needs allowances paid to Medicaid patients can find their way into the nursing home's pocket.

Fourth, some facilities illegally allow outside vendors access to patient records and their beneficiary numbers, opening up possibilities for others to cheat the system; prior to the consolidated billing rules, they could bill Medicare directly, without anyone else authorizing or even being aware of whether or not the services were necessary or actually delivered. Sometimes the owners receive kickbacks from suppliers, including money, vacations, tickets to special events, and other "gifts." Such actions are particularly difficult to prove in criminal cases since prosecutors must show, beyond a reasonable doubt, that there was a quid pro quo (HGR, 1997).[8]

Home Health Care Agencies

As Medicare spending for home health care escalated during the 1990s and the number of agencies—particularly those in the for-profit sector—expanded to take advantage of the new largesse, financial abuse accelerated commensurately. HHAs are particularly susceptible to fraudulent practices because of the isolation of the setting, difficulty in ferreting out falsified or low-quality care, vulnerability of beneficiaries, lack of rigorous requirements for certification in many places, and sorely inadequate government controls.[9] Moreover, although the volume of services expanded, Medicare's inspection of HHA claims by its intermediaries dropped even more dramatically than its overall review rate, from 62 percent in 1987 to only 1–3 percent in 1998 (GAO, 1997b–c; SSCA, 1998g). Consequently, "few claims were subject to medical review and most were paid without questions" (GAO, 2000e, 7). According to the GAO (1997a, 8), this lack of scrutiny has "made it nearly impossible to determine whether the beneficiary receiving home health services qualified for the benefit, needed the care being delivered, or even received the services being billed to Medicare."

Home health agencies are one of the largest provider groups bilking Medicare. A 1995 OIG inspection of Florida firms found that about one-fourth of all services billed to the program should not have been paid (GAO, 1997c). In a 1997 audit of contractors in four states, the GAO reported that fully 43 percent of the Medicare claims were unwarranted. The OIG duplicated the study in 1999: even after two years of concerted national effort and considerable funding, it found that 19 percent of the claims continued to be unjustified, a figure higher than that for Medicare as a whole (HB, 2000a). The evidence suggests that proprietary firms tend to have the most suspect practices.[10]

"Erroneously" paid claims include services that are unnecessary, excessive, or lack supporting documents. Despite Medicare requirements, physicians resist visiting patients at home and tend to be negligent in their supervisory obligations. According to the director of the Homecare Institute, "Many physicians, upon questioning, admit to signing orders on a continuing basis for the home setting without a full appreciation of what is or is not required by their patients" (SSCA, 1998e, 90). Many certifying physicians never see the patient at all (GAO, 1997c). In an audit of 1998 claims for a Florida HHA, the OIG discovered at least $38.3 million in questionable payments, a problem it partly attributed to inadequate physician involvement (OIG, 2001a, April).

Because of the huge sums involved, with an average annual Medicare reimbursement of $1.6 million per company in 1996 (SSCA, 1998a), HHAs are susceptible to massive criminal activities as well. Indeed, they became one of the three primary targets of Operation Restore Trust. From 1997 to 2000, there were 420 investigations related to home health care fraud alone (HB, 2000b). Fraudulent activities range from kickbacks and disguising personal expenses to billing for phantom services and unlicensed personnel (SSCA, 1994).

The largest private home health care agency in the country, First American Health Care of Georgia (formerly ABC Home Health Services), with 15,000 employees in twenty-one states, depended on Medicare for 95 percent of its revenues, or about $616 million annually (GAO, 1995b). From 1989 to 1996, the company and its owners were charged with altering and forging patient records; using Medicare money for personal items; ordering employees to increase home visits, even when not needed; receiving and giving kickbacks; tampering with witnesses; laundering money; and committing a host of other felonies. The company immediately filed for bankruptcy protection and eventually entered into a civil settlement agreement for $255 million, a sum that was paid by Integrated Health Services when it bought out the company in 1996.[11] Though First American Health Care was excluded from Medicare and Medicaid for seven years, it was able to continue its participation in the health care programs under its new owners (OIG, 1996).[12]

In an attempt to deter dishonest businesses, Congress proposed, under BBA 1997, a surety bond of at least $50,000 for HHAs participating in the Medicare and Medicaid programs. Its aim was to render it easier to collect overpayments from these entities, many of which go out of business before the money can be recouped (SSCA, 1998a). However, this was hotly contested by the national and local home health care associations as overly burdensome, and this provision was removed.

Hospitals

Hospitals, most of which are now for-profit institutions, are another leading recipient of "overpayments." Similarly to other providers, they claim that most of the overcharging is due to the difficulty in deciphering Medicare's complicated rules and regulations.[13] These "inadvertent errors" include billing separately for procedures that should be included in the DRG price. For example, a government audit found that most hospitals were double billing for certain diagnostic tests. However, even after they were explicitly told that this was in violation of Medicare regulations, many of them continued the practice until it was referred to the DOJ for possible prosecution (Zaldivar, 1997). They also have made such "mistakes" as concealing the personal expenses of executives in their Medicare charges as well as assorted coding "oversights," nearly all adding substantially to hospital coffers (SJ, 1994).

In an audit of hospital claims from 1992 to 2000, the OIG (2001e) found over 153,000 cases of miscoding patient transfers to subacute settings as discharges instead of relocations as required under Medicare rules. As a result, the hospitals received $233 million more than they were entitled to. In another example, a physician and medical consultant, Richard Newbold, discovered during the course of his research that hospitals were upcoding their fees for pneumonia. With a $2,420 difference in DRG-allowable charges between common viral and bacterial pneumonia, the institutions were consistently billing Medicare and Medicaid for the higher amount, regardless of the actual diagnosis. In 1996, Newbold filed a whistleblower's lawsuit against 100 hospitals under the False Claims Act, which led to multiple financial settlements with HCFA. Despite purposely defrauding the government, none of the hospitals was excluded from participation in the federal health care programs (Taylor, 2001).

Columbia/HCA HealthCare Corporation, Medicare's single largest biller, alone settled for about $800 million in "overpayments" and criminal fines.[14] Its transgressions included upcoding, unbundling, medically unnecessary services, kickbacks, and inflated cost reports (OIG, 2001j; Taylor, 2001). Further investigations found extensive fraud, including financial incentives for physicians to refer clients to their hospitals and associated health care facilities, bribes, and unethical activities related to its acquisition practices. More recently, Quorum Health Group, Inc., which owns a number of acute care hospitals, agreed to a $77.5 million settlement with the government for submitting fraudulent Medicare cost reports (OIG, 2001j).

Hospitals also comprised two of the three most sizable and questionable HCFA settlements in the 1990s.[15] In one case, the hospital had billed Medicare for bad debts and other charges without any documentation. The hospital forced HCFA to accept just $28 million of the $79.4 million owed, threatening to curtail needed community services otherwise. In the other instance, HCFA agreed to a refund of only $25 million out of the $155 million owed. Bruce Vladeck, head of the agency at the time, had previously been a member of that hospital's board of directors. Its assistant vice president for corporate reimbursement services told GAO investigators, "It is common practice for the hospital to use political influence or interference with HCFA to achieve resolution to disputes" (GAO, 2000a, 36). Government attorneys had not even reviewed the final deal nor did HCFA preserve any records, including a copy of the settlement. In both hospital cases, the agreements contained a confidentiality clause at the request of the providers (GAO, 2000a).

Physicians

As a group, physicians have one of the highest levels of billing "irregularities." Yet, they view themselves as subject to a professional morality, insisting that they are the victims of overly zealous government investigators and burdensome regulations. Physician services sometimes can mean the difference between life and death and, as such, they are held in high esteem by large segments of the public. Even convicted doctors "often insist that their crimes were merely the consequence of their being too involved in heady medical matters to attend to the niggling red tape of the programs that were paying them" (Jesilow, Pontell, and Geis, 1993, 11).

The growing commercialization in the practice of medicine has infused business principles into medical ethics, allowing some doctors to rationalize steady but limited cheating of the health care programs. Others defraud the government more blatantly and expansively. In their study of physician Medicaid fraud, Jesilow, Pontell, and Geis (1993) describe numerous illegal practices such as billing for X-rays taken without film, blood and urine specimens that were never tested, and upcoding of services and procedures. Investigators have documented a range of medical "misconduct," including charges for services never rendered, unnecessary treatments and surgery, overutilization of physician-owned equipment and facilities, various methods of upcoding (e.g., cutting toenails but billing for orthopedic surgery), bribery, and kickbacks (Anders, 1997; HGR, 1996; SSCA, 1994).

Four private firms, commissioned by the GAO, analyzed a sample of physician claims submitted to Medicare during 1993 and found that unbundling was one of the most common practices (SA, 1995).[16] Duplicate billing has surfaced as another way in which doctors exploit the system. In a study of physician services in 1998, the OIG scrutinized eighty-six providers, taken from a national sample, who billed more than one Medicare contractor. It reported that nearly 25 percent of the providers had sent identical claims to multiple carriers, a problem that was not detected by any of the contractors' automated screening software. The physicians alleged that they were unaware of the double billings and that they were caused by confusion over policy changes, or they gave other "explanations" for the "mistakes" (OIG, 2001h). In a follow-up study, the OIG analyzed duplicate billings to the same contractors and found $93 million in identical services that were paid for at least twice; some of the doctors who had several offices used separate provider numbers on the claims (OIG, 2001c).

Medical practitioners who focus their practice on frail or otherwise vulnerable beneficiaries tend to be somewhat more unscrupulous than physicians as a whole. And they are also the least likely to get caught (Jesilow, Pontell, and Geis, 1993). Some of their most egregious abuses involve nursing home patients. For instance, gang visits by doctors are common. One podiatrist was paid, without triggering any alarms, for each of the 170 weekly surgical procedures he claimed to have performed on residents (GAO, 1997b). Psychologists and psychiatrists have exploited the institutional setting as well. In one case, a psychiatrist regularly gathered disoriented patients in a group but charged the government for individual therapy sessions (SSCA, 1994). In another instance, a therapist was paid for treating seventeen to forty-two patients per day (GAO, 1997b). The OIG, which in 1996 examined mental health services to nursing home patients, concluded that nearly one-half of the claims should not have been paid. A follow-up study in 1999 found that about one-third of the claims were medically inappropriate and that 12 percent lacked any professional documentation, were highly dubious in other respects, or both (OIG, 2001g).[17]

Physicians who defraud the government generally get away with it: "Few physicians who break the laws are apprehended, prosecuted or convicted" (Jesilow, Pontell, and Geis, 1993, 68). Under Medicare, only the most conspicuous patterns of billing problems involving doctors—about 3 percent in 2000—are subject to complex medical review (GAO, 2001l). If serious irregularities are discovered, the contractors generally request partial or full repayment rather than refer doctors for criminal prosecution (Jesilow, Pontell, and Geis, 1993). Despite their collective outcry against what they view as government harassment of innocent medical practitioners, only 4–5 percent of the 650,000 physicians participating in the Medicare program are investigated annually by the OIG (GAO, 2001l). Moreover, because of the difficulty in prosecuting doctors for health care crimes, there are less than fifty actual litigations against them and only about twelve convictions per year (HWM, 2001).

From the earliest days, physicians insisted on self-review of their practices. In 1972, the professional standard review organizations (PSROs) were established, composed exclusively of physicians, to evaluate complaints against hospitals and their medical practitioners, including any violations of Medicare and Medicaid rules. The PSROs proved to be extremely reluctant to discipline either doctors or hospitals, recommending instead that the providers should receive more information from the government and better explanation of the regulations (Jesilow, Pontell, and Geis, 1993). Physicians tend to be particularly protective of each other, often viewing allegations of fraud against one doctor "as an attack on the whole profession." Consequently, honest doctors often minimize or rationalize cases of financial abuse, refuse to testify against their own, and generally oppose crackdowns against health care fraud (Sparrow, 1996). At the same time,

> State medical regulatory boards often resist revoking a physician's license unless the most egregious behavior has been proved. Medicaid violations, when they are brought to the attention of the licensing authorities at all, are likely to be regarded as peccadilloes, much in the nature of mildly embarrassing pranks. Because Medicaid crimes primarily involve money, they are viewed as irrelevant to the essence of medical practice, which resides in the physical and mental well-being of the patient, not the fiscal integrity of state and federal programs. (Jesilow, Pontell, and Geis, 1993, 197)

Durable Medical Equipment and Supply Firms

Because of the prevalence of large-scale scams, providers of durable medical equipment and other supplies—who received about $6 billion in Medicare money in 2000—also have been among the top three targets of

Operation Restore Trust (HB, 2000a).[18] In fact, the special durable medical equipment regional carriers were established in 1993 specifically to stop the companies from "'shopping' for contractors with the weakest controls and highest payment rates" (GAO, 1995c, 1). DMERCs were assigned a substantially higher goal for prepayment manual medical review (14 percent) than either the regional home health intermediaries (2.05 percent) or regular contractors (2.05 percent) (GAO, 2001l). Among the myriad criminal activities perpetrated by DME establishments against Medicare and Medicaid are invoices for equipment and supplies that are unnecessary, illegally ordered, or not provided; overcharging; duplicate billings; and sham businesses (DOJ, 1994; GAO, 1995c; HB, 2000a).[19]

Medical equipment and supplies have been particularly subject to abuse because firms are not required to list specific items or quantities on their claims. Thus, Medicare can remit thousands of dollars to a DME company without knowing what is being paid for or reviewing any of the bills in detail. Despite some changes in 1993, Congress still allows broad coding for many supplies, especially those provided to nursing home residents and home health care clients (GAO, 1995c). In its investigation of a sample of high-dollar DME claims from 1994 to 1995, the GAO (1995c) discovered that about 60 percent of them should have been denied. Moreover, an in-depth review at one regional carrier revealed that the firms regularly billed Medicare for vastly more supplies per beneficiary than could possibly be required or utilized. And some establishments were receiving reimbursements from both regional carriers and intermediaries for the same items.

Gouging the government through excessive charges has been a chronic problem. For instance, the highly profitable Osmomedic Company of Tampa, Florida, which specialized in TENS units (equipment that eases chronic pain) was paid over seven times the wholesale price per item. The annual cost to Medicare in Florida alone was about $10 million (Sparrow, 1996). Bogus claims for recipients who have died are common in the industry, as well. Of the $20.6 million reimbursed by Medicare in 1997 for services that began after the beneficiaries' deaths, about half was for durable medical equipment and supplies (HGR, 2000a).

Medicaid has experienced "widespread payment for drugs, equipment, and supplies that are not delivered or not needed" (GAO, 2001e, 5). Indeed, there have been numerous con games that have cost Medicare and Medicaid millions of dollars. In one notable illustration, two criminals in New York City hired recruiters to obtain Medicare numbers from elders by holding health fairs in their senior citizen high rises. Subsequently, they billed Medicare $750,000 for equipment that was never provided.[20] In another New York City case, three fictitious companies, which were already in their regional contractor's warning system for bogus MRI services, switched to submitting false claims for ear implants (HGR, 2000a). Deceptive practices related to Medi-Cal, California's Medicaid program, are rampant as well: since 1999, over 350 companies, mostly providers of pharmaceutical products and durable medical equipment, have been investigated, charged with fraud, or both (GAO, 2000b).

In 1996, the OIG sampled thirty-six new DME suppliers applying for Medicare certification and found that thirty-two, or nearly 90 percent, were not even functioning businesses. When the agency enlarged its study to include metropolitan areas in California, Florida, Illinois, New York, and Texas, it discovered that 7 percent of current suppliers and 11 percent of new applicants were phantom companies, most with only mail drop locations (HB, 2000b).

Other Predators

Unprincipled pharmacists have engaged in various ploys to defraud Medicaid. Some of their methods have been to charge the program for brand names when actually providing generic drugs, to short-fill prescriptions, and to participate in kickback arrangements (SJ, 1994). In what has been labeled the "pill mill" scheme, pharmacists join with clinics, labs, patient brokers, and middlemen distributors: Medicaid pays for prescriptions that beneficiaries turn over to buyers on the street for cash; the latter then resell the pills to pharmacists. These mishandled drugs, which may become ineffective or even dangerous, can eventually be disbursed to patients with an actual medical condition (HGR, 2000e).

The pharmaceutical industry has taken advantage of Medicare and Medicaid mostly through excessive and spiraling prices.[21] They not only charge the government and individuals significantly more for the same drugs than do foreign firms conducting business in their own nations, but the prices of American companies' drugs also are lower outside of the United States (SSCA, 1990). Companies such as Eli Lilly also have illegally pressured pharmacists and physicians to use its products, such as Lilly's antidepressant Prozac and its antiulcer medication Axid, over rival products (Hilzenrath, 1997).

Clinical laboratories, too, have exploited the health care programs by ordering tests never prescribed and tacking additional procedures on to legitimate orders (SSCA, 1994). They also have been involved in bribes and other illegal activities such as buying beneficiary numbers or paying older people for undergoing checkups (DOJ, 1994). In one high-profile case, SmithKline Beecham defrauded Medicare and Medicaid by conducting tests that were not ordered, billing for tests performed twice or never, and offering kickbacks to physicians. The company settled for $325 million, claiming it had "problems with ambiguity in the system" (Sparrow, 1996, 17).[22] Another establishment, National Health Laboratories, tripled its billings to the government by redesigning laboratory forms so as to trick doctors into ordering additional diagnostic work; they settled with the government for $111 million (Sparrow, 1996). And, in an even more extreme case—"rolling labs"—the perpetrators set up a chain of mobile medical clinics in Los Angeles, offering free physical examinations for which they billed Medicare and Medicaid. The recipients did not receive any of the results, leaving many elders with undetected health problems (HGR, 1996). The most enormous agreement to date for Medicare fraud—$486 million— was paid by Fresenius Medical Care, the largest provider of kidney dialysis and related products in the world. Its subsidiary had

> submitted false claims seeking payment for nutritional therapy provided to patients during their dialysis treatments, for services that were provided to patients as part of clinical trials, for hundreds of thousands of fraudulent blood testing claims, for kickbacks, and for improper reporting of credit balances. (SSCA, 2001b, 2)

Dishonest individuals also have fleeced community mental health facilities (CMHCs), nearly all of which had been nonprofit entities prior to the inclusion of such services into the Medicare program. For-profit businesses grew rapidly, along with Medicare payments that grew 482 percent between 1993 and 1997; during that same time, average charges per patient increased 530 percent. In many states there are no license requirements or other qualifying procedures. The OIG, which examined Medicare payments to CMHCs in five states during 1997, determined that over 90 percent of the claims were fraudulent; many of the places had disconnected telephones, phony businesses, or shoddy facilities and services. However, HCFA did not even target CMHCs until 1999, leaving many patients with no or low-quality treatment for years (GAO, 2000d).

Operators of substance abuse centers are yet another center of criminal misconduct. National Medical Enterprise (NME), which controlled a large number of psychiatric and substance abuse facilities, was found in 1994 to have bribed doctors and other referral sources as well as to have billed the government for nonexistent and unnecessary services. They settled for $594 million, apportioned between the government and private insurers (HGR, 1996).

Malfeasants abound in other domains as well. Transportation companies have milked the health care programs, for instance, by driving beneficiaries to the doctor but charging for expensive ambulance services (SJ, 1994). Even banks have capitalized on the system. One financial institution, which maintains Medicare accounts for nine contractors, used program money for its own investments, earning well over $12.5 million in profits from 1993 to 2000.

HCFA merely warned it to stop the practice, the government acquiring yet another industry in need of vigilance (SA, 2000b).

Third-party billing has grown increasingly common since the 1980s, generating another opportunity for scamming Medicare and Medicaid. Unscrupulous billing firms have developed complicated schemes for using honest providers without their knowledge. They also have access to vital data, such as provider and beneficiary numbers (HCC, 2000a). At times, providers are partners in the conspiracy. And it is a formidable task to detect fraud when third-party organizations are involved. Since they do not have to enroll in the Medicare and Medicaid programs, there is no official information on ownership, office address, telephone number, criminal history, and the like. They also are difficult to identify since, to meet Medicare regulations, many electronic claims are reformatted by special clearinghouses that substitute their own identification. On the other hand, paper submissions only require provider numbers (HCC, 2000a). Consequently, as with other major fraud cases, one of the largest billing companies in the nation, Medaphis Corporation, was caught submitting duplicate and illegal claims only because of a whistleblower's suit (HCC, 2000b).

Prospective Payment Systems: New Financial Incentives for Fraud

One goal of the new PPS is to reduce incentives for unnecessary services and other financial abuses. Instead, they threaten to foster new forms of fraud for nursing homes, home health agencies, and other providers affected by the payment changes. Specifically, under PPS, HHAs are paid a per episode rate (up to sixty days) for each beneficiary, regardless of the actual number of visits or days of care; the reimbursements are classified into eighty payment groups to adjust for differences in beneficiary care needs.[23] The number of episodes is not controlled. Thus, HHAs will be able to increase their share of Medicare funding by carefully limiting the extent of services per episode, regardless of need. Early indications are not promising: after the implementation of PPS, HHAs enhanced their profits by reducing the number of visits per episode and classifying more patients in the highest-paying categories (GAO, 2002g). In effect, frail elders are suffering from insufficient care while profiteers continue to plunder the system.

The daily rate paid per beneficiary under PPS for nursing homes is supposed to cover all of the costs of care. In order to reduce duplicate billing and prevent nursing homes from shifting costs to outside providers, BBA 1997 established consolidated billing requirements: ancillary vendors, including DME suppliers, are no longer paid separately but must bill the facilities directly. In a recent audit, however, the OIG observed that Medicare is now paying both the nursing home and the firms for the same equipment and supplies, with "overpayments" reaching $48 million in 1999. The DMERCs did not even have computer automated screening software in their processing systems to prevent the fraudulent claims. Another $9 million more in such "inappropriate" reimbursements was paid by the Medicaid program and its beneficiaries (OIG, 2001a, June and August).

Moreover, although the nursing home PPS might reduce the use of unnecessary services, amoral operators can boost profits by avoiding high-cost patients within a RUG group; reducing essential medical and supportive care; eliminating expensive services; substituting less qualified, low-paid staff; and shortchanging residents in other ways, such as discharging them without sufficient rehabilitation (SA, 2000b). Nursing homes receive their per capita allotments without having to detail which services they actually provided; any attempt to force them to itemize has been vigorously opposed by the industry (GAO, 2001m). Indeed, the GAO (2002m) recently found that since the implementation of PPS, the facilities have provided less therapy to nearly two-thirds of their Medicare beneficiaries, and "fewer patients received the highest amounts of therapy associated with each payment group." It also documented that many nursing homes manipulate data so as to classify their new patients into the most lucrative categories, regardless of actual need.

Hospitals also have found ways to use PPS to their advantage, often in innovative ways. For example, a 2001 OIG audit found that the medical facilities were coding transfers of patients to subacute units as discharges, thus shifting costs to Medicaid while reaping the full DRG payment for their care—$2.3 million in "overpayments" from 1996 to 2000 (OIG, 2001a, July).

Managed Care: Et Tu, Brute

As suggested in chapter 2, in an effort to control costs, the Medicare Program was allowed to contract with managed care organizations in 1985, and soon after Medicaid authorized participation in these entities as well. By 1999, about 17 percent of Medicare and 14 percent of Medicaid beneficiaries were participating in some form of MCO. For Medicaid, membership rates vary considerably by state. The Tennessee Medicaid program, for example, consists entirely of MCOs (OIG, 2001b). Moreover, most Medicaid waiver programs for frail elders, including social health maintenance organizations, utilize some form of managed care.

Until the 1980s, most MCOs were nonprofit organizations seeking to provide decent health care at an affordable price; by 1995, over half of them had become proprietary firms. The growth of for-profit MCOs participating in

Medicare and Medicaid has presented new enticements and opportunities for feeding at the public trough. Managed care firms are first and foremost businesses, controlled primarily by commercial ethics and profit maximization. Unlike with physicians and hospitals, one rarely even hears rhetoric lauding their higher medical morality and community services. Their fundamental goal is to divert as high a percentage of Medicare and Medicaid money as possible into the hands of their administrators and stockholders (Sparrow, 1996). And MCOs are extremely lucrative, with exorbitant executive salaries, bonuses, administrative fees, and high profits. Significant resources also have been committed to mergers and acquisitions, allowing them to better control their providers. By 1994, over 23 percent of all MCO premium dollars were devoted to non-patient-related expenses, up from less than 10 percent in earlier decades (Anders, 1997).

In the traditional fee-for-service system, providers have an economic incentive to overutilize services, manipulate codes, engage in double billing, and the like. Since MCOs receive a predetermined capitation fee for each beneficiary, regardless of actual costs, the primary temptation for fraud is underuse of services and reduced quality of care. Under managed care, then, proprietary firms can impede access to care; stint on patient benefits; perform as few tests, treatments, and procedures as possible; avoid expensive services; and deny coverage to high-cost beneficiaries.

Participating physicians often are given financial incentives to treat patients quickly and inexpensively, including authorizing premature discharges from hospitals. Primary care doctors, who serve as gatekeepers, may receive bonuses or penalties, depending on their efforts at controlling referrals to specialists. Some plans have only a limited number of participating specialists, substitute less costly providers whenever feasible, develop bureaucratic and other obstacles to services, and otherwise offer the cheapest treatments possible, often leading to poor quality of care. In some cases, physicians unwilling to skimp on services will be dismissed from the organization.

The curtailing of medical services obviously can have significant adverse health consequences. Patients with severe illnesses or chronic conditions that require costly or ongoing services tend to be the most at risk. A study by Anders (1997) concluded, for example, that although MCOs may have outcomes equivalent to fee-for-service systems when addressing early symptoms of heart disease such as high blood pressure and elevated cholesterol, they are not as effective in treating the condition as it worsens, necessitating increasingly expensive services. A number of MCOs approve only the least expensive hospitals, labs, tests, and procedures for cardiovascular disorders—or what Anders dubs cut-rate heart surgery—regardless of their effectiveness.

Medicare clients experiencing mental illness, such as manic depression, schizophrenia, and dementia, are particularly disadvantaged under managed care; access to psychological services tends to be strictly controlled.

There are few national checks over whether MCOs actually deliver the benefits promised or the number and quality of services provided (SA, 2000b). Though Medicare beneficiaries can appeal any denial of services, relatively few elders take advantage of the opportunity because they are unaware of or confused about the procedures (GAO, 1999f). Those who are frail, seriously ill, or both obviously will have even more difficulty in challenging MCO decisions. The major option for a dissatisfied customer is to withdraw from her plan. In Florida, for instance, in 1999 the disenrollment rate averaged 24 percent. In some of the MCOs, such as Av Med of Jacksonville, Av Med of Orlando, and Av Med of St. Petersburg, well over half of the clients dropped out that year. Across the nation, annual cancellation rates of 25 percent or more are not uncommon.[24]

Clearly, when beneficiaries are denied care and interpretations of medical necessity come into play, the boundary between a financial decision and patient abuse can be quite thin. The issue is further muddied when criminal behavior is added to the mix, since MCOs are subject to the usual types of health care corruption: kickbacks, rebates, bribery, illegal subcontracts, unlicensed providers, and scams (SJ, 1994; SSCA, 1994). They are particularly prone to misleading marketing practices, including sales agents who enlist clients under deceptive circumstances or forge signatures to switch their plans unawares (GAO, 1996b). Some MCOs hire "runners" to recruit patients and buy or steal Medicare and Medicaid beneficiary numbers (SJ, 1994). They also have been caught charging Medicare for patients who actually are enrolled in the regular fee-for-service plan (SA, 2000b).

In an audit of MCOs in Arizona, California, Colorado, and Florida, which represent about 43 percent of the Medicare HMO population, the OIG located $4.1 million in capitation fees paid for deceased elders, a problem it found in other states as well (OIG, 2001a, July).[25] It also exposed illegally obtained "enhanced rates": under Medicare, MCOs are entitled to higher capitation payments for nursing home residents. PacifiCare of California and Penn State Geisinger Health Plan, for instance, were charging the higher price for recipients who were actually living at home (OIG, 2001a, January and March). Other MCOs have fraudulently claimed the "enhanced rates" for clients in retirement communities or other ineligible settings (SA, 2000b).

MCOs also manipulate the system, both legally and illegally, by enrolling only healthy patients, denying coverage to those in need of expensive or intensive services, and forcing out beneficiaries who become high users. More costly participants seeking treatment can be referred to doctors in distant geographic areas or told that there are no appointments for months. On the other hand, some MCOs make it difficult for low-cost clients to disenroll (SJ, 1994).

Managed care has not even controlled Medicare costs. Under risk-based contracts, the per capita payment is based on the adjusted community rate (ACR). Among other factors, the program's price-setting methods have generated exorbitant capitation fees estimated at over $2 billion annually. Though MCOs receive 95 percent of the projected expenditures for a similarly situated beneficiary in the traditional fee-for-service plan, because they tend to attract and recruit healthier patients their actual costs are estimated to be 12 to 37 percent lower. Consequently, they have had a windfall in profits, increasing rather than reducing program expenditures (GAO, 1997d).

In addition, inflated cost reports are a considerable problem. As of 2002, there has been limited control over the items included in the ACR, much of which has been suspect, especially when measured against the "reasonable" standards of the traditional fee-for-service scheme. In audit after audit around the nation from 2000 to 2001, the OIG uncovered millions of dollars in undocumented, highly questionable, and illegitimate charges, including exorbitant salaries; marketing, enrollment, and public relations expenses; charitable donations; political contributions; lobbying; radio and television ads; gifts; travel; alcohol; entertainment and parties; business meetings; souvenirs; and other expenditures unrelated to Medicare per se (see, for example, OIG, 2001a, May, July, August, September, November). Under Medicare rules, any excess of payments to MCOs over their actual costs (with the exception of allowable profits) must be used to provide either more benefits or reduce beneficiary fees such as premiums and copayments. Consequently, not only do these fraudulent charges fleece Medicare, but they also directly harm clients financially. In one Florida Medicare MCO, the $13.8 million in unsupported and excessive "operating expenses" during 2000 could have eliminated entirely participant premiums and copayments (OIG, 2001a, March). In other plans, the ill-gotten gains have precluded the addition of such "extras" as prescription drugs.

Despite the well-documented misuse of Medicare money, there have been no follow-up policies or procedures to curtail these practices (GAO, 2001i). Because of inadequate government checks and sanctions, MCOs have not been accountable to anybody except stockholders. HCFA has been "reluctant to take action against noncompliant HMOs, even when there was a history of abusive sales practices, delays in processing beneficiaries' appeals of their decisions to deny coverage, or poor-quality care" (GAO, 1997b, 13). If MCOs are found guilty of irregular or fraudulent practices, they most often are required to provide corrective action plans; rarely are they cut out of the Medicare program or blocked from enrolling new beneficiaries while they "fix" the problems. In some cases, if the improper activities persist, the MCO simply is required to furnish another corrective plan. In the case of Care Florida, deceptive marketing activities, sorely inadequate services, and deficient quality of care persisted from the company's establishment in 1987 to 1996; the MCO received only warnings and had to furnish a series of corrective plans that were never carried out (GAO, 1996b).

Conclusion: Capitulating to Providers

By 2000, the OIG declared that financial abuse of the federal health care programs was finally being addressed through congressional legislation, Prospective Payment Systems, more provider audits, additional penalties, and the like (HB, 2000a). In fact, the Congressional Budget Office has attributed much of the decline in Medicare's inflation rate since 1997 to the concerted government attacks on program fraud and abuse (SF, 2001b).

The number of health care–related cases under investigation by the DOJ grew steadily after the passage of HIPAA in 1996, as did the recovery of fraudulently gained money. By 2000, it had about 2,000 criminal cases pending and nearly 500 criminal and 230 civil cases filed (GAO, 2001l). In that year, there were 343 cases (467 defendants) that resulted in criminal convictions and over 3,300 providers and health care establishments were excluded from the federal health care programs (GAO, 2001l; HWM, 2001). In 2001 alone, civil monetary penalties for health care fraud amounted to $1.2 billion (OIG, 2001j). But the number of unscrupulous providers and firms charged and the amount of dollars retrieved, although large, pales in comparison to the magnitude of the problem; the unabashed pillaging of the health care programs by both "legitimate" providers and criminals has not been checked to any substantial degree.

Financial fraud and abuse of residents, of course, are inextricably linked: the cost of fraud cannot be measured exclusively in monetary terms; it also poses a threat to the physical and mental health of individuals. Medically unnecessary services or unneeded prescriptions provided to unsuspecting beneficiaries place their well-being in jeopardy. Jesilow, Pontell, and Geis (1993) assert that needless surgery, for example, should be viewed as "equivalent to assault." Similarly, billing for services not rendered, one of the more prevalent health care crimes, deprives people of sometimes urgent diagnostic tests or procedures. Physicians who step up their volume of hourly services to compensate for cuts in reimbursement rates endanger their patients' health, as do agencies that misrepresent the professional qualifications of their staff. According to the OIG, illegal nonphysician practitioner billings are rising, creating vulnerabilities "both from payment and quality of care standpoints"(OIG Audit Report, 2001a, July). Likewise, when a hospital discharges a patient "quicker and sicker" to her home in order to boost its profits, the stability of the recipient's condition is at risk.

By the same token, nursing homes may seriously injure patients or jeopardize their well-being when they don't provide the benefits that Medicare or Medicaid paid for.[26] Such cases abound. Outside suppliers, as suggested above, also may fail to deliver fundamental services to the residents; sometimes these providers are subsidiaries of the facilities themselves. Further, gang visits and phony claims by physicians can seriously harm nursing home patients in need. And, as the last chapter demonstrated, institutions that are reimbursed for substandard and abusive care not only injure the inhabitants, but also can cause their death.

Despite ongoing profiteering and exploitation of Medicare and Medicaid and its detrimental affects on beneficiaries, policymakers have increasingly succumbed to the health and long-term care industries, a surrender that has worsened since the beginning of the George W. Bush administration. Instead of rigorously rooting out financial fraud and abuse, strengthening sanctions, and forcing out unscrupulous providers from the public programs, policymakers have become absorbed in "concerns about Medicare's regulatory and paperwork burden and the cost of doing business with the Medicare program" (SSCA, 2001b, 1). Both Congress and HCFA have turned to "streamlining" regulations, enhancing educational efforts, and improving communication with providers and beneficiaries.

In May 2001, Thomas Scully, the president and chief executive officer of the Federation of American Hospitals, was appointed to head HCFA. Testifying before Congress, he argued that many of the health care programs' rules and regulations were blocking services and should be altered. The new administrator insisted that the government must become "less intrusive to the providers" and more "responsive to their needs." Thus, as one of his first acts, he designated senior-level staff to work with each of the seven health care industry groups "to facilitate information sharing and enhance communication between the Agency and its business partners" (SSCA, 2001b, 1). He also put together a new "regulatory reform" group to seek out which rules need to be condensed or cut and to reduce the paperwork of providers. For program recipients, the approach now is to furnish them with more information about Medicare, Medicare+Choice options, and Medigap policies, including an enhanced website, an extensive (and expensive) multimedia campaign, and a mass mailing of *Medicare and You,* the latest HCFA publication (SSCA, 2001b).

In response to physician complaints about burdensome, complicated, unclear, and inconsistent rules and regulations, in 2001 HCFA revised its policies on medical review of physicians: its progressive corrective action (PCA) initiative directed carriers to focus only on the more risky practices, alter some of its methods for assessing "improper" reimbursements, and increase educational activities. As a result, the following year the amount of "overpayments" repaid by physicians was substantially reduced and fewer of their claims were carefully examined (GAO, 2002d).[27]

HCFA's latest solution to Medicare contractor problems is to provide them and their staff with better education and training or what I would call "train the trainer" sessions along with "monitor the monitor" activities. By 2001, HCFA had commissioned nineteen new, specialized program safeguard contractors to rigorously inspect various aspects of the Medicare program. Commercial firms, which work under cost-based contracts, bid for the tasks. However, the government soon became concerned that these entities, too, would illegally inflate their expenses or, if their bids were too low, perform the job perfunctorily (GAO, 2001h). Consequently, HCFA has been forced to experiment with new mechanisms for "controlling the controllers" and "inspecting the inspectors."

Even some of the relatively weak sanctions objected to by industry groups are being reassessed. In the summer of 2001, the OIG began a series of roundtable discussions and other endeavors to hear complaints from providers subject to CIAs and to "adapt its CIAs to the business realities of the health care industry" (OIG, 2001f, 10). In an open letter to providers a few months later, Inspector General Janet Rehnquist announced modifications to the CIAs that met some of their concerns (OIG, 2001i). At the same time, the OIG has introduced voluntary disclosure: if a provider discovers and reports its own misconduct, it can receive an expedited review of its case and special treatment when penalties are applied. Voluntary compliance programs have been established as well: providers put together their own internal controls and staff training. Currently, there are nine model voluntary plans in place—for hospitals, HHAs, DMEs, hospices, HMOs, nursing homes, physician practices, clinical labs, and third-party billing firms.

An increasing number of legislators also have been actively seeking to appease industry leaders and pander to their needs. In 2000, Congress enacted the Medicare, Medicaid, and SCHIP Benefits Improvement Act that, in addition to providing $35 billion over five years to restore more cuts to providers, curtailed restrictions on them. Among other changes, it extended the advisory opinion process that allows firms to receive binding legal advice as to the legality of their current or future health care operations. It also eased the Medicare appeals process for them, thus exacerbating many of the existing problems (HSB, 2001). The following year, as the previous chapter discussed, the Medicare Education and Regulatory Fairness Act (S. 452, H.R. 868) was proposed to placate providers who were demanding even fewer controls. If enacted, the measure would allow covered firms to remit their "improper" Medicare payments over three years, even if they are able to pay immediately, while also letting them seek new funding from the program;[28] prohibit contractors from requesting supporting documents prior to reimbursement; accord immunity to any provider who voluntarily refunds overpayments within a year or seeks an appraisal of his claims; require HCFA to provide information to companies about its automatic screening processes; and suspend all penalties while a firm is under review for misdeeds.

According to the OIG, these provisions would offer opportunities for providers who owe substantial sums to HCFA to abscond with the money, declare bankruptcy, or close down their business; enable perpetrators "to immunize themselves from investigation and prosecution" simply by returning only a small portion of their debt; coach companies on ways to further circumvent electronic screening devices and exploit the system; and, most importantly, prevent the government from imposing immediate protection to nursing home and home health care patients whose providers are appealing inspection deficiencies that may be endangering their health and safety (GAO, 2001l; HWM, 2001). MERFA also would make it harder to prove unscrupulous behavior in civil cases by requiring "clear and convincing evidence of fraud" in lieu of the "preponderance of the evidence" currently in effect (GAO, 2001, 14).

Overall, the various industries contend that they, in fact, are the victims—of everything from overly burdensome and complex regulations to overzealous government investigations. Providers have been able to successfully lobby and bully political leaders, threaten to withdraw their services from the health care programs, and declare bankruptcy. And public officials in accord with industry views have now achieved substantial power over Medicare and Medicaid matters, fostering an even greater confluence of interests between regulators and the regulated. Beneficiary needs, such as overcoming barriers to services and improving the quality of care, have taken a back seat to industry concerns. Ultimately, yielding to business demands has permitted both relentless profiteering and ongoing patient neglect and abuse in our nation's health and long-term care systems.

Notes

1. Most of the reductions since 1998 have been because providers were forced to furnish better verification of their services (GAO, 1999c; GAO, 2002d).

2. The fraud unit, as I later found out, did, of course, have telephones.

3. A qui tam suit is a legal action against a company brought to the court by an informer on his or her own.

4. In 2001 there were about 450 CIAs in effect (OIG, 2001j).

5. According to a government audit, Medicare paid out over $3 billion for "erroneous" nursing home claims in 1996 alone (Smith, 1998b). The OIG documented that during the first six months of 1999, the program disbursed about $49 million for medically unnecessary, undocumented and inadequately documented therapy (physical, occupational, and speech) with an "error rate" of 25 percent (OIG, 2001j, 2).

Large chains have been particularly audacious in their illegal billing practices. The following are some examples: in July of 1998, the Justice Department began an in-depth investigation of Beverly Enterprises, eventually determining that the company had cheated Medicare out of millions of dollars between 1990 and 1997. In 2000, the company settled with the government for $175 million; it was forced to sell ten facilities in order to pay its obligation (Malone, 2000; Peterson and Stanley, 1998; SSCA, 2000a). Vencor defrauded the program of at least $1.3 billion. In 2001, the Department of Justice settled with the chain for $219 million, of which $104.5 million was for submitting improper claims to Medicare and Medicaid. Vencor also had to submit to a five-year corporate integrity agreement (Malone, 2000; NCC, 2001b; OIG, 2001j). Among other misdeeds, IHS charged Medicare millions for services it never provided and settled with the government for $27 million and a five-year CIA (Salganic, 2000); National Health Care Corporation submitted false cost reports from 1991 to 1996 (OIG, 2001j); and Sunrise Healthcare executives cheated the state of Connecticut by including in its Medicaid cost reports such items as personal trips to Italy and use of a corporate jet, expensive cars, and luxury condominiums. It settled in 1999 for $8.4 million (Julien, 1999).

6. In 1997, about 1.4 million dually eligible beneficiaries resided in nursing homes (HGR, 1997).

7. AHCA has argued that the double billing is because of "bad reimbursement policies," unclear rules, and "confusing interpretations of regulations" (HGRO, 1997).

8. In 1997, the OIG testified that about 13 percent of nursing homes "have been offered inducements for allowing suppliers to provide wound care products in their facility under Medicare" (HGR, 1997, 23). The agency also pointed to the shady marketing methods of vendors selling incontinence supplies; fully half of the $230 million funded for such items by Medicare in 1993 were most likely unnecessary (HGR, 1997).

9. As early as 1975, evidence gathered at congressional hearings showed that there were growing problems among home health providers: "proprietary agencies were harshly described as an unusual concentration of real estate manipulators and quick-buck artists." In Florida, Senator Chiles "decried agencies that had clearly been ripping off the Medicare system and lamented increased patterns of overutilization, padded costs and hidden profits" (Benjamin, 1993).

With the steady rise of proprietary chains, discussed in chapter 2, the quality of care also has continued to be at issue. According to a comprehensive nationwide survey of HHAs from 2001 to 2002 by the GAO (2002e), HCFA's oversight over the agencies has been sorely limited. In order to be certified under Medicare, HHAs must meet fifteen conditions of participation (COPs). The states are supposed to survey the agencies every twelve to thirty-six months, depending on their particular compliance situation. However, not only are HHAs easily certified but the survey processes also tend to be lax and ineffectual. Moreover, states generally do not even survey branch offices, which represent about one-fourth of all HHAs. The GAO concluded that "there is evidence suggesting that the extent of serious care problems may be understated and that situations endangering the health and well-being of home health patients may occur more often than documented."

Moreover, though Congress authorized a variety of sanctions including civil monetary penalties under OBRA 1987, as of 2002 HCFA had not implemented them. For the most part, agencies with serious deficiencies are allowed to generate a "corrective" plan. And, similarly to nursing homes, they go in and out of compliance. HHAs providing substandard care can be terminated from Medicare, but this option is rarely exercised (GAO, 2002e).

10. One study determined that for-profit agencies averaged sixty-nine home health aide visits per client as compared to forty-three and forty-eight for nonprofit and government agencies, respectively (GAO, 2000e).

11. The company paid $154 million in cash and $159 million in contingency payments for the buyout.

12. The convicted proprietor, Jack Mills, received seven and a half years in prison and a $10.2 million fine; his wife, a co-owner, was sentenced to thirty-two months (OIG, 1996).

13. The American Hospital Association testified before Congress, "Our experience with . . . assisting hospitals caught up in the web of government billing investigations reinforces our view that billing issues are usually billing mistakes. Fraud is the exception" (SSCA, 2001b, 12).

14. The proprietary chain had grown rapidly, from 4 hospitals in 1988 to 343 hospitals, 147 outpatient surgical centers, and more than 550 home health agencies in thirty-six states, Switzerland, and Spain by 1997. Columbia/HCA Healthcare Corporation became the ninth-largest employer in the nation, controlling about one-half of for-profit and 7 percent of total hospital beds (Public Citizen Health Research Group, 1997). As a result of the investigation for fraud, the company restructured its operations, reduced its aggressive acquisition policy, and sold off many hospitals and outpatient surgery centers.

15. In the GAO 2000f study, neither hospital is named.

16. They noted, however, that the fraudulent billings were confined to about 8 percent of their sample.

17. Psychiatric services in nursing homes cost Medicare $194 million that year.

18. Durable medical equipment and supplies includes oxygen, wheelchairs, hospital beds, walkers, and the like. The industry tends to depend on Medicare for its income since the program is the major purchaser of such products. Prior to 1987, providers were paid what they charged, subject to local market prices. Reimbursements are now based on a fee schedule for each of 1,900 groups of products. However, "Disparities between fee schedule amounts and market prices developed over time, and Medicare significantly overpaid for some medical equipment and supplies" (SA, 2002, 6).

19. DME suppliers also obtain excess profits legally. For instance, under Medicare part B, beneficiaries can rent equipment such as wheelchairs for up to fifteen months,

after which time the providers are allowed to bill the program semiannually for the maintenance or repair of the objects. An OIG study (2002c), however, found that although the DME suppliers were duly compensated for these costs, totaling $130 million in 2000, only 9 percent of the servicing actually was performed.

20. Eventually, they were convicted of fraud and both sentenced to thirty-three months in prison.

21. Prices for prescription drugs rose by four times the rate of inflation in 1998, at which time the median profit among pharmaceutical firms was 18.5 percent compared to 4.4 percent for industries as a whole. According to the AARP (2002c, 2), drug industry profits are "way above the average 13 percent it spends on research and development. It also spends an average of 35 percent on advertising and administration, which includes the cost of lobbying and lawsuits." In 1997, it spent over $148 million on lobbying alone (AARP, 1999, 2000b).

22. Despite SmithKline Beecham's wrongdoings, in 1997 Mayor Ed Rendell pushed the City Council into granting the company a $4.7 million tax break to entice it to stay in Philadelphia. One of the mayor's largest stock holdings is SmithKline Beecham, valued at between $100,00 and $250,000 in June 2001 (Nicholas, 2001).

23. Rates are based on the national average in 1997 of providing care for each of the groups. In 2001, episode payments ranged from $1,114 to $5,947 (GAO, 2002f).

24. See www.cms.hhs.gov.

25. As of 2001, the government still pays about $700,000 annually to the MCOs (OIG, 2001j).

26. In Pennsylvania, U.S. Attorney David Hoffman has recently employed the Federal False Claims Act, generally used for billing deceptions, to sue nursing homes for cheating Medicare and Medicaid because of substandard care; he has successfully argued that fraud includes the rendering of inferior services (Stark, 2002).

27. At recent congressional hearings, physicians "expressed concern that, because billing rules change frequently, their understanding of them may be obsolete and incorrect, which could lead to inadvertent billing errors" (GAO, 2002c, 2). They favor less medical review of their documents, alleging that "Medicare contractors unfairly pursue and investigate physicians who have made innocent billing errors" (GAO, 2001l, 1).

28. Some groups argued that companies voluntarily admitting the receipt of overpayments should not have to pay the full amount back (HSB, 2001).

9

CONCLUSION: TOWARD
A NEW VISION OF CARE WORK

A GING DOES NOT BEGIN at any one chronological period in the life span; rather, it is a lifelong journey. Early inequalities in income, education, job opportunities, living conditions, health, and access to medical services affect people throughout their lives but are heightened in later years. The intertwining factors of gender, race/ethnicity, and class have a strong influence on the experiences of old age, including the prospects for attaining an adequate income, good health, and independence. Though the vast majority of older U.S. citizens are of White, European descent, the percentage of elderly racial and ethnic minorities is steadily growing, along with their lifelong accumulated socioeconomic disadvantages.

Regardless, even well-off individuals who live to more advanced ages can't sidestep the real risk of functional disabilities and dependency at some point before they die. Older adults are more likely to develop chronic diseases than the general population, conditions that generally lead to functional disabilities requiring long-term care. Though they sometimes can be relieved through medical intervention, they cannot be cured.[1] And, the prevalence of such functional impairments in the United States is increasing because of population aging, technological and medical advances, and increasing numbers of Americans who are reaching age eighty-five and over, necessitating ever greater needs for elder care.[2]

Long-term care has no real place in the U.S. health care system, although it is the most expensive system in the world. Since 1970, the cost of medical services per person has more than doubled, adjusting for inflation; the growth in prices, which tends to outstrip all other consumer items, was nearly 12 percent annually at the turn of the twenty-first century (AARP, 2001c). Nationally, such expenditures totaled over $1.3 trillion in 2000, representing fully 13 percent of the gross domestic product (GDP).[3] It is projected to reach $2.8 trillion in 2011 or 17 percent of the GDP (HCFA, 2001).[4]

Today, just under half (45 percent) of all health care is publicly funded, mostly for the aged through Medicare and Medicaid (HCFA, 2001). The nation's 35 million elders represent about 13 percent of the U.S. population but nearly one-third of its health care costs: per capita spending on older people is about four times that for the under sixty-five age group. As noted in an earlier chapter, Medicare spending has mounted over the years, outstripping both inflation and increases in the overall federal budget. Exclusively a medical program for acute diseases, it does not provide ongoing assistance to older people with chronic disorders. Moreover, though the public costs of their medical services are high, seniors are paying expensive premiums, coinsurance, and deductibles out of pocket.[5] Actual outlays for long-term care amount to only 12 percent of the overall health care tab but a significant percentage of government disbursements through Medicaid, predominantly for nursing homes. Though viewed as belonging in the private sector, in reality these institutional facilities are sustained by a steady, generous flow of money from the public treasury.

The nature of long-term care reflects the political economy in which it is embedded. As with other issues, it is shaped by a nation's social structures and public policies along with the values on which they are based. In the United States, market-based decisions drive solutions to social problems, an approach that has intensified in the even more financialized environment of the post-1980 era (Strobel and Peterson, 1999). We experienced vast corporate restructuring, high and growing federal budget deficits, pressures on state budgets, and greater poverty and economic inequality. With the end of sustained economic growth, the rise of globalism, stagnation in wages, and the escalation of Medicare, Medicaid, and other social program costs, the causes of our economic problems were increasingly deflected from corporate America to the elderly and poor, fostering an anti-entitlement mentality, cutbacks in needs-tested programs, political resistance to developing new initiatives, and new and more conservative social welfare measures generally. Any earlier struggles for economic and social justice gave way to antigovernment rhetoric, along with the dual goals of slashing national spending and helping U.S. firms remain economically competitive in world markets. Public policies became increasingly grounded in fiscal austerity, deregulation, privatization, residualism, devolution, familism, and extreme individualism, strategies that most negatively affect women of all ages, especially racial and ethnic minorities.

Because questions of cost now overshadow all other concerns, increasing government funding for long-term care is, for the most part, not even placed on the public agenda as a topic of debate.[6] There has never been, of course, a national commitment to it: the hodgepodge of policies and programs for the very poor under Medicaid, though funded through federal matching grants, are primarily developed at the state level where resources are most limited and nursing home proprietors have the greatest power. Elder care is heavily and increasingly subject to the twists and turns of state budget priorities, political pressures by provider interests, and the political needs of state legislators and governors.

Devolution has given even more responsibility to the states but without sufficient financial resources to meet them. Any innovative or expanded long-term care programs diverging from the predominant institutional approach must be cost-neutral as they relate to federal payments, thus requiring the states to pick up the additional expenses. Already paying from 20 to 50 percent of their budgets for Medicaid by the 1990s, and with political constraints on raising taxes, their major policy objectives have been driven by cost cutting and cost shifting. Rather than increase the array of services and benefits, most states are struggling to maintain existing ones, often through diversionary schemes aimed at enhancing federal Medicare and Medicaid contributions or, more often, forcing families to take on additional obligations. Since the 1980s, more Medicaid money has been spent on home and community services, and a few states have led the way with some creative programs. Even so, the vast majority continues to warehouse their impoverished elderly in institutions while failing to provide assistance to frail older people ineligible for Medicaid.

Nor have the states been particularly concerned with improving the quality of nursing home care. Though responsible for enforcing national regulations, they have done so haphazardly and ineffectively, leaving the nursing home industry in control. The state agencies have not monitored the facilities vigorously, acted aggressively on serious resident and family complaints, taken strong enforcement actions, or imposed sanctions commensurate with the wrongdoings. In short, the current system allows even the most substandard nursing homes to continue to endanger their patients.

The Future of Elder Care

The Business of Long-Term Care

As suggested throughout this book, we do not have a long-term care system per se or even a sound approach to caring for people who require ongoing help with their basic activities of daily life. Rather, there are numerous self-serving providers, each with their own consolidated turf, feeding from the public trough. Buttressed by population aging and government policies, by

the end of the 1970s old age and its jumble of special interests had emerged as
big business. As noted by Carroll Estes (1979) in her path-breaking *The Aging
Enterprise,* the elderly population had not only become commodities that fueled the nation's immense health and social service industries, but also had become targeted by them for exploitation. For some industries, such as nursing
homes and home health agencies, it became a veritable gold mine. Engaging
in aggressive takeovers, mergers, and acquisitions over the next several
decades, the various establishments evolved into larger and larger chains that
became both horizontally and vertically integrated, including hospitals, physician groups, home health agencies, managed care organizations, and nursing
homes (Herzlinger, 1997).

Their endeavors to grow, expand markets, and improve financial gains had
no relation to patient, family, or community needs or the quality of the services they provided. To the contrary, the commercialization of elder care allowed them to capitalize on older people, their families, workers, and the
Medicare and Medicaid systems. It also provided the organizational context
that defined caregiving itself and how it should be practiced. From experiencing fast-paced, methodical, and efficient modes of care to cost cutting and
profit maximization, frail elders dependent on paid providers were treated as
cost-accountable units subject to business priorities, norms, and needs.

These huge, integrated megachains have been able to wield considerable
political clout, both through carrots and sticks: they fund aggressive and well-
financed lobbying and electoral campaigns, obtain key administrative positions at the national and state levels, and threaten the well-being of their vulnerable charges to achieve their aims. One of their major weapons, actual or
threatened reduction in services, has effectively allowed large-scale providers to
avoid both political controls and severe penalties, even for the most egregious
actions. Ultimately, nursing homes, hospitals, home health agencies, durable
medical equipment suppliers, drug companies, and others have been able to
defend their individual and often interrelated bailiwicks, securing and maintaining huge expenditures of public funding, high profit levels, and control
over the types of service provided, their quality, and how they are delivered.

Revamping Nursing Homes

As this book has established, the nursing home has had a privileged and
dominating role in government long-term care funding. And, though the current situation is appalling, with a significant percentage of facilities providing
inhumane, substandard care, nursing homes are not inherently objectionable
places for frail, dependent people. In some cases, in fact, if they offered decent
care, nursing homes could be a preferred alternative. However, such place-

ments must be based on the needs and preferences of individuals and their families rather than on public budgets, financial constraints, and profit-driven megachains.

Most importantly, we must challenge the assumptions underlying the business ethic of care. The institutions often serve as the elder's permanent home, sometimes for years. Instead of being organized like hospitals, with their bureaucratic structures, medical bias, and systematized, dispassionate care, they must become more patient-oriented. As Gubrium puts it, "Matters of home, family, interpersonal ties, life history, self-worth, dependence, disappointment, and destiny confront residents in ways irrelevant to hospital patients or other short-stay care receivers" (1993, xv).

I would argue for smaller facilities, integrated into communities, that can provide truly homelike environments. The frail elderly need not be warehoused, isolated, and tucked away from previous neighbors, friends, and the larger society. They also are entitled to a room of their own, each one individualized, with items from the elder's past: residents shouldn't have to give up all of their possessions, many of which represent lifelong memories.

The organization, practices, and rules of the current corporate model have to shift away from the concerns of owners and stockholders and to those of the care recipients and their families. This would mean that the residents' desires, needs, and well-being would be substituted for efficiency and profit maximization and the objectification and impersonal treatment they foster. "Bed and body work," which centers on the physical aspects of care, is not enough: residents have social and emotional needs as well (Gubrium, 1975). Affective tasks must take their place among the leading components of an aide's duties: she must be allowed and encouraged to listen to patients, respond to their emotional needs, and provide empathy, warmth, and companionship. Only then can frail elders be known and understood for the unique beings they are. Personal engagement and the establishment of mutual bonds, however, is only possible with high staffing levels and low turnover, allowing greater intensity and continuity of care.

In order to maximize the residents' quality of life, nursing homes must attend to their social needs as well. It is imperative that they move beyond their usual infantilizing, mass activities to the provision of more meaningful, suitable functions, preferably those chosen by the inhabitants themselves. Elders should have settings available for more genuine social interaction as well as the opportunity to pursue their own interests, including an ample supply of books, magazines, and films.

In addition, they should be afforded the chance to reach the highest level of functioning that they are capable of. The development of their physical and mental capacities through myriad rehabilitation and other techniques would entail painstaking, time-consuming, and costly efforts but could engender greater self-reliance and an enhanced sense of well-being. At the same time, by slowing down the pace of daily routines, such as meals and showers, the facilities could foster greater independence among their frail charges. Some disabled patients, including those who are wheelchair bound, are capable of navigating on their own, given sufficient time, adequate room to maneuver, and assistance when required.

Regardless of their vulnerable, disabled state, residents are entitled to maintain their dignity, privacy, basic human rights, and as much autonomy as their personal situation warrants. Nursing homes should find appropriate means for empowering patients, giving them a voice in their own care and in the workings of the home itself, since they have a right to as much self-determination and control over their environment as possible. Greater agency over their lives also implies less regimentation. Needless to say, they also deserve an adequate level of basic care, including decent food, along with meal choices that take into account their ethnic and personal preferences; sufficient and competent medical care; the elimination of protracted waits for meals, the bathroom, showers, and other activities of daily living; and freedom from theft, mistreatment, and abuse.

Deprivatization

In order to improve nursing homes to the extent that they can provide quality care, policymakers must reject their unqualified faith in the virtues of the marketplace, private economic initiative, and profit making as the most effective and fruitful approach to formal care.

From the beginning, vulnerable elders were sacrificed to real estate speculation, investment opportunities, and financial manipulations and later to other profit-making schemes and stockholder needs. Capitalizing on shifting regulatory conditions, proprietors have engaged in both overuse and underuse of services; inflation of charges; excessive executive salaries, bonuses, and administrative costs; self-dealing transactions; and other unsavory practices.

Responding mostly to a vicious cycle of exposés, government studies, congressional hearing, new regulations, conspicuously deficient state enforcement efforts, and even more embarrassing disclosures, policymakers have failed to improve the abominable conditions in nursing homes or the harms inflicted on their residents. A panoply of new rules, inspection procedures, and government sanctions, especially since 1987, have generated little noticeable improvement in the health, safety, and well-being of residents or the quality of their care. Despite financial and other inducements to upgrade staffing levels, one of the most important deficiencies among the facilities, the industry continues to skimp on its help, thus fostering ongoing worker shortages.

Nor does market-based competition and consumer "choice" work effectively for patients and their families who, in reality, can't shop around. For the most part, they are incapable of assessing the quality of the facilities on their own. At the same time, the need for institutional care often occurs unexpectedly, forcing elders to select a nursing home on short notice; beds within decent places generally are scarce, especially for the poor.

Fiscal belt tightening within this overwhelmingly private province of institutional care has been at the expense of the vulnerable nursing home population. National and state cost-cutting measures have only served to trigger threatened—and actual—bankruptcy, lower patient access to services, and reduced quality of care. They have not, however, markedly affected the profits of the facilities or prevented their ongoing drainage of the public treasury.

Indeed, the United States must begin to dismantle the megachains and deprivatize all long-term care services; the privatized system of elder care simply has not worked–and cannot work. Efforts to regulate and improve social protections as well as to curb public expenditures within the context of market relations and a commercial climate only engender new problems and cost-shifting. Not only have there been few appreciable gains for the frail elderly, but the market-based system of care often jeopardizes their well-being and burdens their caregivers. Nor have the attempts at controlling the health and long-term care industries saved the government money: costs are transferred within programs (e.g., Medicare) or passed on to other ones (e.g., Medicaid). The introduction of the hospital prospective payment system, for instance, led to sicker people at home and in nursing homes as well as the promotion and growth of the costly for-profit home health care industry. Restructured payment methods for home health agencies, in turn, have encouraged them to reduce access to the poor and skimp on their care.

Financial fraud, apparently business as usual among the health and long-term care industries, is yet another significant chink in the virtues of the private sector as the preferred agents of formal elder care. The growing commercialism among home health agencies, hospitals, physicians, psychologists, psychiatrists, nursing homes, pharmaceutical companies, clinical laboratories, providers of durable medical equipment, and other firms has escalated the extent and magnitude of fraudulent practices. And some of the government's endeavors to contain public expenditures seem to have ushered in new, innovative, and unscrupulous practices.

Legitimate providers and criminals alike continue to loot the public treasury, taking community money rightly belonging to the sick and needy. Overuse of services, billing for care not rendered or provided by unlicensed, poorly trained personnel, kickbacks, and the like plainly threaten the health, well-being, and safety of elders reliant on others for assistance. On the other hand, managed care organizations, with their eye focused solely on the bottom line, have picked our pockets by obstructing access to care and skimping on patient services. These so-called white-collar crimes, often perpetuated by privileged professionals and major corporations, are neither pursued aggressively nor punished sufficiently. Most offenders are allowed to continue providing publicly funded services, despite the economic and human toll their plundering engenders.

Nevertheless, the dominant rhetoric embracing privatization and antigovernment practices has been reinforced under the George W. Bush administration. In addition to strengthening protections for nursing home operators and diluting regulations for the health and elder care industries overall, HCFA has embarked on an ambitious drive to lighten their paperwork, ease the legal process, lower sanctions, reduce restitution payments, impose fewer government controls, allow greater self-monitoring, and promote other provisions fashioned to placate and bolster provider groups and their interests.

Concomitantly, the current leadership has energetically promoted even more private sector solutions to social problems, including Social Security, Medicare, and a vast array of tax incentives and tax credits for long-term care insurance, caregivers assisting disabled relatives, and medical savings accounts. In accordance with the ideological climate of the times, such policies maintain the antigovernment myth by keeping new programs off budget while simultaneously withholding help to the poor and maintaining the existing, exploitive system of care. Though the middle class can gain some tax relief, the financial gains are sorely short of any meaningful help toward meeting their kin's elder care needs.

Government policy through tax expenditures, though less visible than direct program outlays, is expensive. To illustrate, since the 1980s policymakers have strengthened the privatization of retirement income. In 2001 alone, the federal treasury lost $140 billion from such tax deductions: the public outlay equivalents for Individual Retirement Accounts (IRAs), 401(k) plans, Keogh plans, and employer pension schemes were $24 billion, $55 billion, $8 billion, and $53 billion, respectively.[7] These indirect public costs would skyrocket, of course, if Social Security were to be fully or partially privatized. Whereas the current Social Security system serves over 90 percent of elders in the nation, the private system of retirement income advantages only the more privileged sectors of society, with women and racial/ethnic minorities receiving the least gains. Thus, the antigovernment rhetoric does not preclude government intervention in personal matters; rather, it shifts public benefits to those who need them the least.

Instead of private sector solutions, policymakers must begin to address the underlying structural problems embedded in our usual approaches to health and long-term care and recalibrate how we measure appropriate treatment for dependent people. Any fundamental changes, however, will meet the considerable resistance of the health and long-term care lobby groups, all of which wield formidable power and garner huge campaign war chests.

Revaluation of Care Work

Unarguably, the interplay of gender, race, ethnicity, and class must be treated as central to any discussion of elder care policy. As analyzed in this book, women are the primary individual stakeholders in the world of elder care, whether as family caregivers, paid workers, or the population in need of aid. Since the vast majority of vulnerable elders are on their own, without government assistance, their spouses and adult children are expected to fill in the gaps and provide the help they need. Moreover, policymakers have enacted policies and cost-containment measures that shift ever greater burdens on wives and daughters who increasingly are incapable of meeting the demands placed on them. Caregiving is not only an expectation but now is also a "normal" experience for women, many of whom are single and discharging their responsibility without any financial or other help from anyone. Their charges are sicker and in need of care for longer periods of time than in the past; there may be more of them, both absolutely and relative to available caretakers; and they sometimes live far away.

Females shoulder most household duties, including elder care, yet encounter more hurdles than men in affording paid help or balancing their domestic and workplace obligations. Current policies, premised on the invisibility and low status of the caregiving role, also allow government officials to disregard the actual costs of assisting frail older people. Such caregiving can foster economic hardship; stress; deteriorating health, both physical and psychological; social isolation; and exhaustion. Low-income and racial/ethnic minority women are particularly vulnerable since they tend to have the lowest income and the least autonomy and flexibility at work. Nor can they afford to quit their jobs. Many of them also are pressed into hands-on elder care duties because of cultural and religious mandates, financial imperatives, and discriminatory practices, regardless of their situation or capacity to provide care and often at great sacrifice to themselves. Though likely to have larger support networks than the population at large, Blacks and Latinas, along with Asians, tend to have greater burdens and experience more financial, emotional, and physical strains.

Paid domestic labor mirrors unpaid family assistance in that it is hidden, undervalued, and unrecognized. Increasingly relying on women of color and immigrants, many with transnational families, long-term care employers pay poverty-level wages, offer only limited—or no—health care or other fringe benefits, provide few opportunities for advancement, and keep tight controls over their employees' daily work lives, especially in nursing homes. Though poorly trained and with limited education and medical expertise, aides are expected to take care of patients suffering from multiple, complex physical and mental disorders, many of whom are emotionally needy, resistant, frustrated, or abusive. Their unrealistically high workloads and rigid, harsh working conditions render it difficult to provide decent care, fostering demoralization, discontent, stress, and burnout.

The third key players in the highly gendered long-term care system are functionally incapacitated women, the predominant group among the oldest-old population. Most of them experience low and poverty-level incomes that limit their independence, choices, and control over their lives. Without adequate resources of their own or access to decent and sufficient social services, less-privileged women become subject to the whims of relatives and providers alike. More likely than men to live to an advanced age and less apt to have a spouse or the money to pay for private assistance, they often are dependent on government programs. Since in the United States elder care translates into either family assistance or nursing home placement, dependent female elders without available relatives as well as those who have exhausted their kin supports are warehoused in institutions. Moreover, though the structure of the current system and the policies sustaining it enrich providers, they often impoverish even middle-class women depending on them for care. These institutions symbolize the degree of our collective neglect of the frail aged and the abandonment of the poor. Perhaps hiding them away spares us "a confrontation with our own future" (Rubin, 2000, 75).

Since long-term care is a woman's issue and the structural problems, inadequacies inherent in current programs, gaps and reductions in public offerings, and rising out-of-pocket costs all affect women disproportionately, any new approaches and practices must become more women-friendly. In order to achieve this objective, social welfare measures have to be based on the actual lives and experiences of females, both at younger and older ages (Browne, 1998). And a higher regard by policymakers for care labor itself underlies any improved, more responsive courses of action: caregiving must become more esteemed, honored, and rewarded. In essence, public officials need to appreciate that kin work is as valuable to society as the pursuits that take place in the labor force and adopt an ethics of care as one of the primary foundations of public policy.

At the same time, women should not be forced into elder care, whether by internal or outside pressures. Certainly, some of the inner compulsion stems from the lack of decent alternatives. Society must afford well spouses, as well as adult children, the ability to decide for themselves whether or not to provide hands-on assistance, the amount they are willing to give, and how much additional help they require. Rather than provide patchwork relief that reinforces care labor as a woman's uncompensated, special task and helps her "adjust" to her role, it is essential that available services be structured so as to truly bolster families in their elder care choices and accord carers greater control over their lives (Baines, Evans, and Neysmith, 1998). Consequently, support services should take into account the situation—and wishes—of care providers and care recipients alike. We also must make sure that any specific offerings address real and concrete needs and do not simply hide systemic issues or deflect attention from the underlying economic, political, and social forces that generated the problems in the first place.

It is imperative that policymakers do not ignore the racial and ethnic dimensions of the problems as well. Racial/ethnic older women have some distinct characteristics and confront unique, often formidable problems, much of it compounded by class. More likely to be poor throughout their lives than the dominant population and to lack medical coverage during their younger years, Black and Latino elders have greater incidence of disabling conditions and fewer financial resources with which to seek formal assistance. Substantial structural barriers, including exclusionary and discriminatory practices and restrictive eligibility requirements for public programs, prevent many of them from receiving the care they need. Moreover, certain low-income neighborhoods not only are underserved by in-home and community services, assisted living facilities, and nursing homes, but their quality also tends to be inferior to that found in more privileged areas. Racial and ethnic elders covered under Medicaid often are relegated to the most substandard institutions. Not only are these groups in need of access to affordable, higher-quality local services, but the foreign-born among them require culturally competent programs that take into account their customs, traditions, preferences, distinct lifestyles, and, for many, their lack of fluency in English.

Just as importantly, as we maximize elder care choices for more privileged households, we must be careful not to do so at the expense of economically disadvantaged sectors of society. White middle- and upper-class older females and their families often rely on the cheap labor power of other women. Thus, the care options available to some are dependent on the precarious situation and exploitation of others. Under current conditions, the escalating demand for nursing home aides and home care attendants points to more and more women joining the ranks of the working poor, including those forced from the welfare rolls and immigrants driven out of their home nations.

Accordingly, care labor must be revalued in the labor force as well. Frontline workers, who are responsible for the vast majority of patient care, must be recognized for their considerable contributions to the caring enterprise. Whether employed at a nursing facility or in an elder's home, aides merit respect and adequate rewards for their willingness to take on the enormous challenges that care work entails.

Most obviously, revaluing the importance of formal care implies that front-line elder care workers must earn higher, more decent wages; receive adequate benefits, especially health care and pension coverage; and be offered opportunities for career advancement. Within the nursing home, their conditions of employment must be restructured so that they are not so overburdened, their efforts are deemed worthy, and there is greater control over at least some aspects of their environment. Greater flexibility regarding scheduling, breaks, and leaves, liberal paid sick and vacation allowances, and more family-responsive policies overall also would foster greater job satisfaction.

At a minimum, smaller worker-to-resident ratios and a slower pace of the work itself would benefit the direct care staff and would also allow them to perform more capably and better meet the emotional and psychological needs of their patients. Thus, the federal government must mandate adequate and not just minimum staffing levels. Greater staffing along with injury prevention strategies also are vital to protect the aides. Mechanical and other patient-handling devices, for instance, could reduce the high incidence of back injuries. In addition, the federal ergonomic standards cancelled by Bush in 2000 must be reestablished and perhaps upgraded.

Industry leaders charge that staff shortages, high turnover, and frequent absenteeism are due to external factors that are mostly out of their control. Along with policymakers, they also affix blame on the aides for patient neglect and mistreatment and chatter on about their deficiencies, such as low skill levels, education, training, and experience, again ignoring the fundamental issues. Instead, as chapter 4 has elaborated, most of the problems are rooted in the deficiencies in the workplace, the economizing on care labor, and the exploitation of the frontline workers whose interests, needs, and concerns are largely disregarded. It should be no wonder that nursing homes, home health agencies, and families requiring help confront serious worker shortages and high turnover.

Feminists must begin to give elder care a more prominent place among their central concerns. The socially, economically, politically, and culturally imposed harms to young women can translate into new and sometimes even greater oppressions during old age. The powerlessness of frail aged women is seen most acutely in their potential for losing control over their bodies and their vulnerability to emotional and physical violence, especially in nursing homes but in other situations as well. Their low or poverty-level incomes, functional incapacities, and dependency on others expose them to exploitative individuals and institutions as well as loss of their basic human rights and command over their own lives. In order to fully address the world of elder care and all of its at-risk female participants, feminists will have to traverse difficult, complex ground that includes the basic values and structures of the American political economy and the vast gender, racial/ethnic, and class inequities it engenders.

Toward a National Commitment to Care

Researchers and practitioners alike have described both the appropriate goals of long-term care and various paradigms for meeting them. However, in order to enact more appropriate policies and fully and effectively meet the requirements of the functionally disabled elderly, Americans must first begin to view vulnerable people as a collective responsibility by embracing the notions of interdependence, community, and intergenerational connectedness. In reality, we are all dependent, to a varying extent, on others and share common plights. However, "in modern industrial societies, we tend to acknowledge the truth of our dependence on one another only when illness or another stressful event makes this reality fully evident to us" (Lustbader, 1991, 137).

Self-reliance, always viewed as a virtue by the dominant culture, has now been glorified, intensified, and championed as a leading value upon which we should base all social policies. Even the limited national entitlement to welfare has been revoked, leaving states more financially responsible for benefits while placing time limits and other burdensome constraints on at-risk women and children. Concomitantly, American residualism, based on the idea of using minimal public resources to meet personal needs, promotes a two-tiered strategy whereby benefits for the middle and upper classes are "earned" (e.g., Social Security and Medicare) and those for the poor and disadvantaged are unmerited and undeserved (e.g., Medicaid). The latter services are structured through rigid means-tested programs that segregate, stereotype, and stigmatize beneficiaries. They also provide the bare minimum of aid, assuming that the indigent are not entitled to a decent quality of life at public expense.

The preeminence of extreme individualism and residualism has allowed us to ignore, blame, and burden people in need while diverting attention from the real causes of social ills. Instead of stressing individuals, policymakers must begin to turn to the social causes of personal plights and accept the idea of a collective obligation to resolve them. As such, long-term care should be a universal entitlement, providing help to physically and mentally functionally impaired people of all ages. In a care system based on mutual assistance and the pooling of community resources, high-quality, wide-ranging services would be available to everyone who needs and wants them. They would be affordable; easily accessible; adaptable to accommodate individual needs and circumstances; continuous, but flexible as situations alter; and controlled, as far as possible, by recipients them-selves. Social provisions should take into account consumer preferences, culture, and language; the total person, including her physical, psychological, and social well-being; and the family support system. They also must provide for wide-ranging levels of care needs, including dementia.

Publicly supported consumer options can range from personal and instru-mental services in community settings, including full-time day care when ap-propriate, to nursing homes and other types of facilities such as assisted liv-ing.[8] Adequate funding for home repairs and structural modifications would render dwellings more suitable for disabled occupants. An expansion of af-fordable housing and rent supplements, along with greater property tax relief programs, also would go a long way toward meeting the needs of chronically disabled people.

Significantly, as nearly all students in the field observe, people with func-tional incapacities can only be treated thoroughly and successfully by coordi-nating and integrating health and long-term care programs and services. The current approach, which artificially bifurcates medical intervention and in-strumental/personal assistance, ignores the real and considerable linkages be-tween and among acute illnesses, chronic diseases, disabling conditions, and supportive services.

Providing public funding for long-term care and greater access to services will not be enough to meet the overwhelming needs of our growing physically and mentally impaired population. As Calasanti and Slevin (2001) correctly argue, in addition to upgrading the worth of care work we must "normalize men as carers." It will be impossible to improve measurably the financial and psychosocial well-being of women unless men begin to share equally in care labor and other domestic and household obligations (Aronson, 1992).

The Broader Social Policy Realms

Elder care issues must be viewed in the context of the broader social questions related to age and the interlocking gendered, racialized, and class-based sys-tems of oppression that structure them, both nationally and internationally. I can only briefly sketch a few of these larger political and socioeconomic issues, all of which are rooted in the relations of production and reproduction and the patriarchal power relationships that frame them. A more detailed assess-ment is beyond the scope of this book.

As suggested, the economic vulnerability of older women often stems from patriarchal assumptions, values, and public policies that privilege men over women throughout the life span. Young and middle-aged females confront myriad cumulative disadvantages at home, in the labor market, workplace, private pensions, Social Security system, and social welfare programs generally, all of which foster low incomes in old age, especially for elderly women who are widowed, divorced, or never-married. First and foremost, then, we must address the vast inequalities of income and feminization of poverty among the younger generation that have only worsened with the deep restructuring of the economy over the last several decades.[9] For women, this entails investing in their education and training so that they can obtain decent employment; expanding their access to and opportunities for well-paid work, both in the market and public sectors; offering quality and affordable day care; offering improved and nonstigmatized welfare payments; and advancing other policies that would allow them to earn better wages and improve their financial well-being.

Notably, we must combat the structural racism and anti-immigrant mentality that intersect with gender to impoverish a disproportionate percentage of young Blacks, Latinos, and other minority populations, especially single mothers. The struggle will not be easy within a political economy that is steeped in discriminatory practices—from job markets and pension policies to health care, housing, and social welfare provision generally. As the nation becomes more racially and ethnically diverse and these groups approach old age, their dire situation will translate into even greater pockets of poverty among the future aged.

Economically disadvantaged groups also tend to confront more, earlier, and severer incapacitating diseases. As is widely known, health and socioeconomic status are inextricably linked. Many of the degenerative and chronic conditions prevalent among the aged stem from earlier untreated diseases, poor nutrition, unhealthy living environments, and lack of medical services. Since 1982, a declining percentage of young Americans are privately insured: 42.6 million people, or nearly 16 percent of the population, currently have no health care coverage; many of them are ethnic/minority households (Anders, 1997).

The success of any long-term care system will depend on making generational investments: in order to enhance the health, independence, and well-being of the elderly in coming years, we must not only increase the socioeconomic status of younger women but also provide them access to adequate medical assistance through a universal, affordable, and quality health care system. Among other benefits, it would lower both the incidence and severity of chronic ailments, functional disabilities, and dependency in the future. In order to be effective, the services must be channeled through nonmarket mechanisms, an approach that will demand a fundamental restructuring of the entire U.S. health care system and a reevaluation of the basic assumptions on which it is based. Any attempt to superimpose universal access to services upon the current medical system would only foster higher costs and greater profits without raising the quality of care.

We also must revamp our retirement systems so that they are in accord with the real lives and situations of females as workers and unpaid caregivers. As a case in point, though ostensibly gender neutral, the Social Security system is based on the employment pattern of men, their relatively higher wages, and a traditional family norm that views them as the breadwinners and wives as their dependents. It also counts women's care labor in the home as worthless, penalizing them with zero-income years calculated into their average lifetime earnings. These and other gendered components of the program not only translate into low, often poverty-level incomes for single older women but also render those who are still married only one husband away from impoverishment. At a minimum, in order to improve older women's economic resources, our Social Security system must begin to value kin work as well as take into account women's lower wages, varied work histories, and their generally nontraditional family status, especially among the oldest old.[10] We must also prevent the political penchant for benefit slashing, whether through raising the eligibility age, through cost-of-living reductions, or through across-the-board benefit decreases, since such policies disproportionately place older women at risk.

Instead of merely tinkering with the existing system, however, I would propose a more women-friendly approach that would make the program more equitable and effective as well as more suitable for the twenty-first century. In lieu of the current unstable, three-legged retirement stool, composed of Social Security, personal assets, and a job-based private retirement system, I would offer what I view as more human legs to stand on. I would advocate a flat benefit for all people who reach age sixty and older that would provide a reasonably satisfactory standard of living and be granted as a matter of right. Benefits would be unrelated to contributions or work history. Specially earmarked federal income taxes could subsidize the program, thus shifting from the current regressive, wage-based approach to one that is more progressively financed.

The existent Social Security system could substitute for the hodgepodge of private retirement trusts that, as suggested earlier, serve primarily the pension elite but are partially and generously funded by all taxpayers through indirect means.[11] I would retain Social Security as a supplementary program, though at much reduced benefit and tax levels. Couples would be subject to earnings sharing, thus improving the situation of divorced, widowed, and low-income working-class women. Of course, some households would have additional resources through any savings that they can accrue.

In addition to improving the financial position and health of women of all ages, we must make the labor force itself more family friendly. Consequently, we need to challenge the assumptions underlying the organization of work, the conditions of employment, and the proper place of jobs in the American political economy. The separate, demarcated private household and market spheres are patently unrealistic in a society that expects women to work and families to supply nearly all of the unpaid kin labor. The ability of people to choose hands-on care without becoming emotionally and financially devastated will depend on what changes can be forged in the workplace. As a start, every employed person should be entitled to partially or fully paid family leave for both child and elder care, flexible schedules, and job sharing when practicable. The 1993 Family and Medical Leave Act is not sufficient: the leaves are unpaid and the act only covers companies with fifty or more employees. However, as with my other proposals, this will fly in the face of the ideological tenor of the times as well as the formidable opposition of employers, who are steadily retracting their workers' health and pension benefits and complaining about the ones they still provide.[12]

Some Concluding Thoughts

Other nations are confronting the pressures of age as well: worldwide, the percentage of elderly is increasing rapidly, particularly that of the oldest-old population, and in most places the elderly are outpacing total population growth.[13] As a result, First World nations are scrambling to meet escalating elder care costs but with fewer working-age people to support them. However, many places tend to have more communal, less individualist notions of personal needs and obligations, and a greater foundation of health and social welfare provision than the United States. At a minimum, most other advanced industrial countries have attained near universal health care coverage.[14] Overall, they also have made more progress in fostering social solutions to long-term care problems, even if few places have worked out their policies entirely and their programs fall short of the ideal. Moreover, despite recent economic problems and the subsequent attacks on their welfare states, most First World nations are resisting substantial retrenchment in their provision of fundamental benefits and services.

Regardless of approach, nearly all of Europe, Canada, and Japan have some publicly supported long-term care assistance available for their dependent older population. Though they often have similar percentages of their elders residing in institutions as the United States, not one of these countries has the equivalent of our inhumane, profiteering nursing homes. For the most part, their facilities provide more homelike environments and more compassionate care than we do.[15] Indeed, it is the American dependence on for-profit providers that distinguish us most from the rest of the world (Kane, Kane, and

Ladd, 1998). And most other places provide a panoply of community services, special housing options, and attendant allowances so that disabled elders can purchase and manage at least some in-home services on their own (Keigher, 1995).[16] With differing commitments, emphases, funding levels, and cost-sharing obligations, their efforts range from bolstering family caregivers to full public support, enabling frail elders to live in their communities on their own, when appropriate (Baldock and Evers, 1992; Doty, 1995; Olson, 1994).[17]

I am not optimistic about the United States. The 76 million baby boomers are arriving at old age, prompting concerns that they will steadily overwhelm Social Security, Medicare, and the federal budget generally as early as 2011. The terms of public debate over social welfare provision are circumscribed by the perceived needs of capital in a globalized economy; an antigovernment, antitax mentality; and the sense that federal and state budgets are "overburdened." The reigning ideological beliefs have allowed companies to divert culpability for the social and economic dislocations over the last several decades from themselves to the elderly and the poor as well as to steadily shake off social welfare obligations to their own workers and their families. In such a climate, the nation is in no mood to legislate universal benefits of any kind, despite the unmistakable advantages they would bring to women, children, and the community at large.[18] We lack the political will to provide even basic income support for our vulnerable families, as most recently illustrated by the Personal Responsibility and Work Opportunity Reconciliation Act of 1996.

It is not even clear whether adequate reforms are possible under current structural arrangements and the fundamental precepts that drive them. The key challenge for policymakers is not growing demands on the public treasury and finding sufficient resources for elder care or even for the poor and needy generally. It will be in surmounting deeply embedded ideas and concepts about gender, race and immigrant status, the proper role of government, the family, self-reliance, privatization, the value of caregiving, and the broader issues related to social and economic inequalities in the political economy. Unlike other nations, Americans have an abiding trust in and reliance on the marketplace and the private sector for solving social problems, despite their obvious and persistent failures in meeting the real needs of people, especially its most at-risk sectors of society.

Notes

1. Strokes and arthritis are the leading causes of disability and dependency for older people; other common disabling illnesses include hearing and visual impairments, heart disease, dementia, emphysema, osteoporosis, and diabetes. Women are

more at risk of osteoporosis than men; diabetes is more common among minorities, especially those who are poor.

2. Though disability among the aged has been declining slightly, including among the oldest old, their numerical growth fosters more people in need of assistance (SSCA, 1998e).

3. In contrast, Finland, Germany, and France spend 9 percent of their GDP on health care; Italy and Norway, 8 percent; and Denmark, 7 percent (U.S. Bureau of the Census, 1996).

4. In 1960 and 1980, the United States spent only 5 percent and 9 percent, respectively, of its GDP on health services.

5. Overall, we continue to lead other nations in the percentage of health care costs paid by individuals and families themselves.

6. The issue was briefly discussed from 1993 to 1994 under President Clinton's ill-fated Health Security Act.

7. The $140 billion represents about 38 percent of Social Security outlays for the aged that year.

8. Of course, assisted living facilities must be prevented from becoming just another form of substandard nursing home (Wiener and Stevenson, 1998).

9. In 2001, the overall poverty rate climbed for the first time since 1992, to 11.7 percent of Americans or 33 million people. The richest 20 percent of the population earned more than 50 percent of the nation's total personal income, and the amount accruing to those at the bottom declined since 2000.

10. Though baby boomers overall will be better off than previous generations, single women will continue to suffer from seriously inadequate income, especially Blacks and Latinos. At the time of their retirement, 43 percent of single baby boomer women most likely will be living in poverty or near-poverty conditions. Their average income will be substantially less than that of either married couples or single men. Moreover, though most of them will receive Social Security benefits, "it is likely that baby boom women will contribute more in payroll taxes but actually get less in their old age than their mothers (who most likely did not work outside the home)" (Dailey, 1998, 94–95).

11. It should be noted that the profound restructuring of the industrial sector in recent years has led to fewer plans and less generous benefits even for people who are covered under private retirement plans.

12. On the other hand, according to a Metlife study of working caregivers, in 1997 employers lost $4.9 million in replacement costs for employees who had to quit, $488 million for partial and $398 for full-day absenteeism, and $4.0 million for workday interruptions. They estimate that the total costs to business may range from $11 billion to $29 billion annually (Metlife, 1997).

13. Italy, Greece, Sweden, Belgium, and Spain have the greatest percentage of people aged sixty and over; the United States is in twenty-fifth place (U.S. Bureau of the Census, 1996).

14. Most of them also have achieved greater overall health among their citizens than we have, as measured by longevity or infant and maternal mortality indicators.

15. Denmark, for example, offers private, comfortable accommodations in its facilities (Kane, Kane, and Ladd, 1998). The high quality of care in Scotland, detailed by Kayser-Jones (1981), has already been discussed in chapter 5.

16. In some places, the money can be paid to their caregiving kin.

17. Public generosity varies considerably: as is well known, the Scandinavian countries—Norway, Sweden, Finland, and Denmark—provide extensive home help to their dependent populations. Germany, which has now folded its long-term care program into its universal health insurance system, Japan, and the Netherlands, too, have relatively wide-ranging services (SSCA, 1998e).

18. In point of fact, racial minorities and immigrants increasingly will comprise the bulk of support for the deluge of White, European American aged who will be drawing from the Social Security and Medicare systems.

REFERENCES

Abel, Emily K. 1991. *Who Cares for the Elderly? Public Policy and the Experiences of Adult Daughters*. Philadelphia: Temple University Press.

———. 2000. *Hearts of Wisdom: American Women Caring for Kin, 1850–1940*. Cambridge, Mass.: Harvard University Press.

Aging Research and Training News. 2001. 3 (March 24). Silver Springs, Md.: Business Publishers.

American Association of Retired Persons (AARP). 1998. *Across the States: Profiles of Long-Term Care Systems*. Washington, D.C.: Public Policy Institute.

———. 1999. *Bulletin*. 40, 11 (December).

———. 2000a. *Bulletin*. 41, 2 (February).

———. 2000b. *Bulletin*. 41, 4 (April).

———. 2000c. *Bulletin*. 41, 5 (May).

———. 2000d. *Bulletin*. 41, 10 (November).

———. 2001a. *Bulletin*. 42, 1 (November).

———. 2001b. *Bulletin*. 42, 2 (December).

———. 2001e. "In the Middle: A Report on Multicultural Boomers Coping with Family and Aging Issues." National survey conducted for AARP by Belden, Russonello, and Stewart, Washington, D.C., and Research/Strategy/Management, Great Falls, VA. (July).

———. 2001d. *Bulletin*. 42 (September).

———. 2001e. *Bulletin*. 42, 5 (May).

———. 2002a. *Bulletin*. 43, 3 (March).

———. 2002b. *Bulletin*. 43, 1 (January).

———. 2002c. *Bulletin*. 43, 5 (May).

American Health Care Association (AHCA). 2002. "National Data on Nursing Homes." Retrieved online from www.ahca.org/who/profile4.htm (viewed June 2002).

Anders, George. 1997. *Health against Wealth: HMOs and the Breakdown of Medical Trust.* Boston: Houghton Mifflin.

Angel, Jacqueline, Ronald J. Angel, Judi McClellan, and Kyriakos Markides. 1996. "Nativity, Declining Health, and Preferences in Living Arrangements among Elderly and Mexican Americans: Implications for Long-Term Care." *Gerontologist* 36, 4:464–73.

Angel, Ronald J., and Jacqueline L. Angel, 1997. *Who Will Care for Us? Aging and Long-Term Care in Multi-cultural America.* New York: New York University Press.

Angel, Ronald J., Jacqueline Angel, Geum-Yong Lee, and Kyriakos Markides. 1999. "Age at Migration and Family Dependency among Older Mexican American Immigrants: Recent Evidence from the Mexican American EPESE." *Gerontologist* 39, 1:59–65.

Applewhite, Steven. 1998. "Culturally Competent Practice with Elderly Latinos." In *Latino Elders and the Twenty-First Century,* edited by Melvin Delgado. New York: Haworth Press.

Arizona Republic. 2000. "Unsuitable Workers Still in Nursing Homes." August 31, editorial: 8.

Aronson, Jane. 1992. "Women's Sense of Responsibility for the Care of Old People: 'But Who Else is Going to Do It?'" March. *Gender and Society* 6, 1:8–29.

———. 1998. "Dutiful Daughters and Undemanding Mothers: Constraining Images of Giving and Receiving Care in Middle and Later Life," In *Women's Caring: Feminist Perspectives on Social Welfare,* edited by Carol Baines, Patricia Evans, and Sheila Neysmith, 114–38. New York: Oxford University Press.

Aronson, Jane, and Sheila M. Neysmith. 1996. "You're Not Just in There to Do the Work: Depersonalizing Policies and the Exploitation of Home Care Workers' Labor." February. *Gender and Society* 10, 1:59–77.

Atlanta Journal/Constitution. 2000. "Nursing Home Residents Need Relief." November 17: sec. 26A.

Baines, Carol T., Patricia M. Evans, and Sheila M. Neysmith. 1998. "Women's Caring: Work Expanding State Contracting." In *Women's Caring: Feminist Perspectives on Social Welfare,* edited by Carol Baines, Patricia Evans, and Sheila Neysmith, 3–22. New York: Oxford University Press.

Baldock, J., and A. Evers. 1992. "Innovations and Care of the Elderly: The Cutting Edge of Change for Social Welfare Systems." *Ageing and Society* 12:298–312.

Barusch, Amanda. 1994. *Older Women in Poverty: Private Lives and Public Policies.* New York: Springer.

Barusch, Amanda 1995. "Programming for Family Care of Elderly Dependents: Mandates, Incentives, and Service Rationing." *Social Work* 40:315–22.

Bauer, Julia. 1999. "Nursing Homes Hit with Fines." October 6. *Express* (Easton, Pa.) *Times:* 5.

Belgrave, Linda Liska, May Wykle, and Jung Choi. 1993. "Health, Double Jeopardy, and Culture: The Use of Institutionalization by African Americans." *Gerontologist* 33, 3:379–85.

Benjamin, A. E. 1993. "An Historical Perspective on Home Care Policy." *Milibank Quarterly* 71, 1:129–66.

Berens, Michael J. 1998. "Warehousing the Mentally Ill in Nursing Homes." September to December. *Chicago Tribune*.

Binstock, Robert. 1996. "Issues Affecting the Future of Long-Term Care." In *The Future of Long-Term Care: Social and Policy Issues*. edited by R. H. Binstock, L. E. Cluff, and O. Von Mering, pp. 3–18. Baltimore, Md.: Johns Hopkins University Press.

———. 1998. "Health Care Policies and Older Americans." In *New Directions in Old-Age Policies*, edited by Janie S. Steckenrider and Tonya M. Parrott, pp. 13–35. Albany: State University of New York Press.

———. 1999. "Public Policy and Minority Elders." In *Serving Minority Elders in the Twenty-First Century*, edited by Mary L. Wykle and Amasa B. Ford, pp. 5–24. New York: Springer.

Blancato, Robert, and Brian Lindberg. 1998. "The 1995 White House Conference on Aging: A Tradition Confronts a Revolution." In *New Directions in Old-Age Policies*, edited by Janie S. Steckenrider and Tonya M. Parrott, pp. 89–110. Albany: State University of New York Press.

Brody, Elaine M. 1995. "Prospects for Family Caregiving: Response to Change, Continuity, and Diversity." In *Family Caregiving in an Aging Society*, edited by Rosalie Kane and Joan D. Penrod. Thousand Oaks, Calif.: Sage.

Browne, Colette V. 1998. *Women, Feminism, and Aging*. New York: Springer.

Buhler-Wilkerson, Karen. 2001. *No Place Like Home: A History of Nursing and Home Care in the U.S.* Baltimore: Johns Hopkins University Press.

Calasanti, Toni M. 1996. "Incorporating Diversity: Meaning, Levels of Research, and Implications for Theory." *Gerontologist* 36, 2:147–56.

Calasanti, Toni, and Kathleen F. Slevin. 2001. *Gender, Social Inequalities, and Aging*. Walnut Creek, Calif.: Altamira Press.

Calasanti, Toni, and Anna M. Zajicek. 1993. "A Socialist-Feminist Approach to Aging: Embracing Diversity." *Journal of Aging Studies* 7, 2:117–31.

Calderon, Vanessa, and Sharon Tennstedt. 1998. "Ethnic Differences in the Expression of Caregiver Burden: Results of a Qualitative Study." In *Latino Elders and the Twenty-First Century*, edited by Melvin Delgado, pp. 159–78. New York: Haworth Press.

Calderone, Joe. 2001. "Governor Revives Checks on Nursing Aides." January 7. *New York Daily News:* 39.

Calderone, Joe, and Thomas Zambito. 2000. "Nursing Home Abuse Allegations on Rise." August 1. *New York Daily News:* 8.

———. 2000. "Shame on Nursing Homes." December 17. *New York Daily News*, p. 255.

———. 2001. "Nursing Home Clampdown." January 14. *New York Daily News:* 13.

Caldwell, C. H., L. M. Chatters, A. Billingsley, and R. J. Taylor. 1995. "Church-Based Support Programs for Elderly Black Adults: Congregational and Clergy Characteristics." In *Aging, Spirituality, and Religion: A Handbook*, edited by M. A. Kimble, S. H. McFadden, J. W. Ellor, and J. J. Seeber, pp. 306–24. Minneapolis, Minn.: Fortress Press.

Cancian, Francesca M. 2000. "Paid Emotional Care." In *Care Work: Gender, Labor, and Welfare States*, edited by Madonna Harrington Meyer, pp. 136–49. New York: Routledge.

Cantor, Margarie, and Mark Brennan. 2000. *Social Care of the Elderly: The Effects of Ethnicity, Class, and Culture*. New York: Springer.

————. 1998b. "The Oversight of Nursing Home Care In Pennsylvania: Residents in Jeopardy." A Performance Audit of Pennsylvania's Medical Assistance Long-Term Care as Provided in Nursing Facilities. March. Office of the Auditor General, Harrisburg, Pennsylvania.

Casey, Robert P., Jr. 1998a. "Improving the Quality of Care: A Plan of Action to Improve Long-Term Care in Pennsylvania." November 17. Office of the Auditor General, Harrisburg, Pennsylvania.

————. 1998c. "Residents Still in Jeopardy." A Performance Audit of the Pennsylvania Department of Health's Complaint System for Nursing Home Residents and Their Families. April. Office of the Auditor General, Harrisburg, Pennsylvania.

————. 2000. "A Follow-up Performance Audit of Nursing Home Oversight." October 6. Office of the Auditor General, Harrisburg, Pennsylvania.

Chachere, Vickie. 1998. "Fines Don't Bite Business Hand." November 11. *Tampa Tribune:* 7.

Chang, Grace. 2000. *Disposable Domestics: Immigrant Workers in the Global Economy.* Boston: South End Press, 2000.

Clarette, Aimee, and Pat Johnson. 1998. "Medicaid Long-Term Care: Issues Brief." December 31. Health Policy Tracking Service, National Conference of State Legislators, Washington, D.C.

Clark, Daniel O. 1997. "U.S. Trends in Disability and Institutionalization among Older Blacks and Whites." March. *American Journal of Public Health.* 87, 3:438–40.

Cohen, Elias S. 1997. "Should the Aging Network be Dismantled?—Yes." In *Controversial Issues in Aging,* edited by Andrew E. Scharlach and Leonard W. Kaye, pp. 22–27. Needham Heights, Mass.: Allyn and Bacon.

Cohen, Joel, and William Spector. 1996. "The Effect of Medicaid Reimbursement on Quality of Care in Nursing Homes." *Journal of Health Economics* 15:23–48.

Cohen, Joshua, Matthew Howard, and Martha Nussbaum, eds. 1999. *Is Multiculturalism Bad for Women?* Princeton, N.J.: Princeton University Press.

Cohen, Marion Deutsche. 1996. *Dirty Details: The Days and Nights of a Well Spouse.* Philadelphia: Temple University Press.

Cole, Johnetta. 1986. "Commonalities and Differences." In *All American Women: Lines that Divide, Ties That Bind,* edited by Johnetta B. Cole, pp. 1–30. New York: Free Press.

Collins, Rachel. 2001. "Legislatures Consider Studying Problems Facing Nursing Homes." March. *Boston Globe:* 1.

Congressional Quarterly. 2000. 58 (July 29): 1879.

Connecticut Human Services Committee. 1998. "Final Report of the Nursing Home Work Working Group." February. Hartford: State of Connecticut General Assembly.

Coontz, S. 1992. *The Way We Never Were: American Families and the Nostalgia Trap.* New York: Basic Books.

Costa, Anthony J. 1993. "Elder Abuse." June. *Primary Care.* 20, 2:375–90.

Cowart, Marie E. 1996. "Long-Term Care Policy and the American Family." In *From Nursing Homes to Home Care,* edited by Marie E. Cowart and Jill Quadagno, pp. 169–84. New York: Haworth Press.

Cox, Carole, and Abraham Monk. 1993. "Hispanic Culture and Family Care of Alzheimers Patients," *Health and Social Work* 18, 2:92–100.

Cox, Christopher, and Karen Crummy. 2001. "Lynn Nursing Home Owners Plagued with Problems." August 9. *Boston Herald:* 1.

Crummy, Karen. 2001a. "Care Crisis." January 25. *Boston Herald:* 1, 5.

——. 2001b. "Sun Nursing Homes have History of Patient Attacks," August 10. *Boston Herald:* 12.

Dailey, Nancy. 1998. *When Baby Boom Women Retire.* Westport, Conn.: Greenwood Press.

Daly, Lynne Von Rein. 1998. *A Certain Light: Nursing Home Experiences.* N.l.: Author.

Davis, Henry, and Dan Herbeck. 2001. "Special Report: Nursing Homes." December 9–12. *Buffalo News.*

Deitch, Cynthia H., and Matt L. Huffman. 2001. "Family-Responsive Benefits and the Two-Tiered Labor Market." In *Working Families: The Transformation of the American Home,* edited by Rosanna Hertz and Nancy L. Marshall, pp. 103–130. Berkeley: University of California Press.

De Lollis, Barbara, and Peggy Rogers. 1998. "Neglect, Financial Woes Span Three States." August 16. *Miami-Dade Herald:* sec. A1.

Denver Post. 2000. "Nursing Home Lapses." September 29, editorial: sec. B06.

Detroit Free Press. 2000. "When Bed Rails Kill, Families Go Untold": 1. February 9.

Diamond, Timothy. 1992. *Making Gray Gold: Narratives of Nursing Home Care.* Chicago: University of Chicago Press.

Dilworth-Anderson, Peggye, Ishan Canty Williams, and Sharon Wallace Williams. 2001. "Elderly of African Descent." In *Age through Ethnic Lenses: Caring for the Elderly in a Multicultural Society,* edited by Laura Katz Olson, pp. 95–102. Lanham, Md.: Rowman & Littlefield.

Donovan, Rebecca. 1989. "We Care for the Most Important People in Your Life: Home Care Workers in New York City." *Women's Studies Quarterly* 2:56–65.

Dooley, Pat. 1997. "Medicare Fraud Inquiry Flags $1 Million in Virginia." August 21. *Virginia-Pilot:* A1.

Dorschner, John, and Peter Wallsten. 2003. "Florida Governor Stumps for Medical Malpractice Czars." April 1. *The Miami Herald:* 1.

Doty, Pamela. 1995. "Family Caregiving and Access to Publicly Funded Home Care." In *Family Caregiving in an Aging Society,* edited by Rosalie Kane and Joan D. Penrod. Thousand Oaks, Calif.: Sage.

Dressel, Paula. 1999. "Gender, Race, and Class: Beyond the Feminization of Poverty in Later Life." In *Critical Perspectives on Aging: The Political and Moral Economy of Growing Old,* edited by Meredith Minkler and Carroll L. Estes, pp. 245–52. Amityville, N.Y.: Baywood Publishing Company.

Dribben, Melissa. 2001. "Who Cares for the Caregivers?" October 21. *Philadelphia Inquirer:* 10–15.

DuBois, Barbara C., Carol H. Yavno, and E. Percil Stanford. 2001. "Care Options for Older Mexican Americans: Issues Affecting Health and Long-Term Care Service Needs." In *Age through Ethnic Lenses: Caring for the Elderly in a Multicultural Society,* edited by Laura Katz Olson, pp. 71–85. Lanham, Md.: Rowman & Littlefield.

Dwyer, Jeffrey W., and Raymond T. Coward, eds. 1992. *Gender, Families, and Eldercare.* Thousand Oaks, Calif.: Sage.

Edmonds, Mary McKinney. 1999. "Serving Minority Elders: Preventing Chronic Illness and Disability in the African American Elderly." In *Serving Minority Elders in the Twenty-First Century,* edited by Mary L. Wykle and Amasa B. Ford, pp. 25–36. New York: Springer.

Ehrenreich, Barbara, and John Ehrenreich. 1970. *The American Health Empire: Power, Profits, and Politics.* New York: Vintage.

Ehrenreich, Barbara, and Arlie Russell Hochschild. 2003. "Introduction." In *Global Women: Nannies, Maids, and Sex Workers in the New Economy,* edited by Barbara Ehrenreich and Arlie Russell Hochschild, pp. 1–13. New York: Metropolitan Books.

Eisler, Peter. 1996. "Special Report: Money." November 11. *USA Today:* sec. 11–13B.

Epstein, Helen. 2001. "Time of Indifference." April 12. *New York Review of Books* 43, 6:33–38.

Estes, Carroll. 1979. *The Aging Enterprise.* San Francisco: Jossey-Bass Publishers.

Estes, Carroll, and Charlene Harrington. 1981. "Fiscal Crisis, Deinstitutionalization, and the Elderly," July/August. *American Behavioral Scientist.* 24, 6:811–26.

Eto, Mikiko. 2001. "Confusion in the Introduction of Japan's Long-Term Care Insurance System: Who Is Looking after the Disabled Elderly?" Paper presented at the Northeast Political Science Association Meeting, Philadelphia, November 8–10.

Falcone, David, and Robert Broyles. 1994. "Access to Long-Term Care: Race as a Barrier." Fall. *Journal of Health Politics* 19, 3: 583.

Federal Interagency Forum on Aging-Related Statistics. 2000. *Older Americans 2000: Key Indicators of Well-Being.* August. Washington, D.C.: U.S. Government Printing Office.

Fineman, Martha Albertson. 1995. *The Neutered Mother, The Sexual Family, and Other Twentieth Century Tragedies.* New York: Routledge.

Fingerman, Karen. 2001. *Aging Mothers and Their Adult Daughters: A Study in Mixed Emotions.* New York: Springer.

Foner, Nancy. 1994a. *The Caregiving Dilemma: Work in an American Nursing Home.* Berkeley: University of California Press.

———. 1994b. "Nursing Home Aides: Saints or Monsters?" *The Gerontologist* 34, 2:245–50.

———. 1997. "What's New About Transnationalism? New York Immigrants Today and at the Turn of the Century." *Diaspora* 6, 3:355–75.

Fraser, Nancy. 1994. "After the Family Wage: Gender Equity and the Welfare State." *Political Theory* 22, 4:591–618.

Friedland, Robert B., and Veena Pankaj. 1997. *Welfare Reform and Elderly Legal Immigrants.* Prepared for the Henry J. Kaiser Family Foundation. July. National Academy on Aging, Washington, D.C.

Fulmer, Terry. 1995. "Prevalence of Elder Mistreatment as Reported by Social Workers." In *Elder Mistreatment in the African American Community,* edited by Toshio Tatara, pp. 27– 48. Thousand Oaks, Calif.: Sage.

Fulmer, Terry, and Mildred Ramirez. 1999. "Prevalence of Elder Mistreatment as Reported by Social Workers in a Probability Sample of Adult Day Health Care Clients." *Journal of Elder Abuse and Neglect* 7, 3: 25–36.

Gaines, Atwood D. 1999. "Culture, Aging, and Mental Health." In *Serving Minority Elders in the Twenty-First Century*, edited by Mary L. Wykle and Amasa B. Ford, pp. 180–99. New York: Springer.

Gannon, Linda R. 1999. *Women and Aging: Transcending the Myths.* New York: Routledge.

Garber, Alan. 1995. *To Comfort Always: The Prospects of Expanded Social Responsibility for Long-Term Care.* Working Paper No. 5034. Cambridge, Mass.: Bureau of Economic Research.

Gelfand, Donald, and Charles Barresi. eds. 1987. *Ethnic Dimensions of Aging.* N.Y.: Springer.

Gerace, Cheryl Stewart, and Linda S. Noelker. 1990. "Clinical Social Work Practice with Black Elderly and Their Family Caregivers." In *Black Aged: Understanding Diversity and Service Needs*, edited by Zev Harel, Edward A McKinney, and Michael Williams, pp. 236–58. Thousand Oaks, Calif.: Sage.

Gershman, John, and Alec Irwin. 2000. "Getting a Grip on the Global Economy." In *Dying for Growth: Global Inequality and the Health of the Poor,* edited by Jim Yong Kim, Joyce Miller, Alec Irwin, and John Gershman, pp. 11–43. Monroe, Maine: Common Courage Press.

Gibson, Diane. 1998. *Aged Care: Old Policies, New Problems.* Cambridge: Cambridge University Press.

Gimpel, James G., and James R. Edwards, Jr. 1999. *The Congressional Politics of Immigration Reform.* Boston: Allyn and Bacon.

Glenn, Evelyn Nakano. 1992. "From Servitude to Service Work: Historical Continuities in the Racial Division of Paid Reproductive Labor." *Journal of Women in Culture and Society* 18, 1:1– 43.

Gould, Jean, ed. 1999. *Dutiful Daughters: Caring for Our Parents as They Grow Old.* Seattle, Wash.: Seal Press.

Greene, Vernon, and Patricia Coleman. 1995. "Direct Services for Family Caregivers." In *Family Caregiving in an Aging Society,* edited by Rosalie Kane and Joan D. Penrod. Thousand Oaks, Calif.: Sage.

Greenhouse, Steven. 1999. "The Labor Movement's Eager Risk-Taker Hits Another Jackpot." February 26. *New York Times:* A1.

Groger, Lisa. 1998. "No Target, No Practice: Gerontological Approaches to the Minority Elderly." June. *Journal of Applied Gerontology* 17, 2:119–23.

Gubrium, Jaber. 1975. *Living and Dying at Murray Manor.* New York: St. Martin's Press.

———. 1993. *Speaking of Life: Horizons of Meaning for Nursing Home Residents.* New York: Aldine de Gruyter.

Han, Lein, Charles Barrilleaux, and Jill Quadagno. 1996. "Race and Gender Differences in the Distribution of Home and Community-Based Services in Florida." In *From Nursing Homes to Home Care,* edited by Marie E. Cowart and Jill Quadagno, pp. 93–107. New York: Haworth Press.

Harel, Zev. 2001. "Jewish Aged: Diversity in Need and Care Solutions." In *Age through Ethnic Lenses: Caring for the Elderly in a Multicultural Society,* edited by Laura Katz Olson, pp. 145–59. Lanham, Md.: Rowman & Littlefield.

Harel, Zev, A. McKinney, and M. Williams. 1987. "Aging, Ethnicity, and Services." In *Ethnic Dimensions of Aging,* edited by D. E. Gelfand and C. M. Barresi. New York: Springer.

Harrington, Charlene. 1996. "Nursing Facility Quality, Staffing, and Economic Success." In *Nursing Staff in Hospitals and Nursing Homes: Is It Adequate?* edited by Goolo S. Wunderlich, Frank Sloan, and Carolyne Davis. Washington, D.C.: National Academic Press.

Harrington, Charlene, Helen Carrillo, and J. Mullan. 1998. "Nursing Facility Staffing in the States: The 1991–1995 Period." *Medical Care Research and Review* 55, 3:334–63.

Harrington, Charlene, and Helen Carrillo, 1999. "The Regulation and Enforcement of Nursing Home Standards, 1991–1997." *Medical Care Research and Review* 56, 4: 471–94.

Harris, Bonnie, and Joe Fahy. 1998. "The Tarnished Years: Who Will Protect Our Seniors?" 6-part series, June 19–24. *The Indianapolis Star.*

Harris, Bonnie, and Celeste Williams. 1999. "The Tarnished Years: Who Will Protect Our Seniors?" 4-part series, January 25–28. *The Indianapolis Star.*

Hatch, Julie, and Angela Clinton. 2000. "Job Growth in the 1990s: A Retrospect." *Monthly Labor Review* December:3–18.

Hawes, Catherine, Mirian Rose, and Charles D. Phillips. 1999. "A National Study of Assisted Living for the Frail Elderly: Results of a National Survey of Facilities." December 14. Washington, D.C.: U.S. Department of Health and Human Services.

Hendricks, Jon, Laurie Hatch, and Stephen Cutler. 1999. "Entitlements, Social Compacts, and the Trend toward Retrenchment in U.S. Old-Age Programs." *Hallym International Journal of Aging* 6, 1:14–29.

Hendricks, Jon, and Cynthia A. Leedham. 1999. "Dependency or Empowerment? Toward a Moral and Political Economy of Aging," In *Critical Perspectives on Aging: The Political and Moral Economy of Growing Old,* edited by Meredith Minkler and Carroll L. Estes, 51–64. Amityville, N.Y.: Baywood Publishing Company.

Herbeck, Dan, and Henry Davis. 2001. "Special Report: Nursing Homes." December 9–12. *Buffalo News.*

Herzlinger, Regina E. 1997. *Market-Driven Health Care: Who Wins, Who Loses in the Transformation of America's Largest Service Industry.* Reading, Mass.: Addison-Wesley.

Hilzenrath, David S. 1997. "Drug Firms Said to Pressure Doctors." August 14. *Washington Post.*

———. 1999. "Health Firm in Survival Struggle." November 9. *The Washington Post.*

Hochschild, Arlie Russell. 2003. "Love and Gold." In *Global Women: Nannies, Maids, and Sex Workers in the New Economy,* edited by Barbara Ehrenreich and Arlie Russell Hochschild, pp. 15–30. New York: Metropolitan Books.

Holmberg, R. Hopkins, and Nancy Anderson. 1968. "Implications of Ownership for Nursing Home Care." July/August. *Medical Care.* 6:300–307.

Holstein, Martha, and Thomas Cole. 1996. "The Evolution of Long-Term Care in America." In *The Future of Long-Term Care: Social and Policy Issues,* edited by R. H. Binstock, L. E. Cluff, and O. Von Mering, pp. 19–47. Baltimore: Johns Hopkins University Press.

Hondagneu-Sotelo, Pierrette. 2000. "The International Division of Caring and Cleaning Work." In *Care Work: Gender, Labor and Welfare States,* edited by Madonna Harrington Meyer, pp. 149–63. New York: Routledge.

―――. 2001. *Domestica: Immigrant Workers Cleaning and Caring in the Shadows of Affluence.* Berkeley: University of California Press.

Hooyman, Nancy R., 1999. "Research on Older Women: Where is Feminism?" *Gerontologist* 39:115–18.

Hooyman, Nancy R., and Judith Gonyea. 1995. *Feminist Perspectives on Family Care: Policies for Gender Justice.* Thousand Oaks, Calif.: Sage.

Horner, Joyce. 1982. *That Time of Year: A Chronicle of Life in a Nursing Home.* Amherst: University of Massachusetts Press.

Institute of Medicine (IOM). 1981. *Health Care in a Context of Civil Rights.* Washington, D.C.: National Academy Press.

―――. 1986. *Improving the Quality of Life in Nursing Homes.* Washington, D.C.: National Academy Press.

―――. 1996. *Nursing Staff in Hospitals and Nursing Homes: Is It Adequate?* Edited by Goolo S. Wunderlich, Frank Sloan, and Carolyne Davis. Washington, D.C.: National Academy Press.

Jackson, Jacquelyne Johnson. 1988. "Aging Black Women and Public Policies." May/June *Black Scholar.* 19, 3:31–43.

Jackson, James. 1995. "African American Aged." In *The Encyclopedia of Aging,* 2nd ed., edited by George L. Maddox, pp. 30–80. New York: Springer.

Jesilow, Paul, Henry N. Pontell, and Gilbert Geis. 1993. *Prescription for Profit: How Doctors Defraud Medicaid.* Berkeley: University of California Press.

Jones, Sharon. 1999. "Bridging the Gap: Community Solutions for Black-Elder Health Care in the Twenty-First Century." In *Serving Minority Elders in the Twenty-First Century,* edited by Mary L. Wykle and Amasa B. Ford, pp. 223–47. New York: Springer.

Journal of Health Services Research. 1988. 23, 1.

Julien, Andrew. 1999. "Nursing Home Chain Pays $8 Million, Settles Abuse Charges." February 18. *The Hartford Courant:*1.

Kaffenberger, K. R. 2000. "Nursing Home Ownership: An Historical Analysis." *Journal of Aging and Social Policy* 12, 1:35–48.

Kaledin, Eugenia. 1984. *American Women in the 1950s: Mothers and More.* Woodbridge, Conn.: G. K. Hall.

Kane, Robert L. 1993. "Lessons in Long-Term Care: the Benefits of a Northern Exposure." In *North American Health Care Policy in the 1990s,* edited by Arthur King, Thomas Hyclak, Robert Thorton, and Samuel McMahon. New York: John Wiley and Sons.

Kane, Robert L. 1994. "Long-Term Care in the U.S.: Problems and Promise." In *Economic Security and Intergenerational Justice,* edited by Theodore R. Marmor, Timothy M. Smeeding, and Vernon L. Greene. Washington, D.C.: Urban Institute Press.

Kane, Rosalie A., Robert L. Kane, and Richard C. Ladd. 1998. *The Heart of Long Term Care.* New York: Oxford University Press.

Kane, Rosalie A., and J. Penrod. 1995. "Toward a Caregiving Policy for the Aging Family." In *Family Caregiving in an Aging Society,* edited by R. Kane and J. Penrod. Thousand Oaks, Calif.: Sage.

Kasinitz, Philip. 1992. *Caribbean New York: Black Immigrants and the Politics of Race.* Ithaca, N.Y.: Cornell University Press.

Kay, Julie. 2003. "GOP Falls Back." March 27. *Broward Daily Business:* sec. A1.

Kayser-Jones, Jeanie Schmit. 1981. *Old, Alone, and Neglected: Care of the Aged in Scotland and the United States.* New York: Commonwealth Federation.

Keigher, Sharon M. 1999. "Feminist Lessons from the Gray Market in Personal Care for the Elderly: So What If You Want to Spend Your Own Money?" In *Critical Issues for Future Social Work Practice with Aging Persons,* edited by Sheila Neysmith. New York: Columbia University Press.

Kim, Shin, and Kwang Chung Kim. 2001. "Intimacy at a Distance, Korean American Style: Invited Korean Elderly and Their Married Children." In *Age through Ethnic Lenses: Caring for the Elderly in a Multicultural Society,* edited by Laura Katz Olson, pp. 45–58. Lanham, Md.: Rowman & Littlefield.

King, Violette. 1998. "Nursing Home Abuses Are All Too Real." October 16. *Chicago Tribune:* 28.

Kiyak, H. Asuman, and Nancy Hooyman. 1994. "Minority and Socioeconomic Status: Impact on Quality of Life in Aging." In *Aging and Quality of Life,* edited by Ronald P. Abeles, Helen C. Gift, and Narcia G. Ory, pp. 295–318. New York: Springer.

Knowles, Francine. 2000. "Is Living Wage Enough?" March 1. *Chicago Sun-Times:* 62.

Kosberg, J. I. 1973. "Differences in Proprietary Institutions Caring for Affluent and Nonaffluent Elderly." *Gerontologist* 13:299–304.

Laird, Carobeth. 1982. *Limbo: A Memoir about Life in a Nursing Home by a Survivor.* Novato, Calif.: Chandler and Sharp Publications.

Lee, Philip R., and Carroll L. Estes. 1981. *The Nation's Health.* Sudbury, Mass.: Jones and Bartett Publishers.

Levine, Susan. 1998. "Federal Study Faults Hiring Practices in Nursing Homes." September 15. *Washington Post:* A05.

Levy, Clifford J. 2002. "Mentally Ill Locked Away in Nursing Homes in New York." October 6. *New York Times:* 1.

Lim, Young Mi, Isela Luna, and Sandra L. Cromwell. 1996. "Toward a Cross-Cultural Understanding of Family Caregiving Burden." *Western Journal of Nursing Research* 18, 3:252–66.

Linsk, Nathan, and Sharon Keigher. 1995. "Compensation of Family Care for the Elderly." In *Family Caregiving in an Aging Society,* edited by Rosalie Kane and Joan D. Penrod. Thousand Oaks, Calif.: Sage.

Logan, J. R., and G. Spitze. 1994. "Informal Support and the Use of Formal Services by Older Americans." *Journal of Gerontology: Social Sciences* 49:25–34.

Loucks, Cynthia. 2000. *But This Is My Mother!* Acton, Mass.: Vander Wyk and Burham.

Louie, Kem B. 1999. "Status of Mental Health Needs of Asian Elderly." In *Serving Minority Elders in the Twenty-First Century,* edited by Mary L. Wykle and Amasa B. Ford, pp. 147–59. New York: Springer.

Lustbader, Wendy. 1991. *Counting on Kindness: The Dilemmas of Dependency.* New York: The Free Press.

Macdonald, Barbara, with Cynthia Rich. 1983. *Old Women Aging and Ageism.* Denver, Colo.: Spinsters' Ink Books.

Malone, Julia. 2000. "Nursing Homes Go Hat in Hand to Capital." September 3. *Atlanta Journal/Constitution:* 7P.

Marcell, Jacqueline. 2000. *Elder Rage, or Take My Father . . . Please!* Irvine, Calif.: Impressive Press.

Markides, Kyriakos, and C. H. Mindel. 1987. *Aging and Ethnicity.* Newbury Park, Calif.: Sage.

Markides, Kyriakos, and Christine Stroup-Benham. 1999. "The Health of Mexican American Elderly: Selected Findings from the EPESE." In *Serving Minority Elders in the Twenty-First Century,* edited by Mary L. Wykle and Amasa B. Ford, pp. 72–89. New York: Springer.

Marmor, Theodore R. 1970. *The Politics of Medicare.* London: Routledge and Kegan Paul.

Martin, David. 2002. "Bed-Panning for Gold." October 16. *Cleveland Scene:* 1.

McBarnette, Lorna Scott. 1996. "African American Women." In *Race, Gender, and Health,* edited by Marcia Bayne-Smith, pp. 43–67. Thousand Oaks, Calif.: Sage.

McMullin, Julie Ann. 2000. "Diversity and the State of Sociological Aging Theory." *Gerontologist* 40, 5:517–30.

Meiners, Mark. 1996. "The Financing and Organization of Long-Term Care." In *The Future of Long-Term Care: Social and Policy Issues,* edited by R. H. Binstock, L. E. Cluff, and O. Von Mering, pp. 191–214. Baltimore: Johns Hopkins Press.

Mellor, Jennifer. 2000. "Filling in the Gaps in Long-Term Care Insurance." In *Care Work: Gender, Labor, and Welfare States,* edited by Madonna Harrington Meyer, pp. 202–17. New York: Routledge.

Mendelson, Mary A. 1974. *Tender Loving Freed: How the Incredibly Lucrative Nursing Home "Industry" is Exploiting America's Old People and Defrauding Us All.* N.Y.: Knopf.

Mercer, Susan O., Patricia Heacock, and Cornelia Beck. 1994. "Nurse's Aides in Nursing Homes: A Study of Caregivers." *Journal of Women and Aging* 6:107–20.

Metlife Mature Market Institute. 1997. *Employer Costs for Working Caregivers.* June. Washington, D.C.: Metlife Mature Market Institute and National Alliance for Caregivers.

Meyer, Madonna Harrington, and Michelle Storbakken. 2000. "Shifting the Burden Back to Families?" In *Care Work: Gender, Labor and Welfare States,* edited by Madonna Harrington Meyer, pp. 217–29. New York: Routledge.

Miller, Barbara, and Donald Stull. 1999. "Perceptions of Community Services by African Americans and White Older Persons." In *Serving Minority Elders in the Twenty-First Century,* edited by Mary L. Wykle and Amasa B. Ford, pp. 267–86. N.Y.: Springer.

Millett, Kate. 2001. *Mother Millett.* London: Verso Press.

Min, Pyong Gap. 1998. *Changes and Conflicts: Known Immigrant Families in New York.* Boston: Allyn and Bacon.

Minkler, Meredith, and Thomas R. Cole. 1999. "Political and Moral Economy: Not Such Strange Bedfellows." In *Critical Perspectives on Aging: The Political and Moral Economy of Growing Old,* edited by Meredith Minkler and Carroll L. Estes, 37–49. Amityville, N.Y.: Baywood Publishing Company.

Minkler, Meredith, and Carroll L. Estes, eds. 1999. *Critical Perspectives on Aging: The Political and Moral Economy of Growing Old.* Amityville, N.Y.: Baywood Publishing Co.

Mishel, Lawrence, Jared Bernstein, and John Schmitt. 2001. *The State of Working America 2000/2001.* Ithaca, N.Y.: Cornell University Press.

Montgomery, Rhonda J. V. 1995. "Examining Respite Care: Promises and Limitations." In *Family Caregiving in an Aging Society,* edited by Rosalie Kane and Joan D. Penrod. Thousand Oaks, Calif.: Sage.

Moss, Frank, and Val Halamandaris. 1977. *Too Old, Too Sick, Too Bad: Nursing Homes in America.* Germantown, Md.: Aspen Systems Corp.

Moss, Peter, and Claire Cameron. 2002. "Care Work in Europe: Current Underfundings and Future Directions." October. London: Thomas Coram Research Unit, Institute of Education, University of London. Full report online at 144.82.35.228/carework/uk/reports/index.htm (viewed March 2003).

Mui, Ada C. 1992. "Caregiver Strain among Black and White Daughter Caregivers: A Role Theory Perspective." *Gerontologist* 32, 2:203–12.

Mutran, Elizabeth, and S. Sudha. 2000. "Guest Editorial: Ethnic and Racial Groups, Similar or Different, and How Do We Measure?" *Research on Aging,* Special Issue: Age and Health in a Multiethnic Society 1: Patterns and Methods. November. 22, 6:589–99.

Nalder, Eric, and Kim Barker. 1999. "Throwaway People." 5-part series, December 12–16. *Seattle Times*: 1 (for each date).

National Alliance for Caregiving (NAC) and American Association of Retired Persons (AARP). 1997. *Family Caregiving in the U.S.: Findings from a National Survey.* Final report. June. Washington, D.C.: AARP.

National Center for Health Statistics (NCHS). 1985. *National Nursing Home Survey.* Washington, D.C.: Government Printing Office.

National Citizen's Coalition for Nursing Home Reform (NCC). 2000. *Quality Care Advocate.* Winter. 15, 9/10:1–15.

———. 2001a. *Quality Care Advocate.* April. 16, 1:1–7.

———. 2001b. *Quality Care Advocate.* June. 16, 2:1–11.

———. 2001c. *Quality Care Advocate.* Spring/Summer. 17, 1/2: 8.

Neysmith, Sheila M., and Jane Aronson. 1997. "Working Conditions in Home Care: Negotiating Race and Class Boundaries in Gendered Work." *International Journal of Health Services* 27, 3:479–99.

Nicholas, Peter. 2001. "A Closer Look at Rendell and the SmithKline Deal." June 24. *Philadelphia Inquirer:* sec. A12.

Nohlgren, Nohl. 2001. "Profits and Patients." March 19. *St. Petersburg Times:* 1A.

O'Brien, Mary Elizabeth. 1989. *Anatomy of a Nursing Home: A New View of Resident Life.* Owings Mills, Md.: National Health Publications.

Olson, Laura Katz. 1994. *The Graying of the World: Who Will Care for the Frail Elderly?* Binghamton, N.Y.: Haworth Press.

Parrenas, Rhacel Salazar. 2001. *Servants of Globalization: Women, Migration, and Domestic Work.* Stanford, Calif.: Stanford University Press.

———. 2002. "Human Sacrifices," *The Women's Review of Books.* xix, 5, 5–7.

Pear, Robert. 1997. "Nursing Home Lobbyists Had Access." April 23. *New York Times:* sec. D21.

Peterson, Lindsay. 2000. "Insurers Deserting Nursing Homes." September 22. *Tampa Tribune:* 1.

Peterson, Lindsay, Vickie Chachere, and Doug Stanley. 1998. "Money or Mercy?" November 15. *Tampa Tribune:* 1.

Peterson, Lindsay, and Doug Stanley. 1998. "Profits Can Come at High Costs." November 15. *Tampa Tribune:* 2.

Phillips, Charles, and Kathleen Spry. 2000. "Residents Leaving Assisted Living: Descriptive and Analytic Results from a National Survey." June. Washington, D.C.: Department of Health and Human Services.

Polacca, Mona. 2001. "American Indian and Alaska Native Elderly." In *Age through Ethnic Lenses: Caring for the Elderly in a Multicultural Society,* edited by Laura Katz Olson, pp. 113–22. Lanham, Md.: Rowman & Littlefield.

Powell, Jennifer. 2001a. "Governor's Budget Offers Elderly Aid." January 24. *Boston Herald:* 27.

———. 2001b. "Home's Demise Follows Trend." December 27. *Boston Herald:* 29.

Public Citizen Health Research Group. 1997. *Health Letter.* May. 13, 5:4–5. Washington, D.C.: Author.

Rhoades, Jeffrey A. 1998. *The Nursing Home Market: Supply and Demand for the Elderly.* New York: Garland Publishing.

Robertson, Ann. 1999. "The Politics of Alzheimer's Disease: A Case Study in Apocalyptic Demography." In *Critical Perspectives on Aging: The Political and Moral Economy of Growing Old,* edited by Meredith Minkler and Carroll L. Estes, 135–52. Amityville, N.Y.: Baywood Publishing Company.

Rosenthal, John Terrence. 2000. "Clear and Convincing to Whom? The False Claims Act and Its Burden of Proof Standard: Why the Government Needs a Big Stick." *Notre Dame Law Review.* May:1–74.

Rotstein, Gary. 2002a. "Big Chain Builds Up Long List of Shortfalls in Inspections." September 22. *Pittsburgh Post-Gazette:* sec. A19.

———. 2002b. "Modernizing the Kanes." September 24. *Pittsburgh Post-Gazette:* A6.

———. 2002c. "Nursing Homes Struggling: They Have Too Few Nurses, Aides for Growing Elderly Population." September 22. *Pittsburgh Post-Gazette:* A1.

Rotzoll, Brenda. 2001. "Half of State Home Health Workers Uninsured." March 23. *Chicago Sun-Times:* 21.

Rowbotham, Sheila. 1997. *A Century of Women: The History of Women in Britain and the U.S.* New York: Viking.

Rubin, Lillian B. 2000. *Tangled Lives: Daughters, Mothers, and the Crucible of Aging.* Boston: Beacon Press.

Saghri, E. 2000. "Certified Nursing Assistants and Care Settings in San Diego County." Master's thesis, San Diego State University.

Salganik, M. William. 2000. "U.S. Facing Care-Chain Fraud." December 13. *Baltimore Sun.*

———. 2001. "Nursing Home CEO Gets Departure Deal." January 13. *Baltimore Sun.*

Sanchez, Carmen Delia. 2001. "Puerto Rican Elderly." In *Age through Ethnic Lenses: Caring for the Elderly in a Multicultural Society,* edited by Laura Katz Olson, pp. 86–94. Lanham, Md.: Rowman & Littlefield.

Sanchez-Ayendez, Melba. 1986. "Puerto Rican Elderly Women: Shared Meanings and Informal Supportive Networks." In *All American Women: Lines That Divide, Ties that Bind,* edited by Johnetta B. Cole, pp. 172–86. New York: Free Press.

———. 1998. "Middle-Aged Puerto Rican Women as Primary Caregivers to the Elderly." In *Latino Elders and the Twenty-First Century,* edited by Melvin Delgado, pp. 75–97. New York: Haworth Press.

San Francisco Chronicle. 2000. "A Plan to Curtail Elder Abuse." August 29, editorial: A16.

Sarton, May. 1973. *As We Are Now.* New York: Norton.

———. 1977. *The House by the Sea.* New York: Norton.

Savishinsky, Joel. 1991. *The Ends of Time: Life and Work in a Nursing Home.* New York: Bergin and Garvey.

Scharlach, Andrew E. 1994. "Caregiving and Employment: Competing or Complementary Roles?" *Gerontologist* 34, 3:378–85.

Schiff, Harriet Sarnoff. 1996. *How Did I Become My Parent's Parent?* New York: Penguin.

Schmitt, Christopher H. 2002. "The New Math of Old Age." Special investigative report, September 30. *U.S. News and World Report* 133, 12:67.

Schwartz, Roger A. 1994. "Medicaid Estate Recovery under OBRA 1993: Picking Bones of the Poor." A Report on the Legal Problems of the Elderly. November. Washington, D.C.: American Bar Association.

Service Employees International Union (SEIU). 1997. *Caring Til It Hurts: How Nursing Home Work Is Becoming the Most Dangerous Job in America.* Washington, D.C.: SEIU.

———. 1998. *Rolling the Dice: Quality Failures at Genesis ElderCare.* Washington, D.C.: SEIU.

Shea, Dennis G., Toni Miles, and Mark Hayward. 1996. "The Health–Wealth Connection: Racial Differences." *Gerontologist* 36, 3:342–49.

Shesgreen, Deirdre. 2000. "U.S. Inspectors Find Problems at Nursing Homes Cleared by Missouri." January 28. *St. Louis Post-Dispatch:* sec. A4.

Shibusawa, Tazuko, James Lubben, and Harry H. L. Kitano. 2001. "Japanese American Elderly." In *Age through Ethnic Lenses: Caring for the Elderly in a Multicultural Society,* edited by Laura Katz Olson, pp. 33–44. Lanham, Md.: Rowman & Littlefield.

Shield, Renee Rose. 1988. *Uneasy Endings: Daily Life in an American Nursing Home.* Ithaca, N.Y.: Cornell University Press.

Shulman, Alix Kates. 1999. *A Good Enough Daughter.* New York: Schocken Books.

Simun, April. 1998. "Struggling Home Health Agencies Hope Congress Has a Cure." November 8. *Post-Dispatch* (St. Louis, Mo.): sec. B1.

Skocpol, Theda. 1995. *Social Policy in the United States: Future Possibilities in Historical Perspective.* Princeton, N.J.: Princeton University Press.

Smith, David Barton. 1990. "Population Ecology and the Racial Integration of Hospitals and Nursing Homes in the U.S." *Milbank Quarterly* 68, 4:561–96.

Smith, Elliot Blair. 1998a. "Unheeded Cries for Help Problems at Florida Home Reveal Gaping Holes in Legal Safety Net." October 12. *USA Today:* 1B.

———. 1998b. "Who Will Pay for Medicare Funding Cuts to Elderly?" October 12. *USA Today:* sec. 4B.

Sotomayer, Marta. 1995. "Hispanic Elderly." In *The Encyclopedia of Aging,* 2nd ed., edited by George L. Maddox, pp. 458–59. New York: Springer.

Spalter-Roth, Roberta, and Heidi Hartman. 1988. "Unnecessary Losses: Costs to Americans of the Lack of Family and Medical Leave." Executive Summary, Institute for Women's Policy Research. Washington, D.C.

Sparrow, Malcolm K. 1996. *License to Steal: Why Fraud Plagues America's Health Care System.* Boulder, Colo.: Westview Press.

Spector, W. D., and J. W. Cohen. 1996. "The Effect of Medicaid Reimbursement on the Quality of Care in Nursing Homes." *Journal of Health Economics* 15:23–28.

Stahl, Dulcelina Albano. 2000. "Implications of the Balanced Budget Act of 1997." November 16. *Clinics in Geriatric Medicine* 4, 4:757–75.

Stanford, E. Percil. 1999. "Mental Health, Aging, and Americans of African Descent." In *Serving Minority Elders in the Twenty-First Century,* edited by Mary L. Wykle and Amasa B. Ford, pp. 160–79. New York: Springer.

Stark, Karl. 2002. "Suit Forces Reform of Nursing Homes." August 4. *Philadelphia Inquirer:* sec. E01.

State of Vermont. 2002. "Comparison of State Medicaid Program Costs." November. Retrieved online from www.leg.state.vt.us/jfo/medicaid%20Program%20costs.pdf (viewed February 2003).

Steinhaver, Jennifer. 2000. "Shock but No Longer Surprise over Nursing Home Problems." November 9. *New York Times:* D1.

Steinmetz, Suzanne. 1988. *Duty Bound: Elder Abuse and Family Care.* Newbury Park, Calif.: Sage.

St. Louis Post-Dispatch. 1999. "Largest Union Victory in Decades." February 28: E6.

Stoller, Eleanor Palo. 1993. "Gender and the Organization of Long-Term Care: A Socialist-Feminist Perspective." *Journal of Aging Studies* 7, 2:151–70.

Stone, Deborah. 2000. "Caring by the Book." In *Care Work: Gender, Labor, and Welfare States,* edited by Madonna Harrington Meyer, pp. 89–111. New York: Routledge.

Strobel, Frederick, and Wallace C. Peterson. 1999. *The Coming Class War and How to Avoid It.* Armonk, N.Y.: M. E. Sharpe.

Sudha, S., and Elizabeth Mutran. 2001. "Race and Ethnicity, Nativity, and Issues of Health Care." *Research on Aging,* Special Issue: Age and Health in a Multiethnic Society 11: Health Issues, January. 23, 1:3–13.

Swoboda, Frank. 1999. "A Healthy Sign for Organized Labor." February 27. *Washington Post:* E01.

Tampa Tribune. 2000. "Yet More Nursing Home Complexities." October 6:14.

Taylor, Mark. 2001. "Code Breaker." *Philadelphia Inquirer Magazine.* April 29:12.

Taylor, R. J., C. Ellison, L. M. Chatters, J. S. Levin, and K. D. Lincoln. 2000. "Mental Health Services in Faith Communities: The Role of Clergy in Black Churches." *Social Work* 1:73–87.

Teegardin, Carrie. 2002. "The Bottom Line." 4-part series, July 28–August 1. *Atlanta Journal/Constitution.*

Tellis-Nayek, V., and M. Tellis-Nayek. 1989. "Quality of Care and the Burden of Two Cultures: When the World of the Nurse's Aide Enters the World of the Nursing Home." *Gerontologist* 29, 3:307–13.

Tennstedt, Sharon, Bei-Hung Chang, and Melvin Delgado. 1998. "Patterns of Long-Term Care: A Comparison of Puerto Ricans, African Americans, and Non-Latina

White Elders." In *Latino Elders and the Twenty-First Century,* edited by Melvin Delgado, pp. 179–99. New York: Haworth Press.

Thompson, Mark. 1997. "Fatal Neglect." *Time.* October 27:17.

Tilly, Jane, and Joshua M. Wiener. 2001. "Consumer-Directed Home and Community Services Programs in Eight States: Policy Issues for Older People and Government." *Journal of Aging and Social Policy* 12, 4:1–26.

Time magazine. 1997. "Fatal Neglect." Oct. 27.

Tisdale, Sallie. 1987. *Harvest Moon: Portrait of a Nursing Home.* New York: Henry Holt.

Torres, Sara. 1999. "Barriers to Mental-Health Care Access Faced by Hispanic Elderly." In *Serving Minority Elders in the Twenty-First Century,* edited by Mary L. Wykle and Amasa B. Ford, pp. 200–218. New York: Springer.

Torres-Gil, Fernando. 1987. "Aging in an Ethnic Society: Policy Issues for Aging among Minority Groups. In *Ethnic Dimensions of Aging,* edited by D. E. Gelfand and C. M. Barresi, pp. 239–57. New York: Springer.

———. 1998. "Policy, Politics, Aging: Cross-Roads in the 1990s." In *New Directions in Old-Age Policies,* edited by Janie S. Steckenrider and Tonya M. Parrott, pp. 75–87. Albany: State University of New York Press.

Tran, Thanh Van, Dung Ngo, and Tricia H. Song. 2001. "Caring for Elderly Vietnamese Americans." In *Age through Ethnic Lenses: Caring for the Elderly in a Multicultural Society,* edited by Laura Katz Olson, pp. 59–70. Lanham, Md.: Rowman & Littlefield.

Tress, Judith. 1997. "Older Immigrants and U.S. Welfare Reform." September. *International Journal of Sociology and Social Policy.* 17, 9:8–13.

Tripp-Reimer, Toni. 1999. "Culturally Competent Care." In *Serving Minority Elders in the Twenty-First Century,* edited by Mary L. Wykle and Amasa B. Ford, pp. 235–47. New York: Springer.

Ungerson, Clare. 2000. "Cash in Care." In *Care Work: Gender, Labor, and Welfare States,* edited by Madonna Harrington Meyer, pp. 68–88. New York: Routledge.

U.S. Bureau of the Census. 1996. *Global Aging into the Twenty-First Century.* 1996. International Programs Center, International Data Base. December. Washington, D.C.: U.S. Government Printing Office.

———. 1997. *March Current Population Survey.* 1963–1967, Table 1.1. Washington, D.C.: U.S. Government Printing Office.

———. 2000a. *Number of Families below the Poverty Level and Poverty Rates: 1959 to 2000.* Table 13, Historical Poverty Tables. Washington, D.C.: U.S. Government Printing Office.

———. 2000b. *Population by Age, Sex, Race, and Hispanic or Latino Origin for the U.S.: 2000.* Table 1, Total Population by Age, Race, and Hispanic or Latino Origin for the U.S. Data set: Census 2000 Summary File 1 (PHC-T-9) Washington, D.C.: U.S. Government Printing Office.

———. 2000c. *Profile of Selected Economic Characteristics: 2000.* Supplementary Survey Summary Tables. Washington, D.C.: U.S. Government Printing Office.

———. 2000d. DP-2. *Profile of Selected Social Characteristics: 2000.* Census 2000 Supplementary Survey Summary Tables. Data Set: Census 2000 Summary File 3 (SF 3)—Sample Data. Washington, D.C.: U.S. Government Printing Office.

———. 2000e. *Projections of the Total Resident Population by 5-Year Age Groups and Sex with Special Age Categories: Middle Series.* Selected Years 2000 to 2040. January. Washington, D.C.: U.S. Government Printing Office.

———. 2001a. *Age: 2000. Census 2000 Brief,* October, Julie Meyer. Washington, D.C.: U.S. Government Printing Office.

———. 2001b. *Households and Families: 2000.* Census 2000 Brief. September, Tavior Simmons and Grace O'Neill. Washington, D.C.: U.S. Government Printing Office.

———. 2001c. *Housing Characteristics: 2000.* Census 2000 Brief. October. Washington, D.C.: U.S. Government Printing Office.

———. 2001d. *Population and Housing: 2000.* Profiles of General Characteristics. May. Washington, D.C.: U.S. Government Printing Office.

———. 2001e. *Poverty Guidelines.* Washington, D.C.: U.S. Government Printing Office.

———. 2001f. *Poverty in the U.S.: 2000.* September, Joseph Dalaker. Washington, D.C.: U.S. Government Printing Office.

———. 2001g. *The Sixty-Five Years and Over Population: 2000.* Census 2000 Brief. October, Lisa Hetzel and Annetta Smith. Washington, D.C.: U.S. Government Printing Office.

U.S. Bureau of Labor Statistics. 1999. *Employment and Wages for Selected Health Care Occupations and Industries.* Occupational Employment Statistics. Washington, D.C.: U.S. Government Printing Office.

U.S. Department of Justice (DOJ). 1994. *Health Care Fraud Report: FY 1994.* Washington, D.C.: U.S. Government Printing Office.

U.S. Department of Labor. 1994. *Violence in the Workforce Comes under Closer Scrutiny: Issues in Labor Statistics.* Washington, D.C.: Government Printing Office.

———. 1996. Bureau of Labor Statistics. Survey of Occupational Injuries and Illness, 1994, Summary 96–11. Washington, D.C.: U.S. Government Printing Office.

———. 2000. *OSHA: Final Regulations.* November 14. Washington, D.C.: U.S. Government Printing Office.

U.S. General Accounting Office (GAO). 1991. *Medicare: Improper Handling of Beneficiary Complaints of Provider Fraud and Abuse.* Special Report to the Special Committee on Aging, U.S. Senate. October. Washington, D.C.: U.S. Government Printing Office.

———. 1995a. *Long-Term Care: Current Issues and Future Directions.* Washington, D.C.: U.S. Government Printing Office.

———. 1995b. *Medicare: Allegations against ABC Home Health Care.* Report to the Ranking Minority Member, Committee on Commerce, U.S. House. Washington, D.C.: U.S. Government Printing Office.

———. 1995c. *Medicare: Excessive Payments for Medicaid Supplies Continue Despite Improvements.* Report to the Ranking Minority Member, Subcommittee on Labor, Health and Human Services, Education and Related Agencies, Committee on Appropriations. August. Washington, D.C.: U.S. Government Printing Office.

———. 1996a. *Medicare: Early Resolution of Overcharges for Therapy in Nursing Homes Is Unlikely,* Report to the Ranking Member, Committee on Commerce, U.S. House. August. Washington, D.C.: U.S. Government Printing Office.

———. 1996b. *Medicare: HCFA Should Release Data to Aid Consumers, Prompt Better HMO Performance.* Special Report to the Special Committee on Aging, U.S. Senate. October. Washington, D.C.: U.S. Government Printing Office.

———. 1997a. *Medicaid Fraud and Abuse: Stronger Action Needed to Remove Excluded Providers from Federal Health Programs.* Report to the Chairman, Subcommittee on Human Resources and Intergovernmental Relations, Committee on Government Reform and Oversight, U.S. House. March. U.S. Senate. June. Washington, D.C.: U.S. Government Printing Office.

———. 1997b. *Medicare: Control over Fraud and Abuse Remains Elusive.* Testimony of Leslie Aronovitz before the Permanent Subcommittee on Investigations, Committee on Government Reform, U.S. Senate. June 26. Washington, D.C.: U.S. Government Printing Office.

———. 1997c. *Medicare: Need to Hold Home Health Agencies More Accountable for Inappropriate Billings.* Report to the Ranking Minority Member, Subcommittee on Labor, Health and Human Services, Education, and Related Agencies, Committee on Appropriations, U.S. Senate. June. Washington, D.C.: U.S. Government Printing Office.

———. 1997d. *Medicare HMOs: HCFA Can Promptly Eliminate Hundreds of Millions in Excess Payments.* Report to the Chairman, Subcommittee on Health, Committee on Ways and Means, U.S. House. April. Washington, D.C.: U.S. Government Printing Office.

———. 1998. *California Nursing Homes: Care Problems Persist despite Federal and State Oversight.* Report to the Special Committee on Aging, U.S. Senate. Washington, D.C.: U.S. Government Printing Office.

———. 1999a. *Assisted Living: Quality-of-Care and Consumer Protection Issues in Four States.* April. Washington, D.C.: U.S. Government Printing Office.

———. 1999b. *Medicaid: Federal and State Leadership Needed to Control Fraud and Abuse.* Testimony before the Subcommittee on Oversight, Committee on Commerce, U.S. House. November 9. Washington, D.C.: U.S. Government Printing Office.

———. 1999c. *Medicare: Program Safeguard Activities Expand, but Results Difficult to Measure.* Report to the Ranking Minority Member, Subcommittee on Labor, Committee on Health and Human Services, U.S. Senate. August. Washington, D.C.: U.S. Government Printing Office.

———. 1999d. *Medicare Contractors: Despite Its Efforts HCFA Cannot Ensure Their Effectiveness or Integrity.* Report to the Chairman, Permanent Subcommittee on Investigations, Committee on Government Affairs, U.S. Senate. July. Washington, D.C.: U.S. Government Printing Office.

———. 1999e. *Medicare Home Health Agencies Closures Continue, with Little Evidence Beneficiary Access Is Impaired.* May. Washington, D.C.: U.S. Government Printing Office.

———. 1999f. *Medicare Managed Care: Greater Oversight Needed to Protect Beneficiary Rights.* Report to the Senate Special Committee on Aging, U.S. Senate. April. Washington, D.C.: U.S. Government Printing Office.

———. 1999g. *Nursing Home Care: Enhanced HCFA Oversight of State Program Would Better Ensure Quality.* Report to the Special Committee on Aging, U.S. Senate. November. Washington, D.C.: U.S. Government Printing Office.

———. 1999h. *Nursing Home Oversight: Industry Examples Do Not Demonstrate That Regulatory Actions were Unreasonable*. Report to Charles E. Grassley, Chairman, Special Committee on Aging, U.S. Senate. April 13. Washington, D.C.: U.S. Government Printing Office.

———. 1999i. *Nursing Homes: Additional Steps Needed to Strengthen Enforcement of Federal Quality Standards*. Report to the Chairman and Ranking Minority Member, Special Committee on Aging. March. Washington, D.C.: U.S. Government Printing Office.

———. 1999j. *Nursing Homes: Complaint Investigation Process Often Inadequate to Protect Residents*. Report to the Chairman and Ranking Minority Member, Special Committee on Aging. March. Washington, D.C.: U.S. Government Printing Office.

———. 1999k. *Nursing Homes: HCFA Initiatives to Improve Care Are Under Way but Will Require Continued Commitment*. Testimony of William J. Scanlon before the Special Committee on Aging, U.S. Senate. June 30. 106th Cong., 1st sess. Washington, D.C.: U.S. Government Printing Office.

———. 1999l. *Nursing Homes: Proposal to Enhance Oversight of Poorly Performing Homes Has Merit*. Report to the Special Committee on Aging, U.S. Senate. June. Washington, D.C.: U.S. Government Printing Office.

———. 1999m. *Reported Medicaid Year 2000 Readiness*. Report to the Permanent Subcommittee on Investigations, Committee on Government Affairs, U.S. Senate. Washington, D.C.: U.S. Government Printing Office.

———. 1999n. *Skilled Nursing Facilities: Medicare Payment Charges Require Provider Adjustments but Maintain Access*. Report to the Chairman, Committee on Finance, Special Committee on Aging, U.S. Senate. December. Washington, D.C.: U.S. Government Printing Office.

———. 2000a. *HCFA: Three Largest Medicare Overpayment Settlements Were Improper*. Report to the Chairman, Permanent Subcommittee on Governmental Affairs, U.S. Senate. February. Washington, D.C.: U.S. Government Printing Office.

———. 2000b. *Medicaid: HCFA and States Could Work Together to Better Ensure the Integrity of Providers*. Testimony before the Subcommittee on Oversight and Investigations, Committee on Commerce, U.S. House. July 18. Washington, D.C.: U.S. Government Printing Office.

———. 2000c. *Medicare: HCFA Could Do More to Identify and Collect Overpayments*. Report to the Chairman, Committee on Government Reform, U.S. House. September 7. Washington, D.C.: U.S. Government Printing Office.

———. 2000d. *Medicare: Lessons Learned from HCFA's Implementation of Charges to Benefits*. Report to the Committee on Commerce, U.S. House of Representatives. January. Washington, D.C.: U.S. Government Printing Office.

———. 2000e. *Medicare Home Health Care: Prospective Payment System Will Need Refinement as Data Becomes Available*. Report to Congressional Committees. April. Washington, D.C.: U.S. Government Printing Office.

———. 2000f. *Nursing Homes: Aggregate Medicare Payments Are Adequate Despite Bankruptcies*. Statement of Laura A. Dummit, GAO, before the Special Committee on Aging, U.S. Senate. September 5. Washington, D.C.: U.S. Government Printing Office.

———. 2000g. *Nursing Homes: Sustained Efforts Are Essential to Realize Potential of the Quality Initiatives.* Report to Congressional Requesters. September. Washington, D.C.: U.S. Government Printing Office.

———. 2001a. *Civil Fines and Penalties Debt: Review of CMS' Management and Collection Process.* Report to the Ranking Minority Member, Subcommittee on Investigations, Committee on Government Affairs, U.S. Senate. December. Washington, D.C.: U.S. Government Printing Office.

———. 2001b. *Health Workforce: Ensuring Adequate Supply and Distribution Remains Challenging.* Testimony of Janet Heinrich, GAO, before the Subcommittee on Health, Committee on Energy and Commerce, U.S. House. August 1. Washington, D.C.: U.S. Government Printing Office.

———. 2001c. *Long-Term Care: Baby Boom Generation Increases Challenge of Financing Needed Services.* Statement of William J. Scanlon, Director of Health Care Issues, before the Committee on Finance, U.S. Senate. March 27. Washington, D.C.: U.S. Government Printing Office.

———. 2001d. *Medicaid: HCFA Reversed Its Position and Approved Additional State Financing Schemes.* Report to Congressional Requesters. October. Washington, D.C.: U.S. Government Printing Office.

———. 2001e. *Medicaid: State Efforts to Control Improper Payments Vary.* Report to the Chairman, Committee on Energy and Commerce, U.S. House. June. Washington, D.C.: U.S. Government Printing Office.

———. 2001f. *Medicare: Comments on HHS' Claims Administrative Contracting Reform Proposal.* August 17. Washington, D.C.: U.S. Government Printing Office.

———. 2001g. *Medicare: Cost-Sharing Policies Problematic for Beneficiaries and Program.* Statement of William J. Scanlon, Director of Health Care Issues. May 9. Washington, D.C.: U.S. Government Printing Office.

———. 2001h. *Medicare: Opportunities and Challenges in Contracting for Program Safeguards.* Report to Ranking Minority Members, Subcommittee on Labor, Health and Human Services, Education, and Related Agencies, Committee on Appropriations, U.S. Senate. May. Washington, D.C.: U.S. Government Printing Office.

———. 2001i. *Medicare+Choice Audits: Lack of Audit Follow-Up Limits Usefulness.* Report to Congressional Committees. October. Washington, D.C.: U.S. Government Printing Office.

———. 2001j. Report to Congressional Requesters. *Medicare+Choice: Recent Payment Increases Had Little Effect on Benefits or Plan Availability in 2001.* November. Washington, D.C.: U.S. Government Printing Office.

———. 2001k. *Nursing Workforce: Recruitment and Retention of Nurses and Nurse Aides Is a Growing Concern.* Testimony of William J. Scanlon, Director, Health Care Issues, before the Committee on Health, Education, Labor, and Pensions, U.S. Senate. May 17. Washington, D.C.: U.S. Government Printing Office.

———. 2001l. *Regulatory Issues for Medicare Providers.* Report to Ranking Minority Member, Committee on Finance, U.S. Senate. June 11. Washington, D.C.: U.S. Government Printing Office.

———. 2001m. *Skilled Nursing Facilities: Services Excluded from Medicare's Daily Rate Need to Be Re-evaluated.* Report to Congressional Committees, August. Washington, D.C.: U.S. Government Printing Office.

———. 2001n. Statement of William J. Scanlon, Director of Health Care Issues, before the Subcommittee on Health, Committee on Energy and Commerce, U.S. House. June 14. Washington, D.C.: U.S. Government Printing Office.

———. 2002a. *Long-Term Care: Aging Baby Boom Generation Will Increase Demand and Burden on Federal and State Budgets.* Testimony before the Special Committee on Aging, U.S. Senate, Statement of David M. Walker, Comptroller General. March 21. Washington, D.C.: U.S. Government Printing Office.

———. 2002b. *Long-Term Care: Availability of Medicaid Home and Community Services for Elderly Individuals Varies Considerably.* Report to the Chairman, Special Committee on Aging, U.S. Senate. September. Washington, D.C.: U.S. Government Printing Office.

———. 2002c. *Medicare: Communications with Physicians Can Be Improved.* Report to Congressional Requesters. February. Washington, D.C.: U.S. Government Printing Office.

———. 2002d. *Medicare: Recent CMS Reforms Address Carrier Scrutiny of Physicians' Claims for Payment.* Report to Congressional Committees. May. Washington, D.C.: U.S. Government Printing Office.

———. 2002e. *Medicare Home Health Agencies: Weaknesses in Federal and State Oversight Mask Potential Quality Issues.* Report to Congressional Committees. July 19. Washington, D.C.: U.S. Government Printing Office.

———. 2002f. *Medicare Home Health Care.* Report to Congressional Committees. U.S. Senate. June. Washington, D.C.: U.S. Government Printing Office.

———. 2002g. *Medicare Home Health Care Payments to Home Health Agencies Are Considerably Higher Than Costs.* Report to Congressional Committees. May. Washington, D.C.: U.S. Government Printing Office.

———. 2002h. *Medicare Physician Payments Spending Targets Encourage Fiscal Discipline, Modifications Could Stabilize Fees.* Testimony before the Subcommittee on Health, Committee on Energy and Commerce, U.S. House. February 14. Washington, D.C.: U.S. Government Printing Office.

———. 2002i. *Nursing Homes: Federal Efforts to Monitor Resident Assessment Data Should Complement State Activities.* Report to Congressional Requesters. February. Washington, D.C.: U.S. Government Printing Office.

———. 2002j. *Nursing Homes: More Can Be Done to Protect Residents from Abuse.* Report to Congressional Requesters. March 4. Washington, D.C.: U.S. Government Printing Office.

———. 2002k. *Nursing Homes: Quality of Care More Related to Staffing than Spending.* June 13. Washington, D.C.: U.S. Government Printing Office.

———. 2002l. *Skilled Nursing Facilities: Available Data Show Average Nursing Staff Time Changed Little after Medicare Payment Increase.* Report to Congressional Committees. November. Washington, D.C.: U.S. Government Printing Office.

———. 2002m. *Skilled Nursing Facilities: Providers have Responded to Medicare Payment System by Changing Practices.* Report to Charles E. Grassley, Ranking Minority Member, Committee on Finance, U.S. Senate, August. Washington, D.C.: U.S. Government Printing Office.

U.S. Government, Budget of the U.S. Government 2001a. *Budget, FY 2001.* Washington, D.C.: U.S. Government Printing Office.

————. 2001b. *Historical Tables.* Washington, D.C.: U.S. Government Printing Office.

————. 2003. *Budget, FY 2003.* Washington, D.C.: U.S. Government Printing Office.

U.S. Health Care Finance Administration (HCFA). 1996. *HCFA Study on Appropriateness of Minimum Nurse Staffing Ratios.* Interim Report. Prepared by M. Feuerberg, E. Mortimore and A. Kramer. October. Washington, D.C.: U.S. Government Printing Office.

————. 1998. *Study of Private Accreditation (Deeming) of Nursing Homes, Regulatory Incentives and Non-regulatory Initiatives, and Effectiveness of the Survey and Certification System.* Report to Congress. July. Washington, D.C.: U.S. Government Printing Office.

————. 2000a. *Report to Congress: Appropriateness of Minimum Nursing Staffing Ratios in Nursing Homes.* Staff Report. Spring. Washington, D.C.: U.S. Government Printing Office.

————. 2000b. *Report to Congress: Interim Report on Nursing Home Quality of Care and Implementation of the Nursing Home Initiative.* Staff Report. Washington, D.C.: U.S. Government Printing Office.

————. 2001. "National Health Expenditures Projections: 2001–2011." Retrieved online from www.hcfa.gov/stats/NHE-proj/proj20001/default.htm (viewed March 2001).

U.S. House, Committee on the Budget (HB). 2000a. *Medicare and Medicaid: HHS High Risk Program.* Testimony of June Gibbs Brown, Inspector General. February 18. Washington, D.C.: U.S. Government Printing Office.

————. 2000b. *Medicare Program: Reducing Improper Payments and Fraud.* Testimony of June Gibbs Brown, Inspector General, to the Health Care Task Force. July 12. Washington, D.C.: U.S. Government Printing Office.

————. 2000a. Testimony of Leslie Aronovitz, GAO, before the Subcommittee on Oversight and Investigations. *Medicare: Concerns about HCFA's Efforts to Prevent Fraud by Third-Party Billers.* April 6. Washington, D.C.: U.S. Government Printing Office.

————. 2000b. "Third Party Billing Company Fraud: Assessing the Threat Posed to Medicare." Testimony of Lewis Morris, Assistant Inspector General for Legal Affairs, before the Subcommittee on Oversight and Investigations. *Medicare: Concerns About HCFA's Efforts to Prevent Fraud by Third-Party Billers.* April 6. Washington, D.C.: U.S. Government Printing Office.

U.S. House, Committee on Energy and Commerce (HEC). 2000. Testimony of Michael Mangano, Acting Inspector General, before the Subcommittees on Health and Oversight Investigations. June 28. Washington, D.C.: U.S. Government Printing Office.

————. 2001. Testimony of Michael Mangano, Acting Inspector General, before the Subcommittee on Health and Oversight Investigations. June 28. Washington, D.C.: U.S. Government Printing Office.

————. 2000b. Testimony of Leslie Aronovitz, GAO, before the Subcommittee on Oversight and Investigations, *Medicare: Concerns about HCFA's Efforts to Prevent Fraud by Third-Party Billers,* April 6. Washington, D.C.: U.S. Government Printing Office.

U.S. House, Committee on Government Reform (HGR). 1995. *Health Care Fraud and Abuse.* Hearings before the Subcommittee on Human Resources and Intergovernmental Relations. September 28. 104th Cong., 1st sess. Washington, D.C.: U.S. Government Printing Office.

———. 1996. *Health Care Fraud: All Public and Private Payers Need Federal Criminal Anti-Fraud Protections.* Report to the Committee. July 25. 104th Cong., 2nd sess. Washington, D.C.: U.S. Government Printing Office.

———. 1997. *Health Care Fraud in Nursing Homes.* Hearings before the Subcommittee on Human Resources. April 16. 105th Cong., 1st sess. Washington, D.C.: U.S. Government printing Office.

———. 1999. *Nursing Home Conditions in Los Angeles County: Many Homes Fail to Meet Federal Standards for Adequate Care.* Prepared for Representative Henry Waxman by the Minority Staff, Special Investigations Division. November 22. Washington, D.C.: U.S. Government Printing Office.

———. 2000a. *Medicare Fraud: Continuing Efforts.* Testimony of John E. Harwick, OIG, before the Subcommittee on Government Management, Information, and Technology. July 25. Washington, D.C.: U.S. Government Printing Office

———. 2000b. *Nursing Home Conditions in Texas: Many Homes Fail to Meet Federal Standards for Adequate Care.* Prepared for Representative Ciro D. Rodriguez by the Minority Staff, Special Investigations Division. October 31. Washington, D.C.: U.S. Government Printing Office.

———. 2000c. *Nursing Home Conditions in the San Francisco Bay Area: Many Homes Fail to Meet Federal Standards for Adequate Care.* Prepared for Representatives Stark, Eshoo, Lantos, Lee, Lofgren, Miller, Pelosi, Tauscher, and Woolsey by the Minority Staff, Special Investigations Division. June 8. Washington, D.C.: U.S. Government Printing Office.

———. 2000d. *Nursing Home Staffing Levels Are Inadequate in the 13th Congressional District of California.* Prepared for Representative Fortney Pete Stark by the Minority Staff, Special Investigations Division. December 7. Washington, D.C.: U.S. Government Printing Office.

———. 2000e. Testimony of Robert H. Hast, General Accounting Office, Office of Special Investigations, before the Subcommittee on Government Management, Information, and Technology. July 25. Washington, D.C.: U.S. Government Printing Office.

———. 2001a. *Abuse of Residents Is a Major Problem in U.S. Nursing Homes.* Prepared for Representative Henry Waxman by the Minority Staff, Special Investigations Division. July 30. Washington, D.C.: U.S. Government Printing Office.

———. 2001b. *New York's Nursing Home Enforcement has been Inadequate.* Prepared for Representatives Slaughter and Maloney by the Minority Staff, Special Investigations Division. March 12. Washington, D.C.: U.S. Government Printing Office.

———. 2001c. *Nursing Home Conditions in Oklahoma: Many Homes Fail to Meet Federal Standards for Adequate Care.* Prepared for Representative Brad Carson by the Minority Staff, Special Investigations Division. April 9. Washington, D.C.: U.S. Government Printing Office.

———. 2001d. *Nursing Home Conditions in the 13th Congressional District of Pennsylvania: Many Homes Fail to Meet Federal Standards for Adequate Care.* Prepared for Representative Joseph M. Hoeffel by the Minority Staff, Special Investigations Division. July 23. Washington, D.C.: U.S. Government Printing Office.

————. 2001e. *Nursing Home Staffing Levels Are Inadequate in Chicago: Many Homes Fail to Meet Federal Standards for Adequate Care.* Prepared for Representatives Schakowsky, Blagojevich, and Rush by the Minority Staff, Special Investigations Division. January 16. Washington, D.C.: U.S. Government Printing Office.

————. 2001f. *Nursing Home Staffing Levels Are Inadequate in Oklahoma.* Prepared for Representative Brad Carson by the Minority Staff, Special Investigations Division. May 24. Washington, D.C.: U.S. Government Printing Office.

U.S. House, Committee on Government Reform and Oversight (HGRO), Subcommittee on Human Resources. 1997. *Health Care Fraud in Nursing Homes.* April 16. 105th Cong., 1st sess. Washington, D.C.: U.S. Government Printing Office.

U.S. House, Committee on Ways and Means (HWM), Subcommittee on Health. 2001. *Medicare Reform.* Testimony of George F. Grob, OIG. March 15. Washington, D.C.: U.S. Government Printing Office.

————. 2002. *Medigap: Current Policies Contain Coverage Gaps, Undermine Cost Control Incentives.* Testimony of William J. Scanlon, Director, Health Care Issues, GAO. March 14. Washington, D.C.: U.S. Government Printing Office.

U.S. House, Committee on Small Business (HSB). 2001. *Medicare Operational Changes and Program Integrity.* Testimony of George F. Grob, OIG. July 25. Washington, D.C.: U.S. Government Printing Office.

U.S. Office of the Inspector General (OIG). 1996. *Operation Restore Trust: Review of Home Health Claims Submitted by First American Health Care, Inc., Pennsylvania.* Audit. November 15. Washington, D.C.: U.S. Government Printing Office.

————. 1998. *Safeguarding Long-Term Care Residents: Final Report.* September 14. Washington, D.C.: U.S. Government Printing Office.

————. 1999. *Quality of Care in Nursing Homes: An Overview.* March. Washington, D.C.: U.S. Government Printing Office.

————. 2000. *Self-Disclosure of Provider Misconduct: Assessment of CIA Modifications.* March. Washington, D.C.: U.S. Government Printing Office.

————. 2001b. *Credentialing of Medicaid Providers: Fee-for-Service.* February. Washington, D.C.: U.S. Government Printing Office.

————. 2001c. *Duplicate Medicare Payments by Individual Carriers.* June. Washington, D.C.: U.S. Government Printing Office.

————. 2001d. *Medicare Beneficiary Access to Skilled Nursing Facilities.* July. Washington, D.C.: U.S. Government Printing Office.

————. 2001e. *Medicare Inpatient Hospital Prospective Payment System Transfers Incorrectly Reported as Discharges.* December 4. Washington, D.C.: U.S. Government Printing Office.

————. 2001f. *Medicare Management: CMS Faces Challenges in Safeguarding Payments While Addressing Provider Needs.* Testimony of Lewis Morris before the Special Committee on Aging, U.S. Senate. July 26. Washington, D.C.: U.S. Government Printing Office.

————. 2001g. *Medicare Payments for Psychiatric Services in Nursing Homes: A Follow-Up.* January. Washington, D.C.: U.S. Government Printing Office.

————. 2001h. *Medicare Payments for the Same Service by More Than One Carrier.* March. Washington, D.C.: U.S. Government Printing Office.

———. 2001j. *Semi-annual Report to Congress.* April to September. Washington, D.C.: U.S. Government Printing Office.

———. 2002a. *Audit of Administrative Costs Claimed under Parts A and B of the Health Insurance to the Aged and Disabled Programs.* January, Administar Federal. Indianapolis.

———. 2002b. *Medicare Enrollment of Home Health Providers.* January. Washington, D.C.: U.S. Government Printing Office.

———. 2002c. *Medicare Maintenance Payments for Capped Rental Equipment.* June. Washington, D.C.: U.S. Government Printing Office.

———. 2001a. Audit Reports. http://oig.hhs.gov/oas/reports and "Affairs Public," posted by paffairs@smtp.oig.hhs.gov. January 31, 2001; February 23, 2001; March 13, 2001; April 4, 2001; May 17, 2001; June 8, 2001; July 10, 2001; August 6, 2001; September 5, 2001; October 16, 2001; and November 9, 2001.

———. 2001i. Posts. 2001. "An Open Letter to Health Care Providers." November 20. Posted by eaffairs@os.dhhs.gov.

U.S. Senate, Committee on Appropriations (SA). 1995. *Stopping Abusive and Unnecessary Medicare Payments.* Hearings before Subcommittee, 104th Cong., 1st sess. Washington, D.C.: U.S. Government Printing Office.

———. 2000a. *Medicare: HCFA Faces Challenges to Control Improper Payments.* Testimony of Leslie Aronovitz, Associate Director, Health Financing and Public Health Issues, GAO, before the Subcommittee on Labor, Health and Human Services and Education,. March 9. Washington, D.C.: U.S. Government Printing Office.

———. 2000b. *Medicare: HCFA Faces Challenges to Control Improper Payments.* Testimony of June Gibbs Brown, OIG, before the Subcommittee on Labor, Health and Human Services and Education,. March 9. Washington, D.C.: U.S. Government Printing Office.

———. 2002. Testimony by the GAO, before the Subcommittee on Labor, Health and Human Services, Education, and Related Committees. June 12. Washington, D.C.: U.S. Government Printing Office.

U.S. Senate, Committee on Finance (SF). 2000. *Medicaid: State Financing Schemes Again Drive Up Federal Payments.* Testimony of Kathryn Allen, HHS. September 6. Washington, D.C.: U.S. Government Printing Office.

———. 2001a. *Prescription for Fraud: Consultants Selling Doctors Bad Billing Advice.* Testimony of Lewis Morris, OIG. June 27. Washington, D.C.: U.S. Government Printing Office.

———. 2001b. Testimony of Michael Mangano, Acting Inspector General, OIG. Washington, D.C.: U.S. Government.

U.S. Senate, Committee on the Judiciary (SJ). 1994. *Examining Federal, State, and Local Efforts to Combat Fraud and Abuse in the Health Care Industry and Related Provisions of the Proposed Health Security Act.* May 25. 103rd Cong., 2nd sess. Washington, D.C.: U.S. Government Printing Office.

U.S. Senate, Special Committee on Aging (SSCA). 1975. *Nursing Home Care in the U.S.: Failure in Public Policy.* Subcommittee on Long-Term Care. 94th Cong., 1st sess. Washington, D.C.: U.S. Government Printing Office.

———. 1975a. *Nursing Home Care in the U.S.: Failure in Public Policy.* "The Litany of Nursing Home Abuses and an Examination of the Roots of Controversy," supporting paper #1, Subcommittee on Long-Term Care. January. 94th Cong., 1st sess. Washington, D.C.: U.S. Government Printing Office.

———. 1975b. *Nursing Home Care in the U.S.: Failure in Public Policy.* "Drugs in Nursing Homes: Misuse, High Costs and Kickbacks", supporting paper #2, Subcommittee on Long-Term Care. January. 94th Cong., 1st sess. Washington, D.C.: U.S. Government Printing Office.

———. 1975c. *Nursing Home Care in the U.S.: Failure in Public Policy.* "Doctors in Nursing Homes: The Shunned Responsibility," supporting paper #3, Subcommittee on Long-Term Care. January. 94th Cong., 1st sess. Washington, D.C.: U.S. Government Printing Office.

———. 1975d. *Nursing Home Care in the U.S.: Failure in Public Policy.* "Nurses in Nursing Homes: The Heavy Burden," supporting paper #4, Subcommittee on Long-Term Care. January. 94th Cong., 1st sess. Washington, D.C.: U.S. Government Printing Office.

———. 1975e. *Nursing Home Care in the U.S.: Failure in Public Policy.* "The Continuing Chronicle of Nursing Home Fires," supporting paper #5, Subcommittee on Long-Term Care. January. 94th Cong., 1st sess. Washington, D.C.: U.S. Government Printing Office.

———. 1975f. *Nursing Home Care in the U.S.: Failure in Public Policy.* "What Can be Done in Nursing Homes: Positive Aspects in Long-Term Care," supporting paper #6, Subcommittee on Long-Term Care. January. 94th Cong., 1st sess. Washington, D.C.: U.S. Government Printing Office.

———. 1975g. *Nursing Home Care in the U.S.: Failure in Public Policy.* "The Role of Nursing Homes in Caring for Discharged Mental Patients," supporting paper #7, Subcommittee on Long-Term Care. January. 94th Cong., 1st sess. Washington, D.C.: U.S. Government Printing Office.

———. 1975h. *Nursing Home Care in the U.S.: Failure in Public Policy.* "Access to Nursing Homes by Minorities," supporting paper #8, Subcommittee on Long-Term Care. January. 94th Cong., 1st sess. Washington, D.C.: U.S. Government Printing Office.

———. 1975i. *Nursing Home Care in the U.S.: Failure in Public Policy.* "Profits and the Nursing Home: Incentives in Favor of Poor Care," supporting paper #9, Subcommittee on Long-Term Care. January. 94th Cong., 1st sess. Washington, D.C.: U.S. Government Printing Office.

———. 1990. *Long-Term Care for the Nineties: A Spotlight on Rural America*, August 21. Little Rock, Arkansas. 101st Cong., 2nd sess. Washington, D.C.: U.S. Government Printing Office.

———. 1994. *Medicare Fraud and Abuse.* April 11. Miami, Florida, 103rd Cong., 2nd sess. Washington, D.C.: U.S. Government Printing Office.

———. 1995a. *Medicaid Reform: Quality of Care in Nursing Homes at Risk.* October 26. 104th Cong., 1st sess. Washington, D.C.: U.S. Government Printing Office.

———. 1995b. *Planning Ahead: Future Directions in Private Financing of Long-Term Care.* May 11. 104th Cong., 1st sess. Washington, D.C.: U.S. Government Printing Office.

———. 1997a. *The Risk of Malnutrition in Nursing Homes.* October 22. 105th Cong., 1st sess. Washington, D.C.: U.S. Government Printing Office.

———. 1997b. *The Risk of Malnutrition in Nursing Homes.* Statement of Ms. Catherine Howes, Political Science Director of Program on Aging and Long-Term Care, Research Triangle Institute, North Carolina. October 22. 105th Cong., 1st sess. Washington, D.C.: U.S. Government Printing Office.

———. 1998a. *Access to Care: The Impact of the Balanced Budget Act on Medicare Home Health Services.* March 31. 105th Cong., 2nd sess. Washington, D.C.: U.S. Government Printing Office.

———. 1998b. *Betrayed: The Quality of Care in California Nursing Homes.* July 27, 28. 105th Cong., 2nd sess. Washington, D.C.: U.S. Government Printing Office.

———. 1998c. *The Cash Crunch: The Financial Challenge of Long-Term Care for the Baby Boomer Generation.* March 9. 105th Cong., 2nd sess. Washington, D.C.: U.S. Government Printing Office.

———. 1998d. *Crooks Caring for Seniors: The Case for Criminal Background Checks.* September 14. 105th Cong., 2nd sess. Washington, D.C.: U.S. Government Printing Office.

———. 1998e. *Elder Care Today and Tomorrow.* April 27. 105th Cong., 2nd sess. Washington, D.C.: U.S. Government Printing Office.

———. 1998f. *Everyday Heroes: Family Caregivers Face Increasing Challenges in an Aging Nation.* September 10. 105th Cong., 2nd sess. Washington, D.C.: U.S. Government Printing Office.

———. 1998g. *The Many Faces of Long-Term Care: Today's Bitter Pill or Tomorrow's Cure.* January 12. Las Vegas, Nevada, 105th Cong., 1st sess. Washington, D.C.: U.S. Government Printing Office.

———. 1999a. *Assisted Living: Quality-of-Care and Consumer Protection Issues.* April 26. Testimony of Kathryn Allen, Associate Director Health Financing and Public Health Issues. 106th Cong., 1st sess. Washington, D.C.: U.S. Government Printing Office.

———. 1999b. *The Boomers Are Coming: The Challenge of Family Caregiving.* October 11. 106th Cong., 1st Sess. Washington, D.C.: U.S. Government Printing Office.

———. 1999c. *Long-Term Care for the Twenty-First Century: A Common Sense Proposal to Support Family Caregivers.* March 23. 106th Cong., 1st sess. Washington, D.C.: U.S. Government Printing Office.

———. 1999d. *The Nursing Home Initiative: Results at Year One.* June 30. 106th Cong, 1st sess. Washington, D.C.: U.S. Government Printing Office.

———. 1999e. *Nursing Home Residents: Short-Changed by Staff Shortages.* November 3. 106th Cong., 1st sess. Washington, D.C.: U.S. Government Printing Office.

———. 1999f. *Residents at Risk? Weaknesses Persist in Nursing Home Complaint Investigation and Enforcement.* March 22. 106th Cong., 1st sess. Washington, D.C.: U.S. Government Printing Office.

———. 2000a. *Nursing Home Bankruptcies: What Caused Them.* September 5. 106th Cong., 2nd sess. Washington, D.C.: U.S. Government Printing Office.

———. 2000b. *The Nursing Home Initiative: A Two-year Progress Report.* September 28. Washington, D.C.: U.S. Government Printing Office.

———. 2000c. Testimony of Dr. John F. Schnelle, UCLA School of Medicine and HCFA Contractor. July. *Report to Congress: Appropriateness of Minimum Nursing Staffing Ratios in Nursing Homes.* Washington, D.C.: U.S. Government Printing Office.

————. 2001a. *Long-Term Care: States Grapple with Increasing Demands and Costs.* July 18. Washington, D.C.: U.S. Government Printing Office.

————. 2001b. *Medicare Enforcement Actions: The Federal Government's Anti-fraud Efforts.* July 26. Washington, D.C.: U.S. Government Printing Office.

Villa, M., L. J. Cuellar, N. Gamel, and G. Yeo. 1993. "Aging and Health: Hispanic American Elders." Stanford Geriatric Education Center Working Paper, 5:1–46.

Vitaliano, Peter, Cynthia Dougherty, and Ilene Siegler. 1994. "Bio-Psychosocial Risks for Cardiovascular Disease in Spouse Caregivers of Persons with Alzheimer's Disease." In *Aging and Quality of Life,* edited by Ronald P. Abeles, Helen C. Gift, and Narcia G. Ory, pp. 145–62. New York: Springer.

Vitez, Michael. 1998. "Life's Last Chapter: How Well Will We Care?" 4-part series. March 16–18. *Philadelphia Inquirer:* A01.

Vladeck, Bruce. 1980. *Unloving Care: The Nursing Home Tragedy.* New York: Basic Books.

Vogel, Nancy. 2000. "Davis Signs Bill to Tighten Oversight of Nursing Homes." September 15. *Los Angeles Times:* 3.

Waite, Linda J., and Mark Nielsen. 2001. "The Rise of the Dual-Earner Family, 1963–1997," In *Working Families: The Transformation of the American Home,* edited by Rosanna Hertz and Nancy L. Marshall, pp. 23–41. Berkeley: University of California Press.

Wallack, Stanley. 1997. "Are Private Sector Solutions to Long-Term Care Financing Preferable?—Yes." In *Controversial Issues in Aging,* edited by Andrew E. Scharlach and Leonard W. Kaye, pp. 46–51. Needham Heights, Mass.: Allyn and Bacon.

Waters, Mary C. 1999. *Black Identities: West Indian Immigrant Dreams and American Realities.* Cambridge, Mass.: Harvard University Press.

Watson, William H. 1990. "Family Care, Economics, and Health." In *Black Aged: Understanding Diversity and Service Needs,* edited by Zev Harel, Edward A. McKinney, and Michael Williams, pp. 50–68. Thousand Oaks, Calif.: Sage.

Weissert, William G. 1991. "A New Policy Agenda for Home Care." *Health Affairs.* 10, 2:67–82.

Weissert, William G., and Susan C. Hedrich. 1994. "Lessons Learned from Research on Efforts of Community-Based Long-Term Care." *Journal of the American Geriatrics Society* 42:348–53.

Wichterich, Christa. 2000. *The Globalized Woman: Reports from a Future of Inequality.* New York: St. Martin's Press.

Wiener, Joshua M. 1996. "Financing Reform for Long-Term Care: Strategies for Public and Private Long-Term Care Insurance." In *From Nursing Homes to Home Care,* edited by Marie E. Cowart and Jill Quadagno, pp. 109–27. New York: Haworth Press.

Wiener, Joshua M., and David G. Stevenson. 1998. "State Policy on Long-Term Care for the Elderly." May/June. *Health Affairs* 17, 3:81–100.

Wiener, Joshua M., Catherine M. Sullivan, and Jason Skaggs. 1996. *Spending Down to Medicaid: New Data on the Role of Medicaid in Paying for Nursing Home Care.* Washington, D.C.: Public Policy Institute, American Association of Retired Persons (AARP).

Williams, Celeste. 1999. "Feeding Care." January 27. *Indianapolis Star:* A14.

Williams, Celeste, and Joe Fahy. 1999. "The Tarnished Years." January 26. *Indianapolis Star* A1–3.

Williams, T. Franklin, and Helena Temkin-Greener. 1996. "Older People, Dependency, and Trends in Supportive Care." In *The Future of Long-Term Care: Social and Policy Issues*, edited by R. H. Binstock, L. E. Cluff, and O. Von Mering, pp. 51–74. Baltimore, Md.: Johns Hopkins Press.

Wilmoth, Janet, Gordon DeJong, and Christine Himes. 1997. "Immigrant and Non-Immigrant Living Arrangements among America's White, Hispanic, and Asian Elderly Population." *International Journal of Sociology and Social Policy* 17, 9–10: 57–83.

Wisensale, Steven K. 2001. "What Role for the Family and Medical Leave Act in Long-Term Care Policy?" Paper prepared for the Annual Meeting of the American Political Science Association, San Francisco, August.

Wong, Morrison G. 2001. "The Chinese Elderly: Values and Issues in Receiving Adequate Care." In *Age through Ethnic Lenses: Caring for the Elderly in a Multicultural Society*, edited by Laura Katz Olson, pp. 17–32. Lanham, Md.: Rowman & Littlefield.

Yee, Barbara, and Gayle Weaver. 1994. "Ethnic Minorities and Health Promotion: Developing a 'Culturally Competent' Agenda." *Preventive Healthcare and Health Promotion for Older Adults* Spring: 39–44.

Yee, Donna L. 1999. "Preventing Chronic Illness and Disability: Asian Americans." In *Serving Minority Elders in the Twenty-First Century*, edited by Mary L. Wykle and Amasa B. Ford, pp. 37–50. New York: Springer.

Yeo, Given, and Nancy Kikoyeda. 1995. "Asian and Pacific Islander American Elders." In *The Encyclopedia of Aging*, 2nd ed., edited by George L. Maddox, pp. 80–82. New York: Springer.

Young, Melinda. 2000. "Recognizing the Signs of Elder Abuse." October. *Patient Care.* 30:56–66.

Young, Virginia. 2001. "Aging Dangerously: Inadequate Care in Missouri Nursing Homes." Occasional series, August 5. *St. Louis Post-Dispatch:* A8.

———. 2002. "Elderly Abuse Legislation May Be Put before Missouri Voters." May 22. *St. Louis Post-Dispatch:* B3.

Zaldivar, R. A. 1997. "Eighty-Nine Percent of U.S. Hospitals Found Double-Billing for Inpatient Care." August 26. *Philadelphia Inquirer:* A3.

Zambito, Thomas. 2000. "Shame on Nursing Homes." December 17. *New York Daily News.*

Zebrak, Andrew. 1998. "Assisted Living: Issue Brief." Health Policy Tracking System. October 1. Washington, D.C.: National Conference of State Legislators.

Zielbauer, Paul. 2001. "Workers in Connecticut Conduct a One-Day Walkout." March 21. *New York Times:* B5.

INDEX

CON (certificate of need) restrictions, 33
Congressional Quarterly, 28
Connecticut Human Services
    Committee, 108
consumer-directed programs, 64
continuing care retirement communities
    (CCRCs), 107–8. *See also* assisted
    living facilities; community care;
    nursing homes
Coontz, S., 51, 54, 62, 71, 130
corporate integrity agreements (CIAs),
    208, 227, 229n4
corruption, political, 231n22
Costa, Anthony J., 69
Coward, Raymond T., 52
Cox, Carole, 143
Cox, Christopher, 180, 185
criminals, elder abuse and, 179, 180,
    193n46
Cromwell, Sandra L., 67, 134, 142
Crummy, Karen, 89, 178, 180, 185
Cuban Americans. *See* Latino Americans
Cuellar, L. J., 141
Cutler, Stephen, 99

Dailey, Nancy, 21, 59, 60, 98, 100–101,
    251n10
Daily News (New York), 182, 193n48
Daly, Lynne Von Rein, 80, 83, 111, 114
"Dangerous Bedfellows" (Berens), 181
Davis, Carolyne, 153
Davis, Henry, 181
Deitch, Cynthia H., 61
DeJong, Gordon, 135, 143
Delgado, Melvin, 144
De Lollis, Barbara, 193n50
dementia, 21–22, 53–54, 65, 81, 83, 89,
    111
Denver Post, 180
dependency, leading causes of, 250–51n1
deprivatization, of elder care, 238–41,
    247–48
Detroit Free Press, 181
diagnostic-related groups (DRG) price,
    213

Diamond, Timothy, 43, 75, 78, 93; on
    affective care, 87, 88, 89; on direct
    care workers, 82, 84, 94; on nursing
    home population, 116, 117, 118; on
    nursing home quality of care, 35, 81,
    95, 111, 113, 114, 120
Dilworth-Anderson, Peggye, 138, 139
direct care workers, 73–96; duties,
    82–83, 93; economic circumstances
    of, 89–91; elder abuse and, 94–95,
    193n46; feminism and, 74–75;
    immigrant labor and, 75–79, 93;
    patient abuse of, 83–84; shortage of,
    75–76, 178–79; turnover, 82, 96n8,
    112; wages, 89–90, 93; working
    conditions of, 84–86. *See also* home
    care workers; home health agencies;
    nursing homes
Dirty Details (Cohen), 58
discrimination. *See* racism
DME (durable medical equipment)
    suppliers, 216–18, 230n18, 231n19
DMERCs (durable medical equipment
    regional carriers, 198, 217, 221
DOJ. *See* Justice, U.S. Department of
Dominican Republic, 77
Donovan, Rebecca, 92, 93
Dorschner, John, 184
Doty, Pamela, 250
double billing. *See* fraud
Douherty, Cynthia, 65
Dressel, Paula, 8
DRG (diagnostic-related groups) price,
    213
Dribben, Melissa, 66
DuBois, Barbara C., 140, 142, 145
durable medical equipment (DME)
    suppliers, 216–18, 230n18, 231n19
durable medical equipment regional
    carriers (DMERCs), 198, 217, 221
Dwyer, Jeffrey W., 52

Edmonds, Mary McKinney, 132, 156n14
Edwards, James R., 125, 126, 141
Ehrenreich, Barbara, 77

ABOUT THE AUTHOR

Laura Katz Olson has been a professor of political science at Lehigh University since 1974. She was a scholar at the Social Security Administration, a Gereontological Fellow and a Fulbright Scholar, and has lectured (funded by the Pennsylvania Humanities Council) throughout Pennsylvania on social security, Medicare, and long-term care policies. Her widely published work in the field of aging and women's studies includes: *The Political Economy of Aging: The State, Private Power, and Social Welfare; Aging and Public Policy: The Politics of Growing Old in America* (with William P. Browne); *The Graying of the World: Who Will Care for the Frail Elderly?;* and *Age through Ethnic Lenses: Caring for the Elderly in a Multicultural Society.* Olson resides in Bethlehem, Pennsylvania, with her husband, George. She has one daughter, Alix, who is a performance poet.